VCAP5-DCA
Official Cert Guide

VMware Press is the official publisher of VMware books and training materials, which provide guidance on the critical topics facing today's technology professionals and students. Enterprises, as well as small- and medium-sized organizations, adopt virtualization as a more agile way of scaling IT to meet business needs. VMware Press provides proven, technically accurate information that will help them meet their goals for customizing, building, and maintaining their virtual environment.

With books, certification and study guides, video training, and learning tools produced by world-class architects and IT experts, VMware Press helps IT professionals master a diverse range of topics on virtualization and cloud computing and is the official source of reference materials for preparing for the VMware Certified Professional certification.

VMware Press is also pleased to have localization partners that can publish its products into more than forty-two languages, including, but not limited to, Chinese (Simplified), Chinese (Traditional), French, German, Greek, Hindi, Japanese, Korean, Polish, Russian, and Spanish.

For more information about VMware Press, please visit

www.vmwarepress.com

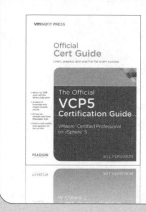

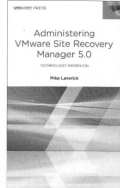
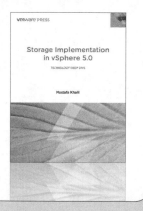

VCAP5-DCA
Official Cert Guide

Steve Baca

John A. Davis

vmware® PRESS

Upper Saddle River, NJ • Boston • Indianapolis • San Francisco
New York • Toronto • Montreal • London • Munich • Paris • Madrid
Capetown • Sydney • Tokyo • Singapore • Mexico City

VCAP-5 DCA Official Cert Guide
VMware® Certified Advanced Professional 5- Data Center Administration

ISBN-13: 978-0-7897-5323-6
ISBN-10: 0-7897-5323-5

Library of Congress Control Number: 2014935439

Text printed in the United States at Courier, Westford, MA.

First Printing: May 2014

Warning and Disclaimer

Special Sales

For information about buying this title in bulk quantities, or for special sales opportunities (which may include electronic versions; custom cover designs; and content particular to your business, training goals, marketing focus, or branding interests), please contact our corporate sales department at corpsales@pearsoned.com or (800) 382-3419.

For government sales inquiries, please contact governmentsales@pearsoned.com.

For questions about sales outside the U.S., please contact international@pearsoned.com.

ASSOCIATE PUBLISHER
David Dusthimer

ACQUISITIONS EDITOR
Joan Murray

VMWARE PRESS PROGRAM MANAGER
Anand Sundaram

DEVELOPMENT EDITOR
Ellie Bru

MANAGING EDITOR
Sandra Schroeder

PROJECT EDITOR
Mandie Frank

COPY EDITOR
Megan Wade-Taxter

INDEXER
Lisa Stumpf

PROOFREADER
Charlotte Kughen

COORDINATOR
Vanessa Evans

DESIGNER
Chuti Prasertsith

COMPOSITION
Jake McFarland

Contents at a Glance

Table of Contents

About the Authors

Steven Baca, VCAP, VCI, VCP, and NCDA, has been in the computer industry for more than 20 years. Originally a computer programmer and a system administrator working on Unix and Windows systems, he migrated over to technical training and wrote a course for Sun Microsystems. He eventually transitioned to VMware about 8 years ago, doing technical training and consulting as well as teaching for Netapp. Currently he lives in Omaha, Nebraska, and does a number of engagements worldwide. He thoroughly enjoys teaching and writing and believes that the constant evolution of the computer industry requires continuously learning to stay ahead. Steve can be found on Twitter @scbaca1.

John A. Davis is a VMware Certified Instructor (VCI) and VMware Certified Professional (VCP). He has been teaching since 2004, when only a dozen or so VCIs existed in the United States. Throughout his tenure, he has taught VMware courses in many U.S. cities and abroad, including in Canada, Singapore, Japan, Australia, and New Zealand. John is a Senior Consulting Engineer at New Age Technologies and splits his time between teaching and consulting. He has most recently been engaged in VMware vCloud, VMware View, and Site Recovery Manager professional services. John has authored several white papers and also holds certifications for VMware Certified Advanced Professional (VCAP) on VMware vSphere (VCAP5-DCA, VCAP5-DCD), VMware View (VCAP5-DTD), and VMware vCloud (VCAP5-CID). John is author of the vLoreBlog.com and can be found on Twitter @johnnyadavis.

Dedications

Steve's dedication

First and foremost, I would like to dedicate this book to my loving wife Sharyl. Your patience and support has been instrumental during the writing of this book. Thank you for believing in me and allowing me to have the time for my many endeavors. I would also like to dedicate this book to my kids: Zachary, Brianna, Eileen, Susan, Keenan, and Maura. I hope to now spend less time glued to a laptop and more time with all of you.

John's dedication

She came to us in such a whirl,

This precious little angel girl.

A fragile life, doctors would say,

Yet perfect to us in every way.

She changed us all from the very start.

Touching each and every heart.

God loves us all, I'll always believe.

He sent his angel of proof to you and me.

Everything I see, Everything I do,

Madison Hope I think of you.

You now see us clearly, that I know,

For God has brought his angel home.

With Love, Grampy

Dedicated to my oldest granddaughter, Madison Hope Stith, 03/20/2000 to 01/17/2012

Acknowledgments

Steve's Acknowledgments

There are so many people to acknowledge and thank for making this book possible. I would like to start with my co-author John Davis, who kept us on track. I cannot have had a better partner. Without your hard work and organization, this book would not have been possible.

Thank you to the technical editors, Brett Guarino and Jon Hall, whose comments and suggestions kept the details straight. I know you guys invested a lot of time on your editing, and it really showed.

Thanks to Ellie Bru, Mandie Frank, and the rest of the team at Pearson Publishing, who do a tremendous amount of work from the initial planning of the book to the final printing.

Finally a special thanks to Joan Murray, who took a chance on a first-time writer. I appreciate your patience and support.

John's Acknowledgments

I would like to thank my wife Delores, who puts up with all my travels, my late-night writing, and all my quirks. I would like to thank my dad Norm, who set an example for me to tackle each challenge with the question "Now, let's see, how can I make this work?"

Thank you to Tom Alves, who hired me and mentored me when I first began my career at the Naval Ordnance Station Louisville in 1988.

Thank you to Charlie Hagerty (president) and Tony Fink (VP) at New Age Technologies for giving me the opportunity to become a consulting engineer at a great company and for encouraging and motivating me in my career development. A big thanks also to Brian Perry, who mentored me on becoming a VMware Certified Instructor. He sets the bar for VCI excellence.

I would like to thank my co-author Steve Baca for bringing me on to write this book with him and our two technical editors, Brett Guarino and Jon Hall, who helped us refine it. Thanks to Joan Murray for coordinating everything.

Finally, I would like to thank my granddaughter, Emma Rosebush, little sister and best friend to Madison Hope. At three years old, she was instrumental in keeping the family sane as we said goodbye to her sister and just weeks later welcomed her baby brother, Jax. She keeps us all entertained and helps me rejuvenate after long stretches on the road.

About the Reviewers

Jon Hall is currently a Senior Technical Certification Developer with VMware. In 2005, Jon joined VMware as an instructor, teaching classes on VMware technologies across the globe. Three years later, he joined the certification team. While continuing to teach, Jon began developing exams and worked to grow VMware's certification program to cover VMware's cloud, end-user computing, and network virtualization technologies. Jon is a VMware Certified Instructor (VCI) and a VMware Certified Advanced Professional in multiple disciplines.

Brett Guarino operates out of Raleigh, North Carolina, and is the founder and CEO of Virtujitsu, Inc. Brett has been a VMware Certified Instructor (VCI) for 4 years and has been working with virtualization products for more than 8 years. He holds multiple VMware certifications, including VMware Certified Advanced Professional (VCAP) in Data Center Design (DCD) and Data Center Administration (DCA).

We Want to Hear from You!

As the reader of this book, *you* are our most important critic and commentator. We value your opinion and want to know what we're doing right, what we could do better, what areas you'd like to see us publish in, and any other words of wisdom you're willing to pass our way.

We welcome your comments. You can email or write us directly to let us know what you did or didn't like about this book—as well as what we can do to make our books better.

Please note that we cannot help you with technical problems related to the topic of this book.

When you write, please be sure to include this book's title and author as well as your name, email address, and phone number. We will carefully review your comments and share them with the author and editors who worked on the book.

Email: VMwarePress@vmware.com

Mail: VMware Press
ATTN: Reader Feedback
800 East 96th Street
Indianapolis, IN 46240 USA

Reader Services

Visit our website at www.pearsonitcertification.com/title/9780789753236 and register this book for convenient access to any updates, downloads, or errata that might be available for this book.

Introduction

John and I both do technical training for VMware, and we have been working with VMware for a number of years. We have spent countless hours learning how vSphere works, and we believe that there is so much to still learn. Together we want to share our knowledge with you.

Before you can take the VCAP5-DCA exam, you must first pass one of the following exams: VCP5-DCV, VCP5-DT, VCP-Cloud, or VCAP4-DCA. So this book does not cover basic vSphere concepts in detail. We recommend that you research any topics mentioned in the exam blueprints guide that you do not fully understand. You can find it on VMware's website, http://vmware.com/certification.

Unlike a lot of certification exams, the VCAP exam is a lab-based exam. I often say that the best way to pass the VCAP exam is what I like to call "stick time." Much like an airplane pilot needs "stick time in the air," you need "stick time in a lab." We recommend you create your own lab environment to practice the procedures we discuss.

This guide is not a brain dump. It might cover specific tasks that are not on your actual exam. It might not cover all the specific tasks that are on the actual exam you take. We expect that once you fully understand all the material covered in this guide to the point where you can quickly perform the associated administration tasks without having to look at the book for guidance, then you should pass the VCAP5-DCA exam.

Who Should Read This Book

This book was written for candidates preparing for the VCAP5-DCA exam. The chapters and the material are focused on accomplishing certification, although the book can be read by VMware system administrators who want to learn more about how vSphere works. Even if they do not plan on taking the exam, they can still sharpen their skills.

Goals and Methods

The goal of this book is to assist you in passing the VCAP5-DCA certification exam, which will allow you to obtain the status of VMware Certified Advanced Professional 5–Data Center Administration (VCAP5-DCA). To help you in this endeavor, each chapter contains examples and scenarios that are based on real-world experiences, where administration tasks that are covered by the exam might need to be applied. Each chapter is organized with the following methods:

- **Do I Know This Already? quiz**—At the beginning of each chapter after the exam objectives is a quiz that is meant to help you gauge your own knowledge on the subject matter of the module. The answers to each chapter's quiz can be found at the back of the book in Appendix A. Although the actual certification exam is not in a multiple-choice format, the questions are based on each module's objectives and will serve as an indicator on how strongly you currently know the topics of the module.

- **Key Topics**—Throughout the module you will find several key topics icons, which will indicate important figures, tables, and lists of information you should know for the exam.

- **Review Tasks**—At the end of each chapter is a list of tasks you should be able to perform after reading the module. The steps for each of the tasks are located within the chapter.

How to Use This Book

Although each chapter contains a "Do I Know This Already?" section, we recommend that you actually read each chapter and practice all the associated administrative tasks.

We recommend that as you use this book to prepare for the exam, you practice each administrative task to the point where you can perform such tasks quickly, without referring to the book. Many VCAP5-DCA candidates fail to do so. Instead, when they encounter a specific task in the guide, they think, "I already know how to do that! I have done that many times in a real environment." We recommend that you stop to think, "Can I do that right now, without looking somewhere for help, and finish it in a couple of minutes?" Understand that during the exam, you will be expected to accomplish these tasks very quickly.

Be sure to examine the Exam Blueprint. Use the Certification Exam and This Preparation Guide table to determine which chapter addresses each specific objective.

Use Chapter 10 as a warm-up before starting any of the practice tests. Don't begin Chapter 10 until you feel comfortable with all the material from Chapters 1–9.

Chapters 1–10, cover the following topics:

- Chapter 1, "Administrator Tools": This chapter focuses on how to implement and use various administrator tools. These tools include the vSphere Client, ESXCLI, vmkfstools, ESXTOP, vCLI, vMA, and PowerCLI.

- Chapter 2, "Network Administration": A number of possible test scenarios can be created for networking. This chapter focuses on the many networking features that are available in vSphere, such as VLAN, PVLANs, and Netflow.

- Chapter 3, "Storage Concepts": This chapter focuses on implementing and managing a number of vSphere features and technologies that can be used to provide solutions to various storage problems. There are discussions on Raw Device Mapping (RDM), VMware DirectPath I/O, and a number of storage features.

- Chapter 4, "Performance": This chapter focuses on performance tuning, optimization, and troubleshooting. It is also intended to ensure that you have the skills to successfully complete the performance analysis, configuration, and troubleshooting tasks.

- Chapter 5, "Clusters": This chapter provides the skills to perform a cluster configuration, troubleshooting, and management of a vSphere Cluster.

Included in this module are vSphere High Availability (HA), Distributed Resource Scheduler (DRS), and other cluster features.

- Chapter 6, "Patch Management": This chapter focuses on gaining the skills to successfully perform patch management and updating of ESXi hosts, virtual machine hardware, VMware Tools, and virtual appliances using VMware Update Manager.

- Chapter 7, "Logging": How logging works for both ESXi hosts and the vCenter Server are discussed in this chapter. The skills to install and configure Syslog and the ESXi Dump Collector are also part of this module.

- Chapter 8, "Security and Firewall" There are different methods to secure your vSphere environment. The chapter begins with a brief discussion on users, groups, and roles. Securing vSphere is more than just looking at passwords and how to strengthen them. There are various other security functions that will be discussed. This module also teaches the skills to configure the ESXi Firewall.

- Chapter 9, "Auto Deploy": This chapter focuses on understanding how Auto Deploy works. There are a lot of parts to Auto Deploy, and the module spends time explaining what the various parts do and how to set them up.

- Chapter 10, "Scenarios": The VCAP exam is based on solving scenarios. This chapter is designed to test your ability to solve several scenarios.

Throughout the book, we provide many terms, acronyms, and abbreviations that are commonly used by VMware and the virtualization community. Each term is identified on its first use. In some cases, the choice for the best term to use in the book is challenging because VMware and the community use multiple terms to refer to a specific item. For example, a standard virtual switch can be referenced as a standard vSwitch or a *vSS*. Don't be alarmed if we use multiple terms to refer to a specific item, but do expect that we clearly identify each term on its first use.

Certification Exam and This Preparation Guide

Table I-1 identifies the chapter in which each exam objective is covered. Chapter 10 is a unique chapter that contains a sample scenario for each exam objective, although it is not included in the following table.

Table I-1 VCAP5-DCA Exam Topics and Chapter References

Exam Section/Objective	Chapter Where Covered
Section 1: Implement and Manage Storage	
Objective 1.1 – Implement and Manage Complex Storage Solutions	Chapter 3
Objective 1.2 – Manage Storage Capacity in a vSphere Environment	Chapter 3
Objective 1.3 – Configure and Manage Complex Multipathing and PSA Plug-ins	Chapter 3
Section 2 – Implement and Manage Networking	
Objective 2.1 – Implement and Manage Complex Virtual Networks	Chapter 2
Objective 2.2 – Configure and Maintain VLANs, PVLANs, and VLAN Settings	Chapter 2
Objective 2.3 – Deploy and Maintain Scalable Virtual Networking	Chapter 2
Objective 2.4 – Administer vNetwork Distributed Switch Settings	Chapter 2
Section 3 – Deploy DRS Clusters and Manage Performance	
Objective 3.1 – Tune and Optimize vSphere Performance	Chapter 4
Objective 3.2 – Optimize Virtual Machine Resources	Chapter 4
Objective 3.3 – Implement and Maintain Complex DRS Solutions	Chapter 5
Objective 3.4 – Utilize Advanced vSphere Performance Monitoring Tools	Chapter 4
Section 4 – Manage Business Continuity and Protect Data	
Objective 4.1 – Implement and Maintain Complex VMware HA Solutions	Chapter 5
Objective 4.2 – Deploy and Test VMware FT	Chapter 5
Section 5 – Perform Operational Maintenance	
Objective 5.1 – Implement and Maintain Host Profiles	Chapter 9
Objective 5.2 – Deploy and Manage Complex Update Manager Environments	Chapter 6
Section 6 – Perform Advanced Troubleshooting	
Objective 6.1 – Configure, Manage, and Analyze vSphere Log Files	Chapter 7

Exam Section/Objective	Chapter Where Covered
Objective 6.2 – Troubleshooting CPU and Memory Performance	Chapter 4
Objective 6.3 – Troubleshoot Network Performance and Connectivity	Chapter 4
Objective 6.4 – Troubleshoot Storage Performance and Connectivity	Chapter 4
Objective 6.5 – Troubleshoot vCenter Server and ESXi Host Management	Chapter 4
Section 7 – Secure a vSphere Environment	
Objective 7.1 – Secure ESXi Hosts	Chapter 8
Objective 7.2 – Configure and Maintain the ESXi Firewall	Chapter 8
Section 8 – Perform Scripting and Automation	
Objective 8.1 – Execute VMware Cmdlets and Customize Scripts Using PowerCLI	Chapter 1
Objective 8.2 – Administer vSphere Using the vSphere Management Assistant	Chapter 1
Section 9 – Perform Advanced vSphere Installations and Configurations	
Objective 9.1 – Install ESXi Hosts with Custom Settings	Chapter 9
Objective 9.2 – Install ESXi Hosts Using Auto Deploy	Chapter 9

Book Content Updates

Because VMware occasionally updates exam topics without notice, VMware Press might post additional preparatory content on the web page associated with this book at http://www.pearsonitcertification.com/title/9780789753236. It is a good idea to check the website a couple of weeks before taking your exam to review any updated content that might be posted online. We also recommend that you periodically check back to this page on the Pearson IT Certification website to view any errata or supporting book files that may be available.

Access to Practice Scenarios and a word about the VDCA511 and VDCA550

This book comes with access to one complete set of practice scenarios that emulate the kind of questions you can expect to encounter on the real exam. You can access these questions by registering the book at PearsonITCertification.com and accessing the files through the book's page at www.informit.com/title/9780789753236.

During the time we were writing this certification guide, VMware announced a new release of the exam, the VDCA550. To help you master the content found on the VDCA511 or the VDCA550 we have provided the foundational topics in the book and have created digital content for you to reference that is specific to the new exam. Content on the practice scenarios maps to the VCAP-DCA blueprint and is relevant to both the **VDCA511** and **VDCA550** exams. All the scenarios are based on real-world experiences that involve administration tasks, which may be covered in the actual exam

Premium Edition

In addition to the free practice exam provided with the book, you can purchase two additional sets of practice scenarios with expanded functionality directly from Pearson IT Certification. The Premium Edition eBook and Practice Test for this title contains an additional two full practice exams and an eBook (in both PDF and ePub format).

If you have purchased the **print** version of this title, you can purchase the Premium Edition at a deep discount. A coupon code in the back of the book contains a one-time-use code and instructions for where you can purchase the Premium Edition.

To view the Premium Edition product page, go to
http://www.pearsonitcertification.com/title/9780133579734

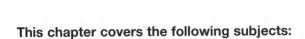

This chapter covers the following subjects:

- **VMware vSphere Client**—This section covers using the vSphere Client to perform vSphere administration.

- **ESXCLI Command Set**—This section covers using the esxcli namespace to perform ESXi server administration.

- **vmkfstools Command**—This section covers using the **vmkfstools** command to perform VMFS and virtual disk administration.

- **esxtop/resxtop**—This section covers the use of the local **esxtop** and remote **resxtop** commands to retrieve real-time metrics regarding the resource utilization of an ESXi host.

- **vCLI and vMA**—This section covers implementing and using the vCLI from the vSphere Management Appliance (vMA). The section covers utilities and options, such as connection options fastpass and vifs, which are useful when executing commands from the vCLI rather than from the ESXi Shell.

- **PowerCLI**—This section covers using the vSphere PowerCLI to run commands and build scripts aimed at managing every aspect of a vSphere implementation, including vCenter Server and vSphere cluster-based services.

The material in this chapter pertains to the VCAP-DCA Exam objectives 8.1 and 8.2.

## CHAPTER 1

Administrator Tools

This chapter describes how to implement and use various administrator tools that are useful in managing large vSphere environments. These tools include the vSphere Client, ESXCLI, vmkfstools, ESXTOP, vCLI, vMA, and PowerCLI. The goal is to ensure you are comfortable with the general use of each tool. In the remaining chapters, procedures will be provided on using these tools for specific purposes.

"Do I Know This Already?" Quiz

The "Do I Know This Already?" quiz allows you to assess how well you already know the material in this chapter. Table 1-1 outlines the major headings in this chapter and the corresponding "Do I Know This Already?" quiz questions. You can find the answers in Appendix A, "Answers to the 'Do I Know This Already?' Quizzes." Because of the advanced and hands-on nature of this particular exam, you should read the entire chapter and practice performing all the described tasks at least once, regardless of how well you do on this quiz. This quiz can help you determine which topics will require the most effort during your preparation.

Table 1-1 "Do I Know This Already?" Foundation Topics Section-to-Question Mapping

Foundations Topics Section	Questions Covered in This Section
VMware vSphere Client	1
ESXCLI Command Set	2
vmkfstools Command	3
ESXTOP	4
vCLI and vMA	5
PowerCLI	6

1. An administrator needs to determine whether a local drive in an ESXi host is malfunctioning. Which method can be used to successfully determine this information?

   a. Use the **esxcli hardware health** namespace on the ESXi host.

   b. Use the vSphere Client to log on directly to the host, and then click the **Hardware Status** tab.

   c. Use the vSphere Client to log on directly to the host, and then click the **Health Status** link on the **Configuration** tab.

   d. Use the vSphere Client to connect to the vCenter Server, and then click the **Summary** tab of the ESXi host.

2. Which command(s) can be used to list all the virtual switches that are controlled exclusively by a specific ESXi host?

   a. From the ESXi Shell, enter **esxcli network vswitch list**.

   b. From PowerCLI, use the **Get-VMHost** and **Get-NetworkAdapter** functions.

   c. From the ESXi Shell, use the **esxcli network vswitch show** namespace.

   d. From PowerCLI, use the **Get-VMHost** and **Get-VMHostNetwork** functions.

3. Which method can be used to create a new virtual disk file on an ESXi host?

   a. Enter the **vmkfstools –c** command.

   b. Enter the **vmkfstools –C** command.

   c. Use the **Add Storage** link on the **Configuration** tab of the ESXi host.

   d. Use the PowerCLI **New-VMGuestFile** cmdlet.

4. Which command can be used to collect performance statistics on an ESXi host and output them to a file?

   a. **esxtop --csv**

   b. **esxtop --filename**

   c. **resxtop -b**

   d. **resxtop -outputfile**

5. An administrator wants to simplify entering commands on a vSphere Management Appliance. Which method will accomplish this task?

   a. Use PowerCLI and run the **Set-FastPass** cmdlet against the vMA.

   b. Use the **Invoke-FastPass** command on the vMA.

   c. Use the **vifp** command on the vMA.

   d. Use the vicfg-fastpass command on the vMA.

6. Which process can be used to successfully deploy a PowerCLI implementation?

   a. Install PowerShell on a Windows virtual machine, and then install PowerCLI on the same VM.

   b. Install PowerShell on a Windows virtual machine. The PowerShell package includes PowerCLI.

   c. Deploy the vMA. The vMA includes a PowerShell implementation.

   d. Install vCenter Server on a Windows virtual machine. The vCenter Server installation also installs PowerCLI.

Foundation Topics

VMware vSphere Client

This section describes how to implement and use the vSphere Client. The vSphere Client, which is often called the vSphere C# Client, is a graphical user interface (GUI) that can be used to connect to a vCenter Server or to ESXi hosts to manage a vSphere environment. It is a Windows-based application. VMware also provides a web-based client called the vSphere Web Client. The vSphere Web Client can perform many of the same tasks performed by the vSphere Client. For the purposes of this book, we will perform vSphere administration tasks using the vSphere Client.

Installation

The vSphere Client can be installed on a Windows-based desktop or server that meets the minimum requirements. The main requirements are one CPU, 1GB RAM, and dot-Net Framework 3.5 or higher. The vSphere Client installer can be downloaded independently from VMware. One way to quickly find a link to download the installer is to use a web browser to browse the default webpage of an ESXi host or vCenter, as shown in Figure 1-1. The Download vSphere Client link on a vCenter Server's home page will download the installer from the vCenter Server, but the same link on an ESXi host's webpage will download the installer from VMware via the Internet. Additionally, the installer named VMware-VIMSetup-all-5.1.xxx (where xxx matches the current build level) contains an option to install the vSphere Client, as well as options to install vCenter Server, Update Manager, the vSphere Web Client, and other modules.

To install the vSphere Client, simply download and run one of the installers to a desktop or other appropriate Windows instance. In most cases, accept all the defaults provided by the installation wizard.

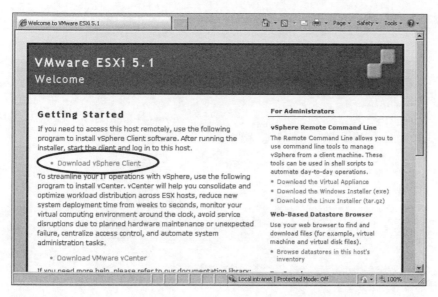

Figure 1-1   Link to download the vSphere Client from an ESXi host.

Usage

To use the vSphere Client, select **Start > Programs > VMware vSphere Client**. At the logon prompt, specify the IP address or hostname of an ESXi host or a vCenter Server and provide user credentials. By default, the **root** account can be used to log on to an ESXi host. The local Windows administrator account or a domain administrator account can used to log on to a Windows-based implementation of vCenter Server. The **root** account can be used to log on to a vCenter Server Appliance.

If the vSphere Client is used to log on directly to an ESXi host, then the **Inventory** pane shows only that host and any objects configured on that host. It does not show other ESXi hosts or vCenter Server, as shown in Figure 1-2.

One commonly utilized step for troubleshooting ESXi host hardware issues is to examine the **Configuration tab > Hardware Health Status**. A healthy system has a normal green check mark indicator for each hardware device, as shown in Figure 1-3. If any items do not have a green check mark, the administrator should address and resolve the issue.

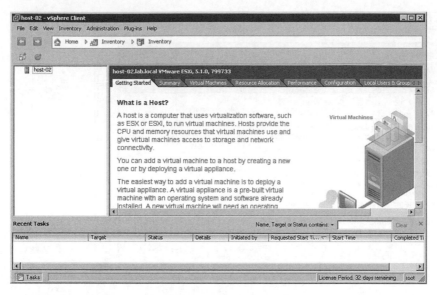

Figure 1-2 vSphere Client logged directly on to an ESXi host.

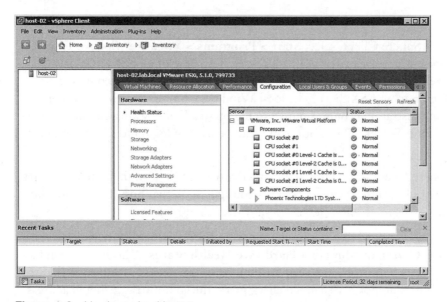

Figure 1-3 Hardware health status.

Most configuration settings can be configured by using the **Configuration** tab and selecting an appropriate option. The **Configuration** tab allows the configuration of items such as **Time Settings**, **DNS and Routing**, and **Licensing**, as shown in Figure 1-4.

Figure 1-4   ESXi host configuration.

The vSphere Client can be used to create a virtual machine (VM) even if vCenter Server is not yet deployed. Frequently, the first VM created by an administrator is a Windows-based VM in which the administrator installs vCenter Server. To create a VM, right-click the ESXi host in the inventory pane, and select **New Virtual Machine**.

The vSphere Client is typically used to connect to a vCenter Server, rather than directly to a specific ESXi host. This provides a single pane of glass to manage the entire vSphere environment, including all ESXi hosts and VMs. When connected to a vCenter Server, the vSphere Client will automatically provide additional options only available when managing the entire environment. For example, the **Home** page might provide as many as 20 options, as shown in Figure 1-5.

In addition to vCenter Server, additional optional server-based modules can be installed. These optional modules include VMware Update Manager and Site Recovery Manager. Each optional module provides a client-based plug-in for the vSphere Client, which enables the use of the vSphere Client to perform all administration tasks without requiring independent clients.

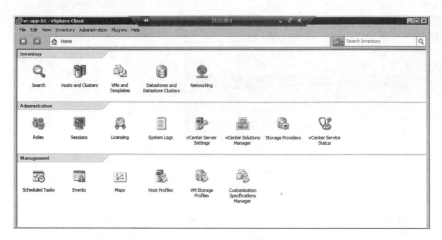

Figure 1-5   vCenter Home page accessed from the vSphere Client.

Use the **Plug-ins > Plug-ins Manager** menu option to manage the plug-ins. Three plug-ins may automatically appear, including vCenter Hardware Status, vCenter Service Status, and VMware vCenter Storage Monitoring, as shown in Figure 1-6.

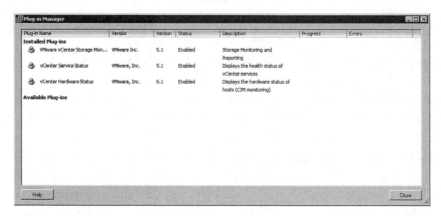

Figure 1-6   vSphere Client plug-ins.

The vSphere Client can be used to perform nearly all the initial configuration tasks for a new vSphere environment. The exception being the majority of new features in vSphere 5.1 and 5.5, such as SSO, Inventory Tagging, Enhanced vMotion, and so on. It can also be used to perform nearly all the daily administrative tasks. When connected to vCenter Server, it provides four options for viewing and managing the vSphere inventory. These options are **Hosts and Clusters**, **VMs and Templates**, **Datastores and Datastore Clusters**, and **Networking**. In an enterprise, administrative tasks are often delegated to various personnel, each having unique responsibilities. Each of the four inventory options provided by vCenter Server is aimed at a specific type of administrator. For example, a Network Administrator would typically use the **Inventory > Networking** option as shown in Figure 1-7.

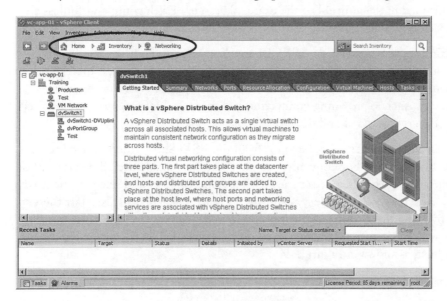

Figure 1-7   Example of the Networking Inventory view.

ESXCLI Command Set

This section describes how to implement and use the ESXCLI command set. The ESXCLI command set is provided in both the ESXi shell and the vSphere Command Line Interface (vCLI). It provides the preferred command set for performing administrative tasks on an ESXi host. The scope of the ESXCLI command set is similar in scope to using the vSphere Client connected directly to an ESXi host, rather than to a vCenter Server. The ESXCLI command set cannot be used to configure vCenter Server or to perform tasks that require vCenter Server.

NOTE   If you want to use a command set for performing administrative tasks that include vCenter Server operations, use PowerCLI.

Getting Started

The vCLI is an interface that provides the ESXCLI command set and other commands, such as the vicfg-* command set. In many cases, vCLI provides more than one command that can accomplish a specific task. Generally speaking, when feasible, you should plan to use esxcli commands because the vicfg-* command set will likely be discontinued in the future. For the exam, plan to use esxcli commands unless an exam task clearly requires you to use another command.

This section focuses on running ESXCLI commands from the ESXi Shell. It describes a method for using the ESXCLI command set and provides examples. It does not provide details for running ESXCLI commands from the vCLI or the vMA. These details, such as providing connection and credential information, are covered in the section on the vCLI and the vMA.

To get started running esxcli commands from the ESXi Shell, you first need to start the ESXi Shell service. For convenience, you could also enable the SSH service. You can enable both of these features by using the vSphere Client and selecting **Security Profile > Services > Properties**, as shown in Figure 1-8. You can also start these services by using the **Troubleshooting** option in the Direct Console User Interface (DCUI), which is a menu of management options provided on the direct console of an ESXi host, as shown in Figure 1-9.

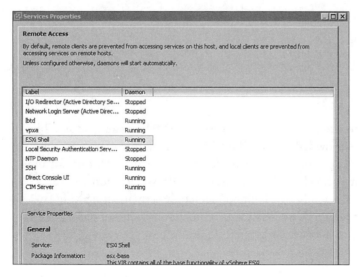

Figure 1-8 Service Properties page of the Security Profile.

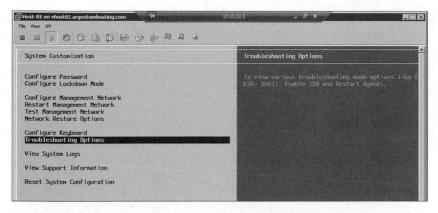

Figure 1-9   The DCUI.

Navigating the Namespace

Generally speaking, the ESXCLI command set is intended to provide a single set of commands to perform all ESXi host-based administrative tasks. It provides a collection of namespaces as a mechanism for an administrator to quickly discover the precise command necessary for a specific task. This command hierarchy groups commands into a parent namespace to which each command relates. For example, all the commands to configure networking exist in the **esxcli network** namespace, and all the commands to configure storage exist in the **esxcli storage** namespace. Each namespace is further divided into child namespaces that comprise various functions performed under the parent namespace. For example, the **esxcli storage** parent namespace contains a **core** namespace that deals with storage adapters and devices and an **nmp** namespace that deals with path selection and storage array types. Therefore, a typical esxcli command is composed of multiple namespaces, where each additional namespace is used to narrow the scope of the command, ending with the actual operation to be performed.

You can use the following method to identify the proper esxcli command to perform a specific task. First, simply enter **esxcli** at the command prompt in the ESXi Shell. Because it is not a command by itself, just the entry point to the namespace hierarchy, the results will show the first level of the namespace hierarchy. The first level of available namespaces includes **esxcli**, **fcoe**, **hardware**, **iscsi**, **network**, **sched**, **software**, **storage**, **system**, and **vm**. The results include a brief description of each namespace as shown in Figure 1-10. Next, identify which namespace is most likely to serve your need. Use the up-arrow key on the keyboard to retrieve the last entered namespace and add the name for the next namespace. For example, if you are seeking a network-related command, you could enter **esxcli network**, which provides the next level of the namespace hierarchy, as shown in Figure 1-11.

Key
Topic

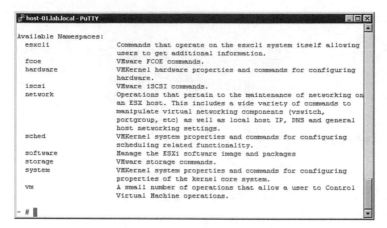

Figure 1-10 First-level hierarchy of the esxcli namespace.

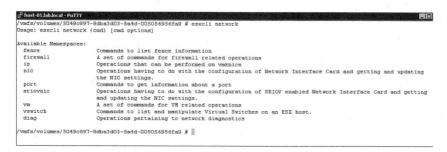

Figure 1-11 Available namespaces at esxcli network.

For a more thorough example, if you are seeking a command to list all standard vSwitches, you could use these steps:

Step 1. Enter **esxcli**, and examine the results shown in Figure 1-10.

Step 2. Enter **esxcli network**, and examine the results shown in Figure 1-11.

Step 3. Enter **esxcli network vswitch**, and examine the results shown in Figure 1-12.

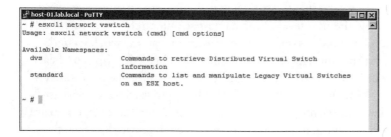

Figure 1-12 Available namespaces at esxcli network vswitch.

Step 4. Enter **esxcli network vswitch standard**, and examine the results shown in Figure 1-13. Notice that at this level, some Available Commands are now displayed. These commands are **add**, **list**, **remove**, and **set**. For this example, the list command seems to be the most appropriate.

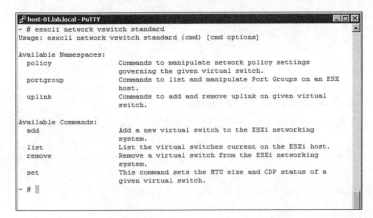

Figure 1-13   Available namespaces and commands at esxcli network vswitch standard.

Step 5. Enter the **esxcli network vswitch standard list** command, which executes the command and produces results, as shown in Figure 1-14.

```
~ # esxcli network vswitch standard list
vSwitch0
   Name: vSwitch0
   Class: etherswitch
   Num Ports: 128
   Used Ports: 4
   Configured Ports: 128
   MTU: 1500
   CDP Status: listen
   Beacon Enabled: false
   Beacon Interval: 1
   Beacon Threshold: 3
   Beacon Required By:
   Uplinks: vmnic0
   Portgroups: VM Network, Management Network

vSwitch1
   Name: vSwitch1
   Class: etherswitch
   Num Ports: 128
   Used Ports: 5
   Configured Ports: 128
   MTU: 1500
   CDP Status: listen
   Beacon Enabled: false
   Beacon Interval: 1
   Beacon Threshold: 3
   Beacon Required By:
   Uplinks: vmnic3, vmnic2
   Portgroups: Production, Test
~ #
```

Figure 1-14   Example of the esxcli network vswitch standard list command.

NOTE   When using the previously discussed approach to discover the appropriate command for a given task, pay attention to commands versus namespaces. Entering a namespace at the command prompt is always safe because it will simply display the next level of available namespaces and commands. However, entering a command at the command prompt will execute that command. You should be careful not to enter a command without fully understanding the consequences.

Scenario—Identifying the Proper Esxcli Command

Determine the proper esxcli command to list all NFS datastores that are accessible by an ESXi host.

This task can be accomplished by performing the following steps:

Step 1.   Using ESXi Shell, enter **esxcli**.

Step 2.   Examine the available namespaces. Notice that the **storage** namespace is probably the best choice for this task.

Step 3.   Enter **esxcli storage**.

Step 4.   Examine the available namespaces. Notice that the **nfs** namespace is probably the best choice for this task.

Step 5.   Enter **esxcli storage nfs**.

Step 6.   Examine the available namespaces and commands. Notice that the **list** command is probably the best choice for this task.

Step 7.   Enter **esxcli storage nfs list**, as shown in Figure 1-15.

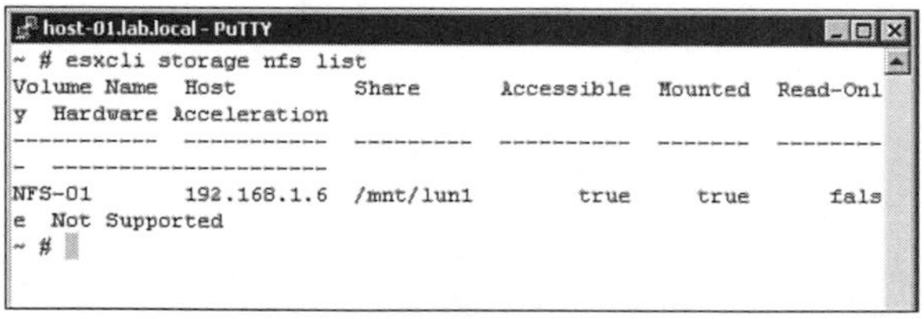

Figure 1-15   Example of the esxcli storage nfs list command.

Formatting ESXCLI Output

The output of an esxcli command can be formatted in different ways. This feature enables the administrator to export the results of an esxcli command into other tools. The **–formatter** argument can be added to an esxcli command to format the output as CSV, XML, or keyvalue. CSV-formatted output can be useful for importing the data into a spreadsheet, whereas XML can be useful for importing the data into web-based reporting tools. Finally, keyvalue can be useful for importing the data into software development tools.

For example, consider the command **esxcli network firewall get command**, which can be used to determine high-level configuration information on the hypervisor-based firewall on an ESXi host. When executed without the **–formatter** option, the default results show the conceptual name and value of some firewall properties, as shown in Figure 1-16.

```
host-01.lab.local - PuTTY
~ # esxcli  network firewall get
    Default Action: DROP
    Enabled: true
    Loaded: true
~ #
```

Figure 1-16 Example of unformatted results.

When executed with the **–formatter** option set to CSV, the same results are formatted in CSV form, as shown in Figure 1-17.

```
host-01.lab.local - PuTTY
~ # esxcli --formatter=csv  network firewall get
DefaultAction,Enabled,Loaded,
DROP,true,true,
~ #
```

Figure 1-17 Example of CSV formatted results.

When executed with the **–formatter** option set to XML, the same results are formatted in XML form, as shown in Figure 1-18.

```
host-01.lab.local - PuTTY
~ # esxcli --formatter=xml  network firewall get
<?xml version="1.0" encoding="utf-8"?>
<output xmlns="http://www.vmware.com/Products/ESX/5.0/esxcli">
<root>
    <structure typeName="Firewall">
        <field name="DefaultAction">
            <string>DROP</string>
        </field>
        <field name="Enabled">
            <boolean>true</boolean>
        </field>
        <field name="Loaded">
            <boolean>true</boolean>
        </field>
    </structure>
</root>
</output>
~ #
```

Figure 1-18 Example of XML-formatted results.

When executed with the **–formatter** option set to keyvalue, the same results are formatted in keyvalue form, as shown in Figure 1-19.

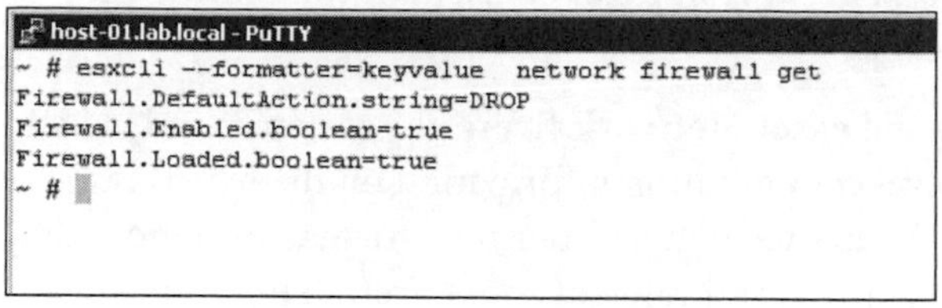

Figure 1-19   Example of keyvalue-formatted results.

vmkfstools Command

This section describes how to use the **vmkfstools** command. The scope of the **vmkfstools** command is the manipulation of datastores and virtual disks. Although some of its features are also provided by esxcli commands, **vmkfstools** is still important. VCAP-DCA candidates are expected to be able to use **vmkfsools**. The **vmkfstools** command set can be used to perform many datastore and virtual disk–related tasks that can be performed in the vSphere Client, as well as some tasks that cannot be performed in the vSphere Client. It is also a good tool for diagnosing and troubleshooting issues that cannot be corrected using the vSphere Client.

Help Information

To get started, you can view the syntax and usage information for **vmkfstools** by using the **vmkfstools –H** command, as illustrated in Figure 1-20. Notice that the results of this command indicate that it can be used for file systems and virtual disks.

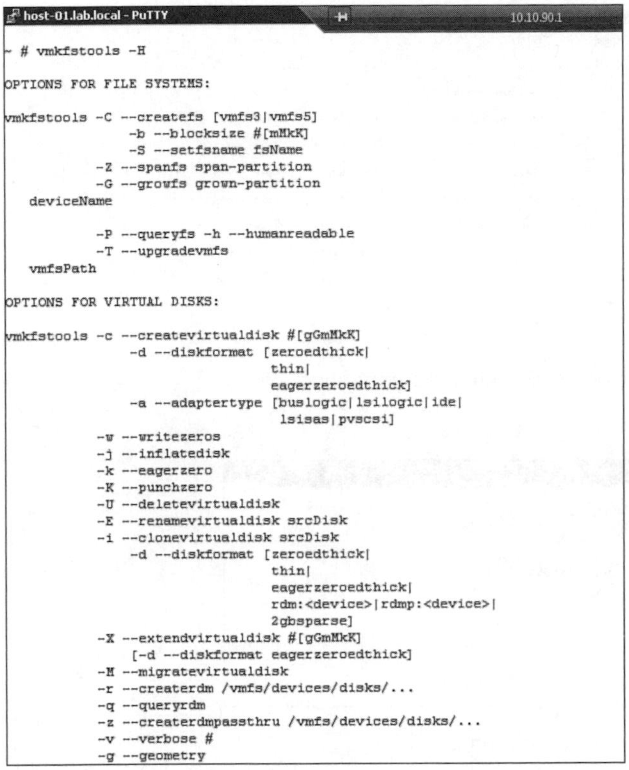

```
host-01.lab.local - PuTTY                          H            10.10.90.1
- # vmkfstools -H

OPTIONS FOR FILE SYSTEMS:

vmkfstools -C --createfs [vmfs3|vmfs5]
              -b --blocksize #[mMkK]
              -S --setfsname fsName
         -Z --spanfs span-partition
         -G --growfs grown-partition
   deviceName

              -P --queryfs -h --humanreadable
              -T --upgradevmfs
   vmfsPath

OPTIONS FOR VIRTUAL DISKS:

vmkfstools -c --createvirtualdisk #[gGmMkK]
              -d --diskformat [zeroedthick|
                              thin|
                              eagerzeroedthick]
              -a --adaptertype [buslogic|lsilogic|ide|
                               lsisas|pvscsi]
         -w --writezeros
         -j --inflatedisk
         -k --eagerzero
         -K --punchzero
         -U --deletevirtualdisk
         -E --renamevirtualdisk srcDisk
         -i --clonevirtualdisk srcDisk
              -d --diskformat [zeroedthick|
                              thin|
                              eagerzeroedthick|
                              rdm:<device>|rdmp:<device>|
                              2gbsparse]
         -X --extendvirtualdisk #[gGmMkK]
            [-d --diskformat eagerzeroedthick]
         -M --migratevirtualdisk
         -r --createrdm /vmfs/devices/disks/...
         -q --queryrdm
         -z --createrdmpassthru /vmfs/devices/disks/...
         -v --verbose #
         -g --geometry
```

Figure 1-20   Results of the vmkfstools help command.

Managing VMFS Datastores

The **vmkfstools** command set can be used to query, create, span, grow, and update VMFS file systems (commonly called VMFS datastores). For example, to view the properties of an existing VMFS datastore, first use **esxcli storage filesystem list** to identify the desired datastore (as illustrated in Figure 1-21); then use **vmkfstools –P** to view its properties. When using **vmkfstools –P**, specify the path name to the datastore in the form of **/vmfs/volumes/<volume-name>**, as illustrated in Figure 1-22. In this example, one of the existing datastores is named **Shared-8**.

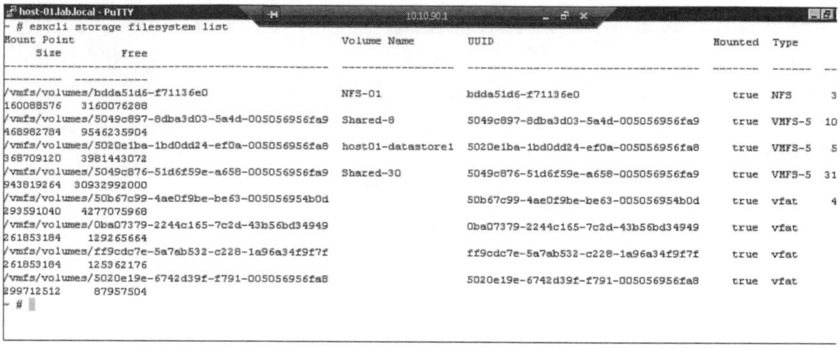

Figure 1-21   Example of the esxcli storage filesystem list command.

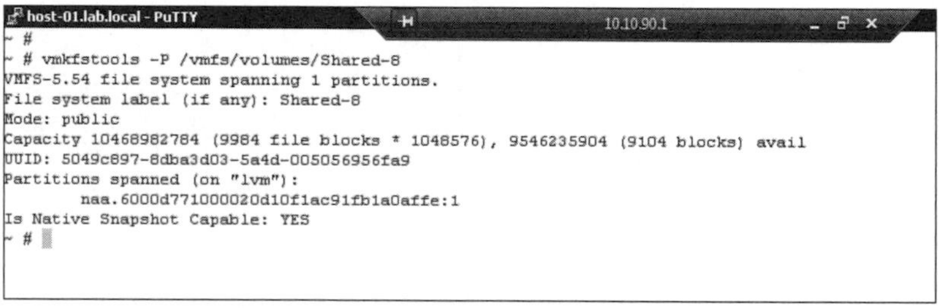

Figure 1-22   Example of the vmkfstools -P command.

To use **vmkfstools** to create a new VMFS datastore, you must first identify an un-used LUN presented by a SCSI-based storage adapter (Fibre channel HBA, local storage controller, or iSCSI initiator), which can be done using the **Storage Views** tab in the vSphere Client connected to vCenter. Follow these steps:

Step 1.   Select **Inventory > Hosts and Clusters**.

Step 2.   Select the ESXi host in the inventory pane.

Step 3.   Select the **Storage Views** tab.

Step 4.   If desired, change the displayed columns by right-clicking any column heading and selecting just the columns you need.

Step 5.   Ensure the **Canonical Name**, **Lun**, and **Datastore** names are displayed.

Step 6.   Identify any SCSI devices (by Lun, Canonical Name, and Runtime Name) that do not have a file system by locating any row whose **Datastore** column is empty, as shown in Figure 1-23. In this example, existing VMFS-formatted datastores reside on SCSI devices whose **Runtime Names** are vmbha1:C0:T0:L0, vmbha33:C0:T0:L8, and vmbha33:C0:T0:L9. All other SCSI devices are unused. Notice in this example that the device whose **Runtime Name** is vmhba33:C0:T0:L0 has the **Canonical Name** naa.6000d771000020f30f1ac91fb1053941.

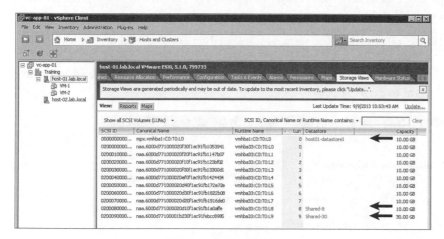

Figure 1-23   Example of identifying unused SCSI devices with the Storage Views tab.

Now that an unused SCSI device has been identified, an available partition on the device needs to be identified or created. This can be accomplished using the **partedUtil getptbl** command. For example, this command can be used to display any existing partitions on the SCSI device identified by canonical name naa.6000d7 71000020f30f1ac91fb1053941, as shown in Figure 1-24. In this example, the device has no partitions.

Figure 1-24   Example of using the partedUtil getptbl command.

The **partedUtil setptbl** command can be used to create a new partition. For example, this command can be used to create a new partition on the SCSI device whose **Canonical Name** is naa.6000d771000020f30f1ac91fb1053941 per these specifications:

1. Partition number = 1

2. Starting sector = 2048 (which is typically recommended by VMware)

3. Ending sector = 20971486 (which happens to be the last available sector on the device used in this example)

4. Type = AA31E02A400F11DB9590000C2911D1B8 (which is a GUID that refers to VMFS-5 file system)

5. Attribute = 0 (which is the same as not specifying any special attributes)

Figure 1-25 illustrates this example. It also illustrates using the **partedUtil getptbl** command again to verify success.

```
host-01.lab.local - PuTTY                                                    _ □ ×
/dev/disks # partedUtil setptbl  /vmfs/devices/disks/naa.6000d771000020f30f1ac91fb1053941 gpt "1
2048 20971486 AA31E02A400F11DB9590000C2911D1B8 0"
gpt
0 0 0 0
1 2048 20971486 AA31E02A400F11DB9590000C2911D1B8 0
/dev/disks #
/dev/disks #
/dev/disks #
/dev/disks # partedUtil getptbl  /vmfs/devices/disks/naa.6000d771000020f30f1ac91fb1053941
gpt
1305 255 63 20971520
1 2048 20971486 AA31E02A400F11DB9590000C2911D1B8 vmfs 0
/dev/disks #
```

Figure 1-25 Example of using the partedUtil setptbl command.

When an empty partition is available, the **vmkfstools** command can be used to create a VMFS datastore in the partition. For example, you can use the following command to create a new VMFS datastore named VMFStest01 in the first partition of a device named naa.6000d771000020f30f1ac91fb1053941:

```
vmkfstools  -C  vmfs5  -S VMFStest01  /vmfs/devices/disks/ naa.6000d77
1000020f30f1ac91fb1053941:1
```

Managing Virtual Disks

The **vmkfstools** command can be used to manipulate virtual disk files. The **–c** option can be used to create a new virtual disk. When creating a new virtual disk, the size of the disk must be specified, typically in megabytes. When creating a virtual disk, the **–d** option can be used to specify the type of disk, such as thin provisioned. For example, the following command can be use to create a thin-provisioned, 4 GB disk named test-1.vmdk in a VMFS named Shared-8:

```
vmkfstools  -c  4096m  -d thin  /vmfs/volumes/Shared-8/test1.vmdk
```

You can use the **vmkfstools** command with the **–X** option to grow (extend) the virtual disk size. For example, the following command can be used to extend the virtual disk that was created in the last example to a new size of 6 GB:

```
vmkfstools  -X  6G  /vmfs/volumes/Shared-8/test1.vmdk
```

esxtop and resxtop Commands

This section describes how to use the **esxtop** and **resxtop** commands. The **resxtop** command is identical to **esxtop**, except that **resxtop** is used remotely from the vCLI and **esxtop** is used locally from the ESXi Shell. This section focuses on **esxtop** and uses **esxtop** exclusively in its examples, but all the following information can also be applied to **resxtop**.

Overview

The **esxtop** utility displays the real-time resource utilization of an ESXi host. It displays CPU, RAM, disk, and network usage. It can present the resource usage for the entire host as well as a detailed breakout of each of the worlds running on the host. Each world (which is similar to a process on other operating systems) performs a specific function on the host. Some worlds, such as **drivers** and **vmotion**, are used directly by the hypervisor to perform necessary tasks. Other worlds belong to VMs. Some worlds represent the workload inside a VM, whereas other worlds represent VM overhead, such as overhead associated with providing a console for the VM.

The concept of **esxtop** is much the same as the concept of the **top** command in Linux, which displays all the processes running on a Linux server in order of resource utilization, with the most resource-intensive process at the top of the list. By default, **esxtop** displays the CPU usage of all the VMs and other worlds running on the ESXi host in order of their current CPU usage, with the world utilizing the most CPU resources listed at the top and the remaining in descending order, as illustrated in Figure 1-26.

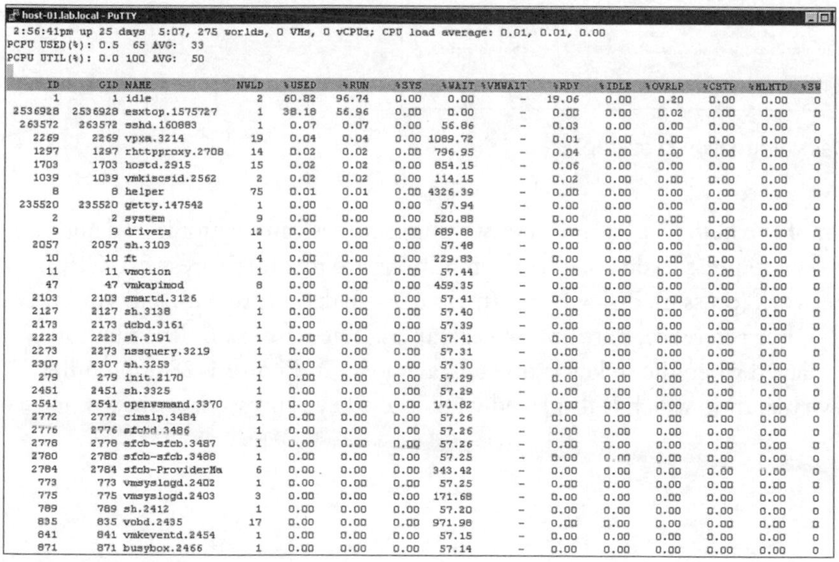

```
host-01.lab.local - PuTTY
 2:56:41pm up 25 days  5:07, 275 worlds, 0 VMs, 0 vCPUs; CPU load average: 0.01, 0.01, 0.00
PCPU USED(%): 0.5  65 AVG:  33
PCPU UTIL(%): 0.0 100 AVG:  50

      ID      GID NAME              NWLD   %USED    %RUN    %SYS   %WAIT %VMWAIT    %RDY   %IDLE  %OVRLP   %CSTP  %MLMTD  %SW
       1        1 idle                 2   60.82   96.74    0.00    0.00       -   19.06    0.00    0.20    0.00    0.00    0
 2536928  2536928 esxtop.1575727       1   38.18   56.96    0.00    0.00       -    0.00    0.00    0.02    0.00    0.00    0
  263572   263572 sshd.160883          1    0.07    0.07    0.00   56.86       -    0.03    0.00    0.00    0.00    0.00    0
    2269     2269 vpxa.3214           19    0.04    0.04    0.00 1089.72       -    0.01    0.00    0.00    0.00    0.00    0
    1297     1297 rhttpproxy.2708     14    0.02    0.02    0.00  796.95       -    0.04    0.00    0.00    0.00    0.00    0
    1703     1703 hostd.2915          15    0.02    0.02    0.00  854.15       -    0.06    0.00    0.00    0.00    0.00    0
    1039     1039 vmkiscsid.2562       2    0.02    0.02    0.00  114.15       -    0.02    0.00    0.00    0.00    0.00    0
       8        8 helper              75    0.01    0.01    0.00 4326.39       -    0.00    0.00    0.00    0.00    0.00    0
  235520   235520 getty.147542         1    0.00    0.00    0.00   57.94       -    0.00    0.00    0.00    0.00    0.00    0
       2        2 system               9    0.00    0.00    0.00  520.88       -    0.00    0.00    0.00    0.00    0.00    0
       9        9 drivers             12    0.00    0.00    0.00  689.88       -    0.00    0.00    0.00    0.00    0.00    0
    2057     2057 sh.3103              1    0.00    0.00    0.00   57.48       -    0.00    0.00    0.00    0.00    0.00    0
      10       10 ft                   4    0.00    0.00    0.00  229.83       -    0.00    0.00    0.00    0.00    0.00    0
      11       11 vmotion              1    0.00    0.00    0.00   57.44       -    0.00    0.00    0.00    0.00    0.00    0
      47       47 vmkapimod            8    0.00    0.00    0.00  459.35       -    0.00    0.00    0.00    0.00    0.00    0
    2103     2103 smartd.3126          1    0.00    0.00    0.00   57.41       -    0.00    0.00    0.00    0.00    0.00    0
    2127     2127 sh.3138              1    0.00    0.00    0.00   57.40       -    0.00    0.00    0.00    0.00    0.00    0
    2173     2173 dcbd.3161            1    0.00    0.00    0.00   57.39       -    0.00    0.00    0.00    0.00    0.00    0
    2223     2223 sh.3191              1    0.00    0.00    0.00   57.41       -    0.00    0.00    0.00    0.00    0.00    0
    2273     2273 nssquery.3219        1    0.00    0.00    0.00   57.31       -    0.00    0.00    0.00    0.00    0.00    0
    2307     2307 sh.3253              1    0.00    0.00    0.00   57.30       -    0.00    0.00    0.00    0.00    0.00    0
     279      279 init.2170            1    0.00    0.00    0.00   57.29       -    0.00    0.00    0.00    0.00    0.00    0
    2451     2451 sh.3325              1    0.00    0.00    0.00   57.29       -    0.00    0.00    0.00    0.00    0.00    0
    2541     2541 openwsmand.3370      3    0.00    0.00    0.00  171.82       -    0.00    0.00    0.00    0.00    0.00    0
    2772     2772 cimslp.3484          1    0.00    0.00    0.00   57.26       -    0.00    0.00    0.00    0.00    0.00    0
    2776     2776 sfcbd.3486           1    0.00    0.00    0.00   57.26       -    0.00    0.00    0.00    0.00    0.00    0
    2778     2778 sfcb-sfcb.3487       1    0.00    0.00    0.00   57.26       -    0.00    0.00    0.00    0.00    0.00    0
    2780     2780 sfcb-sfcb.3488       1    0.00    0.00    0.00   57.25       -    0.00    0.00    0.00    0.00    0.00    0
    2784     2784 sfcb-ProviderMa      6    0.00    0.00    0.00  343.42       -    0.00    0.00    0.00    0.00    0.00    0
     773      773 vmsyslogd.2402       1    0.00    0.00    0.00   57.25       -    0.00    0.00    0.00    0.00    0.00    0
     775      775 vmsyslogd.2403       3    0.00    0.00    0.00  171.68       -    0.00    0.00    0.00    0.00    0.00    0
     789      789 sh.2412              1    0.00    0.00    0.00   57.20       -    0.00    0.00    0.00    0.00    0.00    0
     835      835 vobd.2435           17    0.00    0.00    0.00  971.98       -    0.00    0.00    0.00    0.00    0.00    0
     841      841 vmkeventd.2454       1    0.00    0.00    0.00   57.15       -    0.00    0.00    0.00    0.00    0.00    0
     871      871 busybox.2466         1    0.00    0.00    0.00   57.14       -    0.00    0.00    0.00    0.00    0.00    0
```

Figure 1-26 Example of `esxtop`.

Usage

The **esxtop** utility is interactive. By default, it refreshes its display every few seconds, sorting the rows so that the list appears in descending order with the most active world at the top. Although CPU usage information is displayed by default, the results can be changed to show memory usage, disk usage, and network usage. For each resource type, certain fields are displayed by default. The information displayed can be selected from a list of available fields, by adding or removing individual fields as needed. To make these changes, simply press a specific key while viewing **esxtop**. To learn about the options and appropriate keys, press the H key to get help information, as shown in Figure 1-27.

Figure 1-27   Help information in esxtop.

The bottom of the help section indicates which resources can be monitored and the appropriate key to press to do so. The main options are memory (press m), CPU (press c), network (press n), disk adapter (press d), disk drive (press u), and virtual disk (press v). For reference, here are two examples. The first example is memory, which is displayed when the m key is pressed, as shown in Figure 1-28. The other example is virtual disk, which is displayed when the v key is pressed, as shown in Figure 1-29.

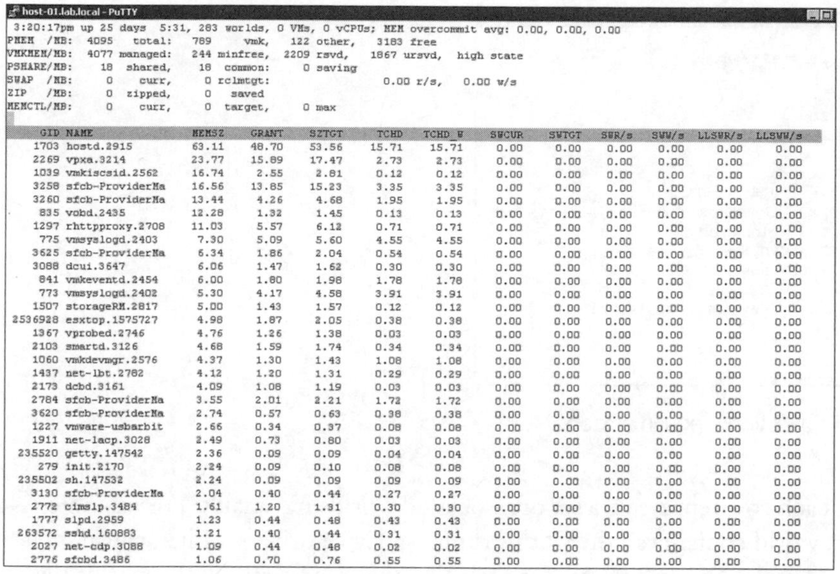

Figure 1-28 Memory display in esxtop.

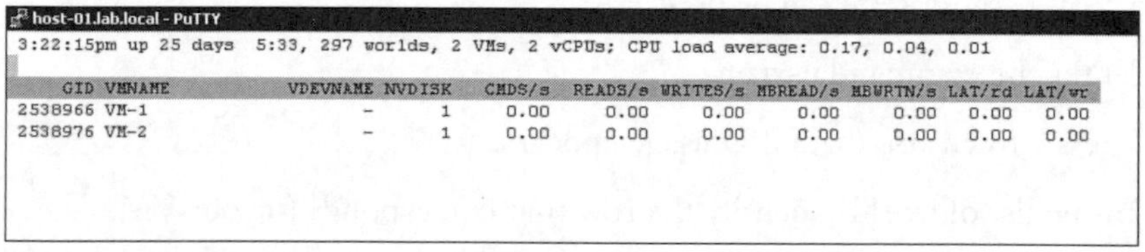

Figure 1-29 Virtual disk display in esxtop.

To change the fields (columns) of a specific resource display in **esxtop**, press the F key while viewing that resource. For example, when displaying CPU resource usage, press the F key to view the CPU-related fields that may be selected. An asterisk at the beginning of the row indicates that the field is included in the current results, as shown in Figure 1-30. To add or remove a column from the currect esxtop view, use the letter keys associated with each field while in the field editor (F while esxtop is running). For example, pressing the B key toggles on or off the display of the Group ID for each world. In Figure 1-30, pressing C would enable the currently disabled field LWID.

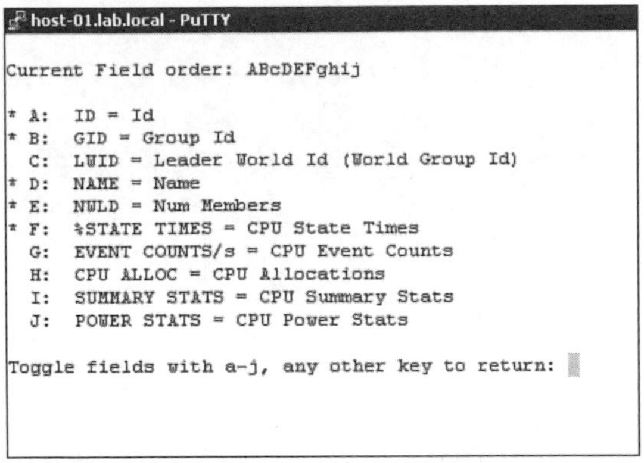

```
host-01.lab.local - PuTTY

Current Field order: ABcDEFghij

* A:  ID = Id
* B:  GID = Group Id
  C:  LWID = Leader World Id (World Group Id)
* D:  NAME = Name
* E:  NWLD = Num Members
* F:  %STATE TIMES = CPU State Times
  G:  EVENT COUNTS/s = CPU Event Counts
  H:  CPU ALLOC = CPU Allocations
  I:  SUMMARY STATS = CPU Summary Stats
  J:  POWER STATS = CPU Power Stats

Toggle fields with a-j, any other key to return:
```

Figure 1-30   Field option menu in esxtop.

In **esxtop**, each row represents a set of associated worlds by default. For example, the **drivers** world contains all the worlds running device drivers. When viewing virtual machine data, a row appears for each VM that represents all the worlds that support the execution of that VM. To expand the parent row and view all the underlying rows, press the E key. For example, to expand the parent row assigned to a VM named VM-1, these steps can be used:

Step 1.   Enter the command **esxtop**.

Step 2.   Press **c** to ensure that CPU usage appears.

Step 3.   In the list of worlds, identify the row that corresponds to your VM.

Step 4.   Make note of the first two columns, ID and Group ID (GID).

Step 5.   For example, a VM named VM-1, whose GID = 2538966, can be expanded by pressing the E key and entering **2538966** for the group to be expanded.

This is shown in Figure 1-31. Notice all the rows whose GIDs are 2538966, indicating they are servicing the same VM. Of these expanded worlds, the world named vm-vcpu-0:VM-1 is the world that best indicates the CPU within the guest OS of this VM. Of these expanded worlds, the world named vm-vcpu-0:VM-1 is the world that best indicates the current CPU usage of the guest OS within this VM.

Often, when diagnosing an issue, the main concern is the resource usage of VMs, not the resources used by system-related processes. To change the **esxtop** view to display only data on VMs and not on worlds belonging to the hypervisor, press Shift+V, as shown in Figure 1-32. On a host running many VMs, this permits you to see more VMs in the display because **esxtop** provides no method by which to scroll up or down through all the available worlds.

```
host-01.lab.local - PuTTY
8:22:43am up 28 days 22:33, 295 worlds, 2 VMs, 2 vCPUs; CPU load average: 0.51, 0.52, 0.51
PCPU USED(%): 3.6 100 AVG:  51
PCPU UTIL(%): 3.8 100 AVG:  51

    ID     GID NAME              NWLD   %USED   %RUN   %SYS  %WAIT %VMWAIT   %RDY   %IDLE  %OVRLP  %CSTP %MLMTD  %
 1576934 2538966 vmx                 1    0.07   0.07   0.00 100.00       -   0.61    0.00   0.00   0.00   0.00
 1578984 2538966 vmast.1578983       1    0.01   0.01   0.00 100.00       -   0.56    0.00   0.00   0.00   0.00
 1576937 2538966 vmx-vthread-4:V     1    0.00   0.00   0.00 100.00       -   0.00    0.00   0.00   0.00   0.00
 1578986 2538966 vmx-vthread-5:V     1    0.00   0.00   0.00 100.00       -   0.00    0.00   0.00   0.00   0.00
 1578987 2538966 vmx-mks:VM-1        1    0.00   0.00   0.00 100.00       -   0.00    0.00   0.00   0.00   0.00
 1576940 2538966 vmx-svga:VM-1       1    0.00   0.00   0.00 100.00       -   0.00    0.00   0.00   0.00   0.00
 1576941 2538966 vmx-vcpu-0:VM-1     1  101.58 102.01   0.00   0.00    0.00   0.01    0.00   0.07   0.00   0.00
 2538976 2538976 VM-2                7    0.23   0.22   0.00 700.00    0.51   2.43  100.56   0.00   0.00   0.00
```

Figure 1-31   Expanding the world of a VM.

```
host-01.lab.local - PuTTY
8:27:10am up 28 days 22:37, 297 worlds, 2 VMs, 2 vCPUs; CPU load average: 0.51, 0.51, 0.51
PCPU USED(%): 2.5 100 AVG:  51
PCPU UTIL(%): 2.6 100 AVG:  51

    ID     GID NAME              NWLD   %USED   %RUN   %SYS  %WAIT %VMWAIT   %RDY   %IDLE  %OVRLP  %CSTP %MLMTD  %
 2538966 2538966 VM-1                7   97.07  97.05   0.00 581.18    0.00   0.55    0.00   0.06   0.00   0.00
 2538976 2538976 VM-2                7    0.22   0.21   0.01 677.36    0.36   1.25   95.70   0.00   0.00   0.00
```

Figure 1-32   VM-only display in esxtop.

Batch Mode

The **esxtop** utility offers other options such as batch mode, sampling period
changes, and the ability to export data to a CSV file for later analysis and playback.
Here is an example of running **esxtop** in batch mode, where it collects all data at
5-minute (300 seconds) intervals and outputs the data to a file named results01.csv:

```
esxtop  -b  -a -d 300 >> results.csv
```

For administrators who have a functional knowledge of the Windows Perfmon utility, the CSV file output from **esxtop** can be imported into this utility. To import a
CSV file into Windows Performance Monitor, right-click the chart, select **Properties**, and select the **Source** tab, as shown in Figure 1-33. Use the **Add** button to
select the CSV file.

After the CSV file is set as the source to Windows Perfmon, the administrator can
select options, such as which counters to display and for what time duration. Perfmon will display a graph containing the selected counters, shown in Figure 1-34.

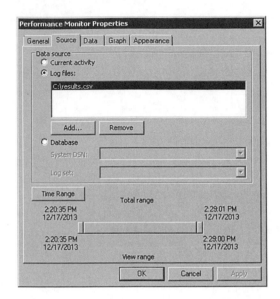

Figure 1-33   Changing the source of Windows Perfmon to a CSV file.

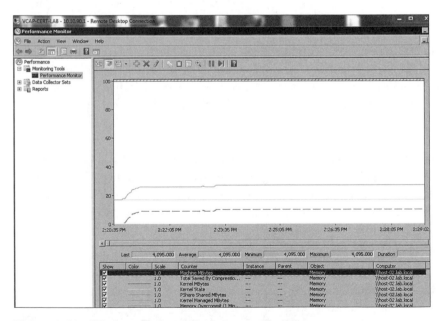

Figure 1-34   Windows Perfmon displaying esxtop data.

vCLI and vMA

This section describes how to implement and use the VMware vSphere Command Line Interface and the VMware vSphere Management Assistant. The main purpose of this section is to enable you to deploy the vMA and utilize it to manage ESXi hosts by executing vCLI commands inside of the vMA.

Overview

The VMware vCLI is a command-line utility that can be installed on Windows- or Linux-based systems. It provides the administrator with the means to use commands to configure, monitor, and manage multiple ESXi hosts from a remote, centralized location. The VMware vMA, on the other hand, is a Linux-based virtual appliance (prebuilt VM) that can be deployed in a vSphere environment. It provides the administrator with a variety of management tools, including the vCLI, and supporting tools, like fastpass. The VMware vMA provides a secure, centralized means for using vCLI commands to manage ESXi hosts. It also provides additional command tools, such as **resxtop**, **svmotion**, **vifs**, **vihostupdate**, **vmkfstools**, and **vmware-cmd**.

VMware provides a vCLI installation package for Windows and Linux, which administrators can download from the VMware website and install in their desktops or servers. The VMware vCLI provides a command utility where legacy **esxcfg-** commands, **vicfg-** commands, and **esxcli** commands can be executed. In other words, it allows the same command sets that are available on the ESXi Shell. VMware recommends not starting the ESXi Shell on the hosts, but instead executing commands from the vCLI. This places less load and less security risk on each ESXi host.

Key Topic

For each **esxcfg-** command that is provided by the ESXi shell, the vCLI provides a corresponding **vicfg-** command that functions identically. So, if you are already familiar with an **esxcli** command, simply change the first three letters from **esx** to **vi**. For convenience, the vCLI also provides a symbolic link (shortcut file) to each **vicfg-** command using the original **esxcfg-** naming convention. This allows any scripts that were developed to run directly in the ESXi Shell to be easily adapted to run in vCLI.

The **vicfg** and **esxcfg** commands are considered legacy because they are being deprecated in favor of the ESXCLI command set. Although this book focuses mostly on **esxcli**, you should practice executing both **esxcli** and **vicfg** commands from the vMA command prompt as you prepare for the exam. As you practice using each **esxcli** command, take a few moments to determine the corresponding **vicfg** command and practice using it.

esxcfg Commands

To get familiar with **esxcfg-** commands, type **esxcfg-** at the prompt in the ESXi Shell and press the Tab key twice. This will display all the commands that begin with those characters, as shown in Figure 1-35.

```
host-01.lab.local - PuTTY
/vmfs/volumes/5049c897-8dba3d03-5a4d-005056956fa9 # esxcfg-
esxcfg-advcfg    esxcfg-hwiscsi   esxcfg-ipsec     esxcfg-nas      esxcfg-resgrp    esxcfg-swiscsi   esxcfg-vswitch
esxcfg-dumppart  esxcfg-info      esxcfg-module    esxcfg-nics     esxcfg-route     esxcfg-vmknic
esxcfg-fcoe      esxcfg-init      esxcfg-mpath     esxcfg-rescan   esxcfg-scsidevs  esxcfg-volume
/vmfs/volumes/5049c897-8dba3d03-5a4d-005056956fa9 # esxcfg-
```

Figure 1-35   List of esxcfg- commands.

To learn about the usage of a specific command, enter the command name followed by **--help**. For example, to obtain usage information for the **esxcfg-rescan** command, enter this command:

```
esxcfg-rescan --help
```

Using **esxcli** commands from the vCLI is similar to using the commands from the ESXi Shell, except that connection information must be added, which is explained later in this section. Using **vicfg** commands from the vCLI is identical to using **esxcfg** commands from the vCLI because the latter is simply a symbolic link to the former.

Deploying the vMA

The remainder of this section focuses on deploying the vMA and using it to execute vCLI commands. It provides steps for simplifying the necessary connection, authentication, and authorization information that must be provided to allow commands to be executed from a remote location to a given ESXi host. Administrators initially might face a challenge when using the vCLI to run **esxcli** commands because the commands are being executed from a remote Windows or Linux instance and require additional connection information for the commands to be executed against the desired ESXi host. For the connection to the ESXi host to occur, user credentials must be provided and authentication must be successful. For the command to be successfully executed, the user must also be authorized to perform the specific task related to the command. One approach to tackling this challenge is to provide host, user, and password parameters with each command, but this is tedious and difficult to script without providing passwords in plain text. The preferred approach, which is defined in this section, is to use the **fastpass** utility included with the vMA.

To get started, download the vMA appliance from VMware's website and deploy it using the **File – Deploy OVF Template** menu option in the vSphere Client.

In the wizard, you then need to deploy the vMA to select the OVF file, provide a name for the VM, select the ESXi host, select a datastore, and select a network port group. After the vMA has been deployed, power on the appliance and respond to the prompts to provide the network configuration, hostname, and password for the vi-admin user. Next, use the console to log in to the vMA using the vi-admin account and the password you created—or for convenience, you can also use Putty or another utility to connect and log in to the vMA using a Secure Shell (SSH) session.

Authentication and Authorization for the vMA

To execute commands from the vMA against a remote host, you must target and authenticate against the host. To simplify this process and enhance security, you can join the vMA to an Active Directory (AD) domain, make fastpass connections, and configure host-level permissions.

To join vMA to an AD domain, use the **domainjoin-cli join** command. This command requires root privileges, so precede the command with the command **sudo.** For example, to join the vMA to an AD domain named lab.local using a user account named administrator, the command shown in Figure 1-36 can be used.

```
vma-01.lab.local - PuTTY                                                        _ □
vi-admin@vma-01:~> sudo domainjoin-cli join lab.local administrator
Joining to AD Domain:    lab.local
With Computer DNS Name: vma-01.lab.local

administrator@LAB.LOCAL's password:
Warning: System restart required
Your system has been configured to authenticate to Active Directory for the first time.  It is recommended that you
restart your system to ensure that all applications recognize the new settings.

SUCCESS
vi-admin@vma-01:~>
```

Figure 1-36 Using the domainjoin command to join an AD domain.

This enables an AD user to log in and use the vMA, but the real goal is to enable AD users to connect to and manage ESXi hosts from the vMA. To authenticate and authorize an AD account to manage an ESXi host, first use the vSphere Client to join the ESXi host to the domain and ensure the AD account is granted the **Administrator** role to the host. This can be accomplished using the following steps. An example is shown in Figure 1-37.

Step 1.   Use the vSphere Client to connect to an ESXi host using the root account.

Step 2.   Select **Configuration tab > Authentication Services**.

Step 3.   Select **Properties**.

Step 4.   In the **Directory Service Type** drop-down menu, select **Active Directory**.

Step 5.   In the **domain** box, enter the full name of the AD domain.

Step 6.   Click the **Join Domain** button.

Step 7.   Provide the credentials of a domain user account with full permissions to the Computers container in Active Directory.

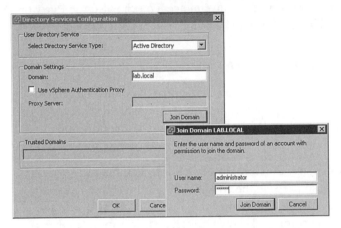

Figure 1-37   Example of Directory Services configuration.

Now that the ESXi host has joined the AD domain, AD user accounts can authenticate with the host, but they might not necessarily be authorized to manage the host. By default, if an AD domain contains a user group named esx admins, then this group is automatically assigned the Administrator role. Regardless, the **Permissions** tab can be used to assign the **Administrator** role to any other AD group, enabling any AD user in that group to have full control of the host. Figure 1-38 illustrates an example of the **Permissions** tab reflecting the default permissions of an ESXi host that has been joined to a domain named Lab.

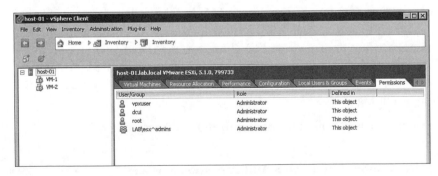

Figure 1-38   Example of the Permissions tab.

Now that the host has joined the domain, AD users who have been granted the **Administrator** can now use the vSphere client to connect to and manage the ESXi host. These users can also use the vMA to manage this host and any other ESXi host that has been similarly configured. To experience this firsthand, you could experiment running a simple command from various user accounts. For example, from the vMA, use the **root** account to run the **esxcfg-nics -l** command to list the physical network adapters in the host. Verify that the command runs successfully. Now run the same command using an AD account that does not have the **Administrator** role on the **Permissions** tab (in the example the user student01a is used). Verify that the command fails. These steps are shown in Figure 1-39.

```
vma-01.lab.local - PuTTY                                                    _ □
vi-admin@vma-01:~> esxcfg-nics -l --server host-01 --username root
Enter password:
Name      PCI      Driver    Link Speed      Duplex MAC Address      MTU   Description

vmnic0  02:00.0 e1000        Up   1000Mbps Full   00:50:56:95:4c:e5  1500  Intel Corporation 82545EM Gigabit Ethernet
Controller (Copper)
vmnic1  02:01.0 e1000        Up   1000Mbps Full   00:50:56:95:4c:e6        Intel Corporation 82545EM Gigabit Ethernet
Controller (Copper)
vmnic2  02:02.0 e1000        Up   1000Mbps Full   00:50:56:95:4c:e7  1500  Intel Corporation 82545EM Gigabit Ethernet
Controller (Copper)
vmnic3  02:03.0 e1000        Up   1000Mbps Full   00:50:56:95:4c:e8  1500  Intel Corporation 82545EM Gigabit Ethernet
Controller (Copper)
vi-admin@vma-01:~>
vi-admin@vma-01:~>
vi-admin@vma-01:~>
vi-admin@vma-01:~>
vi-admin@vma-01:~> esxcfg-nics -l --server host-01 --username lab\\student01a
Enter password:
Error: Permission to perform this operation was denied.
```

Figure 1-39 Examples of using authorized and nonauthorized accounts.

Fastpass

Finally, instead of adding user credentials to each command, utilize the fastpass commands. Fastpass is a utility that prompts the user for credentials once and then stores them for future use. A good practice is to use the **vifp addserver** command to connect to each ESXi host, executing the command once for each host. For example, Figure 1-40 shows the commands you use to create a fastpass connection to ESXi hosts named host-01 and host-02, using the Administrator account in the Lab domain.

Key
Topic

```
vma-01.lab.local - PuTTY
vi-admin@vma-01:~> vifp addserver host-01.lab.local --authpolicy adauth
Enter username for host-01.lab.local: lab\administrator
vi-admin@vma-01:~>
vi-admin@vma-01:~>
vi-admin@vma-01:~> vifp addserver host-02.lab.local --authpolicy adauth
Enter username for host-02.lab.local: lab\administrator
vi-admin@vma-01:~>
vi-admin@vma-01:~>
vi-admin@vma-01:~> vifp listservers
host-01.lab.local        ESXi
host-02.lab.local        ESXi
vi-admin@vma-01:~>
```

Figure 1-40 Example of using fastpass commands to connect to ESXi hosts.

Fastpass allows the user to set one of the ESXi hosts to be the current target. This enables the user to now run vCLI commands without having to specify the host or credentials with each command. The commands are automatically performed on the current target host, and the credentials are already known to fastpass. For example, the fastpass target can be set to host-02; then a set of commands can be run to list the physical adapters and virtual switches on host-02, as shown in Figure 1-41.

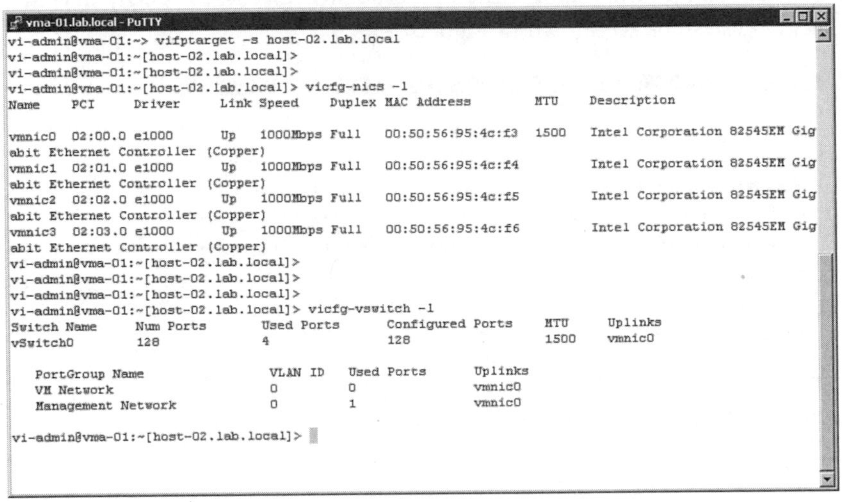

Figure 1-41   Setting and using fastpass targets.

For convenience, the **vifp addserver** command can also be used to make a fastpass connection to the vCenter Server. Although the vCLI commands can be used only to configure ESXi hosts, it is simpler to connect the vMA to the vCenter Server and then select a specific host with each command. To understand this better, think about how you tend to use the vSphere Client. You probably connect and authenticate once to a vCenter Server and then select the ESXi host you want to configure or monitor. You could do the same with the vMA and fastpass by connecting and authenticating to a vCenter Server and then including the **--vihost** parameter with each command to select a specific ESXi host. Another benefit of this approach is that vMA users do no require the ability to log on directly to an ESXi host. In other words, most users use the vSphere Client to log on to vCenter Server to perform their daily tasks. They cannot log on directly to an ESXi host. These users could also use the vMA to connect to vCenter Server to perform the same tasks at the command line just by adding the **--vihost** parameter to each command and specifying the host. Figure 1-42 demonstrates making a fastpass connection to a vCenter Server named vc-app-01, setting it as the target, and using the **--vihost** parameter to list the network adapters on host-02.

```
vma-01.lab.local - PuTTY
vi-admin@vma-01:~[host-02.lab.local]> vifp addserver vc-app-01.lab.local --authpolicy adauth
Enter username for vc-app-01.lab.local: lab\administrator
vi-admin@vma-01:~[host-02.lab.local]>
vi-admin@vma-01:~[host-02.lab.local]>
vi-admin@vma-01:~[host-02.lab.local]> vicfg-nics  -l  --vihost host-02.lab.local
Name    PCI      Driver     Link Speed    Duplex MAC Address        MTU    Description

vmnic0  02:00.0 e1000      Up   1000Mbps Full   00:50:56:95:4c:f3  1500   Intel Corporation 82545EM Gig
abit Ethernet Controller (Copper)
vmnic1  02:01.0 e1000      Up   1000Mbps Full   00:50:56:95:4c:f4         Intel Corporation 82545EM Gig
abit Ethernet Controller (Copper)
vmnic2  02:02.0 e1000      Up   1000Mbps Full   00:50:56:95:4c:f5         Intel Corporation 82545EM Gig
abit Ethernet Controller (Copper)
vmnic3  02:03.0 e1000      Up   1000Mbps Full   00:50:56:95:4c:f6         Intel Corporation 82545EM Gig
abit Ethernet Controller (Copper)
vi-admin@vma-01:~[host-02.lab.local]>
```

Figure 1-42   Example of using vCenter as the fastpass target.

After applying the information in this section, you should now be equipped with the means to execute **vicfg**, **excfg**, and **esxcli** commands without having to specify user credentials with each command. You might find that returning to the **esxcli** section of this guide and practicing using **esxcli** commands and their corresponding **vicfg** commands from the vMA is useful.

File Manipulation with vifs

Most administration tasks can be easily performed from a single vMA appliance, but one challenge an administrator can face is viewing or modifying a text file on an ESXi host. The ESXi shell provides some common commands like **cat**, **tail**, **more**, and **vi** to manipulate files on ESXi hosts, but VMware prefers that the ESXi Shell service remains shut down for security purposes. To manipulate ESXi files from the vMA, begin by using the **vifs** command to download (get) the file. Use common commands to view or edit the file. If you modify the file, use the **vifs** command to upload (put) the file to the host. For example, the following command can be used to download a file named results.csv from the Shared-8 datastore on an ESXi host:

```
vifs    --get   "[Shared-8]results.csv"  /home/vi-admin/results.csv
```

Figure 1-43 illustrates this example, as well as listing the file using the **ls** command and displaying the first page of the file using the **more** command.

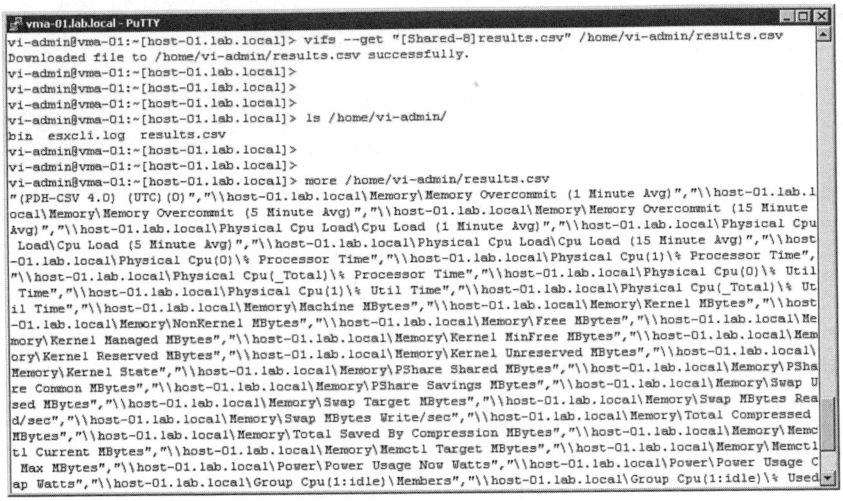

Figure 1-43 Using the vifs command.

PowerCLI

This section describes how to implement and use the VMware vSphere PowerCLI. PowerCLI is a command-line interface that allows administrators to use commands to manage everything in a vSphere environment. The VMware vSphere PowerCLI is a set of commands (typically called cmdlets) that run on top of Microsoft Windows PowerShell. These cmdlets can be used to connect to vCenter Server to monitor and configure all the clusters, ESXi hosts, VMs, and other objects managed by vCenter Server. PowerCLI can be used to perform administrative and operational tasks, such as vMotion. Its primary use is to enable the development of scripts to automate administration processes that require repetitive tasks when using the vSphere Client. Another use is to provide complex reports that are not natively provided by the vSphere Client.

The goal of this section is to introduce you to the steps for implementing PowerCLI and to demonstrate how to perform basic commands. In later chapters, details are provided for performing administration tasks using specific PowerCLI cmdlets. The goal of this chapter is to familiarize you sufficiently with PowerCLI, so you can practice specific PowerCLI cmdlets when encountered in subsequent chapters.

Installation

Here are the steps for implementing PowerCLI:

Step 1. Select a Windows desktop or server to be used to run PowerCLI and to allow scripts to be built and executed. This could be the administrator's desktop or a central Windows server. Most administrators choose to use a Windows VM that can be shared with a team of administrators and accessed via Remote Desktop. Prerequisites are Windows PowerShell (version 2.0 or higher) and dot-Net Framework (version 2.0 SP2 or higher).

Step 2. Install Microsoft Windows PowerShell. The installation steps depend on the version of Windows. For example, to install PowerShell 3.0 on a Windows 2008 R2 Server, the basic steps are to install dot-Net Framework 4.x and Windows Management Framework 3.0. For specific steps, use the PowerShell Installation Guide (http://technet.microsoft.com/en-us/library/hh847837.aspx).

Step 3. Install PowerCLI. The basic steps are to download the installer from VMware's website; run the installer on the selected Windows system; and use the wizard to complete the installation, typically keeping the default values for all options provided by the installer.

Step 4. Select **Start > Programs > VMware > VMware vSphere PowerCLI** to launch PowerCLI.

Step 5. On the first use of PowerCLI, execute this command to enable PowerCLI:

```
Set-ExecutionPolicy RemoteSigned
```

Usage

After PowerCLI has been implemented, you can gain basic familiarity by using it to connect to a vSphere environment and to perform various tasks, such as displaying VM, networking, and storage configuration data. For example, to connect to a vCenter Server named vc-app-01 and identify all the ESXi hosts and VMs that it manages, use the following commands:

Connect-VIServer vc-app-01 (when prompted, provide user credentials)

Get-VMHost

Get-VM

The **Get-VMHost** cmdlet returns a list of all managed ESXi hosts and displays some details for each host. Likewise, the **Get-VM** cmdlet returns a list of all managed VMs with some details for each VM, as illustrated in Figure 1-44.

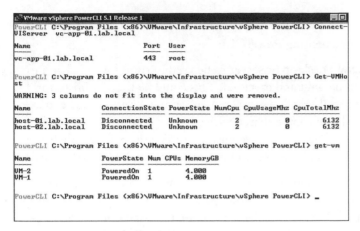

Figure 1-44 Example of Get-VMHost and Get-VM.

Similarly, **Get-VirtualSwitch** can be used to retrieve a list of all managed virtual switches and **Get-Datastore** can be used to retrieve a list of all managed datastores.

PowerCLI is an object-oriented language, meaning that variables can be used to reference real objects, such as ESXi hosts, VMs, virtual switches, and datastores. Operations can be performed on objects. The allowed operations depend on the object type. For example a VM can be powered on, but a datastore cannot be powered on. Generally, the allowed operations (also called methods) for an object are the same operations that are allowed by the vSphere client for the given object depending on the object type and current state. For example, in the vSphere Client, if you right-click a running VM, some available operations are **Migrate** and **Rename**, as shown in Figure 1-45.

Properties can be set on each object. For example, in the vSphere client, if you right-click a VM and select **Edit Settings**, you can make changes to the VM's properties. In object-oriented programming, operations (methods) and properties (attributes) are also called members. To determine the possible members (operations and properties) for a VM using PowerCLI, you can use the **Get-Member** cmdlet. For example, to display a list of all available members for a VM named VM-2, use the following commands:

- **$MyVM = Get-VM VM-2**

- **$MyVM | Get-Member**

In this example, the first command creates an object variable named $MyVM that is used to store the results of the **Get-VM VM-2** command, which retrieves the VM named VM-2. In other words, after the first command finishes, the variable $MyVM represents the VM-2 VM. The second command shows all the available operations and properties for VM-2, as shown in Figure 1-46.

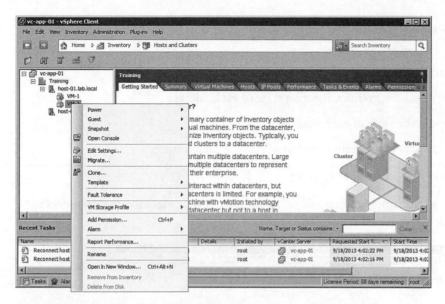

Figure 1-45 Example of available operations for a running VM.

Figure 1-46 Example of Get-Member command.

Object variables can reference a list of objects. The **for-each** command can be used to operate on each object in a list of objects. The **if** command can be used to selectively perform one task when a given condition is true and perform another task otherwise. For example, consider the following scenario.

Scenario – Use PowerCLI to toggle the connection state of all virtual NICs

Use a series of PowerCLI commands to

- Retrieve a list of all virtual network adapters from all VMs

- Display the current connection state of each adapter

- Toggle the state of each adapter

- Re-display the current connection state of each adapter

Figure 1-47 illustrates an example set of commands that meet the requirements in the scenario.

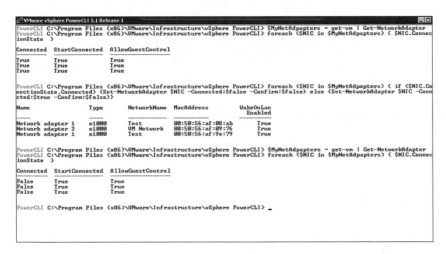

Figure 1-47 Example of PowerCLI commands to toggle the connected state value.

To fully understand this scenario, here are some details:

- In the first command, the object variable **$MyNetAdapters** is set to reference all the discovered network adapters in all the managed VMs.

- Next, the **foreach** command is used to select each adapter from the list one at a time, temporarily use the object variable **$NIC** to reference just the selected adapter, and display the **ConnectionState** value of the adapter.

- Then, another **foreach** command is used to select each adapter from the list one at a time, determine the value of the **ConnectionState**, and change its value to the opposite value. In other words, if the connection state is true, set it to false.

- In the last commands, the object variable **$MyNetAdapters** is refreshed and the value of each adapter's **ConnectionState** is displayed again.

Running Scripts in VMs

Another use case for PowerCLI is to enable the ability to run scripts inside of VMs. This can be accomplished by using the **Invoke-VMScript** cmdlet. This cmdlet involves a guest user as well as a host user. The host user must have at least Read access to the folder containing the VM (Inventory > VMs and Templates view) and Console Interaction to the VM. The guest user must have administrator privileges in the guest operating system. For example, the following command can be used to run the **dir** command within a VM. Notice the host user account is root and the guest user account is administrator:

```
Invoke-VMScript -VM VM -ScriptText "dir" -HostUser root -HostPassword
pass1 -GuestUser administrator -GuestPassword pass2
```

Often a PowerCLI script will need to utilize environment variables in a guest operating system. One use case is the environment variable named **$env:ProgramFiles**, which is used to reference the path to the Program Files folder in a Windows operating system and is commonly needed to locate programs and scripts. Another use case is the environment variable named **$env:Tmp**, which can be used to reference the location of temporary files in Windows. The following example uses these two variables to build a character string containing the full command necessary to run the **msinfo32** command in a VM and save its results in a file named **inforeport** in the temporary folder. The first command builds the character string, and the second command passes the string to VM for execution:

Key
Topic

```
$script = '&"$env:ProgramFiles\Common Files\Microsoft Shared\MSInfo\
msinfo32.exe" /report "$env:Tmp\inforeport"'
Invoke-VMScript -ScriptText $script -VM VM -HostCredential $hostCre-
dential -GuestCredential $guestCredential
```

In the second command, the variables **$hostCredential** and **$guestCredential** should represent the appropriate credentials (username and password) for connecting to the target ESXi host and VM. For brevity, the commands to assign these values are not shown in the example.

Summary

This chapter described how to implement and use the vSphere Client, esxcli, vmkfs-tools, esxtop, vCLI, vMA, and PowerCLI. At this point, you should ensure that you can successfully apply the procedures in this chapter to deploy and utilize each of these tools in your own vSphere environment. The prerequisites for the remaining chapters are that you are comfortable using each tool.

Exam Preparation Tasks

Review All the Key Topics

Table 1-2 provides a list of all Key Topics identified in this chapter along with a few notes intended to refresh your memory of some key details. This may be useful as a quick reference when performing vSphere administration.

Table 1-2 Key Topics for Chapter 1

Key Topic Element	Description	Page
Paragraph	Manage vSphere Client plug-ins	10
Paragraph	Navigating the esxcli command hierarchy	13
Paragraph	Use vmkfstools to create virtual disks	22
Paragraph	Use esxtop in batch mode	27
Paragraph	Understand the use of vCLI	29
Paragraph	Display a list of all esxcfg- commands	30
Paragraph	Join the vMA to an AD domain	31
Step List	Implement fastpass in vMA	31
Paragraph	Use vifs to get a file: vifs -get	33
Step List	Install PowerCLI (prerequisites are dotNet and Powershell)	37
Paragraph	Reference environment variables in PowerCLI	41

Key Terms

Define the following key terms from this chapter, and check your answers in the glossary.

vSphere Client, esxcli, esxtop, vmkfstools, vCLI, vMA, PowerCLI, DCUI, ESXi Shell.

Review Tasks

These Review Tasks allow you to assess how well you grasped the materials in this chapter. Because of the advanced and hands-on nature of this particular exam, a set of tasks are provided instead of a set of questions. You should now attempt to perform each of these tasks without looking at previous sections in this chapter or at other materials, unless necessary. The steps for each task are located within the chapter:

1. Install the vSphere Client.

2. Connect remotely to an ESXi host using SSH, and use an **esxcli** command to display all the NFS datastores available to the host.

3. Use a command-line utility to create a new VMFS datastore on a new, empty LUN that has no existing disk partitions.

4. Use **resxtop** to create a CSV file containing all statistics from an ESXi host taken at 2-minute intervals for 10 minutes. Input the file into Windows Performance Monitor to display graphically.

5. Deploy the vMA and use fastpass to provide credentials and make connections to two ESXi hosts. Set the default target to be the first ESXi host, and use **vicfg** commands to list the network adapters and virtual switches on the host. Then change the default target to the second host, without re-entering credentials, and use **vicfg** commands to list the network adapters and virtual switches on that host.

6. Implement PowerCLI in a Windows desktop, and use it to identify and toggle the current connection state of each virtual network adapter of each VM.

This chapter covers the following subjects:

- **Implement and Manage Complex Virtual Networks**—This section identifies common virtual switch settings and provides steps for configuring and managing standard and distributed virtual switches (vSwitches).

- **Configure and Maintain VLANs, PVLANs, and VLAN Settings**—This section provides steps for configuring VLANs and PVLANs and explains how to recognize potential use cases.

- **Deploy and Maintain Scalable Networking**—This section provides steps for configuring NIC Teaming policies and explains the corresponding physical switch settings.

- **Administrator vSphere Distributed Switches**—This section identifies settings and features that are specific to distributed vSwitches (vDS) and provides steps for implementing each feature.

This chapter covers a portion of the VCAP-DCA Exam objectives 2.1, 2.2, 2.3, and 2.4.

## CHAPTER 2

Network Administration

This chapter is intended to provide you with the knowledge and skills to successfully perform administration of an enterprise network that includes virtual networks built using vSphere. It is also intended to ensure that you have the skills to successfully complete network configuration, troubleshooting, and management tasks that might be part of the VCAP5-DCA exam. As you read this chapter, take time to practice the steps provided until you are confident that you can perform such tasks rather quickly without any assistance. Some steps involve using the vSphere Client; others involve using the vCLI and PowerCLI.

"Do I Know This Already?" Quiz

The "Do I Know This Already?" quiz allows you to assess how well you already know the material in this chapter. Table 2-1 outlines the major headings in this chapter and the corresponding "Do I Know This Already?" quiz questions. You can find the answers in Appendix A, "Answers to the 'Do I Know This Already?' Quizzes." Because of the advanced and hands-on nature of this particular exam, you should read the entire chapter and practice performing all the described tasks at least once, regardless of how well you do on this quiz. This quiz can be helpful to determine which topics will require the most effort during your preparation.

Table 2-1 "Do I Know This Already?" Foundation Topics Section-to-Question Mapping

Foundations Topics Section	Questions Covered in This Section
Implement and Manage Complex Virtual Networks	1, 2
Configure and Maintain VLANs, PVLANs, and VLAN Settings	3, 4
Deploy and Maintain Scalable Networking	5, 6
Administer vSphere Distributed Switch Settings	7, 8

1. Which method can be used to successfully enable SNMP Traps?

   a. Select **Administration > vCenter Server Settings**, and then check the **Enable SNMP Traps** check box.

   b. Use the vSphere Client to log on directly to an ESXi host, and then check the **Enable SNMP Traps** check box on the **Configuration** tab.

   c. Use the **Set_AdvancedSetting** PowerCLI cmdlet.

   d. Use the **esxcli system snmp set** command.

2. Which method can be used to successfully enable Direct Path I/O?

   a. From an ESXi host's **Configuration** tab, check the **Enable Direct Path I/O** box.

   b. From an ESXi host's **Configuration** tab, click **Hardware > Advanced Settings**.

   c. From vCenter Server, enable and configure Network I/O control.

   d. From vCenter Server, enable Direct Path I/O from **Administration > Advanced Settings**.

3. Which method can be used to assign VLAN tagging on a standard vSwitch (vSS) port group?

   a. Use the **Set-Vlan** cmdlet on an object variable that represents a vSS port group.

   b. Select a vSS, choose **Edit**, and enter a VLAN number to assign to the vSwitch.

   c. Use the **esxcli network vswitch standard portgroup set** command.

   d. Select a vSS port group, select **Edit**, and select a VLAN tagging method.

4. Which method can be used to configure the VLAN settings of a vDS port group where a Wireshark VM will be used to inspect network packets to and from all other VMs connected to all other port groups and VLANs on the same vDS?

   a. Set the VLAN on the port group to 4096.

   b. Set the **VLAN Type** to VLAN Trunking.

   c. Set the **VLAN Type** to Promiscuous.

   d. Set the **VLAN Type** to PVLAN.

5. Which method can be used to connect a vSS port group to two uplink ports that are configured with EtherChannel?

   a. Change the Load Balancing Policy to Route based on the originating port ID on the vSS.

   b. Change the Load Balancing Policy to **Route based on the originating virtual switch port ID** on the vSS port group.

   c. Change the Load Balancing Policy to **Route based on Physical NIC Load** on the vSS port group.

   d. Change the Load Balancing Policy to **Route based on IP Hash** on the vSS.

6. Which method can be used to configure a port group to support Microsoft Load Balancing unicast mode?

   a. Set Notify Switches to **No**.

   b. Set Load Balancing Policy to **Route based on IP Hash**.

   c. Set VLAN to **4095**.

   d. Set Beacon Probing to **Link Status Only**.

7. Which method can be used to create user-defined custom network resource pools?

   a. On the properties page of a distributed switch, check the **Enable Network Resource Pools** box. Then use the **Create Network Resource Pool** link.

   b. Use the **New-ResourcePool** cmdlet to create the pool, and use the **Set-ResourcePool** cmdlet to set the pool type to **Network**.

   c. On the **Resource Allocation** tab, check the **Enable Network IO Control** box. Select the **New Network Resource pool** link.

   d. On the Resource Pools tab, click the **Create Network Resource Pool** link.

8. Which of the following summarizes the steps that should be followed to allow a Wireshark VM connected to a vDS to inspect packets to and from just one other specific VM on the same vDS?

   a. Set **VLAN Type** to **Trunking**, and then enable **Promiscuous Mode**.

   b. Configure Port Mirroring.

   c. Edit the settings of the monitored VM and configure port replication.

   d. Configure **NetFlow**.

Foundation Topics

Implement and Manage Complex Networks

This section is intended to provide you with the knowledge and skills to successfully configure and manage virtual switches that are implemented in a complex network. Details on concepts and implementation are provided, along with the steps necessary to perform key configuration and administration tasks. The examples and scenarios in this chapter utilize the vSphere Client, the vCLI, and PowerCLI.

Overview

You should already be familiar with basic vSphere network virtualization concepts and administrative tasks. If any of the following details in this overview are new to you, be sure to research the appropriate information before continuing on to the remainder of this chapter.

vSphere Standard Switches (vSSes) are implemented on each ESXi host in a vSphere implementation. These Layer-2, software-based switches provide the following features: VLAN Tagging, Security, NIC Teaming, Failover, and Traffic Shaping. All these features have settings that can be configured using the vSphere Client. On each vSS, one or more port groups can be configured. These port groups can support virtual machine and management traffic and services like vMotion, IP storage, and FT logging. The default settings for the Security, Teaming, and Shaping policies can be modified per vSS and can be overridden per port group. VLAN settings can be configured on each port group. Some settings, such as Maximum Transmission Unit (MTU) and Cisco Discovery Protocol (CDP), can be configured only at the vSS level.

Prior to attaching virtual machines to a network, a VM port group must be created on a vSS. The port group is then configured with the VLAN, Traffic Shaping, Security, and physical NIC Teaming settings. Finally, the vmnic on the virtual machine is connected to the appropriate port group.

Management traffic and all other network services, including vMotion, IP-based storage, VMware HA heartbeats, and VMware Fault Tolerance logging, require a vmkernel port. When a vmkernel port is created on a vSS, a port group is first created; then a vmkernel virtual adapter is created and placed in the port group. When using the vSphere Client, the port group creation for vmkernel ports is transparent. When using the vCLI, the port group must first be created.

vSphere Distributed Virtual Switches (vDSes) are implemented at the datacenter level, where vCenter Server controls the configuration and management of the vDS.

ESXi hosts are then attached to these vDSes. When a host is connected to a vDS, vCenter Server creates a data plane at the ESXi host level by creating one or more hidden vSwitches. The settings and statistics of the hidden vSwitch(es) are automatically synchronized with those on the vDS. The data plane and packet movement are controlled by the hidden vSwitch(es) at the ESXi host level, which ensures that any disruption of the connection between the ESXi host and vCenter Server does not affect the network connectivity of the VMs. The control plane is handled by vCenter Server. So, any loss of connectivity between the ESXi host and vCenter Server will affect the ability to make modifications to the vDS.

As mentioned earlier, all ports on a vSS or vDS are created from a port group. Although it can appear that a vmkernel port created using the vSphere Client is created without a port group, it is actually created as part of the operation. This port group is used only for the vmkernel port. Policies can be configured for the vmkernel, but they are actually configured on the port group—not the vmkernel virtual adapter. This bit of detail might be new to you concerning vSSes, but it should seem familiar to those who configure vDSes because in the vSphere Client, port groups must first be configured on a vDS prior to attaching vmkernel virtual adapters.

vSSes can be managed by selecting the appropriate ESXi host and using the Configuration Tab > Networking option, as shown in Figure 2-1.

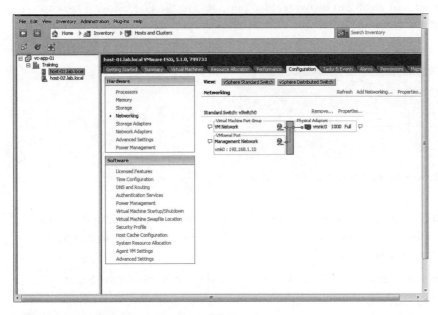

Figure 2-1 Networking page for an ESXi host.

The Add Networking link can be used to launch a wizard to create a new vSS. The first page of the wizard is the Connection Type page, as shown in Figure 2-2.

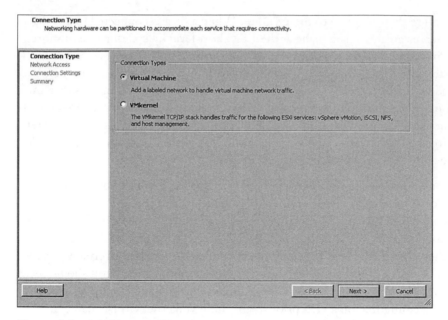

Figure 2-2   Add Network Wizard.

The properties of a vSS can be overridden per port group. The General tab can used to set the Network Label and VLAN ID of the port group, as shown in Figure 2-3.

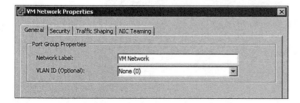

Figure 2-3   General properties of a vSS.

The Load Balancing, Failover Detection, Notify Switches, Failback, and Failover Order settings can be configured on the NIC Teaming properties tab of a port group or the vSS, as shown in Figure 2-4.

Security policy settings, such as Promiscuous Mode, can be set on the Security properties page of a port group or the vSS, as shown in Figure 2-5.

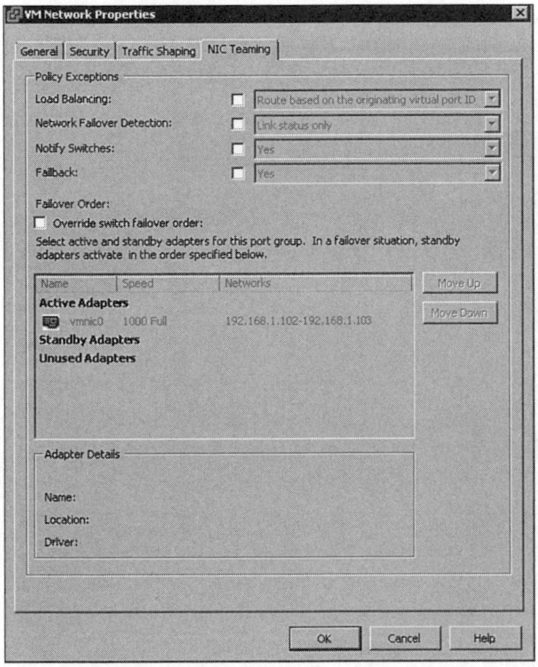

Figure 2-4   NIC Teaming properties page.

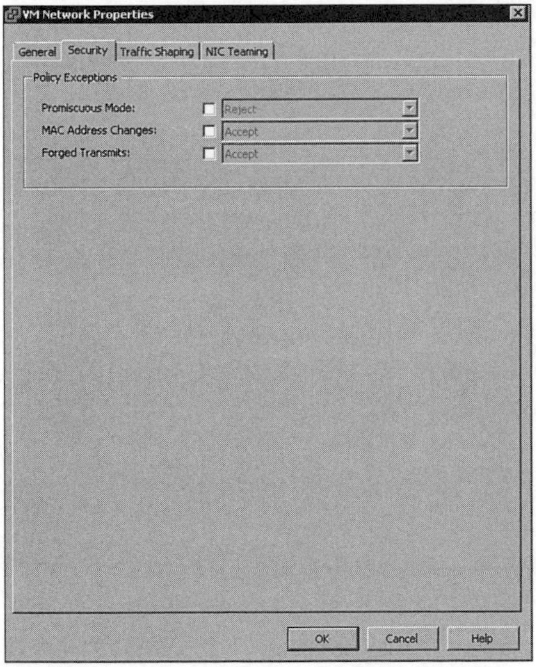

Figure 2-5   Security properties page.

Traffic Shaping policy settings, such as Average Bandwidth and Peak Bandwidth, can be set on the Traffic Shaping properties page of a port group or the vSS, as shown in Figure 2-6.

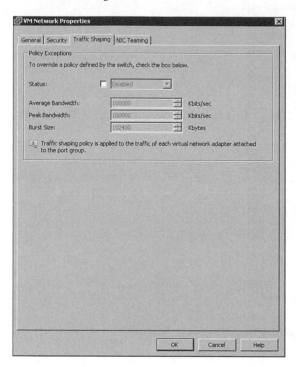

Figure 2-6   Traffic Shaping properties page.

vDSes can be managed using the vSphere Client by connecting to a vCenter Server and navigating to the Inventory > Networking section. You can right-click a data-center object and select New vSphere Distributed Switch to launch the Create vSphere Distributed Switch wizard, as shown in Figure 2-7.

To configure a vDS, right-click the vDS and select **Edit Settings**. General settings, such as the **Name** and **number of uplink ports**, can be set on the **General** properties page of the vDS, as shown in Figure 2-8.

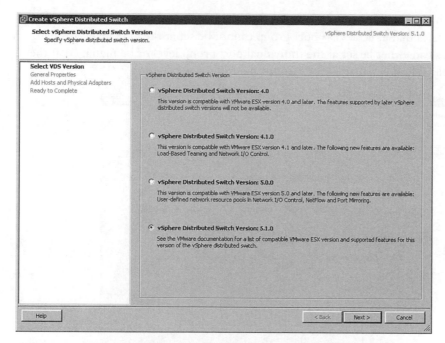

Figure 2-7 Create vSphere Distributed Switch wizard.

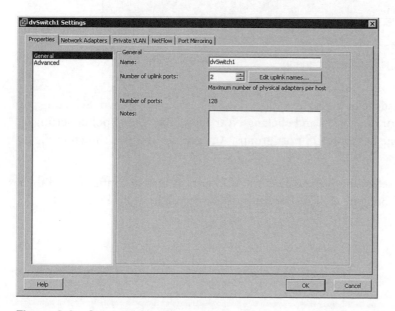

Figure 2-8 General properties page of a vDS.

Policy inheritance on a vDS differs significantly from vSphere Standard Switches. Most policies that affect a vDS port group cannot be set at the vDS level. Instead, properties can either be set at the individual port group level or be managed at the vDS level using the Manage Port Groups menu shown in Figure 2-9.

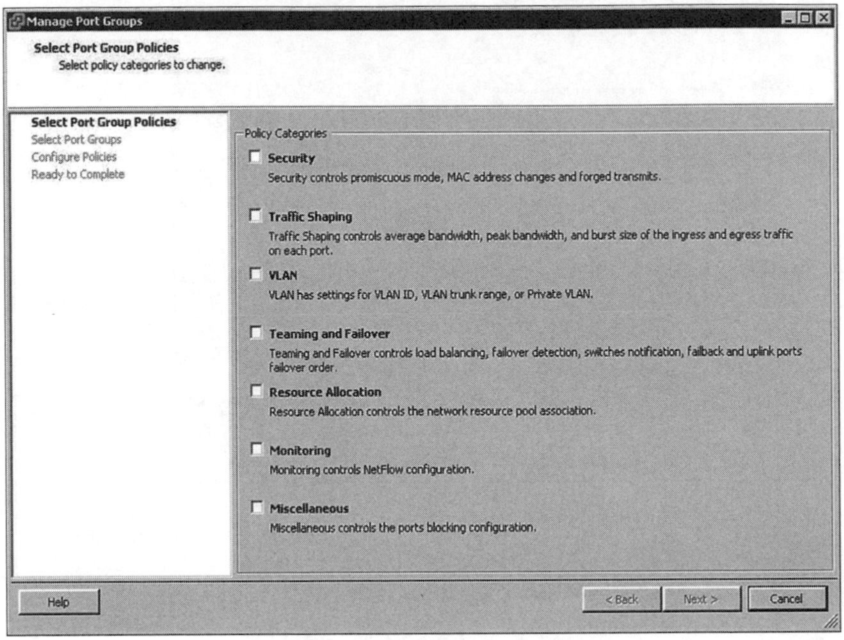

Figure 2-9   vDS Manage Port Groups menu.

All the policies that can be configured on a vDS port group are shown. Selecting any Policy Category (or categories) and clicking Next allows the related policy settings to be applied to one or more vDS port groups. An example of this is shown in Figure 2-10.

To configure the selected policies, select the vDS port groups to configure and then click **Next**. The Configure Policies screen is displayed, as shown in Figure 2-11.

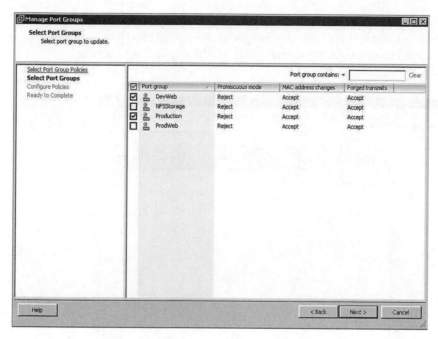

Figure 2-10   vDS Port Group selection page.

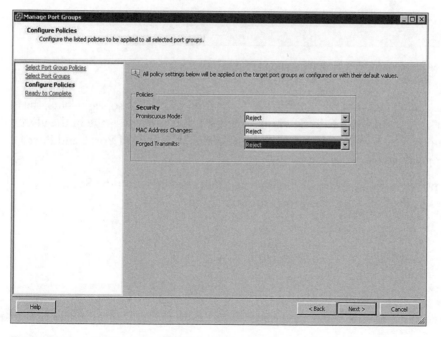

Figure 2-11   vDS Configure Policies page.

The vDS Configure Policies page allows you to adjust the settings for all the policies you selected and will apply those changes to the port groups you have chosen. The final screen summarizes the changes that will be applied, as shown in Figure 2-12.

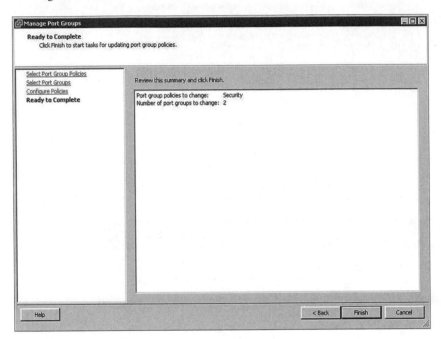

Figure 2-12   vDS Manage Port Groups summary page.

Of course, individual vDS port groups can be configured. To do so, right-click the vDS port group and select **Edit Settings**. The General properties page of the vDA port group is shown and can be used to set the Name, Number of Ports, and Port Binding option, as shown in Figure 2-13.

Security policy settings, such as Promiscuous Mode, can be set on the Security properties page of the vDS port group shown in Figure 2-14.

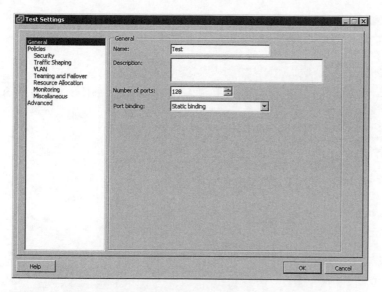

Figure 2-13 General properties page of a distributed port group.

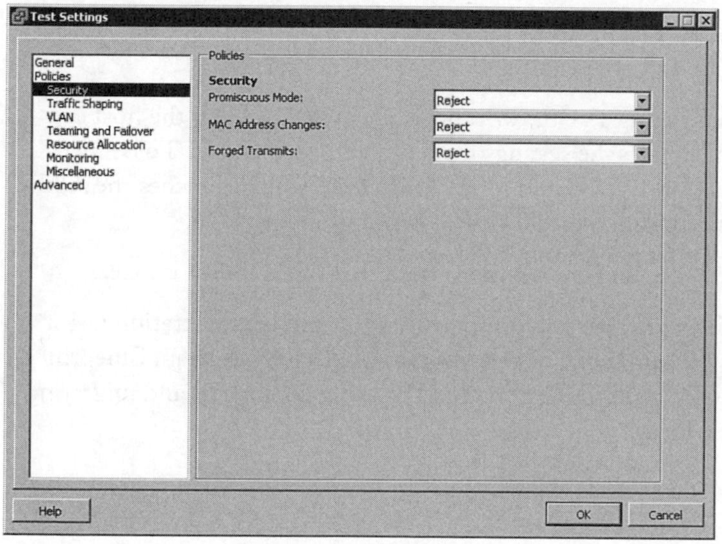

Figure 2-14 Security properties page of a distributed port group.

Traffic Shaping policy settings, such as Average Bandwidth and Peak Bandwidth on ingress and egress traffic, can be set on the Traffic Shaping properties page of a distributed port group, as shown in Figure 2-15.

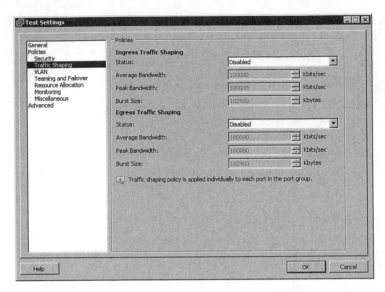

Figure 2-15 Traffic Shaping properties page of a distributed port group.

The same process can be used to adjust the VLAN, Teaming and Failover, Resource Allocation, Monitoring, and other settings.

After creating and configuring a vDS, ESXi hosts are added. Adding the host creates the data plane and applies the settings from the vDS to the host. To connect an ESXi host, right-click the vDSS and select **Add Host**, which launches the **Add Host to vSphere Distributed Switch** wizard shown in Figure 2-16.

Select the hosts to be added and choose the vmnics that the vDS will utilize.

The remainder of this chapter focuses on specific, advanced administration tasks, including commands that are called out on various VCAP5-DCA Exam Blueprint objectives. These tasks include configuring SNMP using commands and migrating objects from vSSes to vDSes.

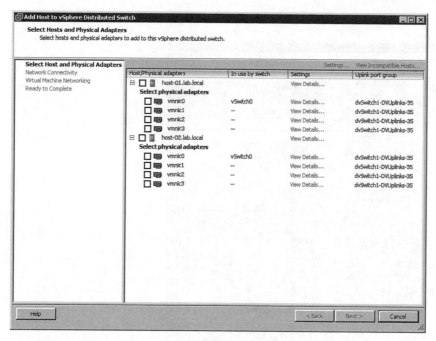

Figure 2-16 Add Host to vSphere Distributed Switch Wizard.

Configure SNMP

Typically, administrators are required to automatically retrieve status information from vSphere and to feed this data to monitoring and management systems. This can be accomplished using SNMP. A vCenter Server can be configured to send SNMP traps to management systems that use SNMP receivers. A maximum of four SNMP receivers can be configured per vCenter Server. The required privilege is Global.Settings.

The procedure for configuring SNMP receivers on a vCenter Server using the vSphere Client is as follows:

Key
Topic

Step 1.   Select **Administration > vCenter Server Settings**.

Step 2.   Select **SNMP**.

Step 3.   In the **Receiver URL** fields, enter the hostname or IP address of the SNMP receiver.

Step 4.   In the adjacent field, enter the port number used by the receiver, which must be between 1 and 65535.

Step 5.   In the **Community** field, enter the community identifier.

Step 6.   Click **OK**.

This is shown in Figure 2-17.

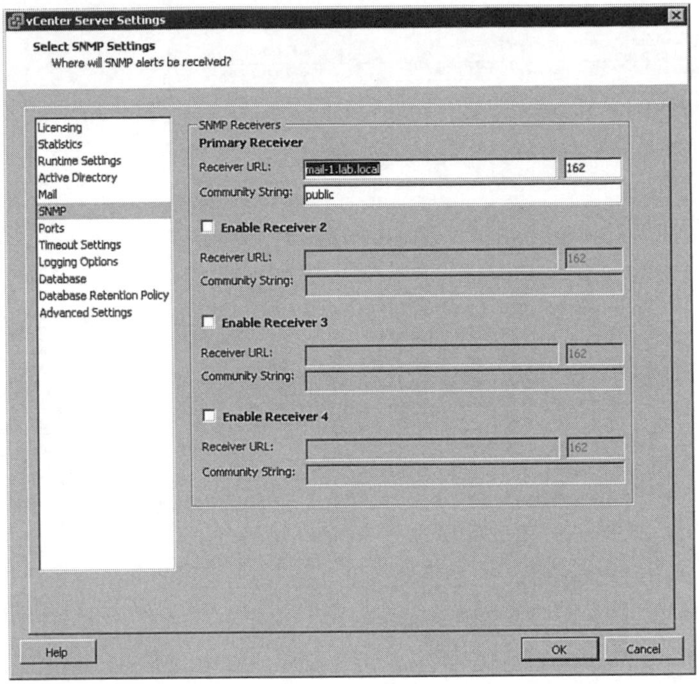

Figure 2-17   SNMP settings.

The **Get-AdvancedSettings** and **Set-AdvancedSettings** PowerCLI cmdlets can be used to query and configure SNMP on a vCenter Server. The value for the **Entity** parameter should be set to the name of the vCenter Server, and the value for the **Name** parameter should match the name of an SNMP receiver.

Scenario—Use PowerCLI to Configure SNMP on vCenter

Examine the current SNMP advanced settings on the vCenter Server named **vc-app-01**. Set the first **SNMP receiver** to 192.168.1.10, the **community** to public, and **Enabled** to true.

The following commands can be used to accomplish this task:

Get-AdvancedSetting –Entity vc-app-01 –Name snmp.*

Get-AdvancedSetting –Entity vc-app-01 –Name snmp. receiver.1.community | Set-AdvancedSetting –Value public

> **Get-AdvancedSetting –Entity vc-app-01 –Name snmp.receiver.1.name |
> Set-AdvancedSetting –Value 192.168.1.10**
>
> **Get-AdvancedSetting –Entity vc-app-01 –Name snmp.receiver.1.enabled
> | Set-AdvancedSetting –Value $true**

SNMP can also be configured on each ESXi host. ESXi 5.1 supports SNMP v1, v2, and v3. The procedure for configuring SNMP v1 on an ESXi host involves configuring the community string, identifying one or more target receivers, enabling SNMP, and testing SNMP using **esxcli system snmp**.

For example, the following set of commands can be used to enable, configure, and test SNMP on an ESXi host, where the **community** is set to public and the **target** is set to esx-01.lab.local on port 161.

> **esxcli system snmp set –communities public**
>
> **esxcli system snmp set –targets esx-01.lab.local@161/public**
>
> **esxcli system snmp set –enable true**
>
> **esxcli system snmp test**

VMware Direct Path I/O

The main use case for implementing VMware Direct Path I/O for a NIC is to support extremely heavy network activity within a VM, when other methods, such as placing the VM on a vSwitch by itself with dedicated NICs, are insufficient. Direct Path I/O, which is often referred to as passthrough, allows the VM to have direct access to the NIC, which in turn allows the VM rather than the vmkernel to own and drive the NIC. Direct Path I/O can also be used for other types of adapters, such as graphic cards.

VMware Direct Path I/O links a virtual machine directly to hardware in a specific ESXi host. This typically introduces limitations for the affected VM, including the inability to utilize common features on the VM, such as vMotion, suspend, and snapshots. These limitations can be mitigated if the virtualization platform is a Cisco Unified Computing System (UCS) using Cisco Virtual Machine Fabric Extender (VM-FEX) distributed switches. The prerequisites for Direct Path I/O are as follows:

- Enable Intel Directed I/O (VT-d) or AMD I/O Virtualization Technology (IOMMU) in the BIOS

- Ensure the VM is utilizing virtual hardware version 7 or higher

The procedure to configure VMware Direct Path I/O involves configuring the PCI device as a pass-through device and assigning it to a specific VM. The steps to configure these settings using the vSphere Client are shown here:

Step 1.   Select the ESXi host.

Step 2.   Select **Configuration tab > Hardware > Advanced Settings**.

Step 3.   Select the **Pass-through** page.

Step 4.   Click **Edit**.

Step 5.   Select the appropriate PCI device.

Step 6.   Click **OK**.

Step 7.   Right-click the VM, and then select **Edit Settings**.

Step 8.   Click the **Hardware** tab.

Step 9.   Click **Add**.

Step 10.   Choose the PCI device.

Step 11.   Click **Next**.

Migrate from Standard to Distributed Virtual Switches

Migrating a virtual network implementation that is based solely on vSSes to one that includes one or more vDSes is typically not very challenging, but it does require some care. More than one method exists to make such a migration. One option is to build a new vDS and then migrate all appropriate items from an existing vSS to the new vDS utilizing a single wizard, available when attaching the ESXi host to the vDS.

The first task when using this method is to the build at least one new vDS. The steps to do this using the vSphere Client are as follows:

Step 1.   Select **Home > Network Inventory view**.

Step 2.   Right-click the appropriate datacenter where the vDS should be created.

Step 3.   Select **New Distributed Virtual Switch**.

Step 4.   In the wizard, enter a name for the vDS (such as dvSwitch0) and enter the maximum number of uplinks allowed per ESXi host (such as 2).

Step 5.   Do not attach any hosts or physical adapters at this time.

Step 6. Accept any defaults related to distributed port groups (this will create a default port group named dvPortGroup that can be renamed and reconfigured later).

Step 7. Click **OK**.

Next, attach the ESXi host and migrate all items, including VMs, NICs, and vmkernel ports, from the vSS to the vDS. This approach works nicely for vSSes configured with IP Hash-based NIC Teaming and Etherchannel. Follow these steps:

Key Topic

Step 1. In the **Inventory** pane, click the vDS.

Step 2. Select the **Configuration** tab.

Step 3. Visually examine the diagram to determine whether any port groups exist on the vDS.

Step 4. Decide which port groups should be configured on the vDS and the specific settings for each port group policy, including VLAN, Security, NIC Teaming, and Traffic shaping policies. These ports will act as the destination port groups during the migration.

Step 5. Modify any existing port groups to match the planned settings for that port group. Create all other port groups as planned. To create a new port group, right-click the vDS and select **New Distributed Port Group**. Provide a port group name and appropriate settings when prompted by the wizard.

Step 6. In the **Inventory** pane, right-click the vDS and select **Add Host**, which launches the **Add Host to vSphere Distributed Switch** Wizard.

Step 7. When prompted by the wizard, select the ESXi host and select all the physical adapters that are currently attached to the vSS that is being replaced, as shown in Figure 2-18. Click **Next**.

Step 8. In the next page of the wizard, choose any vmkernel ports (such as VMotion or Management virtual adapters) that you want to migrate from the vSS, as shown in Figure 2-19. In the **Destination Port Group** column, select the distributed port group where you want to move the vmkernel port.

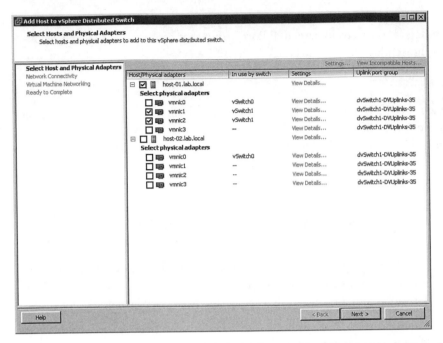

Figure 2-18   The Select Host and Physical Adapter page of the Add Host Wizard.

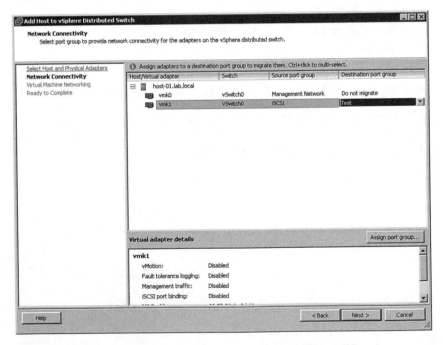

Figure 2-19   The Network Connectivity page of the Add Host Wizard.

Step 9.   In the next page of the wizard, check the box labeled **Migrate Virtual Machine Networking**. In the **Destination Port Group** column, select the target distributed port group for each VM, as shown in Figure 2-20.

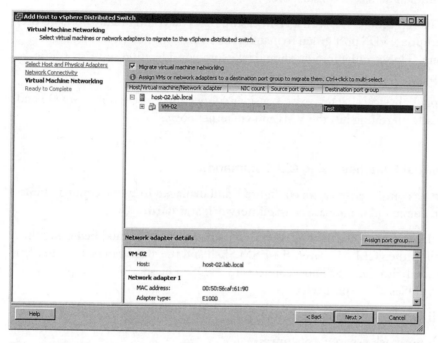

Figure 2-20   The Virtual Machine Networking page of the Add Host Wizard.

Step 10.   Click **Finish**. All the selected VMs, vmkernel ports, and NICs should migrate safely to the new vDS with little or no disruption in network connectivity per VM.

Other options to migrate from vSS to vDS exist. For example, the previous procedure could be modified such that only one NIC (instead of all NICs) from the current vSS is selected in the wizard. By using this method and ensuring that all VMs and vmkernel virtual adapters have migrated successfully to the vDS prior to migrating the remaining NICs, network connectivity is maintained. Even during the midst of the migration, where some VMs are still connected to the original vSS and some to the new vDS, the VMs on either switch are still connected to the network. Do not use this approach if IP Hash-based NIC Teaming and Etherchannel (IEE802.3ad) are currently in use.

For another example, instead of migrating VMs when attaching the ESXi host, the VMs could be migrated after attaching the host. This could be accomplished using the Migrate Virtual Machine Networking wizard. It could also be accomplished by editing each specific VM's virtual NICs.

Some additional details to consider are:

- When replacing a vSS with a vDS, ensure that you configure the ports on the appropriate vDS port group to match the settings on the original vSS port group. These configurations should take into consideration security, traffic shaping, NIC teaming, MTU, and VLAN configurations.

- If spare physical adapters exist, consider connecting those to the new vDS and initially migrating just the VMs and vmkernel ports.

Configure Virtual Switches Using CLI Commands

vSSes can be completely created, configured, and managed from the command line. The main command namespace is **esxcli network standard**.

Because vDSes are created on a vCenter Server, they cannot be modified using the ESXi shell or the vCLI. However, the ESXi Shell and the vCLI can be used to identify and modify how an ESXi host connects to a vDS. The specific namespaces for vSSes and vDSes are respectively:

esxcli network vswitch standard

esxcli network vswitch dvs vmware

The esxcli namespace for vSSes provides commands to allow an administrator to examine and configure all settings of a vSS and its port groups. The volume of commands and options is far too great to provide details and examples for each command, but here is an example of using a set of commands to accomplish a specific task.

Scenario—Create and Configure a Standard Virtual Switch

Create a new vSS named vSwitch1 having 256 ports with support for jumbo frames (**MTU=9000**). Attach vmnic1 and vmnic2 as uplinks. Create a port group named Test. Set its VLAN property to 101, and set its NIC Teaming to iphash. Enable traffic shaping with **average** and **peak bandwidth** set to 100 Mbps. Before beginning, ensure that no vSS named vSwitch1 already exists.

This scenario can be accomplished by using these commands:

esxcli network vswitch standard list

esxcli network vswitch standard add -P 128 -v vSwitch1

esxcli network vswitch standard uplink add –u vmnic1 -v vSwitch1

esxcli network vswitch standard uplink add –u vmnic2 -v vSwitch1

esxcli network vswitch standard set –m 9000 –v vSwitch1

esxcli network vswitch standard portgroup add -p Test -v vSwitch1

esxcli network vswitch standard portgroup set -p Test -v 101

esxcli network vswitch standard portgroup policy failover set -p Test -l iphash

esxcli network vswitch standard port group policy shaping set -p Test -e true -k 100000 –b 100000 –t 100000*

When setting traffic shaping from the ESXi Shell, you must set avg (-b), burst (-t), and peak (-k)

The command to identify all VMware vDSes accessed by an ESXi host is **esxcli network vswitch dvs vmware list.**

Analyze Virtual Switches Using ESXCLI

Commands can also be used to analyze details of existing vSSes and vDSes. For example, to list all vSSes and vDSes, use these commands:

esxcli network vswitch standard list

esxcli network vswitch dvs vmware list

To closely examine properties on a specific vSS, the **–v** argument can be used to identify the vSS. For example, if iSCSI performance is poor and you suspect that jumbo frames is not properly configured, you might want to examine the MTU settings on a vSS. For another example, if a VM fails to connect to a vSS, you might need to determine whether all the ports are already used by comparing Used Ports to Configured Ports. In these and similar cases, you can examine the properties of a vSS named vSwitch1 using this command:

esxcli network vswitch standard list –v vSwitch1.

Configure NetFlow

NetFlow is an industry standard for collecting and analyzing network data. It is a collection of related network packets traveling in sequence in the same direction, sharing specific characteristics, including source IP address, target IP address, source port, target port, and type of service. Ethernet switches that support the NetFlow protocol can be configured to identify net flows and send data about the net flow to net flow receivers. NetFlow analyzers can be used to analyze the collected data and produce reports. Some examples of NetFlow analysis products are Solarwinds NetFlow Traffic Analyzer and OptiView NetFlow Tracker.

vSSes cannot be configured for NetFlow collection, but vDSes can.

The steps to configure a vDS for NetFlow collection using the vSphere Client are as follows:

Step 1.   Drill to **Inventory > Networking**.

Step 2.   Right-click the vDS, and select **Edit Settings**.

Step 3.   Select the **NetFlow** tab.

Step 4.   Define the IP and port ID for the NetFlow Collector.

Step 5.   Define the IP for the vSphere Distributed Switch.

Step 6.   Configure any advanced settings as needed (sampling rate, process internal flows only, and so on).

Step 7.   Click **OK** to save.

Step 8.   Then right-click and select **Edit Settings** on the dvPort Group on which you want to enable NetFlow.

Step 9.   Click **Monitoring**.

Step 10.   Use the drop-down menu to give NetFlow a status of **Enabled on this port** group.

Step 11.   Click **OK**.

Discovery Protocols

Cisco Discovery Protocol (CDP) can be configured on both vSSes and vDSes. Link Layer Discovery Protocol (LLDP) can also be configured on vDSSes, but not vSSes. CDP is a protocol used on Cisco switches to discover identity and configuration information about the switches to which they are attached and broadcast its own information to those switches. CDP can be used by vSwitches to discover and broadcast information in much the same way. In addition, in a vSphere implementation,

CDP can be used to allow attached Cisco switches to discover information about vSwitches and ESXi hosts. Similarly, LLDP—a vendor-neutral implementation of CDP—can be used to discover and broadcast the same information on switches that support LLDP rather than CDP. The main use case for utilizing LLDP is when a network contains non-Cisco switches, but this use case does require vDSes.

The following steps can be used to configure LLDP on a vDS:

Step 1.   Select **Inventory > Networking**.

Step 2.   Right-click the vDS, and select **Edit Settings**.

Step 3.   In the **Properties** tab, select **Advanced**.

Step 4.   In the **Status** drop-down menu, select **Enabled**.

Step 5.   In the **Type** drop-down menu, select **Link Layer Discovery Protocol**.

Step 6.   In the **Operation** drop-down menu, select **Listen**, **Advertise**, or **Both**.

The following command enables CDP and sets it to both on a vSS named vSwitch1:

esxcli network vswitch standard set –c both –v <vSwitch. Name>

Configure and Maintain VLANs and PVLANs

This section is intended to provide you with the knowledge and skills needed to successfully configure Virtual Local Area Networks (VLANs) and private VLANs (PVLANs) in a vSphere network implementation.

Types of VLANs and PVLANs

VLANs are virtual networks that are defined within a LAN. VLANs are often called logical networks and are defined by software within the Ethernet switches. They provide multiple broadcast domains within a LAN without requiring physical separation. vSSes and vDSes support VLANs, VLAN tagging, and VLAN trunking as identified by IEEE-802.1q. Each VLAN is assigned an ID number between 1 and 4094. The VLAN is then typically assigned to a specific IP range. Switches can be configured to allow and control routing between VLANs as desired.

Various methods can be used to connect VMs and vmkernel ports to specific VLANs. The most common method is to configure the physical network port for VLAN trunking and then to assign a desired VLAN number(s) to each virtual port group (or vmkernel port). The VLANs should first be configured on the physical switch if they do not already exist.

This method of VLAN tagging is also known as Virtual Switch Tagging (VST). vSphere supports two other VLAN tagging methods, External Switch Tagging (EST) and Virtual Guest Tagging (VGT). To configure EST, configure the physical Ethernet switch to assign the VLAN numbers. No configuration is performed on the vSS or vDS, and packets are not tagged until they reach the physical switch infrastructure. All virtual machines on all port groups using the vmnic that connects to the physical switch port will reside in that VLAN. VGT is enabled by configuring the VLAN within the guest OS rather than on the virtual port group. Packets are tagged before they leave the guest OS.

VMware recommends network segregation between different types of traffic, such as management, vMotion, and VMs. This can be achieved by using separate VLANs for each network type. For example, a management VLAN can be created on physical switches and configured accordingly on vSwitches.

You can configure VLANs on port groups on vSSes using the vSphere Client by following these steps:

Step 1.   In the **Host and Clusters** Inventory, select an ESXi server.

Step 2.   Select **Configuration > Networking**.

Step 3.   Click the **Properties** link for the desired vSS.

Step 4.   Select the appropriate port group, and click **Edit**.

Step 5.   In the **General Properties** page, enter the appropriate VLAN number.

Step 6.   Click **OK**.

VLANs can be configured with the **esxcli network vswitch standard portgroup** command. For example, to assign VLAN 101 to a port group named Test, the command is

esxcli network vswitch standard portgroup set -p Test -v 101

Determine Use Cases for VLAN Trunking

vSSes permit only one VLAN trunk option on a port group, which is to trunk all VLANs 1 to 4094. To configure a standard port group to trunk all VLANs, set the **VLAN ID** to 4095, which is a special VLAN number designed for this purpose. For example, to connect a VM-based network sniffer (such as Wireshark) to a standard port group and configure it to inspect network packets for multiple port groups that are assigned to various VLANs, set the sniffer port group VLAN to 4095.

> **NOTE** Also set the Security setting of the sniffer port group to allow Promiscuous Mode. This is necessary to allow the Wireshark VM to inspect packets that are not destined for the sniffer VM.

VST (assigning VLAN numbers to virtual port groups) requires VLAN trunking on the physical switch ports. The trunk should include all VLANs that will be assigned to the virtual port groups that share the same physical uplinks. For example, consider this scenario.

Scenario—VLAN Trunking on a Standard Virtual Switch

- The management network is VLAN 101.

- The production network is VLAN 201.

- Both the management vmkernel ports and the production VM port group are configured on the same vSS and share the same NIC team.

In this scenario, the physical switch ports must be configured to trunk VLANs 101 and 201. The Management Network vmkernel port must be set for VLAN 101. The production VM port group must be set for VLAN 201.

VLAN trunking is permitted on vDSes, where it is more configurable than VLAN trunking on vSSes. On vDSes, the VLAN type can be set to VLAN Trunking and the trunk can be set to a combination of specific VLAN values and VLAN ranges. For example, if the Wireshark VM is needed to inspect packets on VLAN 101 and 201, but not on any other VLAN, then it can be attached to a distributed port group that is trunked for just VLANs 101 and 201.

Determine Use Cases for PVLAN Trunking

A PVLAN is typically described as a VLAN within a VLAN. PVLANs are typically referenced using both the primary and secondary VLAN IDs. For example, within primary VLAN 10, you could create secondary PVLANs 1 through 4094 and identify these PVLANs as 10-1 to 10-4094. Private VLANs allow secondary VLANs within a primary VLAN that share the same IP subnet.

PVLANs can be configured as Community, Isolated, or Promiscuous. Objects in the same community PVLAN can communicate with other devices in the same community and in the promiscuous VLAN, but they cannot communicate with other communities. Objects in a promiscuous VLAN can communicate with all objects within the same primary VLAN, including objects in the promiscuous PVLAN, objects in any community PVLAN, and objects in isolated PVLANs. Objects in an isolated PVLAN can communicate with objects in the promiscuous PVLAN but not with any other objects, including objects in the same isolated PVLAN.

Key Topic

Several use cases exist for PVLANs. For example, a public cloud provider might want to provide a separate VLAN for each customer and each customer might require an array of VLANs for their own infrastructure. The combined number of provider and customer VLANs can exceed the standard 4094 VLANs limitation, requiring PVLANs to provide further segmentation by taking each primary VLAN and carving it into multiple secondary PVLANs.

Another use case involves public access to web servers that reside in a DMZ. The goal might be to use a single IP range, but yet protect all objects in the network from malicious activity originating within a compromised web server. In this case, an isolated PVLAN could be used to prevent the web servers from peer communication even though they reside in the same PVLAN.

Scenario—PVLANs for a University

- A university owns a set of servers, including DHCP, DNS, web servers, file servers, and print servers, that need to be reachable from all network ports.

- The university provides hundreds of single workstation areas where students can connect their laptops to the university's network and where they receive IPs automatically via DHCP from within a single Class B network.

- The university provides 20 classrooms and labs where all the PCs in the room can communicate with one another.

- The network must enforce strict security, where PCs in one classroom cannot possibly communicate with PCs in other classrooms. Likewise, a laptop connected to one workstation network port cannot possibly communicate with other laptops or any PC in the classrooms.

- All workstation connections and classrooms must allow all laptops and PCs to access the servers owned by the university.

The solution for this scenario can be implemented by configuring PVLANs on the switches. The university's servers could be connected to a single promiscuous PVLAN—for example, PVLAN 10. Each classroom could be connected to various community PVLANs—for example, PVLANs 10-101 to 10-120, where 10 is the primary and 101–120 are the secondary PVLAN IDs. The hundreds of workstation areas could be connect to a single isolated PVLAN—for example, 10-201. The steps to implement this example on a vDS are as follows:

Step 1.   In the **Networking** inventory view, right-click the vDS and select **Edit Settings**.

Step 2.   Select the **Private VLAN** tab.

Step 3.   Click **Enter Private VLAN ID** here, and enter 10 as the primary private VLAN.

Step 4.   Click anywhere in the dialog box, and then select the **primary VLAN 10** that was just created.

Step 5.   Click **Enter a Private VLAN** here, under Secondary VLAN ID; then enter 201 and select Isolated.

Step 6.   Likewise, select **Enter a Private VLAN** again, enter 101, and select Community. Repeat this for each classroom, providing unique secondary PVLANs ID up to 120.

Step 7.   In the **Network** inventory, right-click the **Workstation** port group and select **Edit Settings**.

Step 8.   Click VLAN. Set **VLAN Type** to **Private VLAN**, and select the Isolated 10-201 PVLAN.

Step 9.   Likewise, right-click the first Classroom port group and select the Community 10-101 VLAN. Repeat this for each classroom port group, selecting a unique community PVLAN previously configured on the vDS (of which there should be 20).

Step 10.   Finally, right-click the servers port group and select the 10 Promiscuous PVLAN.

Command Tools to Troubleshoot and Identify VLAN Configurations

To troubleshoot VLAN-related issues on a vSS, start with the **esxcli network vswitch standard portgroup list** command to list the properties of the vSS. Verify that the VLAN ID is set to the correct value. If the incorrect VLAN ID is assigned to the port group, change it using the **esxcli network vswitch standard portgroup**

set –v command. Ensure the VLAN ID is set to 0 (if no VLAN ID is required), 1–4094 (to connect to specific VLAN), or 4095 (to trunk all VLANs 1 to 4094). Ensure that if a VLAN ID is assigned on the port group, the physical NIC switch port is configured for a VLAN trunk that includes that specific VLAN ID. If a VLAN value is assigned on the port group but is not trunked on the physical connection, then virtual adapters on that port group will not be able to connect because the physical switch might drop the packets.

Deploy and Maintain Scalable Virtual Networking

This section is intended to provide you with the knowledge and skills to successfully configure and troubleshoot scalable vSwitches. It includes understanding NIC teaming, explicit failover, and VMware best practices.

Identify NIC Teaming Policies

The default NIC Teaming policy, which is also called the **Load Balancing** setting, is Route based on the originating virtual port ID. As each running virtual machine connects to a vSwitch; the vSwitch assigns the VM's virtual network adapter to a port number and uses the port number to determine which path will be used to route all network I/O sent from that adapter. Technically, the vSwitches uses a modulo function, where the port number is divided by the number of NICs in the team and the remainder indicates on which path to place the outbound I/O. If the selected path fails, the outbound I/O from the virtual adapter is automatically re-routed to a surviving path. This policy does not permit outbound data from a single virtual adapter to be distributed across all active paths on the vSwitch. Instead, all outbound data from a specific virtual adapter travels through a single path determined by the vSwitch, but might failover, if necessary, to another path. Implementation of this policy on a vSwitch does not require any changes to the connected physical switches.

NOTE   The Route based on the originating virtual port ID algorithm does not consider load into its calculation for traffic placement.

The second NIC Teaming policy available for both vSSes and vDSes is Route based on source MAC hash. This policy is similar to the Route based on the originating virtual port ID policy, except that the vSwitch uses the MAC address of the virtual adapter to select the path, rather than the port number. The vSwitch performs a modulo function, where the MAC address is divided by the number of NICs in the team and the remainder indicates the path to place the outbound I/O.

NOTE   The Route based on source MAC hash algorithm does not consider load into its calculation for traffic placement.

Another NIC Teaming policy available for both switch types is Route based on IP hash. This is the only option that permits outbound data from a single virtual adapter to be distributed across all active paths on the vSwitch. This option requires that the physical switch be configured for IEEE802.3ad, which is often referred to as Etherchannel. Likewise, if Etherchannel is configured to bond a set of paths on the physical switch, then Route based on IP hash must be configured on the vSwitch. This allows inbound traffic to be truly load balanced by the physical switch, which treats all paths in the bond as a single pipe. The outbound data from each virtual adapter is distributed across the active paths using the calculated IP hash, where the vSwitch maintains a table of all current external connections to the virtual adapter and directs the traffic destined for each external connection individually. So, if a virtual adapter is concurrently sending data to two or more clients, the I/O to one client can be placed on one path and the I/O to another client can be placed on a separate path. The outbound traffic from a virtual adapter to a specific external client is based on the most significant bits of the IP addresses of both the virtual adapter and the client. The combined value of these bits is used by the vSwitch to place the associated outbound traffic on a specific path.

NOTE   The Route based on IP hash algorithm does not consider load into its calculation for traffic placement. But, the inbound traffic is truly load balanced by the physical switch.

NOTE   The Route based on IP hash algorithm does require a specific configuration (IEEE802.3ad) on the physical switch. Algorithms using virtual port ID or MAC hash do not require a specific configuration on the physical switch.

A final load balancing policy is available for vDSes only. The Route based on physical NIC load policy is the only load balancing option that factors in the load on the physical NIC when determining traffic placement. It also does not require special settings on the physical switch. Initially, outbound traffic from each virtual adapter is placed on a specific path. Activity is monitored across each path in the team, and when the I/O through a specific vmnic adapter reaches a consistent 75% capacity, then one or more virtual adapters is automatically remapped to other paths. This

Key Topic

algorithm is a good choice for situations in which you are concerned about saturating the bandwidth of some NICs in the team but would rather not configure Etherchannel on the physical switch.

NOTE   The Route based on physical NIC load algorithm does consider load into its calculation for traffic placement. It is available only on vDSes.

You can configure NIC Teaming and Failover policies on a vSS by following these steps:

Step 1.   Select **Inventory > Hosts and Clusters**; then select the ESXi host.

Step 2.   Select **Configuration > Networking**.

Step 3.   Select the **Properties** link of the appropriate vSS.

Step 4.   Select the **NIC Teaming** tab.

Step 5.   Use the drop-down menu to set the **Load Balancing** option to the desired option.

You can set NIC Teaming and Failover policies on vDS by navigating to Inventory > Networking and modifying the vDS. You can also override vSS and vDS settings at the port group level by using the NIC Teaming tab on the individual port group property pages. On vDSes, you can also allow individual ports to override the settings of the port group.

In addition to the Load Balancing option, you can configure other settings on the NIC Teaming tab, such as Failback, Notify Switches, and explicit failover. By default, if a virtual adapter is reconnected to a new path due to a path failure, it will notify the physical switch. One use case where this should be changed is when Microsoft Network Load Balancing (NLB) is used in a unicast mode. In this case, set the **Notify Switches** option to No. Next, when a virtual adapter is placed on a new path due to failover or failback, it notifies the physical switches by default. One use case where this might need to be changed is when a physical network connection is having intermittent issues and you want to ensure that VMs are not using it until it is permanently repaired. Finally, by default, all NICs in a team are active and the selected load-balancing policy determines the appropriate I/O paths for each virtual adapter. One use case where this might need to be changed is when you want to place the Management Network on a specific physical path for normal use but allow it to failover to another specific path if necessary.

Determine and Apply Failover Settings

Another configuration option that can be set on vSwitches is **Use Explicit Failover Order**. A common use case is to modify the default settings on the Management Network such that it has only one active uplink and one or more standby uplinks. Another use case is to provide N+1 failover for a set of port groups and a team of uplinks. In this case, the number of NICs on the team can be one more than the number of port groups. So, each port group can be configured with one unique, active NIC and all port groups can be configured with the same standby adapter.

Scenario—Configure Active and Passive NICS for a Standard Virtual Switch

On a vSS named vSwitch1 that has a team of three NICs (vmnic1, vmnic2, and vmnic3), configure the Production port group to direct its I/O to vmnic1 only, under normal conditions. Likewise, configure the Test port group to direct its I/O to vminic2 under normal conditions. Configure both port groups such that they can failover to vmnic3, if necessary.

This task can be accomplished by performing these steps:

Step 1.   Select **Inventory > Hosts and Clusters**, and then select the appropriate ESXi host.

Step 2.   Select the **Configuration** tab **> Networking**.

Step 3.   Click the **Properties** link on vSwitch1.

Step 4.   Select the Production port group, and click the **Edit** button.

Step 5.   Select the **NIC Teaming** tab.

Step 6.   Check the box to **Override switch failover order**.

Step 7.   By selecting each physical NIC one at a time and using the **Move Up** and **Move Down** buttons, change the Failover Order such that vmnic1 is **Active**, vmnic2 is **Unused**, and vmnic3 is **Standby**, as shown in Figure 2-21.

Step 8.   Repeat the previous steps to modify the **Failover Order** for Test, such that vmnic2 is **Active**, vmnic1 is **Unused**, and vmnic3 is **Standby**.

Step 9.   Click **OK**.

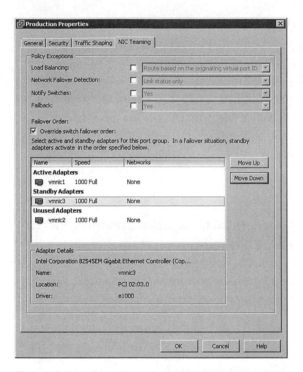

Figure 2-21   Override switch failover order settings.

Scenario—NIC Teaming on a Distributed Port Group

Configure a port group named Production on a vDS named dvSwitch1 to use Up-link-3 to Uplink-6 with the Route based on physical NIC load teaming policy. Set **Failback** to No. On the same switch, configure the Management port group to use Uplink-1, but permit it to failover to Uplink-2 if necessary. Ensure that each port group is configured to notify switches in the event of a failover.

This task can be accomplished by performing these steps:

Step 1.   Select **Inventory > Networking**.

Step 2.   Locate dvSwitch1 in the inventory view and expand its view.

Step 3.   Right-click the Production port group, and select **Edit Settings**.

Step 4.   Select **Teaming and Failover**.

Step 5.   Select the **NIC Teaming** tab.

Step 6.   Set the **Load Balancing** option to Route based on physical NIC load.

Step 7.   Set the **Failback** to No.

Step 8.   Check the box to **Override the Failover Order**.

Step 9.   By selecting each Uplink one at a time and using the **Move Up** and **Move Down** buttons, change the **Failover Order** such that Uplink-3, Uplink-4, Uplink-5, and Uplink-6 are **Active**. Likewise, set Uplink-1 and Uplink-2 as **Unused**.

Step 10.   Click **OK**.

Step 11.   Right-click the Management port group, and select **Edit Settings**.

Step 12.   Select **Teaming and Failover**.

Step 13.   Select the **NIC Teaming** tab.

Step 14.   Check the box to **Override switch Failover Order**.

Step 15.   By selecting each Uplink one at a time and using the **Move Up** and **Move** Down buttons, change the **Failover Order** such that Uplink-1 is **Active**. Likewise, set Uplink-2 as **Standby** and set Uplink-4, Uplink-5, and Uplink-6 as **Unused**.

Step 16.   Click **OK**.

Configure Port Groups to Properly Isolate Network Traffic

VMware recommends that each type of network traffic in vSphere be separated by VLANs and be provided with the appropriate bandwidth. To achieve this, the design typically allocates separate VLANs for management, vMotion, VMs, iSCSI, NAS, VMware HA Heartbeat, and VMware Fault Tolerance logging. Typically, VMs are not placed on a single VLAN, but instead might use multiple VLANs. The implementation requires that the VLANs be created within the physical network. Additionally, each virtual port group might require specific configuration. The most common and flexible means to provide virtual isolation between port groups is to configure each physical switch port with all virtually allocated VLANs configured in the virtual switch. To do so, you "trunk" the VLANs on the physical switch using IEEE 802.1q trunking. For example, if a physical switch port is trunked for VLANs 101–110, then 10 port groups should be created on the connected vSwitch, where each port group is assigned a unique VLAN number in the range from 101 to 110.

Administer vSphere Distributed Switches

This section is intended to ensure that you have the knowledge and skills to perform administration tasks on vDSes. It covers command-line use, port binding settings,

Live Port Moving, configuring vDS settings to satisfy specific network requirements, Network I/O Control, and troubleshooting.

Understand the Use of Command-line Tools to Configure Distributed Virtual Switch Settings on an ESXi Host

Although a vDS cannot be modified via vCLI commands because its control plane resides on a vCenter Server, vCLI commands can be used to control how specific ESXi hosts connect to the vDS.

Determine Use Cases and Apply Port Binding Settings

By default, a vDS port group contains 128 ports with static binding. You can change the number of ports. You can also change the port binding method to dynamic or ephemeral.

Static binding means that existing ports are assigned to virtual adapters immediately when the virtual adapter is attached to the port group. For example, if the port group contains 128 ports, then a maximum of 128 VMs can be connected to the port group regardless of the power state of the VMs.

Dynamic binding means that existing ports are not assigned to virtual adapters until the adapter becomes live. For example, if the port group contains 128 ports, more than 128 VMs can be connected to the port group but no more than 128 of these VMs can actually be running at any given time. As each VM powers on, their virtual adapter becomes live and is then assigned a port on the vDS within the port group. As each VM is powered down or removed from the port group, that port becomes available for reassignment.

With ephemeral binding, ports are not pre-provisioned or assigned, but instead are created and assigned as virtual adapters become live and are connected to the port group. During creation of a port group using the ephemeral port binding method, you do not need to specify a number of ports and no ports are immediately created. As each VM is connected to the port group and started, a port is automatically created and assigned to the virtual adapter. As each VM is stopped, its assigned port is unassigned and destroyed.

To change the binding method, right-click the port group and select **Edit Settings**. Change the binding type from static to either ephemeral or dynamic. In a small environment, the standard approach could be to leave port groups with the default settings, which tends to be easy to configure and support. In larger environments containing multiple port groups, it can be best to lower the number of ports in a port group in cases where you are certain that fewer than 128 virtual adapters will never connect. This frees up otherwise unused ports for assignment to other port groups. In cases where you expect to never have more than a specific number of concurrently running virtual adapters connected to a port group, you could set the port binding method to dynamic. Ephemeral binding is the most flexible and scalable. Ephemeral can be a good choice in most cases due to its flexibility and the fact that it allows additional VMs to be attached to the port group even when vCenter Server is offline.

Live Port Moving

Live Port Moving is a feature of vDSes that enables an active port to be migrated into a dvPortGroup without dropping the connection and while acquiring the settings of the target dvPortGroup. This could be useful for troubleshooting. Enable Live Port Moving on a port group using the following steps:

Step 1.   Select **Inventory > Networking**.

Step 2.   Locate and right-click the appropriate port group; then select **Edit Settings**.

Step 3.   Select **Advanced**, and then select **Allow Override of Port Policies**.

Step 4.   Click **Edit Override Settings**.

Step 5.   Now, use the following PowerCLI commands to set the **LivePortMovingAllowed** property of the port group's policy settings to true:

- **$dvPg = Get-VirtualPortGroup -Name "Test" | get-view**

- **$var = New-Object VMware.Vim.DVPortgroupConfigSpec**

- **$var.Name = "Test"**

- **$var.ConfigVersion = $dvPg.Config.ConfigVersion**

- **$var.policy.LivePortMovingAllowed = "True"**

- **$var.policy.BlockOverrideAllowed = "True"**

- **$taskMoRef = $dvPg.ReconfigureDVPortgroup_Task($var)**

Identify Distributed Virtual Switch Technologies to Satisfy Network Requirements

You should be able to analyze a set of network requirements and decide how to satisfy these requirements by implementing specific vDS features. One way to gain this skill is to examine each available vDS setting and consider possible use cases. Another means is to consider sample scenarios containing network requirements, decide which vDS features might be useful, and determine the best configuration of the feature to fit the requirements. Here are a couple of sample scenarios:

Scenario—Manageability of Distributed Virtual Switches

Configure a vDS such that the administrator can still attach new VMs to the vDS even if vCenter Server is offline due to failure or maintenance.

This can be accomplished by configuring the port groups on the vDS for ephemeral binding, which allows the administrator to connect VMs to the port group using the vSphere Client connected directly to the ESXi host. Static binding and dynamic binding do not allow such changes without involving vCenter Server.

Scenario—Network Sniffing

On a vDS, configure a new port group named Sniffer that allows a VM running Wireshark to successfully inspect network I/O involving two other VMs connected to two other port groups on the vDS whose VLANs are 101 and 102. Do not allow the Wireshark VM to inspect any I/O from any other VMs, port groups, or VLANs.

This can be accomplished by adding a new port group named Sniffer to the vDS and making the following settings:

Step 1. Select **Inventory > Networking**, and right-click the Sniffer port group.

Step 2. Select **Edit Settings**.

Step 3. Set the VLAN Type to **VLAN Trunk**.

Step 4. Enter **101, 102** in the VLAN text box.

Step 5. Click **OK**.

Step 6. Select **Inventory > VMs and Templates**, and then locate the Wireshark VM.

Step 7. Right-click the Wireshark VM, and select **Edit Settings**.

Step 8. Select the network adapter, and change its connection to **Sniffer port group**.

Step 9. Ensure that **Connected** and **Connected at Power On** are selected.

Step 10. Click **OK**.

Step 11. Select **Inventory > Network**, and select the vDS.

Step 12. Select the **Ports** tab, and locate the source and Wireshark VMs.

Step 13. For each of the source VMs, identify and record their port IDs. For example, the port IDs of the VMs could be ports 11 and 21.

Step 14. Identify the port ID of the Wireshark VM. For example, the port ID could be 40.

Step 15. In the inventory view, right-click the vDS.

Step 16. Select the **Port Mirroring** tab, and then click **Add**.

Step 17. Specify a name for the port mirroring session—for example, use Wireshark.

Step 18. Select **Allow normal I/O on destination ports**.

Step 19. Click **Next**.

Step 20. Choose **Ingress / Egress**.

Step 21. Type the port IDs of the source ports, separated by commas. For example, type **11, 21**.

Step 22. Click **Next**.

Step 23. Click the **>>** link and enter the port ID of the Wireshark VM—for example, type 40.

Step 24. Click **Next**.

Step 25. Click **Finish**.

Configure and Administer vSphere Network I/O Control

Network I/O Control is a feature of a vDS that provides the implementation of network resource pools. Network resource pools, which are similar to DRS resource pools, are pools of network ports on which shares and limits can be set. Network resource pools provide a means to control network I/O for specific data types that span multiple port groups. Although port groups on vDSes provide Traffic Shaping policies that enable ingress and egress data to be limited per average bandwidth, peak bandwidth, and burst size settings, Traffic Shaping alone cannot provide sufficient flexibility in certain situations. You might want to control network I/O for a specific type of traffic that spans multiple port groups without having to manage settings on every port group. You also might need to establish a priority level for certain types of traffic, so that critical network traffic is minimally impacted when network contention occurs. For these use cases, Network I/O Control provides an effective solution.

To enable Network I/O Control, select the vDS, select the **Resource Allocation** tab, click **Properties**, and click **Enable Network I/O Control on this vSphere Distributed Switch**. This turns on Network I/O Control and creates system network resource pools that correspond to the types of traffic recognized automatically by vSphere. The system network resource pools are Virtual Machine Traffic,

Key Topic

vMotion Traffic, Management Traffic, iSCSI Traffic, NFS Traffic, HA Heartbeat, Fault Tolerance Traffic, and vSphere Replication Traffic. By default, the Host Limit on each pool is set to Unlimited and the Physical Adapter Shares on each pool is set to Normal. The lone exception is the Virtual Machine Traffic pool whose Physical Adapter Shares is set to High. This is done by default, so if network contention occurs, VM traffic automatically receives a larger portion of the network bandwidth than the other traffic types.

Enabling Network I/O Control provides the administrator with the means to easily control network bandwidth usage by traffic type. For example, consider a case where a cluster of ESXi hosts uses two 10 Gbps NICs and no other network adapters. When vacating all VMs from a host to prepare for maintenance mode, eight concurrent vMotion operations can execute, which expedites the process. However, the administrators might be concerned that if multiple concurrent vMotion operations occur during periods of heavy network activity, network contention could occur and negatively impact the performance of production applications. The goal is to allow vMotion to heavily utilize bandwidth when it is available but to limit the bandwidth usage of vMotion if contention occurs. This can be accomplished by enabling Network I/O Control and setting the Physical Adapter shares on vMotion Traffic to Low.

Network I/O Control also enables the creation of user-defined network resource pools that are containers of vDS port groups. To create this type of pool, click the **New Network Resource Pool** link on the **Resource Allocation** tab. To assign a vDS port group to the pool, click the **Manage Port Groups** link on the **Resource Allocation** tab and use the drop-down menu for each port group to assign each port group to the appropriate network resource pool.

Scenario—User-defined Network Resource Pools

Configure a Network I/O Control to provide **High** shares for all production VMs and **Low** shares for all test VMs. Twenty port groups are used for production VMs and named from Prod101 to Prod120. The VLAN ID of each is uniquely assigned from 101 to 120. Twenty port groups are used for test VMs and named from Test201 to Test220. The VLAN ID of each is uniquely assigned from 201 to 220.

This task can be accomplished by performing the following steps:

Step 1.   Select **Inventory > Networking**, and then select the vDS.

Step 2.   Select the **Resource Allocation** tab.

Step 3. Enable Network IO Control.

Step 4. Click **New Network Resource Pool**, and then name it Production.

Step 5. Set the Shares to High.

Step 6. Click **OK**.

Step 7. Click **New Network Resource Pool**, and then name it Test.

Step 8. Set the Shares to Low.

Step 9. Click **OK**.

Step 10. On the **Resource Allocation** tab, click **Manage Port Groups**.

Step 11. For each port group named Prod101 to Prod120, select the Production resource pool in the drop-down menu.

Step 12. For each port group named Test201 to Test220, select the Test resource pool in the drop-down menu.

Step 13. Click **OK**.

Summary

This chapter described how to perform network administration in vSphere environments. It provided details on administration procedures involving the use of the vSphere Client, the vCLI, and PowerCLI. At this point, you should ensure that you can successfully apply the material in this chapter to perform network administration tasks in an actual vSphere environment.

Exam Preparation Tasks

Review All the Key Topics

Table 2-2 provides a discussion of the key topics. Use this table as a quick reference to sample administrative tasks that you should be capable of performing in preparation for the exam. For each task, ensure that you can accomplish the task using the vSphere Client, the vCLI, and PowerCLI, where appropriate.

Table 2-2   Key Topics for Chapter 2

Key Topic Element	Description	Page
List	Procedure for configuring SNMP receivers on a vCenter Server	59
List	Commands to configure SNMP on an ESXi host	61
List	Procedure for configuring VMware Direct Path I/O	62
List	Migrating VMs, vmkernel ports, and NICs while attaching an ESXi host to a vDS	63
Paragraph	esxcli network vswitch namespace	66
List	Procedure for configuring NetFlow	68
List	Procedure for configuring LLDP	69
List	Commands to configure VLAN on standard port group	70
Paragraph	Use cases for private VLANs	72
List	Procedure for configuring PVLANs	73
Paragraph	Description of Load-Based Teaming	75
List	Procedure for configuring Live Port Moving	81
Paragraph	Procedure for enabling Network I/O Control	83

Definitions of Key Terms

Define the following key terms from this chapter, and check your answers in the glossary.

Standard vSwitch (vSS), Distributed vSwitch (vDS), MTU, Jumbo Frames, SNMP, Traffic Shaping, NIC Teaming, Etherchannel, VLAN, VLAN Trunking, Direct Path I/O, Network I/O Control, network resource pool, Promiscuous Mode.

Review Tasks

These Review Tasks allow you to assess how well you grasped the materials in this chapter. Because of the advanced and hands-on nature of this particular exam, a set of tasks is provided instead of a set of questions. You should now attempt to perform each of these tasks without looking at previous sections in this chapter or at other materials, unless necessary. The steps for each task are located within the chapter.

1. Configure SNMP on vCenter Server and on each ESXi host.

2. Configure Direct Path I/O for one or more network adapters.

3. Build a vDS and host migrate all VMs, vmkernel ports, and network adapters from an existing vSS.

4. Create a vSS, add a virtual switch port group, attach uplink adapters, and assign VLANs using the esxcli namespace.

5. Configure a vSS to support LLDP and Jumbo Frames.

6. Configure PVLANs on a vDS, including at least one isolated PVLAN, one community PVLAN, and one promiscuous PVLAN.

7. Configure Network I/O Control and create a user-defined network resource pool that maps to at least two vSwitch port groups.

This chapter covers the following subjects:

- **Virtual Disk Format Types**—Three types of virtual disks are available to virtual machines. The Lazy-Zeroed Thick Virtual Disk is the default format; Eager-Zeroed Thick Virtual Disk zeros and formats all of its blocks at creation; and Thin Virtual Disk does not preallocate capacity when it is created.

- **Complex Storage Solutions**—With complexity and different storage requirements, there is a need for specialized solutions. Several sections help to solve different needs. As an example, there are sections on VMware DirectPath I/O, NPIV, Storage Filters, SSD Devices, and Software iSCSI port binding, to name a few solutions.

- **Identify Storage Provisioning Methods**—Two types of datastores can be provisioned: block based or file based. The *block-based* storage requires a LUN, which can be accessed by Fibre Channel, Fibre Channel over Ethernet, or iSCSI. The other type is *file-based* storage, which is NFSv3. In addition, there is an additional method called Raw Device Map (RDM), which bypasses the hypervisor due to storage incompatibility.

- **Pluggable Storage Architecture**—This section explains how the Pluggable Storage Architecture provides the ability to determine which storage path to use to access storage and defines how multipathing works within vSphere.

The material in this chapter pertains to the VCAP-DCA Exam objectives 1.1, 1.2, and 1.3

## CHAPTER 3

Storage Concepts

This module is going to look at implementing and managing dedicated storage in a vSphere environment. The system administrator for Windows, Unix, or VMware will need a storage device to house their data. In the case of a VMware system administrator, the storage device is a virtual construct. VMware calls this construct a *datastore*, which can be located either on shared storage or on local disks. If it is located on shared storage, it will be either a NAS or SAN device. The only NAS file system that VMware supports is NFSv3, so in the case of a NAS device, the construct is called an *NFS datastore*. In the case of a SAN device the construct is placed on a LUN and is called a *VMFS datastore*. These virtual datastores are capable of holding media files and virtual machine files. Many files are associated with a virtual machine, but of particular note in this section are the virtual disks. Virtual disks are used by virtual machines to store operating system files and data. These virtual disks can be configured in three different formats: lazy-zeroed thick, eager-zeroed thick, and thin provisioned.

This chapter also highlights a number of vSphere features and technologies that can be used to provide solutions to various storage problems. This includes discussions on Raw Device Mapping (RDM) and VMware DirectPath I/O. Both features can be used to allow virtual machines to bypass the hypervisor and directly access hardware to support specific use cases where this level of access is required. There are also sections on Storage Filters, SSD Devices, Software iSCSI port binding as well as other features. Two important sections on storage APIs are the section on vStorage APIs for Array Integration (VAAI) that enables the ESXi host to offload certain storage operations to the storage array, and the section on the vStorage APIs for Storage Awareness (VASA), which is a set of APIs that a storage vendor can provide to advertise information about a storage array.

The final section details the Pluggable Storage Architecture (PSA), which is really an architecture that defines how multipathing works within vSphere. If a VM sends a SCSI command to access data on a SAN, the VMkernel needs to know how to access the storage and which path it should choose.

"Do I Know This Already?" Quiz

The "Do I Know This Already?" quiz enables you to assess whether you should read this entire chapter or simply jump to the "Exam Preparation Tasks" section for review. If you are in doubt, read the entire chapter. Table 3-1 outlines the major headings in this chapter and the corresponding "Do I Know This Already?" quiz questions. You can find the answers in Appendix A, "Answers to the 'Do I Know This Already?' Quizzes and Troubleshooting Scenarios."

Table 3-1   "Do I Know This Already?" Foundation Topics Section-to-Question Mapping

Foundations Topics Section	Questions Covered in This Section
Virtual Disk Format Types	1
Complex Storage Solutions	2
Identify Storage Provisioning Methods	3
Pluggable Storage Architecture	4, 5

1. Virtual disks created on NFS datastores are?

   a. Thin provisioned

   b. Eager-Zeroed Thick provisioned

   c. Lazy-Zeroed Thick provisioned

   d. In a format dictated by the NFS Server

2. As the VMware system administrator, you are implementing storage profiles. Which are two methods in which storage capabilities can be generated? (Select two.)

   a. They are automatically created through storage filters.

   b. They are automatically determined from the storage array using VMware APIs for Storage Awareness (VASA).

   c. They can be manually generated by an administrator.

   d. They can be automatically created using VM DirectPath I/O.

3. When using shared storage capabilities on an NFS Datastore in ESXi 5.x, which two are true? (Select two.)

  a. Storage vMotion can be used to migrate virtual machines between NFS Datastores.

  b. Microsoft Cluster Server can be used to cluster virtual machines across ESXi hosts.

  c. VMware Storage APIs for Array Integration (VAAI) can be used.

  d. Virtual compatibility mode (RDMs) can be used.

4. You are implementing multipathing using the **Fixed** multipathing policy. You have an ESXi host with four available paths and four configured VMFS datastores. How many paths will be used by the host to send data to the four datastores?

  a. 4

  b. 8

  c. 16

  d. 1

5. When coordinating the VMware NMP and any installed third-party MPPs, the PSA performs which two tasks? (Select two.)

  a. If failover takes too long to complete, it interrupts the I/O to complete failover.

  b. Loads and unloads multipathing plug-ins.

  c. Manages offload creation of linked clones.

  d. Handles physical path discovery and removal.

RAID Levels

One concept that anyone taking the VCAP exam should already have is knowledge of RAID, but in case you are not familiar with RAID or need a refresher, let us begin the storage chapter by discussing RAID. The primary purpose of RAID is to protect data from an underlying hardware failure. With every RAID level above RAID-0, if a disk(s) fails, the RAID volume should continue to remain online and usable. When there is a failure, the RAID volume will operate in a degraded mode until the problem is fixed. The various RAID types available will vary depending on the capabilities of the storage device connected to the ESXi host. Following are examples of some common RAID levels.

Raid-0 (Striping at the Block-level)

A good reason for using Raid-0 striping is to improve performance. The performance increase comes from read and write operations across multiple drives. This is called *parallel access* because all the disk drives in the virtual device are kept busy most of the time servicing I/O requests.

The hardware or software array management software is responsible for making the array look like a single virtual disk drive. Striping takes portions of multiple physical disk drives and combines them into one virtual disk drive that is presented to the application.

The I/O stream is divided into segments called stripe units (SUs), which are mapped across two or more physical disk drives, forming one logical storage unit. The stripe units are interleaved so that the combined space is made alternately from each slice and is, in effect, shuffled like a deck of cards. The stripe units are analogous to the lanes of a freeway. See Figure 3-1.

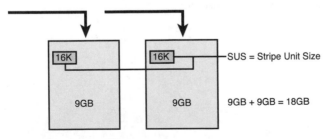

Figure 3-1 Example of striping on disks in a RAID-0 volume.

The advantage of Raid-0 is performance. You can use all of the disks. In addition, striping allows for high data transfer rates because there will be no parity calculations.

The disadvantage of Raid-0 is no redundancy. The loss of one physical disk drive will result in the loss of all the data on all the striped disk drives.

Raid 1 (Mirroring)

The primary reason for using mirroring is to provide a high level of availability or reliability. Mirroring provides data redundancy by recording multiple copies of the data on independent spindles. The mirrored disk drives appear as one virtual disk drive to the application. In the event of a physical disk drive failure, the mirror on the failed disk drive becomes unavailable, but the system continues to operate using the unaffected mirror or mirrors. The array management software takes duplicate copies of the data located on multiple physical disk drives and presents one virtual disk drive to the application. See Figure 3-2.

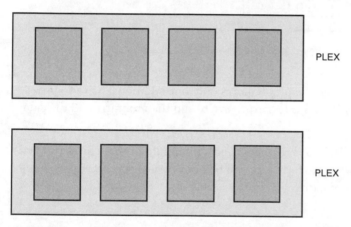

Figure 3-2   Example of data mirroring across two RAID-1 plexes.

The advantage of RAID-1 mirroring is data redundancy. There is a fully redundant copy of the data by having multiple plexes, with each plex being a copy of the data. If the mirror resides on a storage array that is attached to a different interface board, a high level of availability can be achieved. Another advantage is that all plexes can be used for reads to improve performance. Mirroring improves read performance only in a multiuser or multitasking situation where more than one disk drive member can satisfy the read requests.

The main limitation of using a RAID-1 mirrored structure is that mirroring uses twice as many disk drives to have multiple copies of the data. Doubling the number of drives essentially doubles the cost per Mbyte of storage space. Another limitation is that mirroring degrades write performance because the write will have to be done twice.

Raid 5 (Striping with Distributed Parity)

A Raid-5 volume configuration is an attractive choice for read-intensive applications. Raid-5 uses the concept of bit-by-bit parity to protect against data loss. Parity is computed using Boolean Exclusive OR (XOR) and distributed across all the drives intermixed with the data.

Notice in Figure 3-3 how the data (d) and the parity (p) are spread across all the drives in the plex. The data plex can lose a disk and still continue to work, although in degraded mode, until the parity and data can be rebuilt on a new drive.

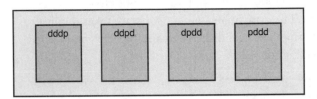

Figure 3-3 Example of data and parity distribution on a RAID-5 volume.

An advantage of Raid-5 is that the plex requires only one additional drive to protect the data. This means Raid-5 is less expensive to run than to mirror all the data drives with Raid-1.

One of the limitations of Raid-5 is that you need a minimum of three disks to calculate parity. In addition, write performance will be poor because every write is going to require a recalculation of parity.

Supported HBA Types

The VCAP exam blueprint mentions that knowledge of how to identify different supported HBA types is required. A Host Bus Adapter (HBA) is a hardware device that presents a connection between a physical ESXi host and a storage array on a Storage Area Network (SAN). The HBA transmits data between the ESXi host and the storage device. There are three types of HBA you can use on an ESXi host. They are Ethernet (iSCSI), Fibre Channel, and Fibre Channel over Ethernet (FCoE). In addition to the hardware adapters, software versions of the iSCSI and FCoE adapters (software FCoE is new with version 5) are available. The maximum number of HBAs of any type that can be installed in an ESXi host is 8. In addition, the maximum number of HBA ports per ESXi host is 16. When selecting HBAs for your vSphere environment, always use supported models, which can be found by going to the Hardware Compatibility Guide webpage VMware provides.

When an HBA is discovered by an ESXi host, a label is assigned to it. Figure 3-4 shows the command-line method to identify an HBA and the label associated with it. To identify an HBA such as a fibre channel adapter or a RAID controller, use the **esxcfg-scsidevs** command. In the output in Figure 3-4, you can see an example of an iSCSI HBA labeled as vmhba33.

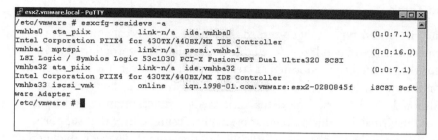

Figure 3-4   Sample output showing the HBAs connected to an ESXi host.

Virtual Disk Format Types

After the storage infrastructure has been successfully configured for use with vSphere, datastores must be created to have a place to store your virtual machines. You begin the process of creating a datastore by asking the storage administrator for a LUN. Once the storage administrator has provisioned the LUN and made it visible to the ESXi hosts, you can begin to create VMFS datastores, which are used to store media and virtual machine files. When creating virtual disks for use with virtual machines, there are three possible disk formats: lazy-zeroed thick, eager-zeroed thick, and thin provisioned. To determine which format to use, it helps to understand the various formats and the differences among them.

Lazy-zeroed Thick

The default virtual disk format used with VMFS datastores is the thick lazy-zeroed disk format. This is the traditional approach that preallocates the capacity of the virtual disk from the VMFS Datastore as it is being created. The blocks and pointers are allocated in the VMFS, but the blocks are not allocated on the array at the time of creation. Also, the blocks are not zeroed or formatted on the array either. Thus, the creation time is very fast because the data blocks are not zeroed out or formatted. At a later point in time when data needs to be written to the disk, the write process must pause while the blocks required to store the data on the storage array are zeroed out and allocated on the storage array. This operation occurs every time a first-time-write needs to occur on any area of the disk that has not been written. Thus, with the lazy-zeroed virtual disk type, the formatting and zeroing out of data blocks happen during the write process. In addition, the lazy-zeroed thick

Key Topic

provisioning process can use VAAI with both SAN and NAS devices to improve the disk's first write performance by offloading the zeroing operation to the storage array.

Eager-zeroed Thick

The second virtual disk type is eager-zeroed thick disk, which is capable of providing better performance than a lazy-zeroed thick disk. Like lazy-zeroed thick, space required for the virtual disk is allocated at creation time. However, the blocks and pointers on the virtual disk are preallocated and zeroed out when the virtual disk is created. Although this increases the virtual disk creation time, it improves the performance of the virtual disk during regular use. When using a SAN that supports VAAI, the zeroing of the blocks can be offloaded to the storage device, reducing the time needed to create the virtual disk.

Thin Provisioned

The thin provisioning format is similar to the lazy-zeroed format in that the blocks and pointers are not zeroed or formatted on the storage area at the time of creation. In addition, the blocks used by the virtual disk are not preallocated for the VMFS datastore at the time of creation. When storage capacity is required by the virtual disk, the VMDK allocates storage in chunks equal to the size of the file system block. The process of allocating blocks from within the datastore occurs on demand any time a write operation attempts to store data in a block range inside the VMDK that has not been written to by a previous operation. This process of allocating blocks is considered a metadata operation. During this process any writes will be suspended as the SCSI locks are imposed on the datastore. At a later point in time when data needs to be written to the disk, the writes will pause as the blocks required to store data are zeroed out. Thin provisioning provides storage on demand, and the amount of space consumed by the virtual disk on the VMFS datastore grows as data is written to the disk. Thin-provisioning must be carefully managed, as multiple virtual machines may be using thin provisioned disks on the same VMFS datastore.

Thin provisioned and lazy-zeroed thick provisioned storage both suspend I/O when writing to new areas of a disk that need blocks to be zeroed out. The difference with thin provisioning is that the virtual disk might have to allocate additional capacity from the datastore because it does not pre-allocate that capacity on creation. Table 3-2 identifies the differences between virtual disk options, including a comparison of the time it takes to create the virtual disk type, how block allocation and zeroing are performed and how the virtual disk is laid out on disk.

Table 3-2 Virtual Disk Format Differences

	Lazy-zeroed Thick	**Eager-zeroed Thick**	**Thin**
Creation time	Fast.	Slow, but faster with VAAI.	Fast.
Zeroing file blocks	File block is zeroed on write.	File block is zeroed when disk is first created.	File block is zeroed on write.
Block allocation	Fully preallocated on datastore.	Fully preallocated on datastore.	File block is allocated on write.

All three types of virtual disk format types can be created using the vSphere Client or the vSphere CLI. To create a virtual disk format type using the vSphere Client, follow these steps:

Step 1. Right-click the Virtual Machine and select **Edit Settings**.

Step 2. From the **Hardware** tab, click **Add > Hard Disk**.

Step 3. At the **Select a Disk** window, select the radio button **Create a new virtual disk**.

Step 4. The Create a Disk window appears, and you can specify the provisioning policy, as shown in Figure 3-5.

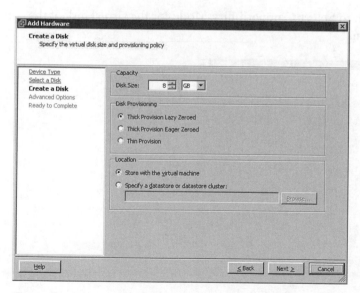

Figure 3-5 Choose the provisioning policy for a new disk.

**Key
Topic**

RDM

Another virtual disk option is Raw Device Mapping. RDM allows a virtual machine (VM) to directly utilize a LUN. Even though the two most common approaches for a VM to access storage are done by using virtual disks created on VMFS or NFS datastores, RDMs can be useful in certain situations. There are special cases where the guest OS or application will not support a VMFS or NFS virtual disk. An example of this is Microsoft Cluster Server, which requires a quorum disk that utilizes the SCSI-3 protocol to provide clustering support. Because VMFS- or NFS-based virtual disks do not support the SCSI-3 protocol, an RDM can be used to bypass the VMware hypervisor and allow the VM to communicate directly with the LUN or SCSI device. The capability of the RDM to directly assign a LUN to a VM is accomplished by using either its virtual SCSI adapter or DirectPath I/O.

The process of adding an RDM to a virtual machine can be done using the vSphere client, like so:

Step 1.   Right-click the VM and select **Edit Settings**.

Step 2.   From the **Hardware** tab, click **Add** > click **Hard Disk**.

Step 3.   On the device type page, select **Raw Device Mappings**.

Step 4.   Select **LUN**.

Step 5.   Select a datastore.

In Figure 3-6 the option to **Select Compatibility Mode** for the virtual disk of the virtual machine is shown.

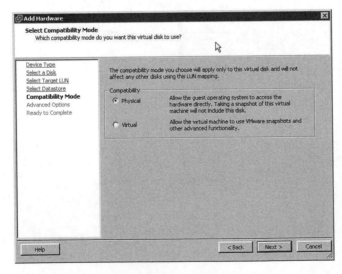

Figure 3-6   Select the RDM Compatibility Mode.

There are two different compatibility modes to choose from when creating an RDM: physical compatibility mode (rdmp) or virtual compatibility mode (rdm). The key difference between these two options is the amount of SCSI virtualization that will occur at the VM level.

The physical compatibility (pass-through) mode is the default format. In this format the SCSI commands pass directly through to the hardware during communication between the guest operating system and the LUN or SCSI device. This allows for unsupported features such as SCSI-3 clustering. Another use case is if the application in the virtual machine is SAN-aware and needs to communicate directly to storage devices on the SAN. However, this mode does not support virtual machine snapshots, VMware cloning, and several other features that require hypervisor support.

Virtual compatibility mode supports a subset of SCSI commands to be passed through the hypervisor for communication between the guest operating system and a mapped physical raw LUN or SCSI disk. Virtual compatibility mode will fully virtualize the mapped device, which enables an RDM virtual disk to appear to the virtual machine as a typical VMFS-based virtual disk. Because this mode allows some SCSI commands to be passed through the hypervisor, VMware features that physical compatibility mode will not allow, such as VMware snapshots, cloning, or storage migration, are supported.

In addition to allowing the pass through of SCSI commands for use cases previously described, the use of an RDM can be beneficial for performance reasons. This is due to the fact that a typical VMFS datastore is shared by multiple virtual machines, which have to share the available I/O operations of the underlying LUN. Some applications might have specific I/O requirements and might be critical enough to require guaranteed I/O. An RDM is presented directly to a single virtual machine and cannot be used by any other virtual machine; it also is presented with the I/O characteristics defined by the storage administrator. It is important to note that similar performance requirements can be gained by placing a single VM on a VMFS datastore that fully utilizes the datastore.

A final reason to use RDMs is if you want to use N-Port ID Virtualization (NPIV), which is covered in the next section.

N-Port ID Virtualization

Key Topic

N-Port ID Virtualization (NPIV) is used when you want a virtual machine to be assigned an addressable World Wide Port Name (WWPN) within a SAN. Normally, the VM uses the ESXi host's physical HBA's WWN. When you configure WWPN's to a virtual machine directly, you can zone storage to a virtual machine's unique WWN. This is a useful feature when you need the physical network interface card (NIC) to have multiple unique WWNs. NPIV also can be useful if you need an ESXi host to have more Fibre Channel connections than VMware normally would allow. Thus, you can go beyond the maximum number of 8 HBAs allowed per host or 16 HBA ports per host. Finally, unique WWPNs can be used with SAN management software to provide storage visibility to each VM.

NOTE   NPIVworks only if the VM has an RDM disk attached, and the HBA and switch used to access the storage must be NPIV-aware.

To begin using NPIV, right-click the virtual machine and select **Edit Settings.** This opens the **Properties** window of the VM. In the **Properties** window, click the **Options** tab and highlight the **Fibre Channel NPIV** setting. By default, no WWNs are assigned. To assign WWNs to the virtual machine, click the radio button **Generate new WWNs** and, using the drop-down boxes, decide how many WWNNs and WWPNs to assign; then click **Next**. Next time you go back to the **Options** tab of the VM, you will see the new WWNs. An example of this is shown in Figure 3-7. Notice in the screenshot the virtual machine now has a Node WWN and a Port WWN.

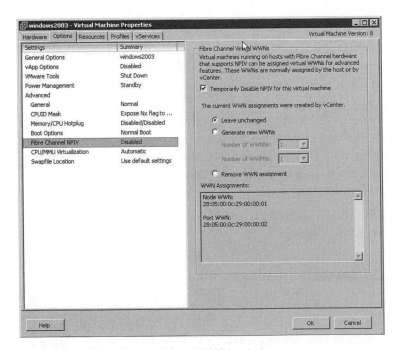

Figure 3-7   Fibre Channel Virtual WWNs window.

VMware DirectPath I/O

Sometimes a virtual machine needs direct control of an adapter installed in an ESXi host. VMware DirectPath I/O enables a virtual machine to directly connect to a physical device such as a network card or storage adapter. Most operating systems are designed with an environment that contains a virtualization system, and the networking and storage I/O has to go through the kernel of the operating system. When VMware was originally designing its operating system environment, the developers had to create a virtualization system for I/O. For an application in VMware to take advantage of virtualization, it would have to go through the kernel, thus all VMs had to go through the kernel. The advantage of this OS design is that it enables the storage and networking bandwidth provided by installed adapters to be used by multiple virtual machine workloads. This enables more efficient use of the hardware. It also allowed VMware to develop features such as vMotion. It should be noted that this virtualization does come at the cost of a little bit of CPU overhead. Fortunately, the additional CPU cycles needed for this virtualization were minor enough to hardly be noticed. However, when 10 GbE network cards were tested and incorporated into vSphere, there was a noticeable issue where 10 GbE NICs used a lot of CPU cycles to manage all the network packets. VMware turned to hardware-assisted virtualization to solve this problem.

Intel Virtualization Technology for Directed I/O (VT-d) in Intel processors and AMD I/O Virtualization (AMD-Vi or IOMMU) in AMD processors are hardware-assisted virtualization technologies that remap I/O DMA transfers and device interrupts to solve the 10 GbE problem of slowdown due to CPU utilization. Using these new CPU technologies can also enable virtual machines to have direct access to hardware I/O devices, such as NICs and storage controllers (HBAs).

This new technology enables VMware to remap DMA areas to virtual addresses and lets a virtual machine have direct access to the remapped DMA areas. This direct connection frees up CPU cycles by bypassing the hypervisor and returns the speed and performance that would otherwise be lost. There is a price to pay for bypassing the hypervisor, though. First, features such as vMotion are no longer available to the virtual machine. Second, the adapter can no longer be used by any other virtual machine in the ESXi host. The exception to this is when ESXi is running on certain configurations of the Cisco Unified Computing System (UCS) platform. In this case, DirectPath I/O is supported with vMotion and other vSphere features that would not normally be supported.

To use DirectPath I/O, the ESXi host has to have Intel Virtualization Technology for Directed I/O (VT-d) or AMD I/O Virtualization Technology (IOMMU) enabled in the BIOS. To check whether DirectPath I/O is supported on the ESXi host, highlight the ESXi host. Select the **Configuration** tab, and under Hardware select **Advanced Settings**. The DirectPath I/O Configuration page then displays, as shown in Figure 3-8.

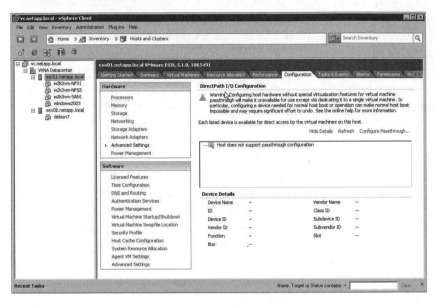

Figure 3-8   DirectPath I/O Configuration page in vSphere Client.

In addition, there are situations where a hardware device needs to bypass the hypervisor. This need to use vSphere DirectPath I/O could be due to the hardware not yet being supported by vSphere, such as an early release of 40 Gbe or 100 Gbe network card. Even though the hardware is not yet supported, there is still a need to test and use the PCI or PCIe device. When DirectPath I/O is enabled, it allows the guest operating system of the virtual machine to bypass the hypervisor and directly access the physical device. In the case of networking, DirectPath I/O enables the virtual machine to access a physical NIC rather than using an emulated device (such as the E1000) or a paravirtualized device (such as VMXNET3). DirectPath I/O for vSphere 5.0 has been enhanced to allow the vMotion of a virtual machine containing DirectPath I/O network adaptors on the Cisco Unified Computing System (UCS) platform. A common use for DirectPath I/O continues to be to reduce CPU usage for network intensive applications using 10 Gbe network cards.

vCenter Server Storage Filters

vSphere provides filters that optimize the use of storage in a mutlihost environment managed by vCenter Server. The vSphere environment provides four storage filters that can affect the action of the vCenter Server when scanning storage. Without these filters, when vCenter Server is scanning for storage, all storage that is found could be presented to vSphere, even if it is in use. The filters prevent this type of unwanted activity. However, some specific use cases can affect the storage devices that are found during scanning. By default, the storage filters are set to true and are designed to prevent specific storage datastore problems. Except for in certain situations, it is best to leave the storage filters in their enabled state. Table 3-3 displays the vCenter Server storage filters and their respective Advanced Setting keys.

Table 3-3   vCenter Server Storage Filters

RDM Filter	config.vpxd.filter.rdmFilter
VMFS Filter	config.vpxd.filter.vmfsFilter
Host Rescan Filter	config.vpxd.filter.hostRescanFilter
Same Host and Transports Filter	config.vpxd.filter.SameHostAndTransportsFilter

- **RDM filter**—Filters out LUNs that have been claimed by any RDM on any ESXi host managed by vCenter Server. This storage filter can be used in a situation such as when using Microsoft Cluster Server. When set to false, the filter is disabled, allowing a LUN to be added as an RDM, even though the LUN is already being utilized as an RDM by another VM. To set up a SCSI-3 quorum disk for MSCS, this storage filter would need to be disabled.

- **VMFS filter**—Filters out LUNs that have been claimed and VMFS formatted on any ESXi host managed by vCenter Server. Thus, in the vSphere client when you go to the Add Storage Wizard, you will not see any VMFS-formatted LUNs. If the setting is switched to false, the LUN would be seen as available by the vSphere Client, and any ESXi host could attempt to format it and claim it.

- **Host rescan filter**—By default, when a VMFS volume is created, an automatic rescan occurs on all hosts connected to the vCenter Server. If the setting is switched to false, the automatic rescan is disabled when creating a VMFS datastore on another host. As an example, you could run a PowerCLI cmdlet to add 100 datastores; you should wait until the cmdlet is finished before scanning all the hosts in the cluster.

- **Same host and transports filter**—Filters out LUNs that can not be used as VMFS datastore extents due to host or storage incompatibility. If the setting is switched to false, an incompatible LUN could then be added as an extent to an existing volume. An example of an incompatible LUN would be adding a LUN as an extent that is not seen by all of the hosts.

NOTE   All storage filters are enabled (TRUE) and are not listed in the Advanced Settings by default.

Figure 3-9 displays the vCenter Server Advanced Settings screen, which is where storage filters can be enabled or disabled. This screen can be reached from the vSphere Client by selecting **Administration > vCenter Settings > Advanced Settings**. To disable a filter, it must first be added to the **Advanced Settings**. At the bottom of the window in the **Key** box, type in one of the four storage filters and add the **Value** of false to enable the storage filter.

Figure 3-9   Enabling a storage filter in the vSphere Client.

Understanding and Applying VMFS Re-signaturing

Every VMFS datastore has a universal unique identifier (UUID), which is used to match a LUN to a specific VMFS datastore. The UUID signature is a hexadecimal number that is shown in Figure 3-10. One way to think of the UUID or signature of the datastore is how a MAC address is a unique identifier for a network interface. A MAC address is used to provide uniqueness within a network so that a network packet is delivered to the correct device. A UUID signature is a way to provide uniqueness for a LUN to associate with a particular datastore. An example of a UUID of a VMFS datastore named **Shared** is shown here and in Figure 3-10.

UUID = 4f870db6-5ed5460c-e0c7-005056370612

```
esxi01.vclass.local - PuTTY
/vmfs/volumes # ls
4e5fc427-1e41de53-3780-0050562e0aa1    7b79d773-82aea955-9ed9-71cef39f6190
4e5fc42f-8757d66d-4357-0050562e0aa1    8651f972-bd76e244-496b-497b9853fa6e
4f870db6-5ed5460c-e0c7-005056370612    Local01
50536e00-4850f3c0-efc5-0050560f080c    Shared
/vmfs/volumes # vmkfstools -P -h Shared
VMFS-5.54 file system spanning 1 partitions.
File system label (if any): Shared              I
Mode: public
Capacity 39.8 GB, 17.1 GB available, file block size 1 MB
UUID: 4f870db6-5ed5460c-e0c7-005056370612
Partitions spanned (on "lvm"):
        naa.6000eb3a2b3b330e00000000000000cb:1
Is Native Snapshot Capable: YES
/vmfs/volumes # █
```

Figure 3-10   Listing of the datastore named Shared that shows its UUID.

A change in the host LUN or SCSI device type causes the VMFS volume's UUID to require a new signature. The ESXi host will notice that the LUN and the signature do not match. The result of a mismatch is that the ESXi host needs to re-signature the VMFS datastore and assign a new UUID.

NOTE   A UUID is stored in the metadata of the inode on a VMFS datastore. Because an NFS datastore's inode resides on the storage device, it does not have a UUID.

One of the main reasons that a VMFS datastore needs to be re-signatured is when a disaster recovery (DR) event occurs. There are two ways to look at a DR event—either an actual DR event is occurring or you are performing a DR test. If an actual DR event is occurring, there is no need to re-signature the VMFS datastore. When an actual DR event occurs, the primary site is no longer functioning, so there is no need to worry about a second datastore with the same UUID. LUNs at the recovery site will be given the same UUID, and there will be no worry about a conflict.

On the other hand, a DR test could lead to an issue. If you are using VMware's DR product called Site Recovery Manager (SRM), re-signaturing is not a concern. SRM has a built-in capability to alleviate any UUID issues. If you are not using SRM, the LUN that is copied and re-created at the recovery site will have the same signature as the datastore at the primary site. This creates a problem where the hosts could see two datastores with the same UUID. If two datastores are mounted with the same UUID, the ESXi host will not know on which VMFS datastore to perform read and write operations, which could lead to corrupted data. Therefore, you need to use datastore re-signaturing to assign a new UUID and a new label to the datastore copy at the recovery site and mount the datastore copy as a new distinct VMFS datastore.

VAAI Hardware Acceleration

VMFS-3 was the version of VMware's file system supplied with VI3 and vSphere 4.x. VMFS-3 was built on the SCSI-2 protocol and followed the SCSI-2 specifications. When vSphere 5 was released, it included a new version of the file system, VMFS-5. The upgrade to VMFS extended the SCSI protocol, which could be referred to as taking SCSI-2 and putting a bandage on it. The bandage that extended the SCSI-2 protocol is called the vStorage APIs for Array Integration (VAAI). VMware began the process of upgrading the file system in vSphere 4.1 by asking storage vendors to add VAAI support to their storage array operating systems, even though it would not be until the vSphere 5.0 release that VAAI would be a fully functional storage feature. VAAI enables the ESXi host to offload certain storage operations to the storage array, where they can be performed faster and consume less CPU and memory resources on the host. The three main built-in capabilities for VAAI are called full copy, block zeroing, and hardware-assisted locking:

- **Full copy**—The SCSI Extended Copy command is replaced by the VAAI XCOPY command, which enables the storage array to perform full copies of data completely within the storage array without having to communicate with the ESXi host during the reading and writing of data. This saves the ESXi host from having to perform the read and then write of data, which reduces the time needed to clone VMs or perform Storage vMotion operations.

- **Block zeroing**—When a new virtual disk is created with VMFS as an eager-zeroed thick disk, the disk must be formatted and the blocks must be zeroed out before data can be written on them. Block zeroing removes this task from the ESXi host by moving the function down to the storage array with VAAI. This increases the speed of the block zeroing process.

- **Hardware-assisted locking**—VMFS is a shared cluster file system that requires file locking to ensure that only one host can write to the data at a time. VAAI uses a single atomic test and set operation (ATS), which is an alternative method to VMware's SCSI-2 reservations. ATS allows a VMFS datastore to scale to more VMs per datastore, and more ESXi hosts can attach to each LUN.

For vSphere to take advantage of VAAI, the storage array has to support VAAI hardware acceleration. One way to check whether the storage array is supported for VAAI hardware acceleration is to check the Hardware Configuration List. It lists all supported storage arrays. Hardware acceleration for VAAI is supported for both SAN and NAS storage devices.

Block Devices Hardware Acceleration

By default, the ESXi host supports VAAI hardware acceleration for block devices, which means no configuration is needed for block devices. If the storage device supports T10 SCSI commands, then by default the ESXi host can use VAAI. If the storage array to which the ESXi host is connected does not support hardware acceleration, then you can disable it using the vSphere Client.

In the Figure 3-11 inventory panel, select the ESXi host, click the **Configuration** tab, and click **Advanced Settings** under **Software**. Then change the value for any of the following three options to 0, which will disable hardware acceleration. Again, this would be done if the storage array did not support hardware acceleration:

DataMover.HardwareAcceleratedMove

DataMover.HardwareAcceleratedInit

VMFS3.HardwareAcceleratedLocking

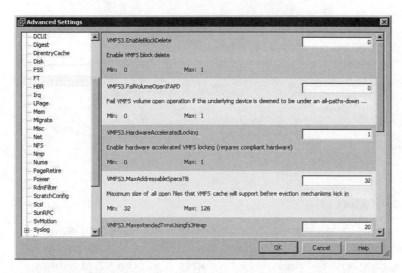

Figure 3-11   VMFS3.HardwareAcceleratedLocking set to 0 to disable.

You can easily check in vSphere whether the storage supports VAAI hardware acceleration. In the Figure 3-12 inventory panel, select the ESXi host, click the **Configuration** tab, and then select **Storage** under **Hardware**. The hardware acceleration status can be seen in the **Datastores** View.

The three possible values for Hardware Acceleration are Supported, Unknown, and Not Supported. The initial value is Unknown, and it changes to Supported after the host successfully performs the offload operation. However, if the offload operation fails, the status changes to Not Supported.

The NFS datastore have an initial value of Not Supported and become Supported when the storage performs an offload operation.

When storage devices are not supported or provide partial support for the host operations, then the host reverts to its native SCSI-2 methods to perform operations.

Figure 3-12   Hardware acceleration status for each datastore.

NAS Hardware Acceleration

Unlike block storage, NAS VAAI hardware acceleration is not set up and enabled by default. Hardware acceleration for NAS devices enables additional hardware operations between the ESXi host and the NAS storage array. The NFS VAAI hardware acceleration is implemented by adding a vendor-specific NAS plug-in to the ESXi hosts. The plug-in is typically created by the vendor and is distributed as a VIB package.

Configuring and Administering Profile-based Storage

The characteristics of the LUN and how the LUN was designed play an important part in picking the proper datastore for the VM. Unfortunately, there is no visibility within vCenter Server into the characteristics of the storage. In addition, there is the issue of Storage DRS, which can allow DRS to migrate the VM files to another datastore. The last thing you want is to migrate an important virtual machine's files to slow storage. You need to keep the important VM files located on the important datastores and the less important VM files on less important, or maybe slower, datastores. These are the kinds of problems that profile-based storage is attempting to solve.

Profile-based storage is achieved by understanding the storage capabilities of the storage devices used in a vSphere implementation and using that information to create virtual machine storage profiles. The main problem is finding the best place for the VM's files; because the files are stored in a datastore, the characteristics of the datastore are important. The VMware system administrator will request a LUN from the storage administrator of a specific size to place the virtual machine's files. The storage then is presented to vSphere as a LUN of the requested size. The problem is that vSphere only knows the size of the LUN. VMware has no idea how many disks make up the LUN or any other characteristics of the LUN other than the size of the LUN.

One feature that can provide storage capabilities is VMware VASA, which is a set of APIs that a storage vendor can provide to advertise information about their storage array. The idea is that with VASA, the storage will be able to advertise its capabilities. It could advertise that it is a RAID-5 disk set, the health of the LUN, and whether any disks in the LUN have failed. The storage vendor creates a component called a VASA Provider that provides the storage capabilities of their devices, so this will probably not be on the exam. But storage profiles, how they are created, and how they are used with virtual machines could be on the exam.

Profile-based storage categorizes storage based on system-defined VASA or user-defined capabilities. You could use any criteria when creating a profile, such as the type of environment—production or test. The production profile would identify all the higher-performing datastores that could be used for production virtual machines, whereas the test profile would contain all the lower-performing datastores that could be used for less important virtual machines. Figure 3-13 shows a vSphere environment where no user- or system-defined storage capabilities have been configured.

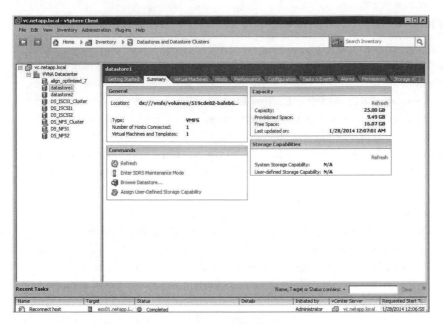

Figure 3-13   Datastore has no system or user-defined storage capabilities.

If no system-defined storage capabilities are present, either the storage is not VASA-aware or the VASA Provider hasn't been added to vCenter Server. If a VASA Provider is available, it should be added before configuring any user-defined capabilities. If no provider is available, an administrator can add capabilities to define the datastore. Because no user- or system-defined capabilities exist for this datastore, we can create some. Right-click the datastore and select **Assign User-Defined Storage Capability**. The **Assign User-Defined Storage Capability** dialog box appears. In the **Name** field, type **Production Tier,** and click **OK** to save the user-defined capability. Verify that the user-defined storage capability has been assigned to the datastore, and if it has not been, click **Refresh** in the **Storage Capabilities** box shown in Figure 3-14.

The next step is to create a virtual machine storage profile. In the vSphere Client, go to the **Home** page, and click **VM Storage Profiles** in the **Management** section. In the toolbar, click **Create**, which opens the **Create New VM Storage Profile** wizard. In the wizard's name field, type **Production Storage Profile**; then click **Next**. The **Select Storage Capabilities** screen appears, which is shown in Figure 3-15. Select **Production Tier**, which is the user-defined storage capability you created earlier. Finally, click **Next**, and click **Finish**.

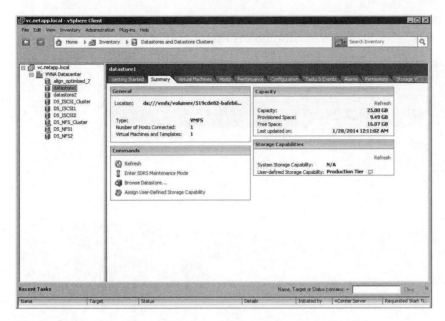

Figure 3-14   User-defined storage capability is now production tier.

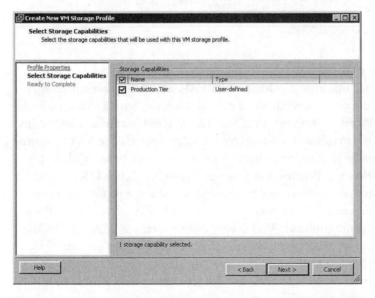

Figure 3-15   Creating a new VM storage profile.

In Figure 3-16 currently no virtual machines are associated with the Production storage profile. Before we can associate virtual machines with the storage profile, we need to enable the ESXi hosts to use virtual machine profiles. In the taskbar shown in Figure 3-16, click **Enable VM Storage Profile.**

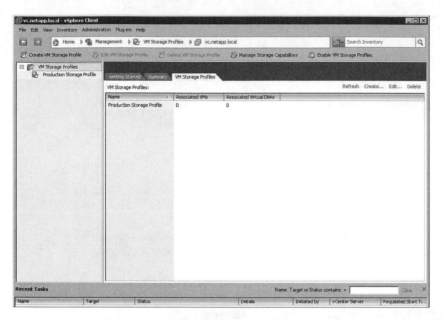

Figure 3-16   Enabling VM storage profiles.

After you enable storage profiles for the ESXi hosts, it is time to associate a storage profile with a virtual machine. Go back to the **VMs and Templates** inventory view, and right-click the virtual machine you want to associate with a storage profile. Select **VM Storage Profile** > **Manage Profiles**. The **Virtual Machine Properties** window appears and the **Profiles** tab is displayed. Underneath **Home VM Storage Profile,** select the storage profile with which you want to associate the VM. In this example you would select the **Production Storage Profile** and click **OK**. When you click the **Summary** tab of the virtual machine after a storage profile has been applied, as shown in Figure 3-17, you might notice that the virtual machine's **Profiles Compliance** is **Noncompliant**. This occurs if the current storage on which the VM is located is not in compliance with the attached profile. To get more information, you can click **Noncompliant.** In this case, the detail would state that there is a "capability mismatch," which confirms that the storage on which the VM is located is not compliant with the profile.

To resolve this problem, the VM needs to be moved to compliant storage. To do so, right-click the virtual machine in the inventory and select **Migrate.** Select the option that allows you to migrate the VM to another datastore. The Storage screen shown in Figure 3-18 lets you select a **VM Storage Profile**. Select the appropriate profile, and the list of datastores will be filtered to show which datastores are compatible with the chosen profile. Selecting a compatible datastore begins the process of storage migration and moves the virtual machine's files to the compliant datastore. After the migration is finished, click **Refresh**, and the **Profiles Compliance** for the VM should now say **Compliant**.

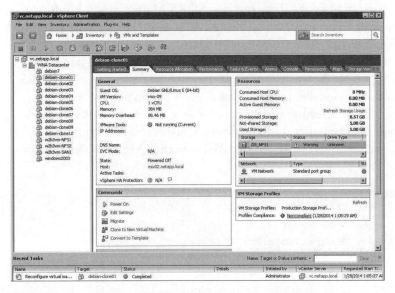

Figure 3-17   A VM showing a Noncompliant profile status.

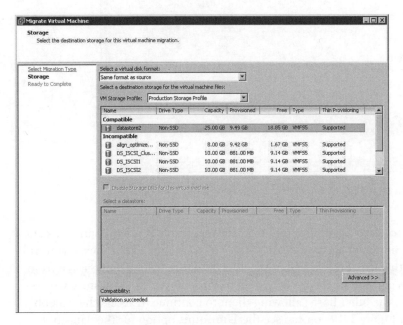

Figure 3-18   Migrating a VM to a compatible datastore.

Preparing Storage for Maintenance

Storage devices might need to be placed into maintenance mode to conduct planned downtime operations. When this is the case, a couple of options are available to place a datastore into this state. If the datastore resides in a Storage DRS-enabled datastore cluster, you can place the datastore into **SDRS Maintenance Mode**. When a datastore enters this mode, the resulting action is similar to a host entering maintenance mode. Every registered VM on the datastore will be migrated to other datastores in the same datastore cluster. When all the VM's files are migrated to other datastores, the empty datastore can be placed into maintenance mode. **SDRS Maintenance Mode** is an excellent feature that enables you to place storage in a maintenance state without affecting client access to data. To enter **SDRS Mainte-nance Mode**, go to the **Datastore and Datastore Clusters** view. Highlight the datastore, right-click, and select **Enter SDRS Maintenance Mode**, which is shown in Figure 3-19.

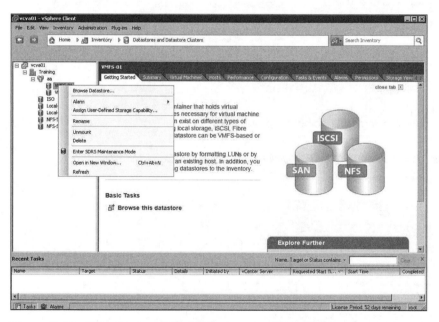

Figure 3-19 Enter Storage DRS Maintenance mode and unmount a datastore.

Another option to place a datastore into maintenance mode is to unmount the datastore. When you unmount a datastore that is shared to multiple ESXi hosts, you will be prompted with a list of the shared hosts. The datastore will be unmounted from all selected hosts and will no longer be visible to those hosts. The datastore will remain mounted to the other hosts, allowing them to continue to access the data on the datastore. In Figure 3-19 you can see the **Unmount** option for the datastore.

When maintenance has been finished on the storage device, you can use the **Mount** option to reconnect to the data.

Upgrading VMware Storage Infrastructure

The current version of VMFS is VMFS-5, which was introduced with vSphere 5.0. The two previous versions of VMFS were VMFS-2 and VMFS-3, with VMFS-3 being introduced with ESX 3.0. For the purpose of the exam you will not need to know how to upgrade from VMFS-2, so we will concentrate on upgrading from VMFS-3. What is interesting is that Storage vMotion was originally created to facilitate upgrading datastores from VMFS-2 to VMFS-3. The original implementation was strictly a command-line operation and was designed to move all VMs from a datastore. This was because, at the time, the datastore had to be empty before it could be upgraded. One advantage with VMFS-5 is that the datastore can be upgraded in place, without migrating the VMs. In fact, the VMs can continue to run while the datastore is upgraded! However, it should be pointed out that an in-place upgrade does not provide all the benefits available to a newly created VMFS-5 datastore. These benefits include optimized block size, optimized sub-block allocation, and the use of VAAI (which requires that the VMFS datastores have the same block size). As a result, it is highly recommended to vacate the datastore using Storage vMotion and reformat it with VMFS-5.

If business requirements necessitate performing an in-place upgrade, it is a very simple and quick process. To upgrade a datastore, highlight it in the vSphere Client, click the **Configuration** tab, and click **Upgrade to VMFS-5**. Then click **OK**, as shown in Figure 3-20.

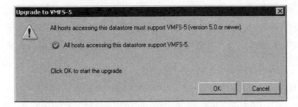

Figure 3-20   Upgrading a datastore to VMFS-5.

The upgrade will be very fast, but the problem is that you have very limited VMFS-5 capabilities. Also, after you upgrade a datastore, you can not revert to the previous version. You are better off upgrading the datastore by using Storage vMotion to vacate the datastore and reformatting it because it is then treated as if you created a brand-new VMFS-5 datastore.

Identifying Storage Provisioning Methods

Two types of storage can be provisioned in vSphere, either block-based storage (local or SAN attached) or file-based storage (NAS attached). Connecting to block-based storage begins by either configuring the local disk space that is directly attached to the ESXi host or partitioning storage on a device accessed through a SAN. SAN devices can be iSCSI, FC, or FCoE based and require the storage administrator to first create a LUN and present it to the ESXi hosts that will use it. The VMware system administrator must then scan for the new storage and create a datastore using that storage, which formats the LUN with the VMFS file system. The easiest method to provision a new datastore is by using the vSphere Client. In the vSphere Client, highlight an ESXi host and click the **Configuration** tab. Underneath the **Hardware** section, select **Storage**; then click the **Add Storage** hyperlink, which will launch the **Add Storage** Wizard. The **Add Storage** Wizard will step you through the process of creating a VMFS Datastore. With block-level SAN LUNs, ESXi creates a file system by writing its own stack on the LUN.

An alternative to SAN-based storage is to use a Network Attached Storage–based device. Network Attached Storage (NAS) devices typically have support for multiple protocols, but to use the device with ESXi, file shares must be configured using NFSv3 because VMware built NFSv3 support into the ESXi disk virtualization layer. Creating an NFS datastore is done using the same process as creating a VMFS datastore—by using the **Add Storage** Wizard. A storage administrator will first create an NFS share on the device, and the VMware system administrator will create a VMkernel port on each ESXi host that will use the storage, on the same network as the NAS device. This enables each ESXi host to access the NFS file share over the network. When this is done, the **Add Storage** Wizard can be used to add the NFS datastore to each ESXi host. NFS is a file-based client-server layout between the ESXi (NFS client) host and a storage device (NFS server). The NFS server manages the file system layout and file structure but still can support all the vSphere features such as HA, DRS, and vMotion.

Finally, you can provision storage using an RDM, which enables storage to be directly accessed by a virtual machine. An RDM uses a mapping file to map a LUN directly to a virtual machine, which bypasses the hypervisor. Although not used very often, an RDM is needed any time VMFS is not supported. An example is when using Microsoft Cluster Server. This requires a SCSI-3 quorum disk, which VMFS does not natively support. Using an RDM for the quorum disk gets around the host SCSI-3 incompatibility.

Configuring Datastore Alarms

Key
Topic

vCenter Server is capable of alerting an administrator when an event occurs that could compromise the availability or performance of a vSphere environment. You can set up alarms that trigger when those events or conditions happen. Different types of alarms can be set up to notify you in response to an event or a condition. A number of these are preconfigured, but they can be modified as needed, or custom alarms can be created when desired.

Five default storage alarms come with vSphere 5.0 and 5.1, with an additional default storage alarm added in vSphere 5.5. The new default storage alarm in vSphere 5.5 is the **Datastore Compliance alarm**. In the **Datastores and Datastore Clusters** view, you can see the default alarms of vSphere 5.5, as shown in Figure 3-21. These can be viewed by highlighting a datastore in the hierarchical view, clicking the **Alarms** tab, and then selecting the **Definitions** view. The default alarms can be modified, but there are different requirements depending on whether the alarm is condition or event driven.

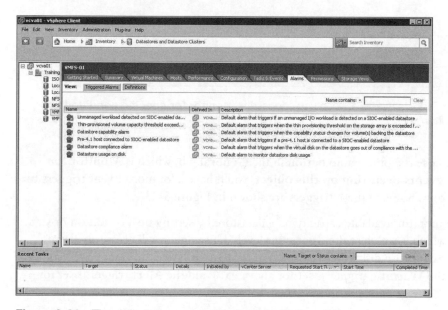

Figure 3-21   The default alarms for datastores in vSphere 5.5.

You can also create a custom alarm by navigating to the **Datastores and Datastore Clusters** view. Highlight a datastore or an object where you want a new datastore alarm created in the hierarchical view, and then click the **Alarms** tab. In the **Definitions** view, right-click underneath the header fields and select **New Alarm**.

The **Alarm Settings** window will then be displayed, as shown in Figure 3-22. Select the **General** tab if it is not already displayed, and begin creating an alarm by providing a name. Next, choose which type of alarm you are setting up by selecting one of the two radio buttons. If you select the **Monitor for specific conditions or state** radio button, the types of triggers you can set up are shown on the **Triggers** tab in Figure 3-22.

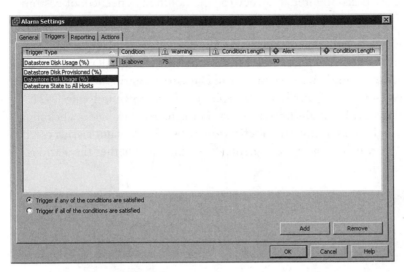

Figure 3-22 Triggers available when you choose the **Monitor for specific conditions or state** radio button.

If you choose the other radio button in the **General** tab, which is **Monitor for specific events occurring on this object,** you'll have a lot more Event triggers to choose from. Some of these triggers are shown in Figure 3-23.

You can monitor available capacity on a datastore by setting up a condition or state trigger, which is set up at the datacenter level. This trigger will create an alarm when the datastore disk usage is above the configured levels. In Figure 3-24 you can see that the **Warning** trigger is set for above 75% and the **Alert** trigger is set for above 85% usage. You can modify these values for your own environment.

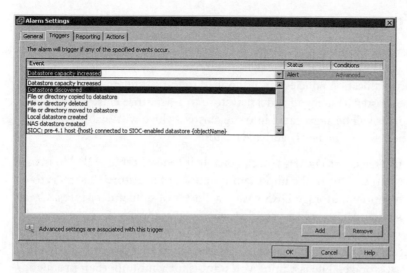

Figure 3-23   Triggers available when you choose the **Monitor for specific events** radio button.

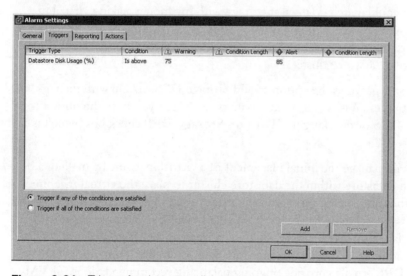

Figure 3-24   Trigger for datastore disk usage.

Configuring Datastore Clusters

A datastore cluster is a grouping of independent datastores designed to function as a single entity. Tasks like virtual machine placement, storage performance optimization, and resource allocation policies can be applied to the cluster and will utilize all datastores in the cluster. When you add a datastore to a datastore cluster object, the datastores resources will be aggregated into the cluster, which will enable you to apply the cluster benefits to the newly added datastore.

When you create a datastore cluster, you can enable it to use Storage DRS to manage datastore resources. One of the important functions of datastore clusters is to support the automation of Storage DRS within a cluster of similar datastores. Creating a cluster of similar datastores ensures that when you automate the balancing of virtual machines across datastores using Storage vMotion for load balancing, you can be sure that your important moneymaking virtual machines will migrate from fast storage to fast storage. The last thing you want is for your important production VM files to be migrated to slow storage. For example, all your fast storage could be in one datastore cluster, and all of your slow storage would be in a separate datastore cluster. Thus, I could match up my fast storage with my moneymaking virtual machines and my slow storage with test and development virtual machines. The ability to control where the virtual machines files could be migrated to is one of the important functions of a datastore cluster.

A datastore cluster provides the option to add Storage DRS to help with managing storage resources. When you create a datastore cluster, you have the option to enable Storage DRS by checking the **Turn on Storage DRS** check box, which is shown in Figure 3-25.

Storage DRS will manage the initial placement of a virtual machine by making a decision on which datastore within the datastore cluster to place the virtual machine's files based on the capacity utilization of each datastore in the cluster. It will attempt to keep space usage as evenly balanced as possible within the datastore cluster. When using a datastore cluster, you assign the storage of the virtual machine's files to the cluster and not to a specific datastore. In addition to providing initial placement, Storage DRS can also provide ongoing balancing recommendations for VMs running within the datastore cluster.

During the setup process for a datastore cluster, you make a decision on how automated you want Storage DRS. In Figure 3-26 you have the option of either **No Automation (Manual Mode)** or **Fully Automated** mode. **Manual mode** will only provide recommendations for the initial placement and migration of the virtual machine's files. **Fully Automated** mode can also migrate VMs to other datastores based on performance and can do so automatically based on settings you can adjust using **SDRS Runtime Rules**. For initial configurations, it is fairly common to leave Storage DRS in **Manual Mode**.

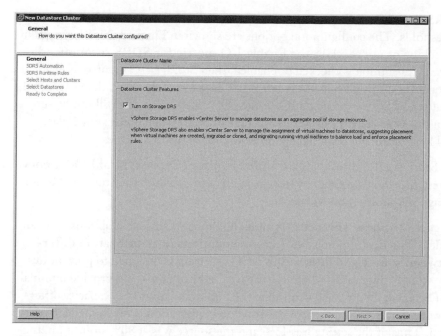

Figure 3-25 Creating a datastore cluster, with the option to turn on Storage DRS.

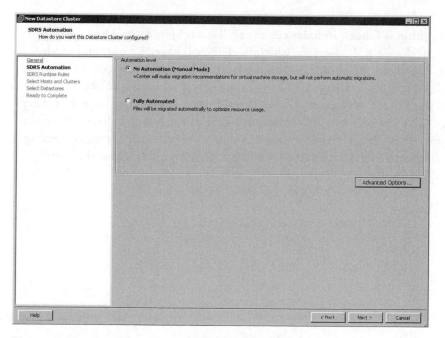

Figure 3-26 Datastore Cluster SDRS automation level.

The **SDRS Runtime Rules** screen is where you define all the values for the Storage DRS thresholds. The configuration options are shown in Figure 3-27. You begin by either checking or not checking the **Enable I/O metric for SDRS recommendations** box. If this option is checked or enabled, then Storage I/O Control is enabled on all datastores in the cluster. If the box is not checked or disabled, then the initial placement for VMs' files based on IOPS and IOPS load balancing will not be supported. In this case, SDRS will still use storage capacity when doing initial placement and load balancing recommendations for virtual machine's files.

The two Storage DRS thresholds are **Utilized Space (Capacity)** and **I/O Latency**. When these thresholds are met by storage, a recommendation for Storage vMotion or a Storage vMotion action will occur.

You can click the **Show Advanced Options** link to view advanced options that can be modified. The first option is **No recommendations until utilization difference between source and destination is.** This setting is designed to prevent unnecessary storage migrations where the capacity adjustment would provide minimal benefit. The value set here will determine the minimum amount of capacity difference between datastores that must be met before a migration is recommended or performed. Thus, if the setting was 15% and the source was at 80% utilization, the target would have to have 65% or less capacity utilization before action would be taken.

The next option is **Check imbalances every**. This option defines how often Storage DRS checks for IOPS latency, which by default is every 8 hours and can be modified. However, you should not set it too small because every check causes an elevated level of CPU activity on both vCenter Server and the ESXi hosts connected to the Datastore Cluster. The **Utilized Space** or capacity is checked every 5 minutes. The last option is **I/O imbalance threshold**, which helps to determine the amount of imbalance that Storage DRS should tolerate. An aggressive setting would result in an increased number of storage migrations, so adjust this setting with care.

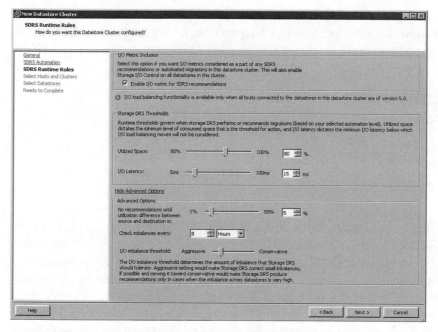

Figure 3-27   SDRS runtime rules for a datastore cluster.

Configuring Software iSCSI Port Binding

The iSCSI protocol provides universal access to both NAS- and SAN-based storage devices over standard Ethernet-based TCP/IP networks. For most implementations, iSCSI storage would be connected to the ESXi hosts and the storage would be used to host virtual machines. In this case, the ESXi host is considered the initiator because it is requesting the storage and the storage device is considered the target because it is delivering the storage. The initiator for the ESXi host can be software or hardware based. A software iSCSI initiator is included and built in to the VMkernel. When using a software iSCSI initiator, a standard 1 gig or 10 gig network adapter is used for storage transport. The advantage to using a software initiator is that there is no need for a dedicated adapter, but some CPU overhead is involved, so in some cases a hardware initiator might be preferable.

A VMkernel port must be configured on the same network as the storage device to use the software iSCSI initiator. The initiator will use the first network adapter port it finds that can see the storage device and use it exclusively for transport. This means that just having multiple adapter ports is not enough to balance storage workloads. However, you can achieve load balancing by configuring multiple VMkernel ports and binding them to multiple adapter ports.

As shown in Figure 3-28, highlight the ESXi host in the vSphere Client. Click the **Configuration** tab and select **Storage Adapters**; then click **Add**. The **Add Storage Adapter** window will appear, and you should click **OK** to create the Software iSCSI Adapter.

Figure 3-28   Add Software iSCSI Adapter.

The next step in configuring iSCSI and port binding is to create the number of desired VMkernel ports and ensure that the same number of network adapter ports are available and can see the iSCSI storage. When this is done, a 1:1 relationship must be established between each VMkernel port and the corresponding network adapter port. By default, the port group policy for network adapters is set to **Active**. This setting attempts to use any and all adapter ports for traffic, which is not desired when configuring port binding. To resolve this, select the **Override switch failover order** option and ensure that the only active adapter port for the VMkernel is the desired port; then move all other ports to **Unused**. Repeat this process for each VMkernel port configured for iSCSI use.

The final step is to bind the adapter ports to the iSCSI initiator. To do this, click the **Properties** of the Software iSCSI Adapter. In the **iSCSI Initiator Properties** dialog box, click the **Network Configuration** tab. Click **Add** and select a VMkernel adapter to bind with the iSCSI adapter. Repeat this process for each VMkernel adapter that will be used with the iSCSI adapter.

Pluggable Storage Architecture Layout

When people ask me what PSA does, I often jokingly tell them that VMware created PSA to make more acronyms. I know it might not be a very funny joke, but PSA does give us a bunch of acronyms. It is nice to know that all the main parts of PSA have an acronym, but PSA is really an architecture that defines how multipathing works within vSphere. If a VM sends a SCSI command to access data on a SAN, the VMkernel needs to know how to access the storage and which path it should choose. Let's start with listing all the acronyms and then discuss how everything works.

PSA—Pluggable Storage Architecture

MPP—Multipathing Plug-in

NMP—Native Multipathing Plug-in

SATP—Storage Array Type Plug-in

PSP—Path Selection Plug-in

VMware changed how they did multipathing when they introduced PSA in vSphere 4.0. The Pluggable Storage Architecture is simply a set of APIs that third-party vendors can use to add their multipathing software into vSphere to manage multipathing and access to storage. Before vSphere 4, the only choices you had for multipathing policies were VMware's **Fixed** or **Most Recently Used** (MRU). The Pluggable Storage Architecture solved this problem by giving third-party storage vendors a means to add policies and to recognize the type of storage deployed. The PSA has two primary tasks. The first task is to discover available storage and the physical paths to that storage. The second task is to assign each storage device a Multipathing Plug-in (MPP) by using predefined claim rules, which are discussed in the next section. Therefore, PSA discovers the storage and then figures out which multipathing driver will be in charge of communicating with that storage. All the error codes, I/O requests, and I/O queuing to the HBA will be handled by the MPP.

MPP

The top-level plug-in in PSA is the Multipathing Plug-in (MPP). The MPP can be either the internal MPP, which is called the Native Multipathing Plug-in (NMP), or a third-party MPP supplied by a storage vendor. Examples of third-party MPPs are Symantec DMP and EMC PowerPath/VE. Therefore, all storage is accessed through an MPP, whether it is VMware's built-in MPP or one of the third-party MPPs. The MPP combines NMP+SATP+PSP, which are really the pieces that make up the process.

As an example, I have a Netapp storage array I want to connect to VMware. I first make sure that the Netapp array is supported by VMware by checking the Hardware Compatibility List (HCL). If it is on the support list, I could simply use the built-in NMP, which will handle all the multipathing and load balancing. The other option is to switch to Symantec's DMP, which is a supported third-party MPP. Symantec's Dynamic Multipathing solution can handle the path discovery and path management of the ESXi host to the Netapp storage array. This third-party MPP solution might provide better load-balancing performance than the built-in solution.

NMP

The Native Multipathing Plug-in (NMP) is the default MPP in vSphere and is used when the storage array does not have a third-party MPP solution. VMware has a default claim rule that applies to storage that has not been claimed by a claim rule; it defaults to NMP. The NMP will contain a Storage Array Type Plug-in (SATP) and a Path Selection Plug-in (PSP). One of the tasks of NMP is to associate physical storage paths with an SATP and associate a PSP that chooses the best available path.

SATP

VMware provides a Storage Array Type Plug-in (SATP) for every type of array that VMware supports in the HCL. As an example, VMware provides an SATP for supported storage arrays such as the IBM SVC, which uses the VMW_SATP_SVC Storage Array Type Plug-in provided by VMware. The SATP monitors the health of each physical path and can respond to error messages from the storage array to handle path failover. There are third-party SATPs that the storage vendor can provide to take advantage of unique storage properties.

PSP

The Path Selection Plug-in (PSP) performs the task of selecting which physical path to use for storage transport. One way to think of PSP is which multipathing solution you are using to load balance. There are three built-in PSPs: Fixed, MRU, and Round Robin (which was added with vSphere 4.1). The NMP assigns a default PSP from the claim rules based on the SATP associated with the physical device. If you need to override the default PSP, you would create a claim rule to assign a different PSP to the device.

Installing and Configuring PSA Plug-ins

The PSA plug-ins are provided by third-party vendors for MPP such as EMC PowerPath or Dell Equallogic MEM. These plug-ins can be installed using vSphere Update Manager or using esxcli commands. Third-party vendors can also supply SATPs or PSPs for Native Multipathing. Figure 3-29 shows the list of default SATPs with their current PSP.

```
esxi01.vclass.local - PuTTY
/vmfs/volumes # esxcli storage nmp satp list
Name                  Default PSP     Description
--------------------  --------------  --------------------------------------------
VMW_SATP_MSA          VMW_PSP_MRU     Placeholder (plugin not loaded)
VMW_SATP_ALUA         VMW_PSP_MRU     Placeholder (plugin not loaded)
VMW_SATP_DEFAULT_AP   VMW_PSP_MRU     Placeholder (plugin not loaded)
VMW_SATP_SVC          VMW_PSP_FIXED   Placeholder (plugin not loaded)
VMW_SATP_EQL          VMW_PSP_FIXED   Placeholder (plugin not loaded)
VMW_SATP_INV          VMW_PSP_FIXED   Placeholder (plugin not loaded)
VMW_SATP_EVA          VMW_PSP_FIXED   Placeholder (plugin not loaded)
VMW_SATP_ALUA_CX      VMW_PSP_RR      Placeholder (plugin not loaded)
VMW_SATP_SYMM         VMW_PSP_RR      Placeholder (plugin not loaded)
VMW_SATP_CX           VMW_PSP_MRU     Placeholder (plugin not loaded)
VMW_SATP_LSI          VMW_PSP_MRU     Placeholder (plugin not loaded)
VMW_SATP_DEFAULT_AA   VMW_PSP_FIXED   Supports non-specific active/active arrays
VMW_SATP_LOCAL        VMW_PSP_FIXED   Supports direct attached devices
/vmfs/volumes #
```

Figure 3-29   Using an esxcli command to list the current SATPs and their default PSP.

Using esxcli commands, you can modify the default PSP for an SATP, as shown in Figure 3-30. Any device that is currently using an SATP that is going to be modified will have to have all its paths unclaimed and then reclaimed. The following esxcli command changes the default Path Selection Plug-in for the VMW_SATP_CX SATP from **MRU** to **Round Robin**.

```
# esxcli storage nmp satp set -s VMW_SATP_CX -P VMW_PSP_RR
```

For this modification to take effect, you still must reboot the ESXi host. After the default PSP has been changed, you can execute the **satp list** command to verify that the default PSP has been changed:

```
# esxcli storage nmp satp list
```

```
esxi01.vclass.local - PuTTY
/vmfs/volumes # esxcli storage nmp satp set -s VMW_SATP_CX -P VMW_PSP_RR
Default PSP for VMW_SATP_CX is now VMW_PSP_RR
/vmfs/volumes # esxcli storage nmp satp list
Name                   Default PSP     Description
--------------------   --------------  ------------------------------------------
VMW_SATP_MSA           VMW_PSP_MRU     Placeholder (plugin not loaded)
VMW_SATP_ALUA          VMW_PSP_MRU     Placeholder (plugin not loaded)
VMW_SATP_DEFAULT_AP    VMW_PSP_MRU     Placeholder (plugin not loaded)
VMW_SATP_SVC           VMW_PSP_FIXED   Placeholder (plugin not loaded)
VMW_SATP_EQL           VMW_PSP_FIXED   Placeholder (plugin not loaded)
VMW_SATP_INV           VMW_PSP_FIXED   Placeholder (plugin not loaded)
VMW_SATP_EVA           VMW_PSP_FIXED   Placeholder (plugin not loaded)
VMW_SATP_ALUA_CX       VMW_PSP_RR      Placeholder (plugin not loaded)
VMW_SATP_SYMM          VMW_PSP_RR      Placeholder (plugin not loaded)
VMW_SATP_CX            VMW_PSP_RR      Placeholder (plugin not loaded)
VMW_SATP_LSI           VMW_PSP_MRU     Placeholder (plugin not loaded)
VMW_SATP_DEFAULT_AA    VMW_PSP_FIXED   Supports non-specific active/active arrays
VMW_SATP_LOCAL         VMW_PSP_FIXED   Supports direct attached devices
/vmfs/volumes # 
```

Figure 3-30   Using an esxcli command to modify a PSP plug-in to Round Robin.

LUN Masking Using PSA-related Commands

In vSphere, LUN masking is used to either block an ESXi host from accessing a storage device or prevent a host from using a storage path. When the LUN is masked, the storage processor blocks the ESXi host from communicating with the LUN. When the VM is created on the ESXi host, the virtual machine's VMDK file is mapped to a SCSI adapter. Each VM will see only the virtual disks that are successfully presented to the VM's SCSI adapter.

A SAN is structured the same way as a traditional SCSI bus and uses the SCSI protocol commands to communicate between initiator and target devices. One difference is instead of using a SCSI cable for communication, the modern-day SAN communicates over a network. This is why LUN masking is needed as the SCSI protocol over the network provides no filtering mechanism to dictate which ESXi host can see a particular LUN. Thus, LUN masking can be used to make a LUN available to some hosts and unavailable to other hosts.

The most common place to do LUN masking is on the back-end storage array. For example, Netapp implements LUN masking through initiator groups, or if you are using an EMC Clarion or VNX device, LUN masking is provided through storage groups. Both methods use the same concept in which you add host(s) and a LUN to the initiator group or storage group and only those ESXi host(s) can see the LUN. A virtual SCSI bus will be created whether you use an initiator group or a storage group. Best practice is to set up LUN masking on the storage array. The exam will only look at setting up LUN masking on the ESXi host using the vSphere CLI.

When you power on an ESXi host or manually choose to rescan for storage devices, the ESXi host will send a signal down the physical bus paths and discover any storage available to the host. The ESXi host will then assign each storage device an MPP based on the claim rules listed in the /etc/vmware/esx.conf file. When the storage device has a proper MPP assigned, the multipathing driver will be responsible for managing the path selection for the storage device. By default, every 5 minutes the ESXi host will resend a signal down the physical bus paths looking for any unclaimed paths to be claimed by the appropriate MPP. This process of associating a storage device with a plug-in is referred to as *claiming the device*, and the MPP claims a storage device by finding an appropriate claim rule in the /etc/vmware/esx.conf file.

The process of LUN masking using PSA commands begins by identifying which LUN you want to mask. The command line **esxcfg-scsidevs –m** will display LUNs with VMFS volumes, which is shown in Figure 3-31. The VMFS datastore named **Shared** is listed here. Using the **Shared** datastore as an example, we find the device id for the datastore which will begin with **naa**:

naa.6000eb3a2b3b330e00000000000000cb

Figure 3-31   The **esxcfg-scsidevs –m** command enables you to find the device ID.

Now that we have the device ID of the datastore, it will need to be copied. The next step is to find all the paths to the LUN. Using the **esxcfg-mpath –L** command and the device ID of the datastore, we discover there is one path to the LUN, which is shown in Figure 3-32.

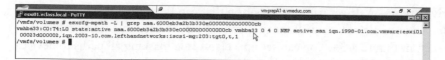

Figure 3-32   The **esxcfg-mpath –L** command shows all of the paths' the device ID.

From the output of the **esxcfg-mpath –L** command, we see the path to the datastore. Now that we have the path to the datastore C0:T4:L0, we can create a new claim rule. To get a list of the current claim rules, use the **esxcli storage core claim rule list** command, as shown in Figure 3-33.

```
 esxi01.vclass.local - PuTTY
/vmfs/volumes # esxcli storage core claimrule list
Rule Class   Rule   Class     Type        Plugin      Matches
----------   ----   -----     ---------   ---------   ------------------------------
MP              0   runtime   transport   NMP         transport=usb
MP              1   runtime   transport   NMP         transport=sata
MP              2   runtime   transport   NMP         transport=ide
MP              3   runtime   transport   NMP         transport=block
MP              4   runtime   transport   NMP         transport=unknown
MP            101   runtime   vendor      MASK_PATH   vendor=DELL model=Universal Xport
MP            101   file      vendor      MASK_PATH   vendor=DELL model=Universal Xport
MP          65535   runtime   vendor      NMP         vendor=* model=*
/vmfs/volumes #
```

Figure 3-33   List the current claim rules for an ESXi host.

Figure 3-33 shows the list of the current claim rules on the ESXi host. You can use any claim rule number that is not being used, with the exception of rules 0–100, which are reserved for VMware's internal use. By default, the PSA claim rule 101 masks Dell array pseudo devices and should not be removed unless you need to unmask these types of devices. Claim rules can be created a number of ways, including manually masking based on the HBA adapter (C:#T:#L:#).

Claim rules can also be created based on the following options:

- **Vendor String**—A claim rule can be set up using the **Vendor** string, which must be an exact match. An example would be **vendor=DELL**.

- **Model String**—A claim rule can be set up using the **Model** string, which must be an exact match. An example would be **model=Universal Xport**.

- **Transport type**—A claim rule can be created to mask all LUNs based on the transport type. Valid transport types are **block**, **fc**, **iscsi**, **iscsivendor**, **ide**, **sas**, **sata**, **usb**, **parallel**, and **unknown**.

■ **Driver type**—A driver name is an option that can be used to create a claim rule. An example of listing all the drivers that can be used in a claim rule can be seen in Figure 3-34. You can set up a claim rule masking all paths to devices attached to an HBA using a driver such as the **iscsi_vmk** driver.

Here is an example of creating a claim rule using a transport type. This example of masking all LUNs that are of transport type fibre channel is shown in Figure 3-34. The example uses rule number 200 because it was not being used and is greater than 100. The first two lines in Figure 3-34 show the successful addition of the claim rule because no error message was given. Line two shows loading the claim rule into the runtime environment. The third line shows that because multipathing was not set up, the host did not want to disconnect the last path. Fortunately, when all the claim rules are listed in the fifth line, we do see that the claim rule was successfully added. This success can be seen by looking at the **Class** field shows file status for the new rule 200.

```
esxi02.vclass.local - PuTTY
~ # esxcli storage core claimrule add -r 200 -P MASK_PATH -t transport -R fc
~ # esxcli storage core claimrule load
~ # esxcli storage core claiming unclaim -t plugin -P NMP
Unable to perform unclaim. Error message was : Unable to unclaim all requested paths. Some paths were bu
sy or were the last path to in use devices.  See VMkernel logs for more information.
~ # esxcli storage core claimrule run
~ # esxcli storage core claimrule list
Rule Class    Rule  Class    Type       Plugin     Matches
----------    ----  -------  ---------  ---------  ------------------------------------
MP               0  runtime  transport  NMP        transport=usb
MP               1  runtime  transport  NMP        transport=sata
MP               2  runtime  transport  NMP        transport=ide
MP               3  runtime  transport  NMP        transport=block
MP               4  runtime  transport  NMP        transport=unknown
MP             101  runtime  vendor     MASK_PATH  vendor=DELL model=Universal Xport
MP             101  file     vendor     MASK_PATH  vendor=DELL model=Universal Xport
MP             200  runtime  transport  MASK_PATH  transport=fc
MP             200  file     transport  MASK_PATH  transport=fc
MP           65535  runtime  vendor     NMP        vendor=* model=*
~ # █
```

Figure 3-34   Steps showing LUN masking for all FC devices on an ESXi host.

One final step is needed because the fibre channel paths originally were claimed by the default NMP plugin (rule 65535). The command shown in Figure 3-35 will unclaim all the paths that are currently claimed by NMP and then reclaim any un-claimed paths using runtime rules.

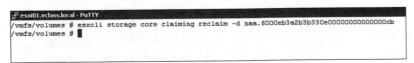

Figure 3-35   The esxcli command that reclaims unused paths for the LUN.

Removing a claim rule is shown in Figure 3-36. The example given is removing rule number 200 that was created to mask fibre channel devices. After the rule is removed, a command needs to be run to unclaim and then reclaim a supported plugin for the device. Finally, a command is run to load the claim rules into the runtime environment.

```
esxi01.vclass.local - PuTTY
/vmfs/volumes # esxcli storage core claimrule list
Rule Class   Rule   Class     Type        Plugin       Matches
----------   ----   -------   ---------   ---------   ----------------------------------
MP              0   runtime   transport   NMP          transport=usb
MP              1   runtime   transport   NMP          transport=sata
MP              2   runtime   transport   NMP          transport=ide
MP              3   runtime   transport   NMP          transport=block
MP              4   runtime   transport   NMP          transport=unknown
MP            101   runtime   vendor      MASK_PATH    vendor=DELL model=Universal Xport
MP            101   file      vendor      MASK_PATH    vendor=DELL model=Universal Xport
MP            200   runtime   transport   MASK_PATH    transport=fc
MP            200   file      transport   MASK_PATH    transport=fc
MP          65535   runtime   vendor      NMP          vendor=* model=*
/vmfs/volumes # esxcli storage core claimrule remove -r 200
/vmfs/volumes # esxcli storage core claiming unclaim -t device -d naa.6000eb3a2b3b330e00000000000000cb
/vmfs/volumes # esxcli storage core claimrule load
/vmfs/volumes # esxcli storage core claimrule list
Rule Class   Rule   Class     Type        Plugin       Matches
----------   ----   -------   ---------   ---------   ----------------------------------
MP              0   runtime   transport   NMP          transport=usb
MP              1   runtime   transport   NMP          transport=sata
MP              2   runtime   transport   NMP          transport=ide
MP              3   runtime   transport   NMP          transport=block
MP              4   runtime   transport   NMP          transport=unknown
MP            101   runtime   vendor      MASK_PATH    vendor=DELL model=Universal Xport
MP            101   file      vendor      MASK_PATH    vendor=DELL model=Universal Xport
MP          65535   runtime   vendor      NMP          vendor=* model=*
/vmfs/volumes #
```

Figure 3-36 The process for removing a claim rule.

Figure 3-37 shows the command to display all the drivers that are loaded on the ESXi host. You can use the information provided to create a claim rule that will mask whichever driver you want to exclude from the ESXi host. The output of Figure 3-37 shows there are two drivers that could be masked: **ata_piix** and **iscsi_vmk**.

```
esxi01.vclass.local - PuTTY
/vmfs/volumes # esxcli storage core adapter list
HBA Name   Driver      Link State   UID                             Description
--------   ---------   ----------   -----------------------------   -----------------------------------------------------
--------   ---------   ----------   -----------------------------   -----------------------------------------------------
vmhba0     ata_piix    link-n/a     ide.vmhba0                      (0:0:7.1) Intel Corporation PIIX4 for 430TX/440BX/MX
IDE Controller
vmhba32    ata_piix    link-n/a     ide.vmhba32                     (0:0:7.1) Intel Corporation PIIX4 for 430TX/440BX/MX
IDE Controller
vmhba33    iscsi_vmk   online       iqn.1998-01.com.vmware:esxi01   iSCSI Software Adapter

/vmfs/volumes #
```

Figure 3-37 The command-line output shows the drivers loaded on the ESXi host.

Multipathing Policies

The PSA is used to take control of the path failover and load-balancing operations for specific storage devices. These multipathing operations do not apply to NFS, which relies on networking over multiple TCP sessions. PSPs are included with the VMware NMP that determine the physical path for I/O requests. By default, three PSPs are included with vSphere: **Round-Robin**, **MRU**, and **Fixed**. They are explained here:

- Round Robin - VMW_PSP_RR

  The ESXi host uses an algorithm that rotates through all the active paths and can be used with active-active and active-passive arrays. On supported arrays multiple paths can be active simultaneously; otherwise, the default is to rotate between the paths.

- Most Recently Used (MRU) – VMW_PSP_MRU

  The ESXi host selects the path that was most recently used. If the active path fails, then an alternative path will take over, becoming active. When the original path comes back online, it will now be the alternative path. MRU is the default for most active-passive storage arrays.

- Fixed – VMW_PSP_FIXED

  The ESXi host uses a designated preferred path, if it has been configured. Otherwise, it selects the first working path discovered at boot time. Fixed is the default for active-active storage arrays.

Changing a Multipath Policy

You can change a multipath policy using either the vSphere Client or esxcli commands. In an earlier section we modified a multipath policy using esxcli commands, so we are now going to concentrate on using the vSphere Client. Select the ESXi host you want to change the multipath policy in the vSphere Client. Click the **Configuration** tab, and underneath the hardware section select **Storage**. In the **Datastores** view, find the datastore you want to change the multipath policy, right-click, and select **Properties**. On the **Volume Properties** page, click the **Manage Paths** button, which will open the **Manage Paths** window shown in Figure 3-38. The **Path Selection** drop-down box presents the PSP options you can use. Select the PSP you want to use, and then click the **Change** button followed by the **Close** button. The **Change** button will modify the PSP for the datastore on the ESXi host.

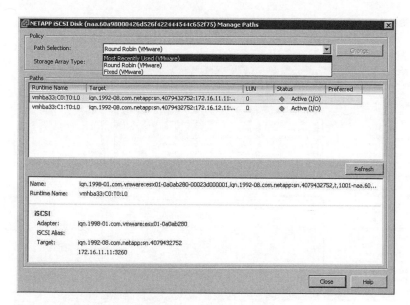

Figure 3-38   Manage paths in the vSphere Client.

Identifying and Tagging SSD Devices

The VMkernel can automatically detect, tag, and enable a Solid-State Drive (SSD) device. SSD devices are detected on the ESXi host using the T10 standard mechanism. This mechanism allows SSD storage devices that are T10 compliant to be automatically detected. You can identify SSD devices in the vSphere Client by highlighting the ESXi host and clicking the **Configuration** tab. Underneath the **Hardware** section you will find the **Storage** link and the **Datastores** view. In Figure 3-39 the **Datastores** view has a column called **Drive Type** that allows you to identify SSD devices (which will be marked SSD, as opposed to Non-SSD or Unknown).

You can use PSA SATP claim rules to tag SSD devices that are not detected automatically.

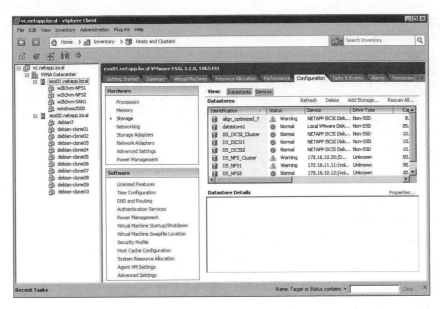

Figure 3-39   Datastores Device Type column shows SSD devices.

Summary

This module discussed how to implement and manage storage in a vSphere environment. The two main datastore types are NFS, which is file based, and VMFS, which
is block based. The NFS datastore uses the storage device to format the storage,
and VMware accesses the NFS data in a file format. The VMFS datastore needs a
LUN to be created on the storage array and formatted by vSphere with VMFS. The
VMFS datastore can be created with three virtual disk formats: lazy-zeroed thick,
eager-zeroed thick, or thin provisioned. The default VMFS format is lazy-zeroed
thick.

The chapter also looked at other features that can affect storage such as VMware
DirectPath I/O, RDM, vCenter Server Storage Filters, and others. In addition, the
module discusses VASA and VAAI and how the two APIs perform important tasks
for storage.

Finally, the section on the Pluggable Storage Architecture (PSA) helped to define
how multipathing works within vSphere. PSA provides the structure that can associate storage with multipathing drivers.

Exam Preparation Tasks

Review All the Key Topics

Table 3-4 provides a list of all Key Topics identified in this chapter along with a few notes intended to refresh the reader's memory of some key details. This can be useful as a quick reference when performing vSphere administration.

Table 3-4 Key Topics Table for Chapter 3

Key Topic	Description	Page Number
Paragraph	Virtual disk formats	95
Paragraph	Raw Device Map (RDM)	98
Paragraph	NPIV	99
Paragraph	DirectPath I/O	101
Paragraph	vCenter Server Storage Filters	102
Paragraph	Create an alarm on a datastore	117
Paragraph	Add iSCSI software adapter	123
Paragraph	Modify default PSP	127
Paragraph	Create a claim rule	130

Key Terms

Define the following key terms from this chapter, and check your answers in the glossary.

Review Tasks

These Review Tasks allow you to assess how well you grasped the materials in this chapter. Because of the advanced and hands-on nature of this particular exam, a set of tasks is provided instead of a set of questions. You should now attempt to perform each of these tasks without looking at previous sections in this chapter or at other materials, unless necessary. The steps for each task are located within the chapter:

1. Create a user-defined storage capability.

2. Create a VM storage profile and name it Production Tier.

3. Enable a VM storage profile.

4. Associate a VM with the Production Tier storage profile.

5. Check that the datastore is compliant.

This chapter covers the following subjects:

- **Tune and Optimize vSphere Performance**—This section covers tuning ESXi host resources and configuring advanced settings.

- **Optimize Virtual Machine Resources**—This section covers tuning and sizing virtual hardware resources for virtual machines.

- **Utilize Advanced vSphere Performance Monitoring Tools**—This section covers utilizing commands to collect and analyze performance data.

- **Troubleshoot CPU and Memory Performance**—This section covers troubleshooting CPU and memory-related issues that affect ESXi host and VM performance.

- **Troubleshoot Network Performance and Connectivity**—This section covers utilizing commands and other tools to troubleshoot network performance and connectivity-related issues.

- **Troubleshoot Storage Performance and Connectivity**—This section covers utilizing commands and other tools to troubleshoot storage performance and connectivity-related issues.

- **Troubleshoot vCenter Server and ESXi Host Management**—This section covers troubleshooting vCenter Server and ESXi host management-related issues.

This chapter contains material pertaining to the VCAP5-DCA exam objectives 3.1, 3.2, 3.4, 6.2, 6.3, 6.4, and 6.5.

## CHAPTER 4

Performance

This chapter is intended to provide you with the knowledge and skills to successfully execute performance tuning, optimization, and troubleshooting. It is also intended to ensure that you have the skills to successfully complete the performance analysis, configuration, and troubleshooting tasks that might be part of the VCAP5-DCA exam. As you read this chapter, take time to practice the steps that are provided until you are confident that you can perform such tasks quickly and without any assistance. Some of these steps involve using the vSphere Client. Others involve using the vCLI and PowerCLI.

"Do I Know This Already?" Quiz

The "Do I Know This Already?" quiz allows you to assess how well you might already know the material in this chapter. Table 4-1 outlines the major headings in this chapter and the corresponding "Do I Know This Already?" quiz questions. You can find the answers in Appendix A, "Answers to the 'Do I Know This Already?' Quizzes and Troubleshooting Scenarios." Because of the advanced and hands-on nature of this particular exam, you should read the entire chapter and practice performing all the described tasks at least once, regardless of how well you might do on this quiz. This quiz can be helpful to determine which topics will require the most effort during your preparation.

Table 4-1 "Do I Know This Already?" Foundation Topics Section-to-Question Mapping

Foundations Topics Section	Questions Covered in This Section
Tune and Optimize vSphere Performance	1
Optimize Virtual Machine Resources	2
Utilize Advanced vSphere Performance Monitoring Tools	3
Troubleshoot CPU and Memory Performance	4
Troubleshoot Network Performance and Connectivity	5
Troubleshoot Storage Performance and Connectivity	6
Troubleshoot vCenter Server and ESXi Host Management	7

1. Which option summarizes the steps that can be taken to ensure that an ESXi host supports SplitRx Mode?

    a. Select the ESXi host, navigate to **Configuration** tab > **Advanced Settings**, and set **Net.NetSplitRxMode** = *true*.

    b. Select the ESXi host, navigate to **Configuration** tab > **Advanced Settings**, and set **SplitRx-Mode** = *true*.

    c. Select the ESXi host, navigate to **Configuration** tab > **Advanced Settings**, and set **Net.NetSplitRxMode** = *1*.

    d. Select the ESXi host, navigate to **Configuration** tab > **Advanced Settings**, and set **SplitRx-Mode** = *true*.

2. Which option summarizes the steps that can be taken to calculate the available remaining memory resources in a DRS cluster that are not reserved for VMs or resource pools?

    a. Choose the cluster, navigate to **Performance** tab > **Overview Graphs**, and select the **Available Memory** graph.

    b. Choose the cluster, navigate to **Performance** tab > **Overview Graphs**, select the **Memory Usage** graph, and manually calculate the available memory by subtracting Memory Used in the graph from the known total memory capacity of the cluster.

    c. Choose the cluster and navigate to the **Resource Allocation** tab.

    d. Choose the cluster and navigate to the **DRS** tab.

3. Which option summarizes the steps that can be taken to save a custom profile in RESXTOP?

    a. Press the **W** key and enter a filename at the prompt.

    b. Press the **w** key and enter a filename at the prompt.

    c. Press the **P** key and enter a filename at the prompt.

    d. Press the **p** key and enter a filename at the prompt.

4. Which option summarizes the steps that can be taken to determine whether a Windows VM needs to be resized with more memory?

    a. Use the vSphere Client to determine whether ballooning is high for the VM.

    b. Use **esxtop** to determine whether the **SWCUR** value is higher than zero for the VM.

    c. Use the vSphere Client to determine whether memory compression or swapping is occurring on the ESXi host where the VM is running.

    d. Log in to the Windows VM and use Windows Performance Monitor to determine whether **Pages per Second** is high.

5. Which option summarizes the steps that can be taken using the ESXi Shell to display configuration and statistics for a dvSwitch?

    a. Use the **esxcli network dvswitch** namespace.

    b. Use the **esxcfg-dvswitch** command.

    c. Use the **esxcli network core dvs** namespace.

    d. Use the **net-dvs** command.

6. Which option summarizes the steps that can be taken to identify all the iSCSI adapters in an ESXi host?

    a. Use the vSphere Client to navigate to **Configuration** tab > **Storage** > **iSCSI Adapters**.

    b. Use the **esxcli iscsi adapter list** command.

    c. Use the **esxcli storage adapter iscsi list** command.

    d. Use the **esxcfg-iscsi –l** command.

7. Which option summarizes the steps that can be taken to restart the vCenter agent on an ESXi host?

    a. In the ESXi Shell, enter **restart vpxa**.

    b. In the ESXi Shell, enter **/etc/init.d/vpxa restart**.

    c. In the ESXi Shell, enter **restart hostd**.

    d. In the ESXi Shell, enter **/etc/init.d/hostd restart**.

Foundation Topics

Tune and Optimize vSphere Performance

This section describes how to tune ESXi host resources. It provides details for optimizing the configuration of ESXi host memory, network, CPU, and storage resources. It provides examples and scenarios that involve the use of the vSphere Client and the vCLI.

Capacity Planning and Peak Workload

The first key to achieving solid performance in a vSphere environment is to ensure that sufficient resources are provided to meet the peak concurrent demand from the virtual machines (VMs) and the system overhead. In this case, *peak demand* refers to the combined workload of a set of VMs at the moment when the combined concurrent workload of the VMs reaches its highest value.

For example, consider a case where you assess a set of 50 physical Windows servers that you plan to virtualize. You could use an assessment tool like VMware Capacity Planner to collect resource usage data from the Windows servers at regular intervals for a duration that you expect to be sufficient to represent the behavior of the servers. In this example, assume that you selected the sampling interval to be 1 hour and the duration to be 30 days. After the collection period is finished, you should use the tool or a spreadsheet to sum the values of the memory usage counter for all the servers at each sampling interval. In other words, use the tool to provide a table or graph that shows the total memory used by all servers at each 1-hour interval taken during the 30-day period. Then determine what is the highest (peak) value of the total memory usage at any particular interval during the 30-day period. Consider this value to be the peak concurrent memory usage. In this example, assume that on the last Friday of the month, several application servers such as payroll, financial reports, and other monthly reporting run concurrently, and the peak concurrent memory usage of the 50 Windows servers is 100GB. If you size a cluster of ESXi hosts to run these 50 Windows servers as virtual machines, then you should plan to provide at least 100GB of physical memory to the VMs—if you want the VMs to perform as well as the original servers. You should include additional physical memory for virtualization overhead, future growth, and redundancy.

Tune ESXi Host Memory Configuration

Although ESXi 5.1 hosts require a minimum of 2GB of physical RAM, each ESXi host should be configured with at least 8GB of RAM to take full advantage of ESXi features and to allow sufficient space to run VMs. Ensure that each ESXi host has sufficient memory resources to meet the peak concurrent demand of its VMs and system services.

Usually, the performance of VMs can be significantly enhanced when hardware-assisted memory management unit (MMU) virtualization is used. Hardware-assisted MMU virtualization is a feature provided by CPUs and is implemented by Intel using extended page tables (EPTs) and by AMD with rapid virtualization indexing (RVI). Hardware-assisted MMU virtualization provides an additional level of page tables in the hardware that maps VM memory (what the guest operating system perceives to be physical memory) to actual host physical memory (commonly called *machine memory*). ESXi hosts that utilize hardware-assisted MMU virtualization do not need to maintain shadow page tables, thus reducing overhead memory consumption and improving the performance of workloads in VMs. VMware recommends that when available, set the system BIOS of the ESXi host to enable hardware-assisted MMU virtualization.

The performance benefit of hardware-assisted MMU virtualization can be negated if a VM's workload causes a high frequency of misses in the hardware translation lookaside buffer (TLB) because the time required for the ESXi host to service a TLB miss is increased in the absence of shadow page tables. In most cases, the additional cost to accommodate TLB misses can be overcome by configuring the guest O/S in the VM and the ESXi host to utilize large pages, which is covered in the Modify Large Memory Page Settings section of this chapter.

Some systems that support non-uniform memory architecture (NUMA) provide a BIOS option to enable node interleaving. In most cases, VMware recommends disabling node interleaving, which effectively enables NUMA and enables ESXi to optimally place each page of each VM's virtual memory.

The BIOS of some ESXi host systems that utilize ECC memory can contain an option to set the memory scrub rate. In these cases, set the memory scrub rate to match the manufacturer's recommendations, which is typically the default setting.

Memory overhead is required for the VMkernel and host agents, such as hostd and vpxa. A new feature in ESXi 5.1 enables the use of a system swap file, which allows up to 1GB of this memory overhead to be reclaimed when the host is under memory pressure. This feature is not enabled by default but can be enabled using an ESXCLI command. For example, to create and enable a system swap file on a datastore named **Local-01**, the following command can be used:

```
esxcli sched swap system set -d true -n Local-1
```

> **NOTE** The system swap file is unrelated to the standard VM swap file (VSWP) file, which is used to enable the VM's guest O/S to consume less physical memory than the configured memory.

Memory overhead is also required for each running virtual machine. The per-VM memory overhead supports the following VM components:

- VM executable (VMX) process, which is needed to bootstrap and support the guest O/S

- VM monitor (VMM), which contains data structures that are used by the virtual hardware, such as the TLB, memory mappings, and CPU state

- Virtual hardware devices, such as mouse, keyboard, SVGA, and USB

- Other subsystems, such as the kernel and management agents

Although the memory requirements for the VMM and virtual devices are fully reserved at the moment the VM is started, the memory reserved for the VMX process can be reduced by the use of VMX swap file. The size of the VMX swap file is typically less than 100MB. Its use typically reduces the VMX memory reservation from about 50MB or more per VM to about 10MB per VM. By default, the ESXi host automatically creates a VMX swap file for each VM in the VM's working directory, but this can be controlled by setting a value for the **sched.swap.vmxSwapDir** parameter in the VMX file. The **sched.swap.vmxSwapEnabled** parameter can be set to **FALSE** in a VM's VMX file to prevent it from using a VMX swap file. To set these parameters, click the **Configuration Parameters** button located on the **Options** tab of the VM's **Properties** pages. In the **Configuration Parameters** dialog box, search the **Name** column for the name of the parameter. If it exists, then modify its value. Otherwise, use the **Add Row** button to create a row for the parameter. When adding a row, be sure to enter the parameter name and value carefully. For example, to modify a VM, such that its VMX swap file is stored in a datastore named *Local-01*, add a row to the Configuration Parameters, where the parameter name is **sched.swap.vmxSwapDir** and the value is */vmfs/volumes/Local-01/*, as illustrated in Figure 4-1.

To verify success, power on the VM and use the vSphere Client to examine the VM's files on the *Local-01* datastore using the **Datastore Browser**, as illustrated in Figure 4-2.

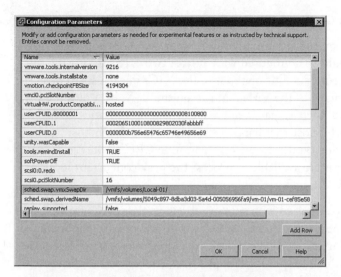

Figure 4-1 VMX swap file configuration parameter.

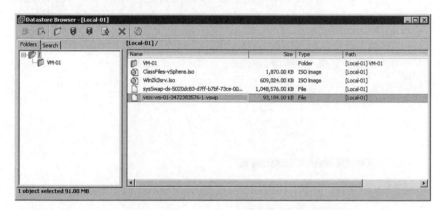

Figure 4-2 VMX swap file.

NOTE The VMX swap file is unrelated to the standard VM swap file (VSWP) file, which is used to enable the VM's guest O/S to consume less physical memory than the configured memory.

Tune ESXi Host Networking Configuration

Although ESXi 5.1 hosts require a minimum of just one network interface card (NIC), each ESXi host should be configured with at least two NICs to provide redundancy. Ensure that the combined throughput of the NICs in each ESXi host is sufficient to meet the demand of the VMs that run on the ESXi host plus the demand from the VMkernel, such as management and vMotion activities. Many networking tasks, particularly those that happen entirely with an ESXi host (such as VM-to-VM communication on the same host), consume CPU resources. Ensure that sufficient CPU resources are available to process the peak concurrent levels of network for the VMs and VMkernel.

Each ESXi host should be configured with supported server-class NICs for best performance. Ensure that the network switches, switch ports, and other components of the network infrastructure are properly configured to support the capabilities of the NIC. For example, ensure that the speed and duplex are properly set on the switch ports and physical NICs. To set the speed and duplex on a physical adapter using the vSphere Client, navigate to the vSwitch, select **Properties**, select the **Network Adapters** tab, select the physical adapter (such as vmnic3); then click **Edit**, as illustrated in Figure 4-3.

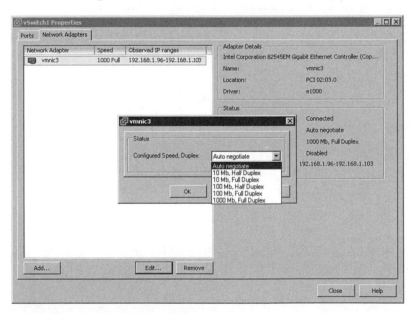

Figure 4-3   NIC speed and duplex.

In some rare cases, Direct I/O might be desired to meet the high throughput demand of a virtual machine. In these cases, ensure that the BIOS settings of the ESXi host system are configured to enable the appropriate hardware-assisted virtualization support, such as Intel VT-d or AMD-Vi.

SplitRx mode is an ESXi feature that uses multiple physical CPUs to process network packets from a single network queue. This feature can improve the performance of specific workloads, such as multiple VMs receiving multicast traffic from a single source. By default, the feature is automatically enabled on VMXNET3 virtual network adapters whenever vSphere 5.1 detects that a single network queue on a physical NIC is heavily utilized and servicing at least eight virtual network adapters with evenly distributed loads. SplitRx mode can be enabled or disabled by adjusting the value of the *NetSplitRxMode* parameter. This setting can be viewed and modified by using the vSphere Client to navigate to the ESXi host's **Configuration** tab > **Advanced Settings** > **Net.NetSplitRxMode**, as illustrated in Figure 4-4. The default value is 1, which means SplitRx mode is enabled. If the value is set to 0, then SplitRx mode is disabled.

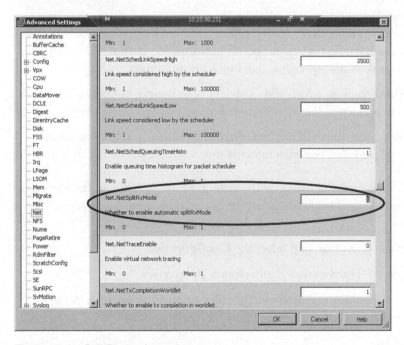

Figure 4-4 SplitRx mode setting.

Tune ESXi Host CPU Configuration

ESXi 5.1 should be installed only on system hardware containing CPUs that are supported for ESXi 5.1 and having at least two CPU cores. Ensure that each ESXi host has sufficient CPU resources to meet the peak concurrent demand of its VMs and system services. VMware recommends using modern CPUs that provide the latest features, such as hardware-assisted virtualization.

The performance of VMs can be significantly enhanced whenever hardware-assisted instruction set virtualization is used. Instruction set virtualization is a feature provided by CPUs that support Intel VT-x or AMD-V, where the hardware traps sensitive events and instructions eliminating the need for hypervisor to do so. VMware recommends that when available, set the system BIOS of the ESXi host to enable hardware-assisted instruction set virtualization. As mentioned in other sections, VMware also recommends enabling the hardware-assisted MMU virtualization features: Intel EPT and AMD RVI.

VMware also recommends making the following settings in the system BIOS when available:

- Enable all installed CPU sockets and cores.

- Enable Intel Turbo Boost, which allows the CPU to run at faster than its thermal design power (TDP) configuration specified frequency whenever the hypervisor requests the highest processor performance state and the CPU is operating below its power, current, and temperature limits.

- Enable hyperthreading, which allows each core to behave as two logical CPUs, permitting two independent threads to run concurrently on the core.

- Disable any devices that will not be utilized. For example, if the system includes a serial port that you plan to never use, disable it in the BIOS.

By default, ESXi automatically uses hyperthreading if it is available on the hardware and enabled in the BIOS. This behavior can be changed by using the vSphere Client:

Step 1.   Select the ESXi host and select the **Configuration** tab.

Step 2.   Navigate to **Hardware > Processors > Properties**.

Step 3.   In the dialog box, set the **hyperthreading** status to either *enabled* or *disabled*.

Step 4.   Click **OK**.

Tune ESXi Host Storage Configuration

If the ESXi host is configured to boot from local storage, ensure that a supported RAID controller is used and the selected RAID type includes redundancy, such as RAID-1. If the local storage is equipped with write-back cache, enable the cache and ensure it has a functional battery.

Ensure that only supported host bus storage adapters (HBAs) are installed and that each HBA is installed in slots with enough bandwidth to support their expected throughput. For example, a dual-port 16 Gbps Fiber Channel HBA should be installed in, at a minimum, a PCI Express (PCIe) G2 x8 slot, which can support up to 40Gbps in each direction. Ensure that the maximum queue depth of the HBA is configured to meet manufacturer and VMware recommendations, which are unique depending on the combination of ESXi version and HBA model and version. Here are some useful examples of using ESXCLI commands to manage HBA queue depth:

- To view all currently loaded modules, use this command:

```
esxcli system module list
```

- To view all currently loaded Qlogic HBA modules, use this command:

```
esxcli system module list | grep qla
```

- To view all currently loaded Emulex HBA modules, use this command:

```
esxcli system module list | grep lpfc
```

- To view all currently loaded Brocade HBA modules, use this command:

```
esxcli system module list | grep bfa
```

To determine the current queue depth for an HBA, first use the vSphere Client to navigate to the **Storage Adapters** configuration page for the ESXi host and identify the device name of the HBA. Then use the **esxtop** command to determine the queue depth size. For example, to determine the queue depth for *vmhba33*, the following steps can be used:

1. In the ESXi Shell, enter **esxtop**.
2. Press the **d** key to display statistics for storage adapters.
3. Press the **f** key to display the available fields.
4. Press the **d** key to select the **Queue_Stats** field. Press the **f** and **g** keys to hide two other columns.
5. Examine the value for the AQLEN field for device vmhba33, as illustrated in Figure 4-5.

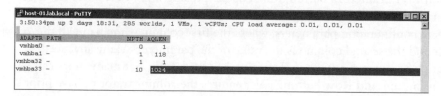

Figure 4-5   AQLEN field in ESXTOP.

The name of the parameter to set the queue depth on an HBA depends on the HBA module. To determine the available parameters for a particular HBA module, use the **esxcli system module parameters list** command. For example, to list the available parameters for the qla2xxx module, use this command:

```
esxcli system module parameters list -m qla2xxx
```

In this example, by examining the results you might determine that the appropriate parameter name is *ql2xmaxqdepth*. To set the maximum queue depth for the qla2xxx module, use this command:

```
esxcli system module parameters set -p ql2xmaxqdepth=64 -m qla2xxx
```

VMware recommends maintaining uniform configuration settings for all the HBAs used in an ESXi host cluster. You should ensure that any changes to a specific HBA's queue depth in one ESXi host is also implemented to all identical HBAs throughout that host and all hosts in the cluster.

Configure and Apply Advanced ESXi Host Attributes

ESXi hosts provide many advanced attributes that could be configured in specific situations, such as the **Mem.AllocGuestLargePage** and the **Net.NetSplitRxMode** attributes described elsewhere in this chapter. To view the existing advanced attributes for an ESXi host using the vSphere Client, select the host and navigate to the **Configuration** tab > **Software** > **Advanced Settings**. To change the value of one of the advanced parameters, navigate to the parameter, enter its new value in the provided box, and click **OK**.

Configure and Apply Advanced Virtual Machine Attributes

You can use the vSphere Client to modify many advanced options. For example, you can right-click a VM; select **Edit Settings**; select the **Options** tab; and use it to view and edit **Advanced** attributes, such as **CPUID Mask**, **Memory/CPU Hotplug**, and **CPU/MMU Virtualization**. For example, Figure 4-6 illustrates the **Options** tab for a VM named *VM-04*.

Additionally, you can select **Advanced** > **General** on the **Options** tab and click the **Configuration Parameters** button, which opens a dialog box where these advanced configuration parameters can be viewed and edited. The dialog box contains a table with rows of configuration parameters, where the first column is the name of the parameter and the second column is the value of the parameter. Many advanced configuration parameters appear in the dialog box by default, but many more can be added by using the **Add Row** button. This requires the administrator to have prior knowledge of the exact parameter name and its acceptable values. The administrator should enter parameter names and values carefully. All parameters that are added and all values that are set using this dialog box are automatically added to the VM's VMX file.

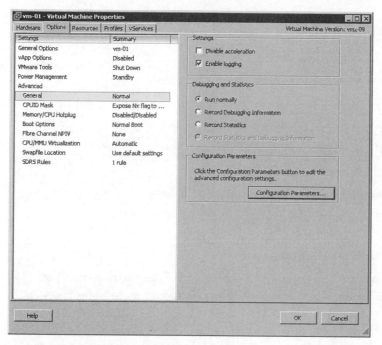

Figure 4-6 VM Properties Options tab.

Scenario—VM Advanced Configuration Parameters

An administrator has difficulty using the console of a specific VM named *vm-04* because characters are repeated as he types into the console. The root cause of the problem is that latency in the wide area network (WAN) is high enough to trigger the VM to begin to auto-repeat characters.

To fix this problem, add a configuration parameter named *keyboard.typematic-MinDelay* and set its value to *2000000*, which effectively configures the VM console to wait 2,000,000 microseconds (two seconds) for a key to be held before triggering auto-repeat. This can be accomplished by using the **Add Row** button in the **Configuration Parameters** dialog box, as shown in Figure 4-7.

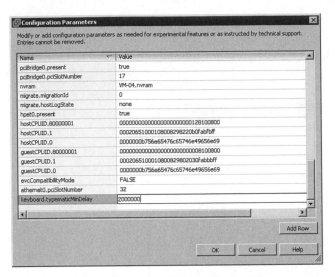

Figure 4-7   Add the VM configuration parameter Keyboard Min Delay.

Scenario—Disable VM Copy and Paste

You want to follow VMware best practices to harden a vSphere environment. You notice that one VM currently allows you to copy and paste into its console. You want to disable this ability.

To fix this problem, add configuration parameters named *isolation.tools.copy.disable* and *isolation.tools.paste.disable* to the VM and set both parameters to *true*, as shown in Figure 4-8.

Scenario—VM Advanced Configuration Parameters

Although VMware recommends enabling the hardware-assisted MMU virtualization features Intel EPT and AMD RVI, in some cases you might want to configure some VMs differently. For example, assume you suspect that the unique workload in a specific VM might perform better by disabling the hardware-assisted MMU.

To test this, use the **Options** tab of the VM's Properties page to modify the **CPU/ MMU Virtualization** attribute. Set its value to **Use Intel VT/AMD-V for instruction set virtualization and software for MMU virtualization**, as shown in Figure 4-9.

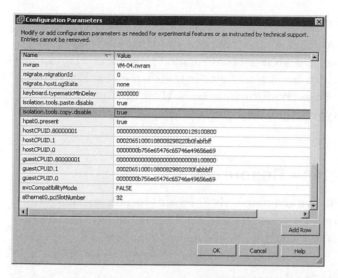

Figure 4-8 Additional VM configuration parameters.

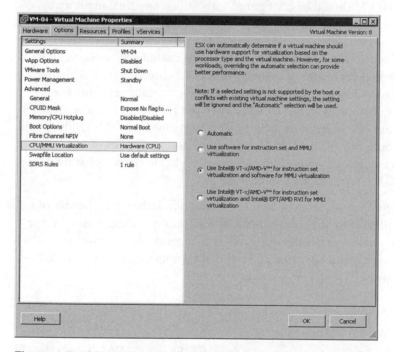

Figure 4-9 CPU/MMU virtualization attribute.

Configure Advanced Cluster Attributes

DRS clusters provide a means to set advanced options, much like ESXi hosts and VMs provide advanced setting and advanced configuration parameters. Many of the ESXi host and VM advanced attributes are covered in this chapter, but DRS cluster advanced attributes, such as **PowerPerformanceRatio**, **HostMinUptimeSecs**, **PowerPerformanceHistorySecs**, and **MinPoweredOnCpuCapacity**, are covered in Chapter 5, "Clusters."

Optimize Virtual Machine Resources

This section describes how to size and tune VMs. It provides details on configuring VM hardware, calculating available resources, and configuring the swap file. It provides examples and scenarios involving the vSphere Client and the vCLI.

Tune Virtual Machine Memory Configurations

At a minimum, each VM should be configured with sufficient virtual memory to meet the O/S and application manufacturers' recommendations for the VM. This includes meeting the manufacturers' recommendations to accommodate the expected peak workload for the VM. In most cases, a VM should not be configured with a significantly higher amount of memory than it is expected to use. Although ESXi is designed to intelligently manage memory and is typically capable of reclaiming any excess memory assigned to VMs when the ESXi host is under memory pressure, the practice of continuously assigning excess memory to VMs tends to lead to issues. For example, if a specific VM is expected to need only 2GB of memory but you choose to configure it with 4GB memory, then a side effect is that the VM's swap file is also 4GB, which can waste disk space.

If a VM is not performing well due to memory contention rather than the size of its memory, you might want to increase its memory reservation to determine whether the performance improves. A sensible approach is to increase the reservation gradually to a point at which further increases do not make a noticeable performance improvement to the user.

Scenario—Determine the VM Memory Size

Your customer wants to run vCenter Server 5.1 in a Windows 2008 VM. The vCenter Server database, vCenter Single Sign On, Inventory Service, and VMware Update Manager will run elsewhere. She plans to use vCenter Server to manage 2 ESXi hosts and 50 VMs. She seeks your advice on the amount of memory to configure for the VM.

To meet this requirement, you can examine the Installing VMware vCenter Server 5.1 Best Practices knowledgebase article (KB 2021202), which reveals that the minimum supported memory for running just vCenter Server 5.1 in a Windows VM is 4GB and no additional memory is required in deployments with fewer than 50 ESXi hosts and fewer than 500 VMs. Based on this information, you might decide to configure the VM memory for 4GB.

Tune Virtual Machine Networking Configurations

VMware recommends that you choose to use VMXNET3 virtual network adapters for all your VMs that run a supported guest O/S for VMXNET3 and have VMware Tools installed. The VMXNET3 virtual adapter is optimized, such that it provides higher throughput, lower latency, and less overhead than other virtual adapter choices. But, operating system vendors do not provide the driver for the VMXNET3 virtual adapter. The VMXNET driver is supplied by VMware Tools.

Tune Virtual Machine CPU Configurations

At a minimum, each VM should be configured with enough virtual CPU resources to meet the O/S and application manufacturers' recommendations for the VM. This includes meeting the manufacturers' recommendations to accommodate the expected peak workload for the VM. In most cases, a VM should not be configured with more virtual CPU cores than it is expected to need. Although ESXi is designed to intelligently schedule CPU activity and fairly grant CPU access to VMs using shares, when the ESXi host is under CPU pressure, the practice of continuously assigning excess virtual CPU cores to VMs tends to lead to issues. For example, consider a case where the CPUs in an ESXi host are currently being stressed and the contention is causing one of the VMs to perform poorly. It is possible that if you add more virtual CPU cores to the VM that its performance could actually worsen, due to the extra burden of scheduling more virtual CPUs.

If a VM is not performing well due to CPU contention rather than the number of virtual CPU cores, you might want to increase its CPU reservation to see if the performance improves. A sensible approach is to increase the reservation gradually to a point at which further increases do not make a noticeable performance improvement to the user.

Scenario—Determine the VM CPU Core Count

Your customer wants to run vCenter Server 5.1 in a Windows 2008 VM. The vCenter Server database, vCenter Single Sign On, Inventory Service, and VMware Update Manager will run elsewhere. He plans to use vCenter Server to manage 2 ESXi hosts and 10 VMs. He seeks your advice on the number of virtual CPU cores to configure for the VM.

To meet this requirement, you can examine the Installing VMware vCenter Server 5.1 Best Practices knowledgebase article (KB 2021202), which reveals that the minimum number of CPU cores supported for running just vCenter Server 5.1 in a Windows server is 2 and no additional CPU cores are required in deployments with less than 50 ESXi hosts and less than 500 VMs. Based on this information, you might decide to configure the VM with 2 virtual CPU cores.

Tune Virtual Machine Storage Configurations

When addressing VM performance, you might need to address and tune its storage configuration. In many cases the placement of the VM onto a particular datastore has a significant impact on its performance. Ensure the VM is not experiencing high I/O latency due to overworked LUNs. Ensure that the LUN on which the datastore resides is configured with appropriate disks, RAID type, and cache to meet the concurrent peak I/O requirements of all the virtual machines housed on the datastore. If I/O becomes constrained on the datastore, the issue might be resolved by using Storage vMotion to migrate one or more VMs to datastores that have fewer competing workloads or that are configured for better performance.

Another storage configuration option to consider is the virtual SCSI controller type. In most cases, the default virtual SCSI controller type, which is based on the guest O/S type, is adequate. If a VM's disk throughput is not adequate, you could consider modifying its virtual SCSI controller type to *VMware Paravirtual*, as illustrated in Figure 4-10. This choice does require the installation of VMware Tools in the VM to provide the appropriate driver, and it requires a supported guest O/S.

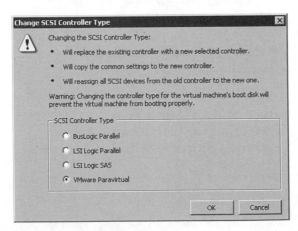

Figure 4-10 Changing the SCSI controller type to VMware paravirtual.

You should ensure the file system used by the guest O/S is properly configured for proper track alignment. In a modern guest O/S, the default settings should properly align the tracks of the file system, but this should be verified—preferably before creating VM templates. The steps for proper track alignment are unique in each guest O/S type. For example, in Windows 2003, the diskpart command could be used to properly align the NTFS partitions.

When configuring a VM for maximum performance, configure the virtual disk type as thick provision eager-zeroed, which preallocates the disk space and pre-zeroes the bits in the virtual disk. This is the best performing virtual disk type because it does not have to obtain new physical disk blocks or write zeros to newly accessed blocks at runtime.

In rare cases, VMs could be configured to use raw device mappings (RDMs) to remove the VMFS layering.

Calculate Available Resources

Prior to deploying new VMs or increasing the size of existing VMs, you should examine the target ESXi host, resource pool, and cluster for available resources. For an ESXi host, you could use the **Overview** graphs on the **Performance** tab to determine CPU and memory utilization. The CPU(%) graph could be used to determine how much CPU capacity is being utilized and how much CPU capacity is available. Likewise, the Memory(%) graph could be used to determine how much memory capacity is being utilized and how much memory capacity is available. These are good tools to use when making decisions based on actual unused resources. But, in many cases, the main concern is to guarantee that VMs and applications receive sufficient resources to ensure that certain performance levels are met. In these cases, the best tool to determine the available resources can be the **Resource Allocation** tab of the associated resource pool or cluster. The resource allocation tab provides the **Total**, **Reserved**, and **Available Capacity** for the entire cluster or resource pool. It also provides details on each VM, including the **Reservation**, **Limit**, and **Shares** for both **CPU** and **Memory**. The information on the **Resource Allocation** tab enables you to size VMs based on reservations rather than on actual usage. Figure 4-11 illustrates an example of the **Resource Allocation** tab for a resource pool named *Test*, where the memory reservation of one VM is 512MB and the available memory reservation of the pool is 3338MB.

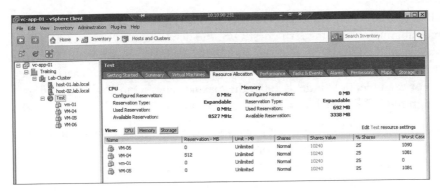

Figure 4-11   Memory resource allocation for the test resource pool.

Properly Size a Virtual Machine Based on Application Workload

First, size each VM according to vendor recommendations for the guest O/S, application, and workload. As mentioned in previous sections, ensure that the virtual memory size and the number of virtual CPU cores in each VM is at least as large as any supported minimum requirements identified for the software application in the VM. Additionally, ensure that the VM's memory and CPU are sized accordingly with any vendor recommendations based on the expected workload. For example, Microsoft might publish memory and CPU recommendations for Exchange servers based on the number of mailboxes or concurrent users. Next, adjust the memory and CPU size of each VM based on measured usage. For example, if a VM consistently uses 80% or more of its available CPU resources, then you should consider adding more virtual CPU cores. Or if a VM's guest O/S is swapping internally, you should consider adding more virtual memory. In either case, making these increases would be warranted only if the current utilization is causing the VM to perform badly. High utilization does not always correlate to poor performance.

As a general rule, don't size the memory and CPU of many VMs much higher than necessary. Doing so can cause performance issues for those and other VMs. For example, configuring excess virtual CPUs for a VM makes the job of scheduling its virtual CPUs much more difficult for the VMkernel. If a VM already suffered from poor performance due to CPU contention for available ESXi host resources, increasing its number of virtual CPU can make it run more slowly. If most VMs are configured with twice as many virtual CPU cores as needed, it might reduce the number of VMs that you could place on the ESXi host before performance is noticeably degraded. If Windows 2008 VMs are configured with more memory than needed, the memory consumption on the ESXi host might be extremely high because the VMs might be using large pages, which cannot be shared by the VMkernel. This can cause the ESXi host to enter soft and hard memory states with fewer VMs running on the hosts than necessary, which in turn triggers ballooning, swapping, and compression.

Scenario—Size a VM Based on Workload

Your customer wants to run vCenter Server 5.1 in a Windows 2008 VM. The vCenter Server database, vCenter Single Sign On, Inventory Service, and VMware Update Manager will run elsewhere. She plans to use vCenter Server to manage 150 ESXi hosts and 1,000 VMs. She seeks your advice on the amount of memory and the number of virtual CPU cores to configure for the VM.

To meet this requirement, you can examine the Installing VMware vCenter Server 5.1 Best Practices knowledgebase article (KB 2021202), which reveals that the minimum supported memory for running just vCenter Server 5.1 in a Windows Server is 4GB and the minimum number of cores is 2. But, it also reveals that VMware recommends configuring at least 8GB memory and 4 CPU cores if the deployment includes between 50 and 300 ESXi hosts and between 500 and 3,000 VMs. Given this information, you might choose to configure the VM with 8GB virtual memory and 4 virtual CPU cores.

Modify Large Memory Page Settings

Many modern guest operating systems are configured to use large memory pages by default. Likewise, ESXi is configured to support and deliver large memory pages by default. In other words, in many cases today, no additional effort is needed to enable ESXi hosts to successfully deliver large memory pages for guest O/S use. However, some guest operating systems might be unable to utilize large memory pages or might require some configuration to use large memory pages. For example, in Windows Server 2003, the system administrator must grant a privilege called "lock pages in memory" to user accounts that run applications where the use of large memory pages would be beneficial. To accomplish this, the following steps can be performed:

Step 1.   Log on to Windows using the Administrator account.

Step 2.   Select **Start > Control Panel > Administrator Tools > Local Security Policy**.

Step 3.   In the left pane, expand **Local Policies** and select **User Rights Assignment**.

Step 4.   In the right pane, right-click **Lock pages in memory** and select **Properties**.

Step 5.   In the **Local Security Setting** dialog box, click **Add User or Group**.

Step 6. Enter the appropriate username, and click **OK**.

Step 7. On the **Ready to Complete** page, click **Finish**.

The interfaces used in this procedure are illustrated in Figure 4-12.

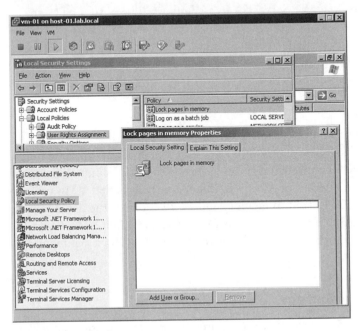

Figure 4-12   Configuring a Windows Server 2003 user to support large memory pages.

Large memory page support is enabled in ESXi 5.x by default. The advanced setting named **Mem.AllocGuestLargePage** can be used to view and modify support for large memory pages per ESXi host. Likewise, the setting **monitor_control. disable_mmu_largepages** can be set in a VM's configuration file to control its capability to use large pages. One use case for modifying this setting involves its impact on transparent page sharing.

Scenario—Disable Large Memory Pages

In a specific vSphere environment running Windows 2008 R2 VMs, the administrator observes that memory consumption is higher than expected on an ESXi host. His investigation reveals that the host is not benefitting from transparent page sharing because the ESXi host is incapable of sharing large memory pages and all the VMs are utilizing large pages. He learns that VMware intends for VMs and ESXi hosts to use large pages, when feasible, to improve the performance and reduce overhead memory usage. He theorizes that given the current workload, the performance of the VMs on the ESXi host would not be noticeably impacted if he disabled the use of large memory pages, although this can cause an increased number of TLB misses for the hardware-assisted MMU virtualization. To test his theory, he decides to disable large memory page support on the host.

To accomplish this task, the administrator can perform the following steps:

Step 1. Using the vSphere Client, navigate to **Inventory > Hosts and Clusters** and select the ESXi host.

Step 2. Click the **Configuration** tab.

Step 3. Select **Software > Advanced Settings**.

Step 4. In the Advanced Settings dialog box, select **Mem**.

Step 5. In the right pane, set **Mem.AllocGuestLargePage** to 0.

Step 6. Click **OK**.

Understand Appropriate Use Cases for CPU Affinity

By default, the VMkernel is permitted to schedule the VM's virtual CPU cores to run on any of the logical CPUs provided by the ESXi host hardware. You can modify this behavior and force the ESXi host to restrict the logical CPUs that can be used for running a VM. Using the vSphere Client, you can select **Edit Settings** to modify the settings of a VM and use the **Resources** tab to modify the **Advanced CPU** settings of a VM. You can use the **Advanced CPU** settings to configure **Scheduling Affinity** for the VM's virtual CPUs. In the provided text box, you can specify the logical CPUs that are permitted for use by the VM by listing individual logical CPU numbers and ranges of logical CPU numbers. For example, on an ESXi host with 16 logical CPUs, numbered from 0 to 15, a valid setting for Scheduling Affinity is "1,3,5,7-10". Figure 4-13 is an example of a VM's **Advanced CPU** settings page.

VMware recommends that you use CPU scheduling affinity only in very rare cases. One primary reason is that vMotion is not functional with VMs configured with CPU scheduling affinity. If a VM resides in a DRS cluster, enabling CPU scheduling affinity is disabled. One valid use case for using CPU scheduling affinity is for troubleshooting purposes. If you are troubleshooting the performance of a CPU intensive VM, you might wonder if its performance would improve if you migrated it to CPU hardware that is not used by other VMs. If you do not have the flexibility of temporarily running just one VM on an ESXi host, the next best choice might be to use CPU scheduling affinity to configure the VM to use specific logical CPUs and to configure all other VMs to use the remaining logical CPUs.

CPU scheduling affinity is also a useful tool for testing and capacity planning purposes. For example, you might be interested in measuring a VM's throughput and response time when it is pinned along with a set of competing VMs to a specific set of logical CPUs.

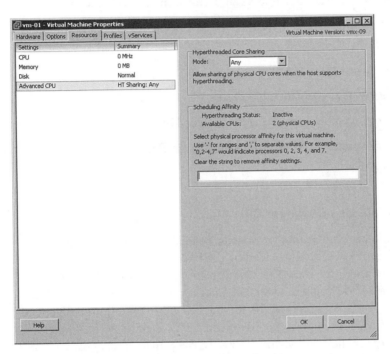

Figure 4-13 The CPU scheduling affinity setting page.

Configure Alternative Virtual Machine Swap Locations

The location of the VM's swap file can be set at the VM level, ESXi host level, and cluster level. You can use the **Options** tab > **Advanced** > **General** > **Configurations Parameters** in the VM's properties to add a row for the **sched.swap.dir** parameter. Set its value to the full path to relocate the VM's swap file. This setting will not take effect until the VM is power cycled.

Alternatively, you can change the VM swap file location for an entire cluster. The first step is to edit the settings of the cluster and set the **Swap File Location** to **Store the swap file in the datastore specified by the host**. The next step is to use the **Configuration** tab for the ESXi host to select **Software** > **Virtual Machine Swapfile Location** and click **Edit**. In the **Virtual Machine Swapfile Location** dialog box, select the datastore to use to store the swap file for all VMs on the host and click **OK**, as illustrated in Figure 4-14.

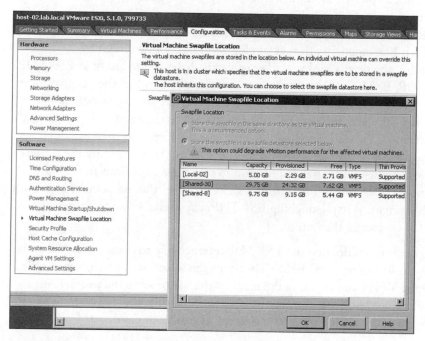

Figure 4-14   VM swap file location setting.

NOTE   The standard VM swap file (VSWP) file is unrelated to the VMX swap file, which is used to reduce the memory requirement for the VM's VMX process when the ESXi host experiences memory pressure.

Utilize Advanced vSphere Performance Monitoring Tools

This section describes how to collect and analyze performance data for VMs and ESXi hosts using advanced methods. It provides details on using advanced features available in ESXTOP and RESXTOP and on utilizing the vscsiStats utility. It also provides examples and scenarios of using these utilities in specific use cases.

Configure ESXTOP/RESXTOP Custom Profiles

As described in Chapter 1, "Administrator Tools," in this guide, ESXTOP is a tool that can be used in the ESXi Shell to interactively display resource usage statistics per world. RESXTOP is a nearly identical command that is designed for remote use from the vCLI. For simplicity, the remainder of this section will refer to the ESXTOP utility, but the details in this section can actually be applied to both ESXTOP and RESXTOP. ESXTOP enables the user to interactively select the resource type to be monitored. For example, the user can press the **n** key to display network statistics. It enables the user to select the fields to include in the display. For example, when monitoring CPU statistics, the user can press the **f** key and then use the **h** key to toggle the display of the **CPU Summary Stats** fields. After selecting the resource type and selecting fields, the user might want to save these selections to facilitate making identical selections in the future. ESXTOP allows the use of custom profiles to save such changes. When launching ESXTOP, any available custom profiles can be specified to customize the output.

To create a custom profile, first use ESXTOP interactively to make all the desired selections for resource type and fields. Then save the selections in a custom profile by pressing the **W** key and entering the name of the file to store the profile. After creating the custom profile, to use it with ESXTOP, provide the **–c** switch followed by the filename of the profile when entering the **esxtop** command.

Key Topic

For example, to create a custom profile named *jad-03* that can be used to display just memory swap statistics, the following steps can be used. In this example, the host name is *host-01.lab.local*:

Step 1. In the ESXi Shell, enter **esxtop**.

Step 2. Press the **m** key to display memory statistics.

Step 3. Press the **f** key to display the available memory fields.

Step 4. Press the **k** key to select the **SWAP STATS** fields. Press the **h** key, the **l** key, and the **o** key to deselect some other statistics.

Step 5. Press the **V** key to display only the VM worlds.

Step 6. Press the **W** key to save the settings in a custom profile.

Step 7. When prompted, enter *jad-03*, as illustrated in Figure 4-15. The file is saved in the present working directory because *jad-03* is not a fully qualified name. Alternatively, a fully qualified name could have been used.

Step 8. Press the **q** key to quit RESXTOP.

Step 9. Enter this **esxtop -c jad-03** to open ESXTOP with the custom profile, which must be in the present working directory because it is not a fully qualified name.

Step 10.   Verify that ESXTOP opens to the memory statistics and that only the swap statistics fields are displayed. Notice that the selection to display only VMs was not saved as part of the custom profile.

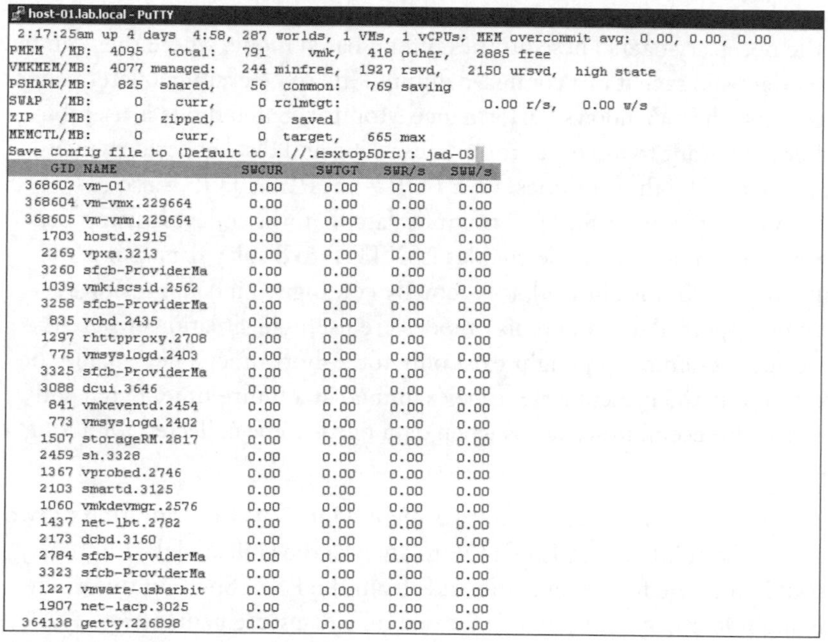

Figure 4-15   Saving a custom profile in ESXTOP.

You can maintain multiple custom profiles for use with ESXTOP. You can also modify the default ESXTOP profile, which enables you to control the data that is displayed by ESXTOP when it is opened without specifying a custom profile. To modify the default profile for ESXTOP, enter **esxtop** to open ESXTOP without using a custom profile, make the desired selections, and then use the **W** key to save selections without entering a filename. This allows the settings to be saved in the default profile, which is stored at */.esxtop50rc*. (The default profile for RESXTOP is */home/vi-admin/.esxtop50rc*.)

ESXTOP Interactive, Batch, and Replay Modes

ESXTOP and RESXTOP are not typically required for daily activities by most vSphere administrators. Instead, administrators typically use the performance graphs in the vSphere Client and the vSphere Web Client to examine resource usage and to troubleshoot performance issues. The main use case for utilizing ESXTOP and RESXTOP is when the administrator needs more granular information than the data provided by the performance graphs. For example, if data samples need to be taken at a higher frequency than every 20 seconds, RESXTOP is a better choice than performance graphs.

The interactive mode provided by ESXTOP and RESXTOP is useful in situations where the current workload is rather steady and the administrator has ample time to examine all the necessary data. These utilities offer a batch mode, where they can be used to collect data and save it in a comma-delimited file to be examined later using third-party tools, such as Windows Performance Monitor. Batch mode is useful in situations where you want to use other tools to examine and display performance data that was collected by these utilities. ESXTOP—not RESXTOP—also offers a replay mode that allows ESXTOP to input data that was collected using the **vm-support** command. Replay mode enables ESXTOP to display data as if it was coming from a live ESXi host; instead, it is actually coming from data previously collected by vm-support. Batch and replay modes are useful in situations where the workload that needs examination might exist only for a short time. They enable the data to be collected in the present time to be examined at a future time. Batch and replay modes are also useful in scenarios when data needs to be collected for a long period of time.

For example, if you want to collect data at two-second intervals for a duration of two minutes and have the ability to use ESXTOP to analyze the collected data in replay mode, you could enter the following commands from the ESXi Shell. In this example, a preexisting folder named *tmp* that it located on a datastore named *Shared-30* is used to store the data files produced during the collection:

Step 1.   Change the folder to the temp folder by entering

```
cd /vmfs/volumes/Shared-30/tmp
```

Step 2.   Generate the batch collection by entering

```
vm-support -p -d 120 -i 2 -w /vmfs/volumes/Shared-30/tmp
```

Step 3.   Locate the output file using the **ls** command.

Step 4.   Extract the file by entering

```
tar -xzf esx-host-01.lab.local-2014-01-14--13.18.tgz
```

Step 5.   Locate the appropriate folder using the **ls** command.

Step 6.   Change the folder to the appropriate location using

```
cd esx-host-01.lab.local-2014-01-14--13.18/
```

Step 7.   Execute the reconstruct script using

```
./reconstruct.sh
```

Step 8.   Change to the parent folder and replay the batch collection using:

```
esxtop -R esx-host-01.lab.local-2014-01-14--13.18
```

Figure 4-16 contains a screenshot illustrating these commands.

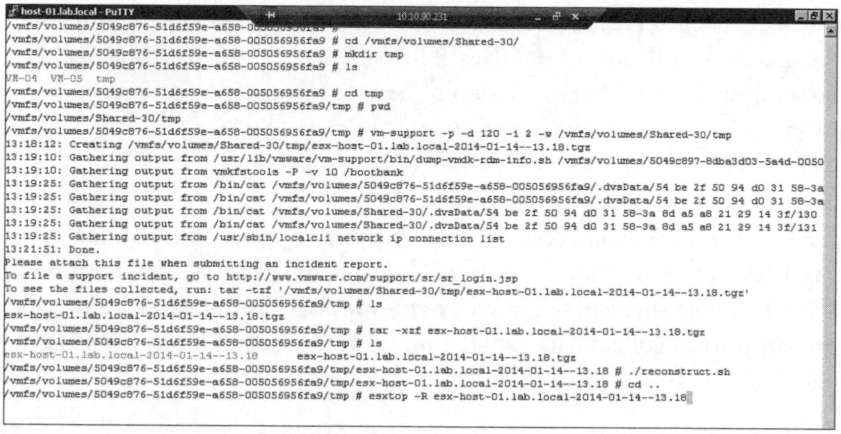

Figure 4-16   ESXTOP replay mode.

In this example, the **–p** parameter is used with the **vm-support** command to instruct it to collect performance data. The **–d** parameter is used to set the duration to 120 seconds, and the **–i** parameter is used to set the interval to 2 seconds. The **–w** parameter is used to set the target directory for the output file. In Figure 4-16, after the **vm-support** command completes, a message appears that identifies the output TGZ file. This filename is then used in the **tar** command that extracts the contents of the TGZ file, using the **–xzf** parameters. The **ls** commands are used to illustrate the files and folders that exist in the **tmp** folder prior to and after the execution of the **tar** command. After the **tar** command execution completes, the **cd esx-host-01.lab.local-2014-01-14--13.18/** is used to change the default directory into the directory produced by the **tar** command. Next, the files used for replay are prepared by executing the **reconstruct.sh** script. Finally, **esxtop –R** is used to open ESXTOP in replay mode using the prepared data, which is identified by using the directory name.

Chapter 1 of this guide contains an example of using ESXTOP in batch mode to collect data and display it using the Windows Performance Monitor.

Scenario—ESXTOP Replay Modes

You need to troubleshoot an issue where certain VMs experience poor performance during each night during a time period when backup operations are in a vSphere 5.1 environment. You want to collect performance data on a specific ESXi host during the peak time of the backup and then have the ability to examine the data carefully and repeatedly using ESXTOP for several days. The peak time of the backup begins at 2 a.m. and lasts for about one hour. You want to be able to examine the data at up to 10-second intervals.

Key Topic

To address these needs, you could collect data using **vm-support** and examine the data using ESXTOP replay mode. You could decide to use a VMFS datastore named *VMFS-01* to hold the data prepared by **vm-support**. Promptly at 2 a.m., you could use **vm-support** to collect data for 60 minutes at 10-second intervals, using this command.

```
vm-support -p -d 3600 -i 10 -w /vmfs/volumes/VMFS-01
```

After the collection is finished, you can use the steps provided in the previous example to finish preparing the data using the **tar** command and **reconstruct.sh** script. After the data is prepared, use the ESXTOP replay mode to examine the data with the **esxtop –R** command and the name of the folder where the prepared data resides.

Use vscsiStats to Gather Storage Performance Data

The vscsiStats utility, which is available in the ESXi Shell, can be used to troubleshoot VM storage performance-related issues. It can be used to collect data at the virtual SCSI device level in the VMkernel and report the data using histograms. It collects data on each I/O operation and reports on I/O metrics such as length, seek distance, number of outstanding I/Os, I/O latency, and inter-arrival time. So, it covers more storage statistics than ESXTOP, which covers only latency and throughput statistics. Because it works at the virtual SCSI device level, it can be used to analyze the storage activity of virtual disks regardless of storage type. For example, it can be utilized to analyze latency for NFS traffic.

This data can be useful for characterizing the associated workload. For example, if vscsiStats reports that seek distance for a large majority of the IOs during a specific sampling period is very small, the workload can be sequential. This information can be useful in determining the best choice for the RAID type that services the workload.

The first step for using vscsiStats is to determine the world ID and handle IDs associated with the VM you intend to monitor. You can use the **vcsiStats –l** command to list information on all currently running VMs and their virtual disks, including the *worldGroupID* of each VM and the *handleID* of each virtual disk. The second step is to start the data collection for a specific single virtual disk or for all virtual disks associated with a specific VM. To start the data collection for all virtual disks used by a specific VM whose *worldGroupID* is 1000, use this command:

```
vscsiStats -s -w 1000
```

To start the data collection for a specific virtual disk whose *handleID* is 2000 that is used by a specific VM whose *worldGroupID* is 1000, enter this command:

```
vscsiStats -s -w 1000 -i 2000
```

The data collection runs in the background. While the data collection is running, you can use **vscsiStats -p** option to print a histogram for a specific statistic. The choices for statistics are *iolength*, *seekDistance*, *outstandingIOs*, *latency*, and *interarrival*. For example, this command can be used to print a histogram for the latency statistic:

```
vscsiStats -p latency
```

Figure 4-17 shows the results of a sample execution of this command. In this example, for the first disk, no I/Os completed in 100 microseconds or less; no I/Os took longer than 15,000 microseconds; and 55 I/Os experienced latency between 100 and 500 microseconds.

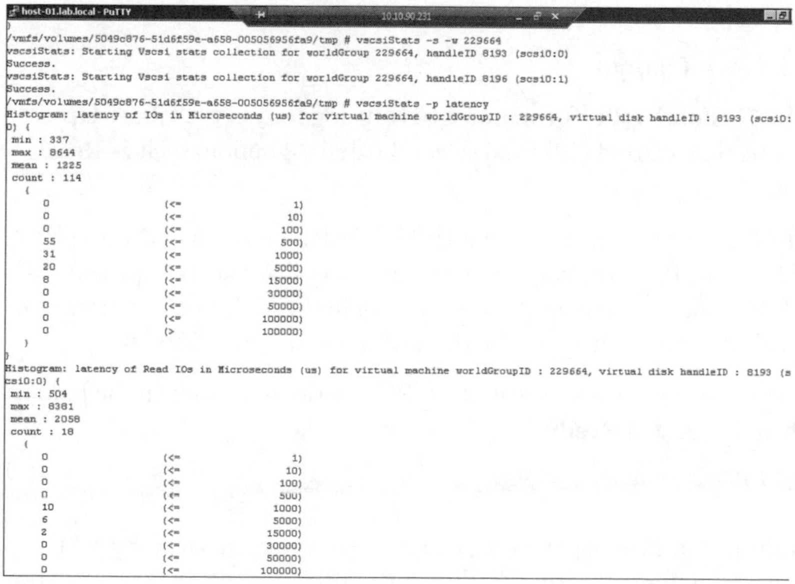

Figure 4-17 Latency histogram by vscsiStats.

By default, the data collection will run for 30 minutes, but you can stop it by entering the following command:

```
vscsiStats -x
```

Troubleshoot CPU and Memory Performance

This section describes how to troubleshoot CPU- and memory-related issues that affect ESXi host and VM performance. It provides details on performance metrics that can be used to identify specific performance issues. It includes examples that involve the use of the vSphere Client and the vCLI.

Troubleshoot CPU Performance Issues

You can use the vSphere Client, as well as other tools like ESXTOP and RESXTOP, to troubleshoot CPU performance issues that impact ESXi hosts and VMs. The vSphere Client provides two types of performance graphs for ESXi hosts and VMs, overview and advanced. The advanced graphs, which provide the most granular data, are typically more useful for CPU troubleshooting than the overview graphs. The steps for using the vSphere Client advanced graphs to analyze CPU performance issues are as follows:

Step 1.   In the inventory pane, select either the ESXi host or VM.

Step 2.   Select the **Performance** tab.

Step 3.   Select **Advanced**.

Step 4.   Click **Chart Options**.

Step 5.   In the **Customize Performance Chart** dialog box, in the **Chart Options** section, expand CPU and select the desired option, such as **Real Time**.

Step 6.   In the **Objects** section, select the CPU objects to include in the graph. For example, for VMs, you can select an object that matches the name of the VM, which represents all CPU activity in the VM. You can also select individual virtual CPUs used by the VM, such as virtual CPU **0**.

Step 7.   In the **Counters** section, select the CPU metrics to include in the graph, such as **Usage** and **Ready**.

Step 8.   Click **OK**.

Figure 4-18 illustrates an example of customizing a performance chart for a VM named *vm-01* that is configured with a single virtual CPU.

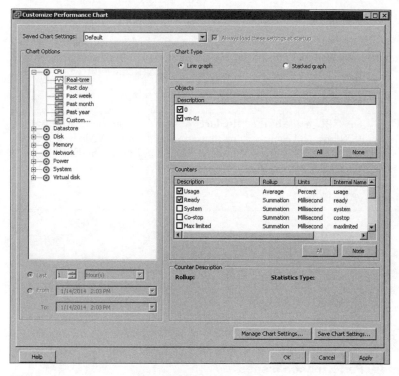

Figure 4-18 Custom VM CPU chart options.

The vSphere Clients offer many CPU-related counters for use with advanced performance graphs. Certain counters are more useful than others for troubleshooting specific CPU-related issues. For example, for a poorly performing VM, high *CPU Ready Time* indicates that CPU contention exists, where the VM is contesting with other VMs for scheduled CPU time. Table 4-2 contains a set of potential CPU-related performance issues. For each potential issue, the table includes an Indicators column that contains details on using specific CPU counters in real graphs identify the issue. Also, for each potential issue, the table includes a column that lists some potential resolutions.

Table 4-2 Potential CPU Issues and Resolutions

Potential Issue	Indicators	Potential Resolutions
The VM is experiencing CPU contention.	CPU ready time for one or more of the VM's virtual CPUs is frequently 1000ms or more.	Migrate the VM to an ESXi host with available CPU resources. Increase the CPU shares or CPU reservation of the VM. Stop some competing VMs or migrate the VMs to other ESXi hosts. Decrease the CPU shares or CPU reservation of competing VMs.

Potential Issue	Indicators	Potential Resolutions
The VM's virtual CPU resources are insufficient to meet the current demand.	The CPU usage of the entire VM and of each of the VM's virtual CPUs are frequently 80% or higher.	Reconfigure the VM with additional virtual CPUs. Migrate the VM to an ESXi host with faster CPUs. Reduce the workload in the VM.
The ESXi host's CPU resources are insufficient to meet the current demand from its VMs.	The CPU usage of the ESXi host and each of its CPU cores are frequently 80% or higher. CPU latency is 5% or higher.	Reduce the workload on the ESXi hosts by migrating some of the VMs to less busy hosts. Add more CPUs to the ESXi host.

NOTE   Table 4.2 does not contain all the potential resolutions, just a few examples. Other potential resolutions exist. Likewise, it does not contain all the indicators, just a few of the strongest indicators.

Troubleshoot Memory Performance Issues

You can use the vSphere Client, as well as other tools like ESXTOP and RESX-TOP, to troubleshoot memory performance issues that impact ESXi hosts and VMs. The vSphere Client provides two types of performance graphs for ESXi hosts and VMs, overview and advanced. The advanced graphs, which provide the most granular data, are typically more useful for memory troubleshooting than the overview graphs. The steps for using the vSphere Client advanced graphs to analyze memory performance issues are shown here:

Step 1.   In the **Inventory** pane, select either the ESXi host or VM.

Step 2.   Select the **Performance** tab.

Step 3.   Select **Advanced**.

Step 4.   Click **Chart Options**.

Step 5.   In the **Customize Performance Chart** dialog box, in the **Chart Options** section, expand **Memory** and select the desired option, such as **Real Time**.

Step 6.   In the **Objects** section, select the memory objects to include in the graph. For example, for VMs, you can select an object that matches the name of the VM, which represents all memory usage of the VM.

Step 7.   In the **Counters** section, select the memory metrics to include in the graph, such as **Balloon** and **Active**.

Step 8.   Click **OK**.

Figure 4-19 illustrates an example of customizing a performance chart for a VM named *vm-01* that is configured with 1GB virtual memory.

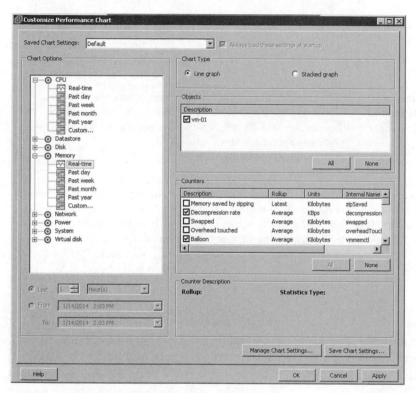

Figure 4-19   Custom VM memory chart options.

A number of memory-related counters are available for use with advanced performance graphs. Certain counters are more useful than others for troubleshooting specific memory-related issues. For example, for a poorly performing VM, a high *Swap in rate* indicates that memory contention exists, where the VM is competing with other VMs for access to physical memory. Table 4-3 contains a set of potential memory-related performance issues. For each potential issue, the table includes an Indicators column that contains details on using specific Memory counters in real-time graphs to identify the issue. Also, for each potential issue, the table includes a column that lists some potential resolutions.

Table 4-3   Potential Memory Issues and Resolutions

Issue	Indicators	Potential Resolutions
The VM is experiencing memory contention.	Memory Ballooning, Memory Decompression Rate, and/ or Memory Swap In Rate is greater than zero.	Migrate the VM to an ESXi host with available memory resources. Increase the memory shares or memory reservation of the VM. Stop some competing VMs or migrate the VMs to other ESXi hosts. Decrease the memory shares or memory reservation of competing VMs.
The VM's virtual memory resources are insufficient to meet the current demand.	The memory usage of the VM is about 100%. Memory latency is 5% or higher, which indicates that the VM is waiting to access swapped or compressed data.	Reconfigure the VM with additional virtual memory. Reduce the workload in the VM.
The ESXi host's memory resources are insufficient to meet the current demand from its VMs.	Memory state is 3 (hard) or 4 (low), which indicates that the ESXi host is swapping and compressing memory. Memory latency is 5% or higher.	Reduce the workload on the ESXi host by migrating some VMs to ESXi hosts with available memory resources. Add more memory to the ESXi host.

Other indicators that a VM's virtual memory resources are insufficient to meet the demand from its current workload can be found within the guest O/S. For example, the Performance Monitor on a Windows VM could be used to examine the **Pages per sec** counter, which indicates that Windows is actively swapping data in from its page file.

Use Hot-Add Functionality to Address CPU and Memory Performance Issues

As indicated in the previous sections, CPU and memory can be added to VMs to resolve certain performance issues. In many cases, CPU and memory can be added to running VMs without user interruption, by making use of the vSphere feature to hot-add CPU and memory to a VM. Naturally, the guest O/S in the VM must be capable of accepting memory increases or CPU additions while the guest O/S is running. An ESXi host will allow the configured memory of the VM to be increased if the guest O/S supports the increase and the VM is configured to permit memory hot-add. Likewise, an ESXi host will allow virtual CPUs to be added to a VM if the guest O/S supports the increase and the VM is configured to permit CPU hot-add.

To configure memory and CPU hot-add for a VM, use the vSphere Client and follow these steps:

Step 1. Ensure the VM is powered down.

Step 2. Right-click the VM and select **Edit Settings**.

Step 3. Select the **Options** tab.

Step 4. Click **Memory/CPU Hotplug**.

Step 5. Check the **Enable memory hot add for this virtual machine** option. Then check either **Enable CPU hot add only for this virtual machine** or **Enable CPU hot add and remove for this virtual machine**.

Step 6. Click **OK**.

After successful completion of these steps, the VM will be able to increase its memory and/or add virtual CPUs while the VM is running. Figure 4-20 illustrates an example of what the **Options** tab shows for a VM whose guest operating system (in this case Windows 2003 Standard 32-bit) does not support CPU hot-add.

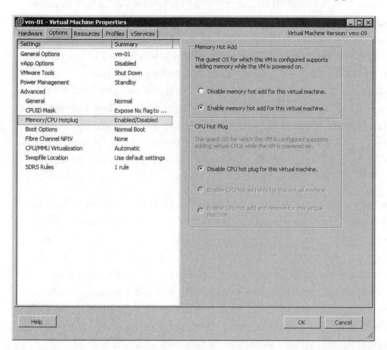

Figure 4-20 Hot-add CPU and RAM.

NOTE   The setting to enable hot-add of CPU and memory is disabled by default for each VM. This setting can be enabled only while the VM is powered off. So, if you want to use this feature for a VM, be sure to enable the hot-add feature shortly after creating the VM.

Troubleshoot Network Performance and Connectivity

This section describes how to use commands and other tools to troubleshoot network performance and connectivity issues. It provides details on troubleshooting distributed virtual switches, private VLANs, and DNS issues. It provides details for using the net-dvs utility, the Direct Console User Interface (DCUI), and port mirroring for troubleshooting. It provides examples and scenarios of where each of these tools can be applied.

Use net-dvs to Troubleshoot vSphere Distributed Switch Configurations

Key Topic

The **net-dvs** command can be used from the ESXi Shell or the vCLI to display information about a distributed vSwitch (dvSwitch) configuration for an ESXi host. As explained in Chapter 2, "Network Administration," the configuration of dvSwitches is managed by vCenter Server, but each ESXi host that connects to a dvSwitch receives details about the configuration and stores this data in a local file named **/etc/vmware/dvsdata.db**. The ESXi host ensures the data in the **dvsdata.db** file is kept current by updating its contents at five-minute intervals. When executed, the **net-dvs** command examines this file and displays configuration details for the dvSwitch, distributed port groups, and ports. It also displays details on port statistics, much like the vSphere Client does on the **Ports** tab for a dvSwitch or distributed port group.

One use case for **net-dvs** is when networking troubleshooting is necessary but the vCenter Server is unavailable or unreachable. If the vCenter Server is not available and you need to examine the configuration of a dvSwitch, you could use the **net-dvs** command. To do so, you could simply enter **net-dvs** from the ESXi Shell, but the amount of information returned by the command is typically too much to easily process. You might prefer to enter **net-dvs | less**, which enables you to scroll forward and backward through the results. Or, you might prefer to output the results to a file and then use traditional commands like **grep**, **less**, **more**, **cat**, or **vi** to view the file. For example, to export the results of **net-dvs** to a file named **net-dvs-results**, use this command:

```
net-dvs  >> net-dvs-results
```

To use the **vi** text editor to view the **net-dvs-results** file, use this command:

```
vi net-dvs-results
```

Typically, the first line of this file begins with the string **switch**, which indicates the first row in a section that provides details on a specific dvSwitch. The following lines contain details about the configuration of the dvSwitch, such as *max ports* and *global properties*. To quickly find the first line for next dvSwitch section, press the **/** key and enter **switch** at the prompt (including a space character at the end). To navigate through each dvSwitch section, use the arrow keys on the keyboard. Each section contains many attribute names and corresponding values. Table 4-4 provides information for a few of the attributes, including a brief description.

Table 4-4 Attributes in **net-dvs** Results

Attribute Name	Description
com.vmware.common.alias	Name of the dvSwitch.
com.vmware.common.uplinkPorts	List of the dvSwitch's uplink port groups.
com.vmware.common.port.block	Indicates whether the port is blocked. For example, the value *false* indicates the port is not blocked.
com.vmware.common.port.teaming.load balancing	Load-balancing type assigned to a particular port. For example, one permitted value is *source virtual port id*.
com.vmware.common.port.statistics.pktsInDropped	Inbound dropped packets statistics for a particular port.

After using **vi** to view the file, you can close the file without changes. To do so, type the **:** key and enter **q!** at the prompt.

Use vSphere CLI Commands to Troubleshoot ESXi Network Configurations

Chapter 2 of this guide describes using the vCLI to configure and manage virtual networks. The information is also useful for troubleshooting ESXi network configurations. In many cases, the vCLI provides more than one command choice for performing certain network tasks, but the commands provided by the ESXCLI command set are typically preferred over other choices. The ESXCLI command set is available in the ESXi Shell as well as in the vCLI. During efforts to troubleshoot issues that affect the ESXi management network, access to the ESXi host from the vSphere Client, an SSH client, the vCLI, or the vMA might be unavailable. Troubleshooting ESXi network issues can require using ESXCLI commands from the ESXi Shell accessed directly from the ESXi host console. This section focuses on troubleshooting ESXi network issues using ESXCLI commands from the ESXi Shell, but it could be applied to using the vCLI, if available.

Chapters 1 and 2 of this guide provide details for using the ESXCLI command set, the ESXi Shell, and specific network-related commands. This section provides scenarios and sample solutions for troubleshooting specific ESXi network configuration issues.

Scenario—Troubleshoot the Management Interface

Using the vSphere Client connected to a vCenter Server, you see that a particular ESXi host is not responding. You perform several tests including attempts to connect a vSphere Client directly to the ESXi host and to ping the host from a node on the management network. These tests are unsuccessful. You want to examine the configuration of the VMkernel port used for management on the ESXi host and the associated standard vSwitch.

To address this challenge, you could access the ESXi Shell directly from the console and enter the following commands. The first command displays information on all of the ESXi host's vSwitches. The second command displays information on all the ESXi host's VMkernel ports:

```
esxcli network vswitch standard list
esxcli network vswitch standard portgroup list
```

Scenario—Configure VLAN

To correct a certain connectivity issue, you need to set the VLAN for the Management Network port group on a standard vSwitch to 100.

To address this need, you could access the ESXi Shell directly from the console and enter the following command:

```
esxcli network vswitch standard portgroup set -p 'Management Network'
-v 100
```

Scenario—View Speed and Duplex

You suspect that speed and duplex are set incorrectly on the physical network adapter vmnic1. You want to use the vCLI to examine these settings.

To address this challenge, you could use CLI to enter the following command:

```
esxcli network nic list
```

Troubleshoot Private VLANs

Configuring private VLANs (PVLANs) is covered in the Chapter 2 of this guide. Troubleshooting PVLAN issues mostly involves testing communication between virtual adapters that use the PVLANs and examining the configuration of the associated distributed port groups and associated physical switch ports. For VMs in a community secondary PVLAN, troubleshooting might involve using **ping** commands in the VMs to ensure they can communicate with each other, can communicate with VMs in promiscuous PVLANs, and cannot communicate with VMs any other PVLANs. For VMs in an isolated secondary PVLAN, troubleshooting can involve using **ping** commands in the VMs to ensure they can communicate with VMs in promiscuous PVLANs but cannot communicate with each other or with VMs in any other PVLANs. For VMs in a promiscuous secondary PVLAN, troubleshooting might involve using **ping** commands in the VMs to ensure they can communicate with each other and with VMs in all the PVLANs.

For example, consider a case in which the virtual network design calls for the use of three secondary PVLANs identified as 70-101, 70-102, and 7-103. 70-101 is a promiscuous secondary PVLAN, 70-102 is a community secondary PVLAN, and 70-103 is an isolated secondary PVLAN. During implementation testing, none of the associated distributed virtual port groups appear to work. You could begin troubleshooting by using the vSphere Client to examine the PVLAN settings of the dvSwitch and ensure that each of the three PVLANs is properly numbered and properly configured with the appropriate PVLAN type as in the design. You could then examine the configuration of each of the associated distributed port groups and ensure that each is assigned the appropriate PVLAN settings as stated in the design. You could also examine the configuration of the physical switch and ports where the dvSwitch uplinks connect and ensure that the switch and ports are also properly configured for these PVLANs.

As another example, consider the same network design used in the previous example. In this case, assume that multiple ESXi hosts and multiple VMs are successfully using all the PVLANs. But on one particular ESXi host, the VMs connected to the distributed port group assigned to the 70-102 PVLAN cannot successfully communicate with other VMs running on other ESXi hosts and connected to the same distributed port group. Because the VMs on the troubled ESXi host connect to the same distributed port group as VMs that are communicating successfully, you should be able to eliminate improper PVLAN type configuration as a potential root cause. In other words, if the wrong PVLAN type is assigned to the 70-102 PVLAN on the dvSwitch and the 70-102 PVLAN is assigned to a distributed port group, it would affect all VMs on all ESXi hosts that are connected to the distributed port group. A better fit for the root cause of the problem could be the configuration of the physical network ports, where the physical adapters from the troubled ESXi host are connected. If one of these ports is misconfigured, it could impact just the VMs on this specific ESXi host. Perhaps one of these ports is not properly configured to accept the 70-102 PVLAN.

Troubleshoot VMkernel-related Network Configuration Issues

Some examples of troubleshooting VMkernel configuration issues have already been provided in this chapter, but they focused on using the commands. This section covers other examples and provides a methodology.

Troubleshooting VMkernel-related network issues could begin with steps aimed at narrowing the scope of potential root causes, such as testing connectivity and examining settings. The tests typically involve using the **vmkping** command to test connectivity from a VMkernel port to another network end point. The settings to examine include those on the VMkernel virtual adapter, virtual port groups, vSwitches, and physical network infrastructure. Other troubleshooting steps, such as examining log files, can also be used. Here is a high-level methodology that could be applied for identifying the root cause of a networking issue that involves a VMkernel port on an ESXi host:

Step 1.   Use **vmkping** to test connectivity from a VMkernel port to other VMkernel ports on the same network and to other known working addresses on the network. Determine whether communication is successful with some end points and not successful with other end points.

Step 2.   Determine whether connectivity is successful with VMkernel ports and VMs connected to the same distributed virtual port group, which might require temporarily attaching VMs for test purposes. Determine whether communication is successful with virtual adapters on the same ESXi host, but not with virtual adapters on other ESXi hosts.

Step 3. If the issue seems to be isolated to just one VMkernel port, examine its IP address, mask, gateway settings, and other direct settings.

Step 4. If the problem appears to be isolated to a specific ESXi host, examine the corresponding virtual port group, vSwitch, and uplink settings. For example, ensure that the appropriate physical adapters are configured as **Active** uplinks.

Step 5. If the problem appears to be isolated to a specific virtual port group (standard or distributed), examine its settings, such as VLAN and Load Balancing policies.

Scenario—Test VMkernel Network Connectivity

You are troubleshooting an issue where vMotion migrations hang when the progress is near 10 percent and eventually fail with a connection timeout error. You suspect that the problem might be related to network connectivity issues between the vMotion VMkernel ports on the source and target hosts. To test connectivity, you need to use the ESXi Shell on the source ESXi host to ping the vMotion IP address of the target host, and vice versa. During these tests, you should ensure that the **ping** command uses the vMotion VMkernel port and not the management or other VMkernel ports on the ESXi host. The VMkernel port that is used for vMotion on each ESXi host is identified as *vmk1*. In this scenario, the IP address of the source vMotion port is 192.168.2.10 and the IP address of the target vMotion port is 192.168.2.11.

To address this need, you could begin by accessing the ESXi Shell on the source ESXi host and enter the following command to see whether the target VMkernel port responds:

```
vmkping -I vmk1 192.168.2.11
```

Scenario—Test VMkernel Network Connectivity

You are troubleshooting an issue where vMotion migrations between two particular ESXi hosts (*host-01* and *host-02*) always fail, but vMotion migrations between either of these two ESXi hosts and other ESXi hosts succeed occasionally. For example, you successfully migrated a couple VMs between ESXi hosts *host-01* and *host-03*, but many of the attempts to use vMotion between these two hosts fail. In your attempts to use **vmkping** to test connectivity between the vMotion VMkernel port on *host-01* and the vMotion VMkernel ports on *host-02* and *host-03*, the tests to *host-02* always fail, but tests to *host-03* occasionally fail and occasionally succeed with no recognizable pattern.

This scenario could be caused by duplicate IPs on the vMotion VMkernel ports on *host-01* and *host-02*. When troubleshooting VMkernel network connectivity issues where tests fail and succeed intermittently, consider whether duplicate IP addresses could be the root cause. This could be determined by first temporarily disconnecting, disabling, or deleting one the associated VMkernel ports and then pinging its address to see whether some other network node responds to the ping. Another approach is to examine the events and logs of the ESXi hosts to search for messages indicating duplicate IP addresses.

Troubleshoot DNS- and Routing-related Issues

Many DNS-related issues can be identified by performing tests that involve IP addresses instead of hostnames. For example, if you suspect that the DNS settings on an ESXi host are incorrect or that their DNS servers are not successfully resolving some names, you could begin by using **vmkping** tests from the ESXi Shell on the host. First, use **vmkping** to test connectivity to known servers on the management network and networks that are reachable from the management network. For these tests, use the hostnames of the target servers and ensure the target servers can be pinged from other sources. If these tests fail, repeat the tests, but this time use the IP address of each target server. If the second test succeeds but the first test fails, then the problem might be DNS related. You can also use the **nslookup** command to determine whether specific hostnames are properly being resolved to the correct IP addresses. Figure 4-21 illustrates an example from the ESXi Shell, where **nslookup** is used to test the resolution for a hostname *vma-01*. In this example, the hostname is resolved to IP address 192.168.1.12 by the DNS server at IP address 192.168.1.1.

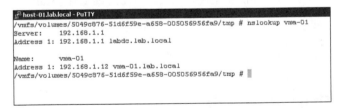

Figure 4-21 Nslookup example.

To determine the root cause of routing issues, first examine the mask and gateway settings of the VM or VMkernel port. Then use the **traceroute** command in the ESXi Shell (or similar command in a VM, such as **tracert** in a Windows VM) to examine the network route that is being traversed. The **traceroute** command provides the **–s** parameter, which can be used to identify the source IP address. Figure 4-22 illustrates an example in which **traceroute** displays details for successfully reaching a server named *vma-01* from a VMkernel management network interface, whose IP address is 192.168.1.10.

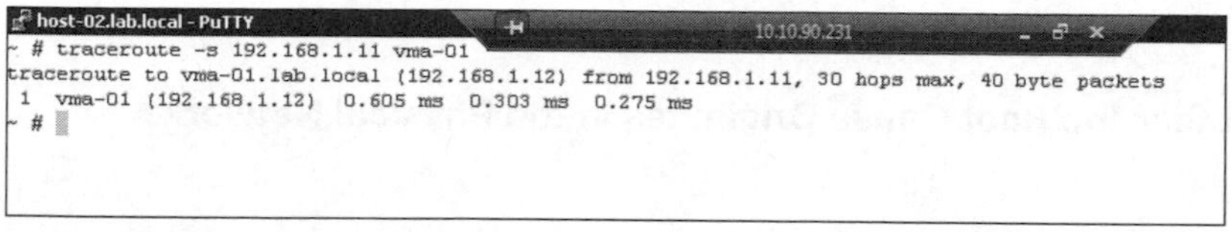

```
host-02.lab.local - PuTTY                      H          10.10.90.231        _  ☐  x
~ # traceroute -s 192.168.1.11 vma-01
traceroute to vma-01.lab.local (192.168.1.12) from 192.168.1.11, 30 hops max, 40 byte packets
 1  vma-01 (192.168.1.12)  0.605 ms  0.303 ms  0.275 ms
~ #
```

Figure 4-22   Traceroute example.

Use ESXTOP/RESXTOP to Identify Network Performance Problems

To use ESXTOP or RESXTOP to analyze network performance-related issues, press **n** to display network statistics. If VM or VMkernel virtual adapters are experiencing poor performance, the problem could be related to network contention, where the physical uplinks are struggling to process the outbound traffic from a set of VMs. Use the *USED-BY* column to locate the row in the display that corresponds to the troubled virtual adapter (VMkernel virtual adapter or VM virtual adapter) and determine whether the *%DRPTX* is higher than zero, which indicates that outbound network contention is present. The problem could be related to a lack of CPU resources, which prevents efficient processing of inbound network packets. Determine whether *%DRPRX* is higher than zero, which indicates that CPU resources are insufficient to process the inbound packets.

If no packets are dropped, examine the *PKTTX/s* (packets transmitted per second), *MbTX/s* (megabits transmitted per second), *PKTRX/s* (packets received per second), and *MbRX/s* (megabits received per second) to determine whether the expected throughput is being achieved. If necessary, consider placing a test network load in one or more VMs to measure the maximum throughput. Figure 4-23 illustrates an example of using ESXTOP to examine network statistics.

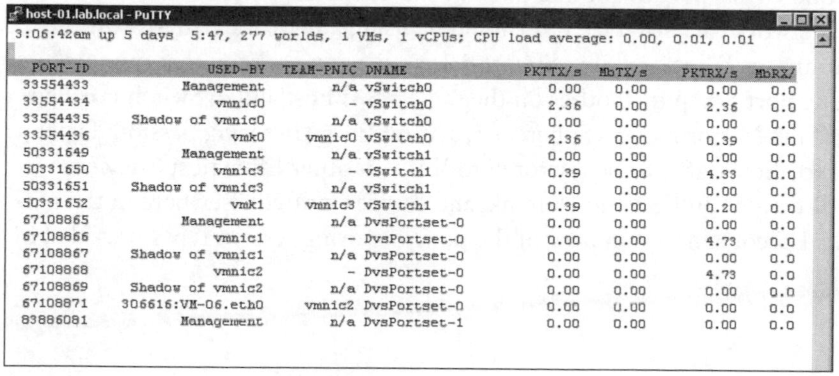

```
host-01.lab.local - PuTTY                                                      _ ☐ x
 3:06:42am up 5 days  5:47, 277 worlds, 1 VMs, 1 vCPUs; CPU load average: 0.00, 0.01, 0.01

   PORT-ID           USED-BY   TEAM-PNIC DNAME           PKTTX/s  MbTX/s    PKTRX/s  MbRX/
   33554433       Management   n/a vSwitch0                 0.00    0.00       0.00    0.0
   33554434          vmnic0     - vSwitch0                  2.36    0.00       2.36    0.0
   33554435 Shadow of vmnic0   n/a vSwitch0                 0.00    0.00       0.00    0.0
   33554436            vmk0    vmnic0 vSwitch0               2.36    0.00       0.39    0.0
   50331649       Management   n/a vSwitch1                 0.00    0.00       0.00    0.0
   50331650          vmnic3     - vSwitch1                  0.39    0.00       4.33    0.0
   50331651 Shadow of vmnic3   n/a vSwitch1                 0.00    0.00       0.00    0.0
   50331652            vmk1    vmnic3 vSwitch1               0.39    0.00       0.20    0.0
   67108865       Management   n/a DvsPortset-0             0.00    0.00       0.00    0.0
   67108866          vmnic1     - DvsPortset-0              0.00    0.00       4.73    0.0
   67108867 Shadow of vmnic1   n/a DvsPortset-0             0.00    0.00       0.00    0.0
   67108868          vmnic2     - DvsPortset-0              0.00    0.00       4.73    0.0
   67108869 Shadow of vmnic2   n/a DvsPortset-0             0.00    0.00       0.00    0.0
   67108871 306616:VM-06.eth0 vmnic2 DvsPortset-0           0.00    0.00       0.00    0.0
   83886081       Management   n/a DvsPortset-1             0.00    0.00       0.00    0.0
```

Figure 4-23   ESXTOP network statistics.

If dropped packets or low throughput is discovered for a VM or a VMkernel port, examine the dropped packets and throughput statistics for the associated physical NIC.

Determine Whether the Root Cause Originates in the Physical Network Infrastructure

To determine whether the root cause for a given network connectivity problem originates in the physical infrastructure, begin by using ping tests from within VMs or **vmkping** tests from the ESXi Shell to determine whether connectivity is successful using end points on the same ESXi host, same virtual port group, and same vSwitch. If you determine that tests succeed whenever they involve VMs on the same ESXi host but tests fail whenever they involve the physical infrastructure, the root cause might be in the physical infrastructure or in the ESXi host's connection to the infrastructure. You should check settings, such as the speed and duplex of the physical adapter, as mentioned previously in this section. You should also check settings such as the **NIC Teaming Load Balancing** policy, **MTU,** and **VLAN** to ensure that the configuration is compatible with the physical switch port settings. For example, verify that the *route based on IP Hash* load-balancing policy is configured only on the virtual port group in cases where Etherchannel is configured on the associated physical ports. For another example, if the virtual port group is configured with a VLAN ID, ensure that the physical port is configured to allow that VLAN ID in its VLAN trunk.

Configure and Administer Port Mirroring

Port mirroring can be a useful troubleshooting tool for dvSwitches in cases where you need to analyze network packets for a particular VM. As described in Chapter 2 of this guide, you can create a port mirror session on a dvSwitch that mirrors packets on one virtual port to another port on the dvSwitch, where a VM is used to analyze the network packets. The VM should be using a network analysis software application, such as Wireshark. In vSphere 5.1, a mirroring session that mirrors data from one port group to another on the same ESXi host and dvSwitch is called Distributed Port Mirroring. In vSphere 5.1, several Port Mirroring Session Types can be used to allow traffic to be mirrored to VMs on other ESXi hosts, devices connected directly to an ESXi host uplink, and devices located elsewhere in the network. Table 4-5 contains a summary of the port mirroring session types provided by vSphere 5.1.

Table 4-5 Port Mirroring Session Type in vSphere 5.1

Port Mirroring Session Type	Description
Distributed Port Mirroring	Mirroring occurs from a source distributed port to another target distributed port on the same dvSwitch.
Remote Mirroring Source	Mirroring occurs from a source distributed port to a target uplink port on the same distributed dvSwitch.
Remote Mirroring Destination	Mirroring occurs from a source VLAN to a target distributed port.
Encapsulated Remote Mirroring (L3)	Mirroring occurs from a source distributed port to a target IP address.
Distributed Port Mirroring (legacy)	Intended to support ESXi 5.0

Utilize the DCUI and the ESXi Shell to Troubleshoot ESXi Networking

This section focuses on using the direct console user interface (DCUI) to troubleshoot and configure ESXi networking. Previous sections and chapters have provided details on using the ESXi Shell to troubleshoot, configure, and monitor ESXi networking, but in some cases, the DCUI might need to be used.

For example, consider a case where no ESXi management interfaces are responding to attempts to use the vSphere Client, the vCenter Server, or an SSH client to access an ESXi host. Or consider a case where **Lockdown Mode** is enabled and vCenter Server loses connection to an ESXi host. In these cases, you will likely need to use the DCUI to address the problem.

To get started using the DCUI to troubleshoot ESXi networking issues, access the ESXi console either directly or by an available remote access connection, such as HP ILO, Dell DRAC, or KVM. At the ESXi 5.x splash screen, press **F2** to open the login prompt and enter credentials for the *root* account—or another appropriate **Login Name**. The DCUI should appear and provide a menu of options that can be used for troubleshooting, configuring, and monitoring the ESXi host, as illustrated in Figure 4-24.

The first ESXi management network troubleshooting step is typically to select the **Test Management Network** option. This option provides a dialog box, as illustrated in Figure 4-25, where you can choose to ping up to three addresses and resolve a hostname. By default, it will ping the gateway and resolve its own fully qualified hostname, but you can modify these values and add more addresses.

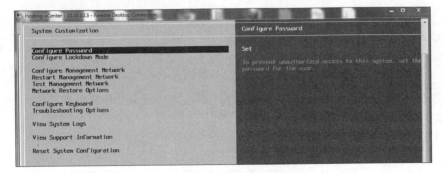

Figure 4-24   The DCUI.

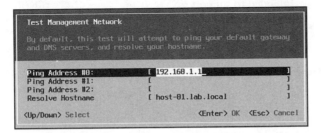

Figure 4-25   The DCUI Test Management Network option.

Another step is to examine the configuration of the management network and make corrections, if necessary. To perform this step, select the **Configure Management Network** option, which enables you to change the physical network adapter, IP address, gateway, mask, and VLAN that is used for the management interface. Regardless of whether you reconfigure the management network, the next step should be to select the **Restart Management Network** option to see if the issue still exists.

ESXi 5.1 provides some new **Network Restore Options**, as illustrated in Figure 4-26. These options are useful in scenarios in which a management network issue was caused by a recent configuration change to port group or vSwitch. These options provide a means to undo or correct the misconfiguration. One choice is the **Restore Network Settings** option, which reverts all network settings back to the original default configuration. The other choices are the **Restore Standard Switch** and **Restore vDS** options, which revert changes made to virtual switches.

Other troubleshooting steps could involve selecting the **Troubleshooting** option to enable the ESXi Shell, which allows you to enter the ESXi Shell from the DCUI by typing **Alt-F1**. From the ESXi Shell, you can use the ESXCLI command set as described elsewhere in this chapter to perform troubleshooting tasks. To return to the DCUI, type **Alt-F2**. From the **Troubleshooting** menu, which is shown in

Figure 4-27, you can also select the **Restart Management Agents** option if you suspect the root cause is actually related to the agent itself and not the management network.

Figure 4-26   Network restore options.

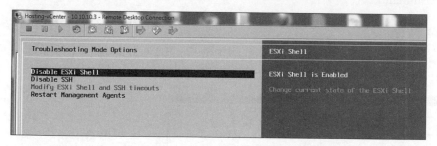

Figure 4-27   The DCUI Troubleshooting Mode Options menu.

From the DCUI, you can also select the **System Logs** option and choose the specific logs you want to view, as shown in Figure 4-28.

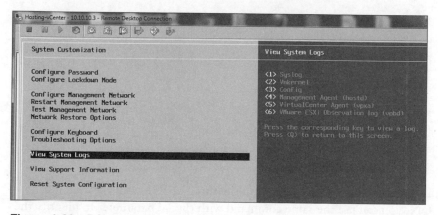

Figure 4-28   DCUI system logs.

Troubleshoot Storage Performance and Connectivity

This section describes how to troubleshoot storage performance and connectivity issues. It provides details for using commands to resolve storage-related issues for ESXi hosts such as multipathing, NFS, and VMFS-related issues. It includes examples and scenarios that involve the use of the ESXCLI command set, ESXTOP, and vscsiStats.

Use ESXCLI Commands to Troubleshoot Multipathing- and PSA-related Issues

The first step for using the ESXCLI command set to troubleshoot storage issues, such as issues related to mulitpathing and Pluggable Storage Architecture (PSA), is to use it to identify storage devices (LUNs). To identify storage devices, use this ESXCLI command:

```
esxcli storage core device list
```

The results of this command tend to be long, so you might with to add | **more** to the end of the command to display one page at a time, as shown in Figure 4-29.

```
vma-01.lab.local - PuTTY
vi-admin@vma-01:~[host-01.lab.local]> esxcli storage core device list | more
naa.6000d771000020d30f1ac91fb1822b08
   Display Name: FALCON iSCSI Disk (naa.6000d771000020d30f1ac91fb1822b08)
   Has Settable Display Name: true
   Size: 10240
   Device Type: Direct-Access
   Multipath Plugin: NMP
   Devfs Path: /vmfs/devices/disks/naa.6000d771000020d30f1ac91fb1822b08
   Vendor: FALCON
   Model: IPSTOR DISK
   Revision: v1.0
   SCSI Level: 4
   Is Pseudo: false
   Status: degraded
   Is RDM Capable: true
   Is Local: false
   Is Removable: false
   Is SSD: false
   Is Offline: false
   Is Perennially Reserved: false
   Queue Full Sample Size: 0
   Queue Full Threshold: 0
   Thin Provisioning Status: yes
   Attached Filters:
   VAAI Status: supported
   Other UIDs: vml.02000600006000d771000020d30f1ac91fb1822b08495053544f52
   Is Local SAS Device: false
   Is Boot USB Device: false
```

Figure 4-29   Using an ESXCLI command to list storage devices.

If you want to focus on troubleshooting multipathing or PSA issues related to a specific LUN, you can use the same command with the **–d** parameter to identify the LUN, as shown in Figure 4-30. In this example, the results show that the **Multipath Plugin** used to access this LUN is *NMP*, which is the VMware Native Multipath Plugin. This information is useful in troubleshooting PSA-related issues. In this example, you might determine that *NMP* is not the best or desired multipath plug-in for this LUN. Typically, this can be resolved by following the storage manufacturer's recommendations to install vendor-specific multipath plug-ins and modify claim rules.

```
host-01.lab.local - PuTTY
~ # esxcli storage core device list -d naa.6000d77100001b230f1ac91febcc8985
naa.6000d77100001b230f1ac91febcc8985
   Display Name: FALCON iSCSI Disk (naa.6000d77100001b230f1ac91febcc8985)
   Has Settable Display Name: true
   Size: 30720
   Device Type: Direct-Access
   Multipath Plugin: NMP
   Devfs Path: /vmfs/devices/disks/naa.6000d77100001b230f1ac91febcc8985
   Vendor: FALCON
   Model: IPSTOR DISK
   Revision: v1.0
   SCSI Level: 4
   Is Pseudo: false
   Status: on
   Is RDM Capable: true
   Is Local: false
   Is Removable: false
   Is SSD: false
   Is Offline: false
   Is Perennially Reserved: false
   Queue Full Sample Size: 0
   Queue Full Threshold: 0
   Thin Provisioning Status: yes
   Attached Filters:
   VAAI Status: supported
   Other UIDs: vml.02000900006000d77100001b230f1ac91febcc8985495053544f52
   Is Local SAS Device: false
   Is Boot USB Device: false
~ #
```

Figure 4-30 Using an ESXCLI command to obtain details on a specific storage device.

Another typically useful troubleshooting step is to identify all the paths to LUNs that are available on an ESXi host, using this command:

```
esxcli storage core path list
```

The results of this command contain every path that is known to the ESXi host. You could use this information to determine all the known paths for a particular LUN, but it would be challenging due to the size of the results.

A more convenient way to identify all the paths for a given LUN is to use the **esxcg-mpath** command. For example, to list all the paths for a LUN whose identifier is *naa.6000d771000020d40f1ac91fb172e72e*, use this command:

```
esxcfg-mpath -l -d naa.6000d771000020d40f1ac91fb172e72e
```

To troubleshoot multipathing issues, you might want to closely examine the details of a particular path. To see the details for a specific path, you can use the previous command with the **–path** parameter to identify the path using the **Runtime Name**, as shown in Figure 4-31. In this example, the results show that the **State** of the path is *active*. If any other value appeared for the **State**, it could be the sign of a problem or a misconfiguration.

Figure 4-31   Using an ESXCLI command to list multiple paths for a LUN.

If you are concerned that a particular path has some health or performance issues, you could examine the statistics for the path by using the ESXCLI command set. For example, the following command can be used to retrieve the statistics for a specific path identified by the runtime name *vmhba33:C0:T0:L9*:

```
esxcli storage core path stats get --path vmhba33:C0:T0:L9
```

Figure 4-32 shows a sample of the results for this command. In this example, the results include many statistics for the path, such as 759 successful commands; 42,584 blocks read; 2 failed commands; and 0 failed write operations. When troubleshooting performance issues for a LUN, any non-zero values for the any of the *Failed* statistics could indicate issues with the path or the storage.

Figure 4-32   Using an ESXCLI command to get statistics for a LUN.

As mentioned previously in this section, you might need to modify claim rules to resolve PSA-related issues. For example, you might need to modify claim rules to allow a custom multipath plug-in or custom path selection policy to claim a LUN. Another purpose for modifying claim rules is to configure the MASK_PATH plug-in to claim all the paths to a LUN, which effectively prevents the ESXi host from accessing the LUN. For example, if you suspect that one ESXi host is experiencing unreliable connection issues to a datastore and are concerned that it could impact the performance of VMs running on other ESXi hosts, you could modify the ESXi host to allow the MASK_PATH plug-in to claim each path to the LUN. To accomplish this, first examine the current claim rule list by using this command:

```
esxcli  storage core claimrule list
```

An example of this command is shown in Figure 4-33, which indicates that MASK_PATH is initially configured to claim a couple of specific DELL devices, but all other devices are claimed by NMP. In this case, you could create new rules that are assigned rule numbers in the acceptable range between 150 and 199. Each new rule should assign a specific path to the MASK_PATH plug-in.

```
host-01.lab.local - PuTTY
~ # esxcli  storage core claimrule list
Rule Class   Rule   Class     Type         Plugin       Matches
----------   -----  -------   ----------   ----------   ------------------------------------
MP               0   runtime   transport    NMP          transport=usb
MP               1   runtime   transport    NMP          transport=sata
MP               2   runtime   transport    NMP          transport=ide
MP               3   runtime   transport    NMP          transport=block
MP               4   runtime   transport    NMP          transport=unknown
MP             101   runtime   vendor       MASK_PATH    vendor=DELL model=Universal Xport
MP             101   file      vendor       MASK_PATH    vendor=DELL model=Universal Xport
MP           65535   runtime   vendor       NMP          vendor=* model=*
~ #
```

Figure 4-33   Using an ESXCLI command to list claim rules.

Scenario—LUN Masking

You discover that one of your ESXi hosts is having a high volume of failed reads and writes to a particular LUN, but no other ESXi host is having such issues. You migrate all VMs that access the LUN from the troubled ESXi host to other ESXi hosts. You now want to temporarily prevent the ESXi host from attempting to access the LUN. You decide to add new claim rules to allow the MASK_PATH plug-in to claim each path to the LUN. The ESXi host has two paths to the LUN that are identified by the runtime names *vmhba33:C0:T0:L5* and *vmhba33:C1:T0:L5*.

Key
Topic

To address this need, you could create a claim rule numbered *192* that claims the path with MASK_PATH, as shown in Figure 4-34.

```
host-01.lab.local - PuTTY
~ # esxcli storage core claimrule list
Rule Class   Rule  Class    Type       Plugin     Matches
----------   ----  -------  ---------  ---------  -----------------------------------
MP              0  runtime  transport  NMP        transport=usb
MP              1  runtime  transport  NMP        transport=sata
MP              2  runtime  transport  NMP        transport=ide
MP              3  runtime  transport  NMP        transport=block
MP              4  runtime  transport  NMP        transport=unknown
MP            101  runtime  vendor     MASK_PATH  vendor=DELL model=Universal Xport
MP            101  file     vendor     MASK_PATH  vendor=DELL model=Universal Xport
MP          65535  runtime  vendor     NMP        vendor=* model=*
~ #
~ # esxcli storage core claimrule add --rule 192 -t location -A vmhba33 -C 0 -T 0 -L 5 -P MASK_PATH
```

Figure 4-34   Using ESXCLI commands to create a claim rule.

After creating the claim rule, use this command to load the rule into the active working set and to reclaim the LUN. In this example, the LUN identifier is *naa.600 0d771000020d40f1ac91fb172e72e*:

```
esxcli  storage core claimrule load
esxcli storage core claiming reclaim -d naa.6000d771000020d40f1ac91fb
172e72e
```

You can then use this command to verify that one path has been removed:

```
esxcfg-mpath -l -d naa.6000d771000020d40f1ac91fb172e72e
```

You can then repeat these steps for the second path, whose runtime name is *vmhba33:C1:T0:L5*:

Use ESXCLI Commands to Troubleshoot VMkernel Storage Module Configurations

Troubleshooting issues related to storage modules typically begins with identifying all the storage adapters (HBAs) in an ESXi host. To do this, use the following command, which identifies the driver and other details for each HBA:

```
esxcli storage core adapter list
```

Figure 4-35 shows an example of this command. In this example, the second column identifies the driver for each HBA. You should ensure that the correct driver is assigned to each adapter by following the manufacturer's recommendations. If you suspect that a driver or adapter is not functioning well, you could display adapter statistics using this command:

```
esxcli storage core adapter get
```

Figure 4-35 also shows an example of using this command, which shows statistics, including failure statistics. In this example, no failed commands appear on *vmhba0*.

```
host-01.lab.local - PuTTY
~ # esxcli iscsi adapter list
Adapter  Driver     State   UID                                         Description
-------  ---------  ------  ------------------------------------------  ----------------------
vmhba33  iscsi_vmk  online  iqn.1998-01.com.vmware:host-01-2f6ec656     iSCSI Software Adapter
~ #
~ #
~ # esxcli iscsi adapter get --adapter vmhba33
vmhba33
   Name: iqn.1998-01.com.vmware:host-01-2f6ec656
   Alias:
   Vendor: VMware
   Model: iSCSI Software Adapter
   Description: iSCSI Software Adapter
   Serial Number:
   Hardware Version:
   Asic Version:
   Firmware Version:
   Option Rom Version:
   Driver Name: iscsi_vmk
   Driver Version:
   TCP Protocol Supported: false
   Bidirectional Transfers Supported: false
   Maximum Cdb Length: 64
   Can Be NIC: false
   Is NIC: false
   Is Initiator: true
   Is Target: false
   Using TCP Offload Engine: false
   Using ISCSI Offload Engine: false
~ #
```

Figure 4-35 Using ESXCLI commands to list storage adapters and statistics.

A commonly used troubleshooting tactic is to rescan the paths accessible by an HBA, which can be done using the following command. In this example, the adapter identified as *vmhba33* is scanned:

```
esxcli storage core adapter rescan --adapter vmhba33
```

Use ESXCLI Commands to Troubleshoot iSCSI-related Issues

The ESXCLI command set includes several commands that are specifically intended for configuring and troubleshooting iSCSI storage. These commands are in the namespace **esxcli iscsi**. Troubleshooting often starts by using the following command to display a list of all iSCSI adapters used by the ESXi host:

```
esxcli iscsi adapter list
```

The results of this command include the **Name**, **Driver**, **State**, **Unique ID** (UID), and **Description** of each iSCSI adapter. To display more details on a specific iSCSI adapter, such as an adapter named *vmhba33*, the following command can be used:

```
esxcli iscsi adapter get --adapter vmhba33
```

These commands, shown in Figure 4-36, can be used to examine details like the **Hardware Version** and **Firmware Version** of hardware iSCSI adapters, which can be useful for troubleshooting.

Figure 4-36   Using ESXCLI iSCSI commands.

The **esxcli iscsi adapter set** command can be used to modify the **iSCSI Quali-fied Name** (IQN) and the **Alias** of the adapter. The **esxcli iscsi adapter auth chap** namespace can be used to view and configure CHAP settings, whereas the **esxcli iscsi adapter discovery** namespace can be used to manage targets. These commands could be useful for modifying the adapter, its CHAP authentication, and its targets in an attempt to troubleshoot problems where the adapter is not properly discovering LUNs that have been presented to an ESXi host.

Troubleshoot NFS Mounting and Permission Issues

Troubleshooting NFS issues primarily involves examining the related settings in vSphere. For example, consider a case in which the vSphere Client is used to configure an ESXi host to connect to an NFS datastore presented by a storage device whose IP address is *192.168.1.6* using the folder */mnt/lun1*, as shown in Figure 4-37.

In this example, if the ESXi host has problems connecting to the datastore, you can begin troubleshooting by verifying that each of these settings is correct. Next, you can check the configuration of the VMkernel network port that is used. This port must be able to establish a network connection to the NFS server. You can test this by using the **vmkping** command as described earlier in this chapter.

Other potential issues can exist in the physical network infrastructure or on the NFS storage device. For example, you should work with your storage administrator to ensure that the NFS folder is properly exported to allow access by the ESXi host. The **esxcli storage nfs namespace**, which contains commands for adding, listing, and removing NFS datastores, can also be used for troubleshooting. For example, this namespace can be useful for creating scripts that can be quickly applied from the vMA to large groups of ESXi hosts to either retrieve data or make configuration changes that are needed to troubleshoot NFS issues. Figure 4-38 illustrates using the **esxcli storage nfs add** command to add an NFS datastore to an ESXi host, using the same configuration as in the last example.

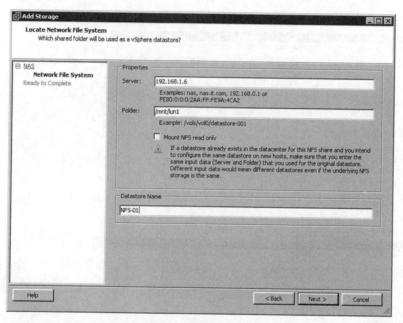

Figure 4-37 An example of adding an NFS datastore to an ESXi host.

```
~ # esxcli storage nfs list
~ #
~ #
~ # esxcli storage nfs add -v NFS01 -H 192.168.1.6  -s /mnt/lun1
~ #
~ #
~ # esxcli storage nfs list
Volume Name  Host         Share       Accessible  Mounted  Read-Only  Hardware Acceleration
-----------  -----------  ---------   ----------  -------  ---------  ---------------------
NFS01        192.168.1.6  /mnt/lun1        true     true      false  Not Supported
~ #
```

Figure 4-38 Using ESXCLI commands to add an NFS datastore.

Use ESXTOP and vscsiStats to Identify Storage Performance Issues

The best set of performance statistics for identifying storage performance issues would consist of all statistics that report the latency of related objects, such as virtual disks, storage adapters, and LUNs. ESXTOP and RESXTOP can be used to examine these statistics. For example, to examine the latency for I/O that occurs on storage adapters, use ESXTOP, press the **d** key, and examine the **GAVG/cmd** column, as shown in Figure 4-39.

```
host-01.lab.local - PuTTY                                                         _ □
 3:58:52pm up  5:57, 286 worlds, 1 VMs, 1 vCPUs; CPU load average: 0.01, 0.01, 0.01

ADAPTR PATH              NPTH   CMDS/s   READS/s  WRITES/s  MBREAD/s  MBWRTN/s  DAVG/cmd  KAVG/cmd  GAVG/cmd
vmhba0 -                    0     0.00     0.00     0.00     0.00     0.00     0.00     0.00     0.00
vmhba1 -                    1     0.00     0.00     0.00     0.00     0.00     0.00     0.00     0.00
vmhba32 -                   1     0.00     0.00     0.00     0.00     0.00     0.00     0.00     0.00
vmhba33 -                  18     0.00     0.00     0.00     0.00     0.00     0.00     0.00     0.00
```

Figure 4-39 Using ESXTOP to examine storage adapter statistics.

To examine the I/O latency for a particular LUN, press the **u** key and examine the **GAVG/cmd** column, as shown in Figure 4-40.

```
host-01.lab.local - PuTTY
 3:58:25pm up  5:57, 286 worlds, 1 VMs, 1 vCPUs; CPU load average: 0.01, 0.01, 0.01

DEVICE                              PATH/WORLD/PARTITION  DAVG/cmd  KAVG/cmd  GAVG/cmd  QAVG/cmd
mpx.vmhba1:C0:T0:L0                         -               0.00     0.00     0.00     0.00
mpx.vmhba32:C0:T0:L0                        -               0.00     0.00     0.00     0.00
naa.6000d77100001b230f1ac91febcc8985       -               0.00     0.00     0.00     0.00
naa.6000d771000020d10f1ac91fb1a0affe       -               0.00     0.00     0.00     0.00
naa.6000d771000020d20f1ac91fb1916de0       -               0.00     0.00     0.00     0.00
naa.6000d771000020d30f1ac91fb1822b08       -               0.00     0.00     0.00     0.00
naa.6000d771000020ef0f1ac91fb1424434       -               0.00     0.00     0.00     0.00
naa.6000d771000020f00f1ac91fb13300d1       -               0.00     0.00     0.00     0.00
naa.6000d771000020f10f1ac91fb123bf02       -               0.00     0.00     0.00     0.00
naa.6000d771000020f20f1ac91fb1147b07       -               0.00     0.00     0.00     0.00
naa.6000d771000020f30f1ac91fb1053941       -               0.00     0.00     0.00     0.00
(NFS)NFS01                                  -                 -        -      0.00       -
```

Figure 4-40 Using ESXTOP to examine LUN statistics.

To examine the latency for I/O that occurs for a virtual disk, press the **v** key and examine the **LAT/rd** and **LAT/wr** columns, as shown in Figure 4-41.

```
host-01.lab.local - PuTTY
 3:54:44pm up  5:53, 284 worlds, 1 VMs, 1 vCPUs; CPU load average: 0.03, 0.01, 0.01

   GID VMNAME        VDEVNAME NVDISK  CMDS/s   READS/s  WRITES/s  MBREAD/s  MBWRTN/s  LAT/rd  LAT/wr
 27949 VM-06              -       1     0.00     0.00     0.00     0.00     0.00     0.00     0.00
```

Figure 4-41 Using ESXTOP to examine virtual disk statistics.

In most cases, these latency values should be less than 5 milliseconds. Whenever the **GAVG/cmd** value for a particular storage adapter or LUN is high, you should determine the root cause. **GAVG/cmd** is the metric that indicates the latency for each I/O from the guest operating system's perspective. It includes VMkernel Latency (**KAVG/cmd**) and device Latency (**DAVG/cmd**). So, the next step is to examine the **KAVG/cmd** and **DAVG/cmd** values for the troubled adapter or LUN. High **KAVG/cmd** values indicate CPU contention within the VMkernel. High **DAVG/cmd** values indicate slowness in the physical storage infrastructure, including the storage adapters, storage network, and storage arrays.

As described previously in this chapter, the **vscsiStats** utility is useful for analyzing storage activity. It can be used to troubleshoot storage performance by producing histograms of latency, seek distance, I/O size, number of outstanding I/Os, and inter-arrival time whenever this data is useful. For example, if you determined that high device latency exists, you might want to learn details about the characteristics of the I/O of the VMs that are involved. This information might lead you to move some VMs to a datastore backed by a different RAID type.

Scenario—Using vscsiStats

Several VMs are performing poorly, and you have determined that the root cause is high latency for a particular LUN. You want to move some workloads off the LUN to LUNs backed by physical drives that are not part of the currently used LUN. But the only available LUNs are built on RAID-5, which you fear will not perform well enough for some workloads. You are curious about the characteristics of the disk I/O produced by a VM named *vm-01*, which has two virtual disks, but you are only concerned about the activity of the second virtual disk. You theorize that if *vm-01* is mostly performing sequential reads, it might perform adequately on the RAID-5 LUN. You know you can use the **v** key in ESXTOP to examine the READ/s and WRITE/s of the virtual disks to determine whether the I/Os are mostly reads. You need to use **vscsiStats** to report on the *seekDistance* to determine whether the I/O is mostly sequential.

Key Topic

To determine the *seekDistance* of the I/O for the second virtual disk used by *vm-01*, you can use **vscsiStats** to produce a histogram, as shown in Figure 4-42. In this example, 10,178 operations out of a sample of 14,068 had a *seekDistance* equal to or less than 1 LBN. This indicates the data is mostly sequential.

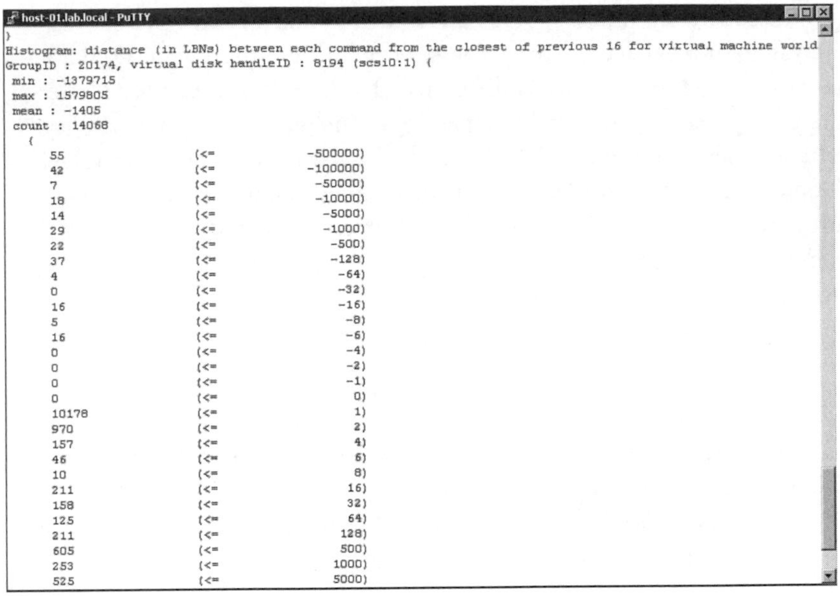

Figure 4-42 A seek distance histogram example.

Configure and Troubleshoot VMFS Datastores Issues Using VMKFSTOOLS

Chapter 1 of this guide contains instructions and examples of using **vmkfstools** to configure VMFS datastores. In this section, details are provided on using **vmkfstools** for troubleshooting VMFS datastores. Typically, the first step is to identify the properties of specific VMFS datastores, which can be done with this command:

```
vmkfstools -P /vmfs/volumes/Shared-30
```

In this example, the name of the VMFS datastore is *Shared-30*. The fully qualified path is */vmfs/volumes/Shared-30*. Technically, this is the path to a file that is a symbolic link to the actual VMFS datastore. Each VMFS datastore is assigned a **unique ID** (UID), which in many cases should be used to reference the datastore. In this example, the */vmfs/volumes/Shared-30* symbolic link references a VMFS datastore whose UID is *5049c876-51d6f59e-a658-005056956fa9*. You can use this command to learn the mapping between symbolic links and VMFS UIDs:

```
ls -la /vmfs/volumes
```

Figure 4-43 shows a sample execution of this command.

```
host-01.lab.local - PuTTY
/vmfs/volumes # ls -la /vmfs/volumes
drwxr-xr-x    1 root     root           512 Jan 16 17:47 .
drwxr-xr-x    1 root     root           512 Jan 16 10:01 ..
drwxr-xr-x    1 root     root             8 Jan  1  1970 0ba07379-2244c165-7c2d-43b56bd34949
drwxr-xr-x    1 root     root             8 Jan  1  1970 5020e19e-6742d39f-f791-005056956fa8
drwxr-xr-t    1 root     root          1820 Jan 16 16:12 5020e1ba-1bd0dd24-ef0a-005056956fa8
drwxr-xr-t    1 root     root          1680 Jan 14 13:17 5049c876-51d6f59e-a658-005056956fa9
drwxr-xr-t    1 root     root          1540 Jan 14 20:55 5049c897-8dba3d03-5a4d-005056956fa9
drwxr-xr-x    1 root     root             8 Jan  1  1970 50b67c99-4ae0f9be-be63-005056954b0d
lrwxr-xr-x    1 root     root            35 Jan 16 17:47 Local-01 -> 5020e1ba-1bd0dd24-ef0a-005056956fa8
lrwxr-xr-x    1 root     root            17 Jan 16 17:47 NFS01 -> bdda51d6-f71136e0
lrwxr-xr-x    1 root     root            35 Jan 16 17:47 Shared-30 -> 5049c876-51d6f59e-a658-005056956fa9
lrwxr-xr-x    1 root     root            35 Jan 16 17:47 Shared-8 -> 5049c897-8dba3d03-5a4d-005056956fa9
drwxr-xr-x    1 root     root           512 Sep  9  2012 bdda51d6-f71136e0
drwxr-xr-x    1 root     root             8 Jan  1  1970 ff9cdc7e-5a7ab532-c228-1a96a34f9f7f
/vmfs/volumes #
/vmfs/volumes #
```

Figure 4-43 Mapping symbolic links to VMFS UIDs.

To retrieve the properties of this VMFS datastore, use the UID with this command:

```
vmkfstools -P /vmfs/volumes/ 5049c876-51d6f59e-a658-005056956fa9
```

The results of the command are identical to the results of the last command, as shown in Figure 4-44. The results contain details on VMFS UID, capacity, and spanned partitions.

```
host-01.lab.local - PuTTY
~ # vmkfstools -P /vmfs/volumes/Shared-30
VMFS-5.54 file system spanning 1 partitions.
File system label (if any): Shared-30
Mode: public
Capacity 31943819264 (30464 file blocks * 1048576), 7441743872 (7097 blocks) avail
UUID: 5049c876-51d6f59e-a658-005056956fa9
Partitions spanned (on "lvm"):
        naa.6000d77100001b230f1ac91febcc8985:1
Is Native Snapshot Capable: YES
~ #
~ #
~ #
~ # vmkfstools -P /vmfs/volumes/5049c876-51d6f59e-a658-005056956fa9
VMFS-5.54 file system spanning 1 partitions.
File system label (if any): Shared-30
Mode: public
Capacity 31943819264 (30464 file blocks * 1048576), 7441743872 (7097 blocks) avail
UUID: 5049c876-51d6f59e-a658-005056956fa9
Partitions spanned (on "lvm"):
        naa.6000d77100001b230f1ac91febcc8985:1
Is Native Snapshot Capable: YES
~ #
```

Figure 4-44 VMFS properties of VMKFSTOOLS.

The **vmkfstools** utility can also be used to troubleshoot issues with creating and upgrading VMFS datastores. For example, if you experience issues trying to create a new VMFS volume using the vSphere Client, you could try to do so using **vmkfstools –C**, as explained in Chapter 1. Likewise, if you have issues using the vSphere Client to upgrade a VMFS-3 volume to VMFS-5, you could try using the **vmkfstools –T** command, as shown in Figure 4-45. In this example, the VMFS UID is *52d81f5d-6726097b-b2bb-005056954ce5*; the VMFS name is *VMFS-003*; the original VMFS version is *3.58*; and the updated VMFS version is *5.58*.

Figure 4-45   Upgrading a VMFS datastore using VMKFSTOOLS.

Troubleshoot Storage Snapshot and Resignaturing Issues

Key Topic

Many storage systems allow the administrator to create replicas of LUNs, which might contain VMFS datastores. When an ESXi host accesses a LUN replica, it detects that the SCSI_DiskID information in the VMFS metadata does not match the SCSI_DiskID information stored in the Logical Volume Manager (LVM) header and classifies the LUN as a snapshot. This is done by design because corruption issues could occur if any ESXi host is presented with both the original LUN and the replica. An ESXi host cannot determine the difference between two VMFS volumes that contain the same VMFS UID in its metadata. The administrator should en-sure that no ESXi host is ever permitted to mount two LUNs containing the same VMFS UID.

For this reason, if any ESXi host attempts to mount a VMFS datastore that it de-tects as a replica, it prompts the user to choose one of two options to complete the mount operation. One option is the **Keep the existing signature**, which maintains the VMFS UID but updates other VMFS metadata. This option can be used if the replica is not presented to any ESXi host that accesses the original LUN. This can be useful when SAN replication is used for disaster recovery (DR). The other option is to use **Assign a new signature**, which updates the UID in the VMFS metadata. This option must be selected if the replica will be presented to an ESXi host that ac-cesses the original LUN.

When troubleshooting issues exist where an ESXi host has difficulty mounting a new VMFS datastore, you can check the VMkernel log. If it contains a message with a string similar to *Device vmhba1:0:5:1 is a snapshot*, the ESXi host is deliberately not mounting the VMFS datastore. If the vSphere Client is also not prompting you to keep the signature or assign a new signature, you might need to use an ESXCLI command to fix the issue. In this case, use this command to determine whether the ESXi host truly detects a snapshot:

```
esxcli storage vmfs snapshot list
```

If a snapshot is detected for a VMFS datastore, whose UID is *52d81f5d-6726097b-b2bb-005056954ce5*, then you can use the following ESXCLI command to resigna-ture the VMFS datastore.

```
esxcli storage vmfs snapshot resignature -u=52d81f5d-6726097b-b2bb-
005056954ce5
```

Analyze Log Files to Identify Storage and Multipathing Problems

Troubleshooting storage and multipathing issues often requires the examination of VMkernel log files. The VMkernel log file can be viewed from the DCUI as de-scribed in a previous section. It can be examined from a vSphere Client that is con-nected directly to an ESXi host. It can also be examined from the ESXi Shell using traditional commands, like cat, less, more, and grep. For example, you can use the grep command to search the VMkernel log file for any rows containing the string "error" using this command:

```
grep  error /var/log/VMkernel.log
```

Here are a few examples of error messages that might appear in the log file.

The VMkernel log file might contain an entry similar to following sample, which indicates that a LUN, whose runtime name is vmhba33:C1:T0:L5, is detected to be a replica:

```
Jan 18 11:15:41 Host-01 VMkernel: 0:14:17:59.787 cpu13:1046)LVM:5670:
Device vmhba33:1:0:5 is a snapshot
```

The VMkernel log file might contain an entry similar to the following sample, which indicates a SCSI error. In this example, the portion marked as bold (in this guide, not in the actual log file) is a **Device Status** number that identifies the issue. In this example, the **Device Status** is **0x8**, which indicates the SCSI device was too busy to accept the SCSI command, which the VMkernel will automatically resend again. A number of these messages could indicate the LUN is overloaded.

```
VMkernel: 1:02:02:02.206 cpu3:4099)NMP: nmp_CompleteCommandForPath:
Command 0x28
(0x410005078e00) to NMP device "naa.6001e4f000105e6b00001f14499bfead"
failed on
physical path "vmhba1:C0:T0:L100" H:0x0 D:0x8 P:0x0 Possible sense
data: 0x0 0x0
0x0.
```

The VMkernel might contain other entries with similar codes that indicate the meaning of the error. Table 4-6 shows a few examples of **Device Status** codes and a brief description of each. Each of these can indicate that the LUN is overworked. One possible solution is to migrate one or more VMs to other datastores.

Table 4-6   SCSI Device Status Codes Examples

SCSI Device Status Code	Description
0x8	VMK_SCSI_DEVICE_BUSY
0x18	VMK_SCSI_DEVICE_RESERVATION_CONFLICT
0x28	VMK_SCSI_DEVICE_QUEUE_FULL

Troubleshoot vCenter Server and ESXi Host Management

This section describes how to troubleshoot vCenter Server and ESXi host management-related issues. It includes details on troubleshooting issues related to services and connections involving the vCenter Server, the vCenter Server database, and the ESXi host management network. These steps involve the use of the vSphere Client and the ESXi Shell. Although this section does not directly cover performance troubleshooting, it is placed in the same chapter mainly because issues that impact ESXi host management could impact the availability of tools that are useful for performance troubleshooting.

Troubleshoot vCenter Server Service and Database Connection Issues

Database connection issues will cause the vCenter Service to fail and prevent it from starting. A symptom of this is that the vCenter Service cannot be started or fails shortly after being started. Another symptom is that the *vpxd.log* file contains one or more "ODBC error" messages. When troubleshooting issues exist where the vCenter Server fails to start or immediately crashes after starting, you can begin by testing the database connection. Log on to Windows on the vCenter Server and select **Administrator Tools** > **Data Source (ODBC) Connections**. Locate and select the **System DSN** connection for the vCenter Server database. Click the **Configuration** button and then verify the settings such as database server name, database name, and user credentials. Click the **Test Connection** button.

Also from Windows on the vCenter Server, select **Administrator Tools** > **Services** to check the status of the **VMware VirtualCenter Server** service. If necessary, right-click the service and select **Start**, **Stop**, and/or **Restart** as needed to troubleshoot. If you suspect that a database connection issue involves improper user authentication or authorization, right-click the **VMware VirtualCenter Server** service and select the **Properties** > **Logon** tab to configure the user account used to run the service. Also from Windows on the vCenter Server, select **Administrator Tools** > **Services** to examine and manipulate other vCenter Server–related services that might be installed, such as the **VMware vCenter Inventory Service** and the **VMware VirutalCenter Management Webservices.** Issues with these services might not always cause complete vCenter Server failure, but they will certainly have some impact. For example, if the **VMware VirutalCenter Management Webservices** fails, the symptom might be that although the vCenter Server is functioning, some features such as Overview Graphs, the Storage View tab, and Hardware Health might not be functional. To troubleshoot such issues, begin by restarting the **VMware VirutalCenter Management Webservices** service.

Troubleshoot ESXi Firewall Issues

You can use the **Security Profile** in the vSphere Client to examine and configure the ESXi firewall. To do so, select the ESXi host in the inventory, select the **Configuration** tab, and select **Software** > **Security Profile**. In the **Firewall** section, click **Properties**. Use the **Firewall Properties** page to enable (check) each required traffic type to permit through the firewall. For example, if NTP is not working correctly, ensure the **NTP Client** is checked, as shown in Figure 4-46.

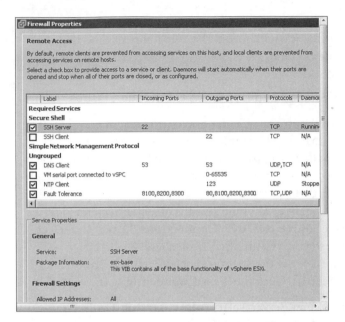

Figure 4-46   Examine an ESXi host's firewall properties.

For more extensive troubleshooting needs, you can use the **Firewall Properties** page to examine and verify that the correct **Incoming Ports** and **Outgoing Ports** are identified for each service. You can use the **Options** button to start and stop the corresponding services manually and to configure the corresponding services to automatically start with the ESXi host or automatically start when the ports are enabled. For example, the NTP Client service can be configured to start manually, automatically start when the ESXi host restarts, and automatically start when the *NTP Client* is enabled in the firewall, as shown in Figure 4-47.

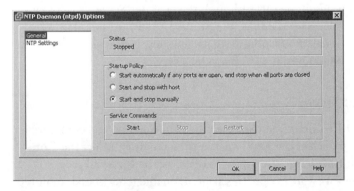

Figure 4-47   Modifying the NTP daemon options in the ESXi firewall.

The ESXi firewall provides the ability to restrict the networks that are permitted to connect per service type. For example, to restrict the networks that can connect to the **VMware vCenter Agent**, such that only the vCenter Server IP address is allowed, click the **Firewall** button and specify the vCenter Server IP address in the **Only allow connections from the following networks** box, as shown in Figure 4-48.

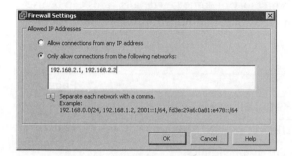

Figure 4-48 Restricting IP addresses in the firewall.

Troubleshoot ESXi Host Management and Connectivity Issues

The ESXi hosts have management agents named *vpxa* and *hostd*. The *vpxa* agent is responsible for communicating with the vCenter Server, whereas the *hostd* agent is responsible for most other management functions on the ESXi host. If vCenter Server reports that an ESXi host is *Not Responding*, the problem could be that one or both of the management services on the ESXi host needs to be restarted. To restart these agents using the DCUI, select **Troubleshooting Options** and then select **Restart Management Agents**. You can also use the ESXi Shell to restart the agents by using the following commands:

```
/etc/init.d/hostd restart
/etc/init.d/vpxa restart
```

Summary

You should now have the knowledge and skills to successfully perform administration tasks focused on monitoring, optimizing, and troubleshooting VM performance in a vSphere environment. You should also be able to successfully complete cluster configuration, troubleshooting, and management tasks that might be part of the VCAP5-DCA exam. Be sure to take time to practice the steps that are provided in this section until you are confident that you can perform such tasks quickly and without any assistance.

Exam Preparation Tasks

Review All the Key Topics

Table 4-7 provides a list of all Key Topics identified in this chapter along with a few notes intended to refresh the reader's memory of some key details. This can be useful as a quick reference when performing vSphere administration.

Table 4-7   Key Topics for Chapter 4

Key Topic Element	Description	Page
List	VMware recommended BIOS settings	148
Paragraph	List the storage HBAs in an ESXi host	149
Step List	Configure ESXTOP custom profiles	164
Paragraph	Use ESXTOP replay mode	168
Step List	Customize performance charts for memory troubleshooting	172
Step List	Configure memory/CPU hotplug	175
Paragraph	Use net-dvs for network troubleshooting	176
Step List	Network troubleshooting methodology	180
Table	Port mirroring types	185
Paragraph	Using the esxcfg-mpath command	189
Paragraph	Masking LUNs with MASK_PATH	191
Paragraph	Using ESXTOP for storage performance analysis	196
Paragraph	Using vscsiStats for storage performance analysis	197
Paragraph	Troubleshooting resignaturing issues	200

Definitions of Key Terms

Define the following key terms from this chapter, and check your answers in the glossary.

Storage replica, storage snapshot, vscsiStats, net-dvs, performance graphs, DCUI, VMkernel log, guest latency, VMkernel latency, device latency

Review Tasks

These review tasks enable you to assess how well you grasped the materials in this chapter. Because of the advanced and hands-on nature of this particular exam, a set of tasks is provided instead of a set of questions. You should now attempt to perform each of these tasks without looking at previous sections in this chapter or at other materials, unless necessary. The steps for each task are located within the chapter:

1. Configure a swap file for the ESXi system (not a VM swap file, but an ESXi system swap).

2. Change a VM to use the best performing virtual SCSI driver instead of the virtual SCSI driver that was selected by default based on the guest O/S type.

3. Use vm-support to collect performance data, and then use ESXTOP in replay mode.

4. Use the vSphere Client to create a custom performance chart that can be used for a single VM to show just a single counter that best indicates whether the VM is experiencing CPU contention where it is contesting with other VMs for access to CPU resources.

5. Use the DCUI to restore network settings back to the original, default configuration.

6. Use the **esxcfg-mpath** command to list all the paths for a specific LUN.

7. Configure the ESXi firewall to permit only VMware vCenter Agent traffic to communicate with a specific IP address.

This chapter covers the following subjects:

- **VMware High Availability (HA)**—This section covers configuring and supporting VMware HA.

- **VMware Distributed Resource Scheduler (DRS)**—This section covers configuring and supporting VMware DRS.

- **VMware Storage DRS**—This section covers configuring and supporting VMware Storage DRS.

- **VMware Distributed Power Management (DPM)**—This section covers configuring and supporting VMware DPM.

- **VMware Enhanced vMotion Compatibility (EVC)**—This section covers configuring and supporting VMware EVC.

- **VMware Fault Tolerance (FT)**—This section covers configuring and supporting VMware FT.

This chapter contains material pertaining the VCAP5-DCA exam objectives 3.3, 4.1, and 4.2

## CHAPTER 5

Clusters

This chapter is intended to provide you with the knowledge and skills to successfully perform cluster administration in a vSphere virtualized datacenter. It is also intended to ensure that you have the skills to successfully complete the cluster configuration, troubleshooting, and management tasks that might be part of the VCAP5-DCA exam. As you read this chapter, take time to practice the steps that are provided until you are confident that you can perform such tasks quickly and without any assistance. Some of these steps involve using the vSphere Client. Others involve using the vCLI and PowerCLI.

"Do I Know This Already?" Quiz

The "Do I Know This Already?" quiz allows you to assess how well you might already know the material in this chapter. Table 5-1 outlines the major headings in this chapter and the corresponding "Do I Know This Already?" quiz questions. You can find the answers in Appendix A, "Answers to the 'Do I Know This Already?' Quizzes." Because of the advanced and hands-on nature of this particular exam, you should read the entire chapter and practice performing all the described tasks at least once, regardless of how well you do on this quiz. This quiz can be helpful to determine which topics will require the most effort during your preparation.

Table 5-1   "Do I Know This Already?" Foundation Topics Section-to-Question Mapping

Foundations Topics Section	Questions Covered in This Section
VMware High Availability (HA)	1
VMware Distributed Resource Scheduler (DRS)	2
VMware Storage DRS	3
VMware Distributed Power Management (DPM)	4
VMware Enhanced vMotion Compatibility (EVC)	5
VMware Fault Tolerance (FT)	6

1. Which option summarizes the steps that can be taken to ensure that virtual machines continue to run on ESXi hosts that become disconnected from the management network but remain connected to storage?

   a. Use the **Set-Cluster** PowerCLI cmdlet and set the **-HAIsolationResponse** parameter to DoNothing.

   b. Use the **Set-Cluster** PowerCLI cmdlet and set the **-HAIsolationResponse** parameter to LeaveVMsRunning.

   c. Use the **esxcli cluster ha set** command.

   d. Use the **esxcli cluster ha isolation** command.

2. Which option summarizes the minimum steps that can be taken to configure DRS Automation to automatically place and migrate VMs as necessary to enforce DRS rules but not to just balance the workload?

   a. Edit the cluster settings, set the **DRS Automation Level** to **Fully Automated**, and move the **Migration Threshold** slider to the extreme left (Conservative) setting.

   b. Edit the cluster settings, set the **DRS Automation Level** to **Fully Automated**, and move the **Migration Threshold** slider to the extreme right (Aggressive) setting.

   c. Edit the cluster settings, set the **DRS Automation Level** to **Partially Automated**, and move the **Migration Threshold** slider to the extreme left (Conservative) setting.

   d. Edit the cluster settings, set the **DRS Automation Level** to **Partially Automated**, and move the **Migration Threshold** slider to the extreme right (Aggressive) setting.

3. Which option summarizes the steps that can be taken to configure an SDRS datastore cluster?

   a. Select **New Datastore Cluster**. In the wizard, check the **Turn on Storage DRS** box, select the ESXi hosts or clusters, and then select the datastores.

   b. Select **New Datastore Cluster**. In the wizard, check the **Turn on Storage DRS** box, select the datastores, and then select the ESXi hosts or clusters.

    c. Use the **New-Cluster** PowerCLI cmdlet with the **–SdrsEnabled $True** option.

    d. Use the **New-Cluster** PowerCLI cmdlet with the –**SdrsConfig $Enable** option.

4. Which option summarizes the steps that can be taken to properly configure Distributed Power Management?

    a. Select **New Cluster**. In the first page of the wizard, check the **Turn on DPM** box.

    b. For each ESXi host in the cluster, check the **Turn on DPM** box on the **Configuration** tab.

    c. Use the **New-Cluster** PowerCLI cmdlet with the –**DPM $Enable** option.

    d. Select **New Cluster.** Set the default power management state to **Manual** or **Automatic**.

5. Which option summarizes the steps that can be taken to properly configure EVC on a cluster containing some Intel Nehalem processors and some Intel Westmere processors?

    a. Set the **VMware EVC** properties of the cluster to **Enable**.

    b. Set the **VMware EVC** properties of the cluster to **Enable EVC for Intel Hosts**, and set the **EVC Mode** to **Westmere**.

    c. Set the **VMware EVC** properties of the cluster to **Enable EVC for Intel Hosts**, and set the **EVC Mode** to **Nehalem**.

    d. Set the **VMware EVC** properties of the cluster to **Intel**.

6. Which option summarizes the steps that can be taken to implement vSphere Fault Tolerance?

    a. Edit the cluster settings and check the **Turn on Fault Tolerance** box.

    b. For each participating ESXi host, use the **Configuration** tab and select **Turn on Fault Tolerance.**

    c. Configure a vmkernel virtual adapter on each participating ESXi host to support **FT Logging**.

    d. Use the **FT-Enable** PowerCLI cmdlet with the –**Logging** option.

VMware High Availability

This section provides details for configuring and managing VMware High Availability (HA) Clusters. It includes details on procedures and concepts related to VMware HA administration. It provides examples and scenarios that involve the use of the vSphere Client and PowerCLI.

Overview

You should already be familiar with the following details in this overview. If any of this information is new to you, be sure to conduct the appropriate research before continuing on to the remainder of the section.

VMware HA is a vSphere cluster feature that provides automated high availability for virtual machines (VMs) and applications. Its main feature is to provide automated recovery of VMs that fail as a result of an unplanned ESXi host downtime event. When an ESXi host becomes nonresponsive, VMware HA automatically cold migrates the failed VMs to surviving ESXi hosts in the cluster and restarts them. HA requires these VMs to be hosted on shared datastores, which allows them to be immediately registered on the surviving hosts in the cluster without the need to copy any files. Typically, when a host fails, HA migrates and restarts all failed VMs within a few minutes.

VMware HA also offers other forms of protection, such as VM Monitoring and Application Monitoring, which are not enabled by default. When configured for VM Monitoring, VMware HA listens to the heartbeat of each VM, which is generated by VMware Tools. If at any point the heartbeat cannot be detected, VMware HA restarts the affected VMs. When configured for Application Monitoring, VMware HA listens to heartbeats that are generated by applications that are customized to interface with VMware Tools. If at any point the heartbeat cannot be detected, VMware HA restarts the affected VMs.

VMware HA has many configurable settings, such as Admission Control, Restart Priority, and Host Isolation Response. It has a highly available architecture, including ESXi host-based agents and network and datastore heartbeats. Although vCenter Server is required for configuration as well as maintaining the protected VM list, VMware HA is not dependent on vCenter Server availability for its failover operation. A minimum licensed edition of vSphere Essentials Plus to use VMware HA in a vSphere implementation.

Implement and Maintain Complex HA Solutions

VMware completely redesigned HA for vSphere 5. It no longer uses a host-based agent derived from Legato AAM. It now uses a host-based agent known as Fault Domain Manager (FDM) that was developed by VMware. It uses a model with a single master and multiple slaves. The master monitors the status of the slaves and receives the list of protected VMs from the vCenter Server. Communication between agents now includes datastore heartbeats in addition to network heartbeats. VMware HA allows for and accommodates network partitions. The HA status link on the cluster summary tab indicates the current number of protected VMs.

These architectural changes should be considered when creating a complex HA design. For example, when designing HA clusters involving two blade enclosures, you no longer need to be concerned about the placement of primary and secondary nodes as you would have been in vSphere 4.x. Instead, HA will elect one of the ESXi hosts to be the master, and if that host's hypervisor, blade hardware, or enclosure should fail, HA will initiate an election for a new master and begin the cold migration of all failed VMs. You also do not need to be concerned about the potential loss of network connectivity between the two enclosures because HA also monitors datastore heartbeats and can easily recognize network partition conditions and differentiate them from host failure or host isolation conditions.

In complex environments, it usually is important to set VM restart priorities. There are two reasons priority settings might be changed. First, mission-critical and tiered virtual machines might need to start up before other VMs. Second, if circumstances result in insufficient resources to start all VMs, the restart priority can ensure that critical VMs are started first. By default, the cluster's **VM Restart Priority** is set to **Medium**, but it can be changed to **High, Low**, or **Disabled**. Each VM's restart priority is set to the cluster's default, but individual VMs can be modified as needed. Examples of VMs that might be set to High are DNS servers, domain controllers, and vShield Edge appliances. An example of using restart priorities to reflect application importance would be to set the Restart Priority of production VMs to High and test VMs to Low. Unfortunately, HA does not provide a means to set restart priorities on vApps, but priorities could be set on the individual VMs that comprise a vApp. For example, a web vApp could have a database VM set to High, an application server VM set to Medium, and a web server VM set to Low. This would ensure that the power-on operations happen in the order necessary to enable the web vApp.

The following topics provide details on configuring, monitoring, and managing specific components of HA such as admission control, slot size, heartbeats, dependencies, isolation response, resource calculation, and alarms.

Admission Control Policies and Determining the Best Policy

Admission Control is an HA mechanism that controls the number of VMs that can be powered on in a cluster. It is used to ensure that sufficient resources exist to failover VMs if an unplanned downtime event occurs. After Admission Control has been configured, any attempt to power on a VM that violates the established policy setting will be prevented. The Admission Control Policy can be based on CPU and memory reservations, dedicated failover hosts, or slot size calculation. Admission control is applied as attempts are made to power on VMs, revert VMs to powered-on snapshots, increase the reservation of running VMs, and migrate VMs into the cluster. HA depends on vCenter Server for Admission Control.

Key Topic

If Admission Control is enabled, HA decides whether to allow a VM to power on based on the available resources in the cluster. Resources in the cluster are diminished when an unplanned downtime event occurs, and the remaining resources might be insufficient to power on all VMs. Although there are several ways to reserve spare capacity in a cluster, the preferred setting for the Admission Control Policy is to reserve a specific percent of CPU and memory resources. When this setting is chosen, VMs can power on successfully if sufficient unreserved CPU and memory resources exists to support VM overhead and any reservations on the VM. For example, if 25% CPU is reserved for HA spare capacity, then only 75% of the cluster resources can actually be used for currently running VMs.

An alternative to reserving resources is to set the Admission Control Policy to specify the number of host failures the cluster tolerates. This setting, and only this specific setting, instructs HA to calculate and use a slot size to determine the amount of resources to reserve. The slot size is calculated utilizing a worst-case approach that allocates a specific amount of CPU and memory resources per VM based primarily on the currently running VMs that have the greatest CPU and memory reservation. The default Admission Control Policy sets the Host failures the cluster tolerates to 1.

Scenario—N+1 HA Cluster Size

Without allowing for spare capacity for scheduled maintenance or unplanned host failures, capacity planners estimated that six ESXi hosts are needed to provide sufficient resources for a specific vSphere-based workload. The customer is now requesting to add one more active host to the cluster to allow sufficient spare capacity in the cluster to tolerate one host failure. The customer would like to maintain the equivalent of one spare host over time, even if the workload in the cluster increases and more hosts are added to the cluster over time. The client prefers to configure the cluster to guarantee sufficient resources for a single host failure, and they prefer not to have to recalculate and reconfigure spare CPU and memory capacity.

In this scenario, the administrator might decide to enable Admission Control and set the **Host failures the cluster tolerates** to 1.

Finally, the Admission Control Policy can be set to use one or more specified hosts for failover events. In this case, the selected ESXi hosts sit idle and do not run VMs unless an ESXi host failure occurs in the cluster. To configure this option, select the **Failover ESXi Hosts** option and select which hosts will be used for HA failover.

Create a Custom Slot Size Configuration

If Admission Control is enabled and the **Host failures the cluster tolerates** is set, then HA uses an algorithm based on slots to ensure that sufficient spare resources are reserved to tolerate host failures. In this case, HA calculates the slot size. It examines the CPU reservation for each running VM in the cluster, determines the highest current value, and sets the CPU size for the slot to that value. It then sums the memory reservation and memory overhead for each running VM in the cluster, determines the highest current value, and sets the memory size for the slot to that value. HA then uses the slot size to make several calculations using this algorithm:

- HA determines the entire CPU and memory capacity of the cluster.

- HA calculates the number of slots in the cluster by dividing the total CPU and memory capacity of the cluster by the CPU and memory size of the slot.

- HA calculates the number of slots for each host by dividing the total available slots in the cluster by the number of hosts in the cluster.

- HA calculates the number of slots that must be reserved for HA by multiplying the **Host failures the cluster tolerates** value by the slots per host.

- HA calculates the maximum available slots for running VMs by subtracting the number of slots that must be reserved for HA from the total number of slots in the cluster.

- HA sets the number of currently used slots to the number of currently running VMs.

- HA calculates the number of available (unused) slots by subtracting the number of currently used slots from the maximum available slots.

HA displays the results on the Advanced Runtime Info page, as illustrated in Figure 5-1. The Advanced Runtime Info page is accessible from the **Advanced Runtime** link on the cluster's Summary tab.

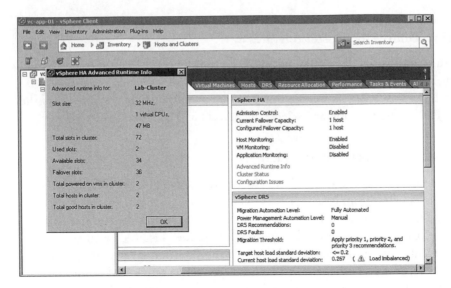

Figure 5-1 HA Advanced Runtime Info.

By default, the slot size is automatically set to reflect the VM with the highest CPU reservation and the VM with the highest memory reservation. This might not always be desirable. Consider a case where one VM has 8 GB of memory reserved and all the other VMs in the cluster have 0 GB reserved. In this case, HA effectively allocates 8 GB for all VMs in the case of a host failure. As a result, under normal conditions Admission Control will allow very few VMs to start. It is possible to manually control the slot size by setting advanced options in HA to establish minimum and maximum slot sizes. The options **das.vmCpuMinMHz** and **das.vmMemoryMinMB** are used to configure the minimum allowed slot size. The options **das.vmCpuInMHz** and **das.vmMemoryInMB** are used to configure the maximum allowed slot size. The names of these options must be carefully entered in the Advanced Options page of the HA cluster settings along with their values, as illustrated in Figure 5-2.

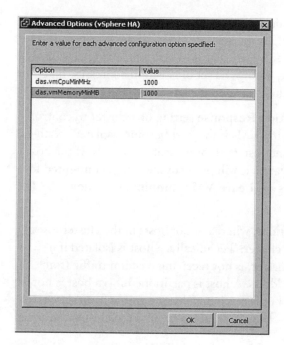

Figure 5-2   HA Advanced Options.

Heartbeats and Dependencies

VMware HA uses three types of heartbeats, which are network, datastore, and VMware Tools. Historically, network heartbeats have been the main mechanism used for host failure detection. By default, ESXi hosts send network heartbeats to other hosts in the cluster via the Management Network. Additional vmkernel management ports can be added to create redundant network heartbeats. Technically, the master server sends network heartbeats to all slaves and each slave responds. The master simultaneously uses all available vmkernel ports configured for management traffic to send heartbeats. The slaves send responses using only one vmkernel port but can failover to a different vmkernel port configured for management traffic if necessary.

In vSphere 5, an added measure of resiliency for HA is the datastore heartbeat. If the master does not receive a network heartbeat response from a specific slave, it then checks for a datastore heartbeat. VMFS datastores contain a heartbeat region, where each host accessing the datastore frequently updates a time stamp to indicate the host is healthy. On NFS datastores, HA adds a file for each host named **host-<X>-hb**, which is used for similar purposes. If needed, the master can check the time stamps on the designated HA heartbeat datastores. If no network heartbeats, no ping responses, and no datastore heartbeats are detected for a given slave,

Key Topic

then it is considered to have failed. If datastore heartbeats are received from a slave host, but no network heartbeats or ping responses are received, the host is considered to be isolated from the network. If a particular host is not receiving heartbeats or election traffic from any other host, it pings its set of isolation addresses. If at least one isolation address responds, the host is not isolated from the network.

You can preconfigure the **Host Isolation Response** setting of a cluster to control which action should be taken on running VMs if the host becomes isolated. Naturally, if a host fails, HA will migrate and restart all of its protected VMs. If the host does not fail, but instead becomes isolated, it will perform the action configured for Host Isolation Response. The options are **Leave VMs Running**, **shut down VMs**, or **Power down VMs**.

HA can now recognize network partitions, where a set of hosts in the cluster loses connectivity to the other hosts in the cluster. Technically, a host is isolated if it is not receiving heartbeats from the master, is not receiving election traffic from slaves, and cannot ping its isolation address. A host is partitioned if is a host is not receiving heartbeats from the master but is receiving election traffic from slaves. In this case, the hosts in the partition re-elect a second master and the cluster continues to provide high availability.

Customize Isolation Response Settings

When choosing the appropriate Host Isolation Response setting, be sure to consider the configured network and datastore redundancy described in the next topic. For example, if two networks and two datastores are used for HA heartbeats, then the likelihood of isolation is minimized but possible. Consider if one host is isolated from both of the heartbeat networks, what is the likelihood that users can still reach its VMs? If this scenario is likely, set the **Host Isolation Response** to **Leave VMs Running**. Otherwise, configure the setting to **shut down VMs**. Another approach is to configure a vmkernel port tagged for management traffic on the same network as the VMs and set the **Host Isolation Response** to **shut down VMs**. The reasoning behind this configuration is that if this management port cannot reach the network, it is doubtful the VMs on the same network can do so.

Configure HA Redundancy

The networks and the datastores used for HA should be as resilient as possible. Redundancy should be configured for the HA network heartbeat and the datastore heartbeat. Placing additional vmkernel ports on each host and enabling them for management traffic can achieve network heartbeat redundancy. This allows HA heartbeats to traverse multiple networks, so that HA does not mistake a loss of connectivity on one network for host failure or host isolation. Additionally, each vmkernel port used for heartbeats can be configured to use NIC teaming to increase resiliency for each network.

HA datastore heartbeats are automatically assigned to two datastores that are available to all hosts in the cluster, if available. To change this assignment, do the following:

Step 1. Select **Inventory > Hosts and Clusters**.

Step 2. Right-click the HA cluster, and select **Edit Settings**.

Step 3. Select **Datastore Heartbeating** as shown in Figure 5-3.

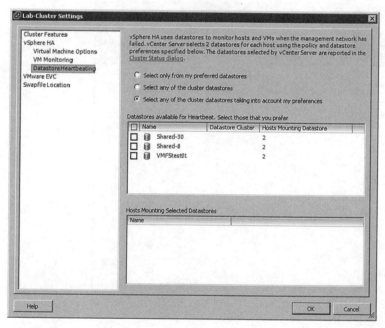

Figure 5-3   HA datastore heartbeats.

The best choices for heartbeat datastores typically involve datastores with as much separation as available. Optimal choices are datastores on separate arrays, separate spindles, separate RAID groups, or separate LUNs. If a host is successfully updating its heartbeat region on either selected datastore, the host has not failed.

A best practice to improve redundancy is to add more isolation addresses. By default, a single isolation address is used and is set to the default gateway of the management network. It is recommended to have at least one isolation address for each heartbeat network and a minimum of two isolation addresses. Isolation addresses can be added by using the **Advanced Options** button on the HA Cluster Settings, as discussed previously. Use the option names **das.isolationaddressX**, where X is any integer between 0 and 9, and set each option to an appropriate IP address. When testing for isolation, the host will first ping the IP assigned to **das.isolationaddress0** and then continue pinging the remaining isolation addresses in order until a response is received or the list is exhausted.

Calculate Host Failure Requirements

One way to determine the spare capacity required for a host failure is to analyze the **Resource Allocation** tab of the cluster, as shown in Figure 5-4.

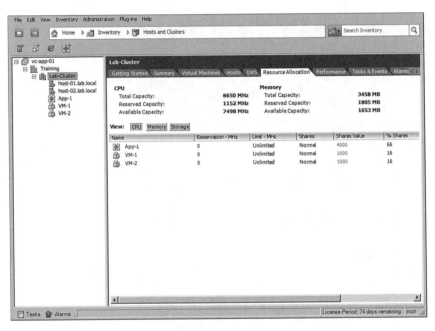

Figure 5-4   Resource Allocation tab.

Key Topic

Examine the total capacity, reserved capacity, and available capacity of the cluster. For example, a cluster contains two hosts and the HA Admission Control is set to allow one host failure. This resulted in about 50% of the total memory capacity being reserved. You can use the **View > Memory** button to examine the memory reservation for each VM, sum these values, and verify that the reserved amount is sufficient.

If the capacity reserved for HA is either too low or too high, consider changing the Admission Control policy to use specific percentages of CPU and memory resources. If the previous example is changed to reserve 25% CPU and 25% memory resources for failover, the resulting resource allocation would look like the example in Figure 5-5.

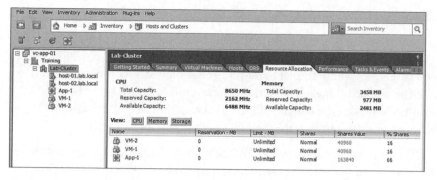

Figure 5-5   The Resource Allocation tab after reserving memory.

Configure HA-related Alarms and Monitor HA Clusters

VMware HA provides many alarms, such as these:

- Insufficient vSphere HA failover resources

- vSphere HA failover in progress

- Cannot find vSphere HA master agent

- vSphere HA host status

- vSphere HA virtual machine failover failed

Configure an action for each of these alarms to automatically notify administrators via email or SNMP traps. When triggered, each of the alarms deserves immediate attention. For example, the **Insufficient vSphere HA Failover resources** alarm indicates that not all protected VMs might be able to failover if a host failure was to occur.

Whenever performing maintenance tasks that can disrupt network heartbeats or datastore heartbeats, it is best to temporarily disable HA host monitoring. If you plan to disconnect an ESXi host from vCenter Server, reconfigure a virtual switch (vSwitch) used for management traffic, change physical management network connections, or modify physical network switches, you should consider unchecking **Enable Host Monitoring** on the cluster settings page until the work is completed. This will avoid any unintended HA activity while these changes are taking place. But, this will also prevent HA from responding to actual failures while these changes are taking place.

Interactions Between DRS and HA

To support and troubleshoot VMware Distributed Resource Scheduler (DRS) and HA, you should fully understand how they interact. For example, when a host failure occurs, HA decides where to place and restart each failed VM. Because HA is not aware of the workload in each VM, this can result in unbalanced workloads on the surviving ESXi host in the cluster. If DRS is also configured, it can balance these workloads to provide the best possible conditions during the HA event.

The basic DRS affinity rules are strictly DRS rules, not HA rules. HA ignores those rules. But HA does comply with the VM DRS group to host DRS group affinity rules.

Scenario—Anti Affinity Rule

A DRS/HA cluster contains two ESXi hosts. A DRS rule is implemented for a pair of Active Directory domain controller VMs, with the setting **Separate Virtual Machines**.

In this scenario, if an administrator wants to shut down one host for maintenance, she will need to manually migrate one of the domain controllers because DRS cannot do so due to the rule. However, if one of the hosts unexpectedly failed, HA will migrate all VMs including the failed domain controller to the surviving host and restart them. After the failed host is repaired and is successfully reconnected to the cluster, DRS will immediately apply the rule and migrate one of the domain controllers to the reconnected host.

If HA admission control is set to designate one or more failover hosts, DRS will not make recommendations to migrate VMs to those hosts. If Distributed Power Management (DPM) is enabled and an HA failover event occurs, DPM will likely ask hosts to start up and exit standby mode.

Use PowerCLI to Configure HA

The **New-Cluster** PowerCLI cmdlet can be used to create new HA clusters. For example, to create a new cluster named Cluster-01 in a datacenter named DataCenter-01, the following command can be used:

```
New-Cluster -Location (Get-Datacenter "Training") -Name Cluster-01
```

The **Set-Cluster** PowerCLI command can be used to configure the cluster. For example, to configure a cluster named Cluster-01 to enable HA and set **HA Isolation Response** to Leave VMs Running, the following command can be used:

```
Set-Cluster Cluster-01 –HAEnabled $True
-HAIsolationResponse DoNothing
```

In this PowerCLI example, the value DoNothing corresponds to the Leave VMs Running value provided by the vSphere Client for HA Isolation Response. Other acceptable values for **–HAIsolationResponse** are PowerOff and Shutdown.

VMware Distributed Resource Scheduler

This section describes how to manage a DRS cluster. It covers many specific elements and provides details on concepts, implementation, and management. It provides steps, examples, and scenarios involving the vSphere Client and PowerCLI.

DRS Overview

You should already be familiar with the following details in this overview. If any of this information is new to you, be sure to conduct the appropriate research before continuing on to the remainder of the section.

DRS is a vSphere feature that provides automatic balancing of CPU and memory workloads across a cluster of ESXi hosts. It achieves this balancing by intelligently placing VMs on hosts as they are powered on and by migrating running VMs to less used hosts in the cluster using vMotion. The key requirements for DRS are a proper license for vSphere Enterprise edition or higher and a properly configured vMotion network. For optimal workload balancing, each ESXi host and each VM should meet vMotion requirements as well. DRS also provides cluster-based resource pools allowing CPU and memory resources to be reserved for groups of VMs.

DRS Configuration

The DRS Automation Level can be set to Manual, Partially Automated, or Fully Automated. When set to Manual, DRS only makes recommendations, which then require manual approval to actually apply the placements or migrations. When set to Fully Automated, DRS automatically performs some placements and migrations that it recommends, dependent on a configured threshold setting. When set to Partially Automated, DRS automatically performs initial placements but only makes recommendations for migrations. You can set the DRS Automation Level by using the Cluster Settings page, selecting vSphere DRS on the left side, and the appropriate level on the right side, as shown in Figure 5-6.

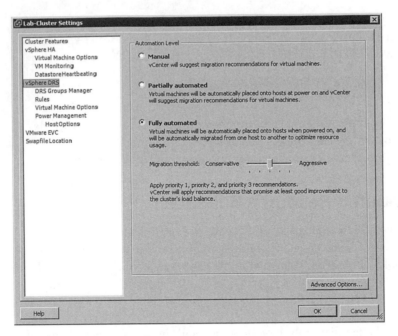

Figure 5-6 The DRS automation level.

When set to Fully Automated, DRS only applies recommendations that are allowed based on the **Migration Threshold**. This setting controls how aggressively recommendations are applied. Recommendations are priority based from priority levels 1 to 5. The most aggressive setting results in applying all recommendations. The default threshold applies only priority 1–3 recommendations. If the threshold is set to Conservative, it applies only priority 1 recommendations, which effectively means it applies only the DRS rules and does not balance based on workload. Each priority maps to an allowed level of deviation between the workload levels of each host in the cluster, as illustrated in Figure 5-7 and Figure 5-8.

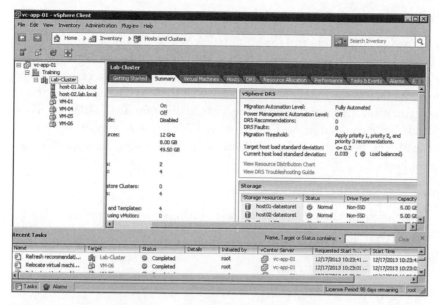

Figure 5-7   The target host load std dev for default threshold.

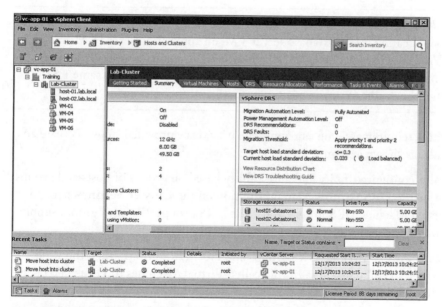

Figure 5-8   The target host load std dev for Priority 2 threshold.

DRS Affinity and Anti-affinity Rules

Rules can be used in DRS to control the affinity of VMs. By default, no rules exist and DRS is free to put VMs on any active host in the cluster. You can create an affinity rule to force DRS to keep a set of VMs on the same host. In this case, if DRS decides to place one VM on a specific host, it places all the VMs in the rule on the same host. If you manually migrate one of the VMs to different host, DRS will likely migrate it back, but it could migrate the remaining VMs in the rule to the other host. You can also create an anti-affinity rule to force DRS to separate a set of VMs onto different hosts.

To configure an affinity rule, follow these steps:

Step 1.   Right-click the cluster and select **Edit Settings**.

Step 2.   Select **VMware DRS > Rules**.

Step 3.   Supply a name for the rule.

Step 4.   Select **Keep VMs Together**.

Step 5.   In the VMs section, select the appropriate VMs.

Scenario—Affinity Rule

A three-tier application uses a database server VM, an application server VM, and a web server VM. Due to high network traffic between the application server and the other two VMs, you are tasked to ensure that the three VMs run on the same ESXi hosts, allowing this traffic to stay inside the host.

To meet this requirement, you can apply the previously provided steps to create an affinity rule, as shown in Figure 5-9.

You can also configure affinity and anti-affinity based on groups of hosts and groups of VMs. Use the **DRS Groups Manager** option on the **Cluster Settings** page to create Virtual Machine DRS groups and Host DRS groups. For each group, supply a logical name and select its members, as illustrated in Figure 5-10.

If you create Virtual Machine DRS groups and Host DRS groups, then the Rule page will offer an additional type of rule called Virtual Machines to Hosts. To create VMs to Hosts affinity rules, select this option, select one VM DRS group, select one host DRS group, and select the affinity designation. The choices are as follows:

- Should run on hosts in group
- Must run on hosts in group
- Must not run on hosts in group
- Should not run on hosts in group

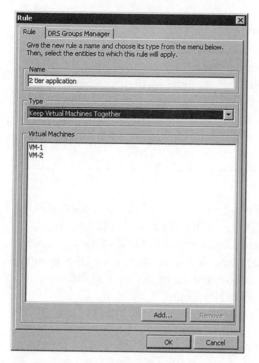

Figure 5-9   DRS Affinity Rule example.

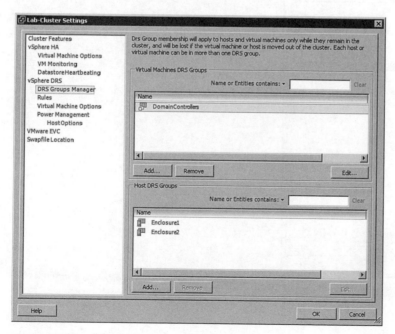

Figure 5-10   The DRS Groups Manager page.

Scenario—Domain Controller VMs Running on Blades

A DRS/HA cluster contains 16 ESXi hosts running on blades in two chassis. A DRS rule is implemented for a pair of Active Directory domain controller VMs, with the setting **separate virtual machines**. You realize that it would be better to ensure the domain controllers run not just on separate blades, but in separate chassis. You also want to ensure that when you place all hosts in one chassis into maintenance mode, that you can easily, temporarily allow both domain controllers to run in the same chassis.

Key Topic

To meet this requirement, you can create two Host DRS groups—one for each chassis—containing the corresponding ESXi hosts. Create two VM DRS groups, containing one domain controller VM each. Create a VM to Host affinity rule for one of the VM DRS groups specifying that it should run the first host DRS group as shown in Figure 5-11. Likewise, create a second rule for the other VM DRS group specifying that it should run in the other host DRS group.

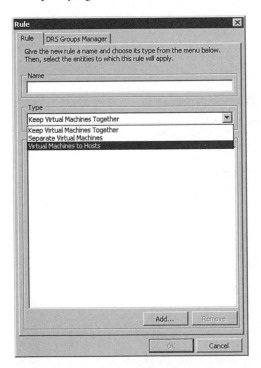

Figure 5-11   An example of VM to Host affinity rule.

DRS Alarms

No DRS-specific alarms are defined by default in vSphere, but you should consider creating some custom alarms. You can create new alarms at any point in the vCenter Server hierarchy, but by creating the alarms on the vCenter Server (root) object, they can then be easily applied to any DRS cluster. Setting the Alarm Type to monitor clusters enables you to choose DRS specific triggers, such as **DRS disabled** and **DRS enabled**, as illustrated in Figure 5-12.

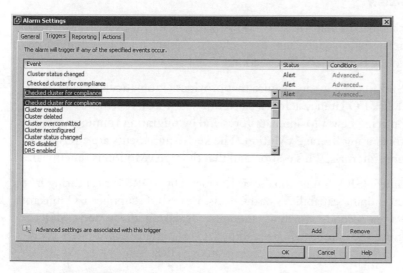

Figure 5-12   DRS alarm triggers.

You might want to create alarms to trigger on **Cluster status changed** and **Cluster overcommitted** and assign actions to notify administrators via email or SNMP for immediate attention.

Use PowerCLI to Configure DRS

The **New-Cluster** PowerCLI cmdlet can be used to create new clusters, where HA, DRS, or both can be enabled and configured. The **Set-Cluster** PowerCLI cmdlet can be used to configure the cluster. For example, to configure a cluster named Cluster-01 to enable DRS and set DRS Automation to Fully Automated, the following command can be used:

```
Set-Cluster Cluster-01 –DRSEnabled $True -DrsAutomationLevel
FullyAutomated
```

VMware Storage DRS

This section describes how to configure and manage VMware Storage DRS. It covers many specific elements providing details on concepts, implementation, and management. It provides steps, examples, and scenarios utilizing the vSphere Client and PowerCLI.

Storage DRS Overview

You should already be familiar with the following details in this overview. If any of this information is new to you, be sure to conduct the appropriate research before continuing on to the remainder of the section.

Storage DRS (SDRS) is a vSphere feature that provides automatic balancing of disk space usage and disk I/O latency across a cluster of datastores. It achieves balancing by intelligently placing new VMs on datastores and by migrating running VMs to less-used datastores using Storage vMotion. The key requirements are a proper license for vSphere Enterprise Plus edition and that Storage vMotion is functional.

Storage I/O Control (SIOC) functionality is leveraged by SDRS for capturing I/O statistics and determining capabilities of the datastores. SIOC supplies I/O injectors, which generate a few seconds' worth of random reads during idle periods. SIOC measures and stores the number of outstanding I/Os and the latency. These statistics are then used in the load-balancing algorithm of SDRS.

By default, SDRS analyzes I/O latency statistics once every 8 hours but uses the past 24 hours' worth of statistics to make migration recommendations. If 90% of the collected statistics of the 24-hour period are above the current I/O latency threshold, the datastore is overloaded.

If you select the **Enable Storage I/O Control** check box, SIOC will work with the injector to estimate the datastore latency when it operates at 90% of its peak throughput. SDRS will automatically set its IO Latency threshold to that value, but you can override this setting if desired. In most cases, the calculated value is acceptable.

SDRS will not begin to evaluate any IO statistics until at least 16 hours after implementation.

Storage DRS Configuration

To create a datastore cluster and configure Storage DRS for full automation, the following steps can be used:

Step 1.   Select **Inventory > Datastores and Datastore Clusters**.

Step 2. Right-click a datacenter object and select **New Datastore Cluster**, which starts a wizard.

Step 3. On the **General** page, provide a name for the cluster, ensure the **Turn on Storage DRS** box is selected, and click **Next**.

Step 4. On the **Automation** page, select **Full Automation**. Click **Next**.

Step 5. On the **Runtime Rules** page, leave the default settings and click **Next**.

Step 6. On the **Select Hosts and Clusters** page, select a DRS cluster containing the ESXi hosts that will participate in Storage DRS. Click **Next**.

Step 7. On the **Datastores** page, select the datastores that will participate in the cluster. Click **Next**.

Step 8. On the **Ready to Complete** page, click **Finish**.

Settings on an existing cluster can be performed by right-clicking the cluster and selecting **Edit Cluster**.

Storage DRS is useful for balancing capacity utilization in a datastore cluster and for preventing a datastore from becoming full. It enables the administrator to set a **Used Space Threshold**, which can be set from 50% to 100%. Typically, this threshold should be set to the target maximum capacity utilization that has been determined based on a given vSphere design. A best practice is to target filling the datastores to 80%, leaving 20% spare capacity for snapshots and for growth of thin-provisioned virtual disks. If these values are used, the Storage DRS disk space threshold should likewise be set to 80%. Whenever a datastore's disk space usage reaches that threshold, SDRS will immediately invoke disk space usage balancing and potentially use Storage vMotion to migrate one or more VMs from the datastore to other datastores that are significantly below the threshold. It might make sense to set disk space usage alarms on the cluster at a slightly higher value, such as 85%. If the alarm is then triggered, it can indicate that all the datastores in the cluster are becoming full and additional datastores might need to be added to the cluster. When datastores are added to the cluster, SDRS can automatically make use of the space and migrate any VMs from data stores that are too full.

Storage DRS can also be configured to balance workload based on I/O latency, by editing its settings and selecting **Enable I/O metric for SDRS recommendations**. Selecting this feature enables Storage I/O Control, if it is not already enabled. Use the **I/O Latency** option to set an allowed threshold. If latency exceeds this threshold on a datastore, then SDRS might determine that VMs should be migrated to a less active datastore. Typically this threshold should be set per established SLAs or per storage vendor recommendations.

Key
Topic

The Storage DRS Automation Level can be set to **No Automation (Manual Mode)** or **Full Automation**, as shown in Figure 5-13.

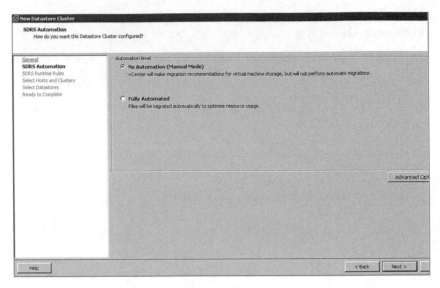

Figure 5-13 Storage DRS automation level.

When set to Manual, SDRS only makes recommendations, which require manual approval before SDRS will apply the placements or migrations. When set to Full Automation, SDRS automatically makes the placements and migrations that it recommends, which requires no manual activity.

Advanced options are available to granularly control SDRS behavior. Select the **Show Advanced Options** link on the settings page of the datastore cluster. Use the **No recommendations until utilization difference between source and destination is** option to instruct SDRS to ensure that the target datastore utilization is lower than the source datastore utilization by a specified percentage. For example, if the usage threshold is 80%, a datastore is 81% full, and the difference threshold is 5%, then the selected target utilization must be 76% or less. Notice this setting impacts only disk space usage balancing. Another advanced option is the **Check imbalances every** setting, which defines how often SDRS invokes I/O latency and disk space usage balancing. The default setting is 8 hours. Notice this option mainly impacts I/O latency balancing because disk space usage balancing is also automatically triggered whenever the **Utilized Space** threshold is exceeded on one or more datastores in the datastore cluster. Another advanced option is the **I/O imbalance threshold** setting, which defines the aggressiveness of I/O Latency balancing. An example of the Advanced Options page is shown in Figure 5-14.

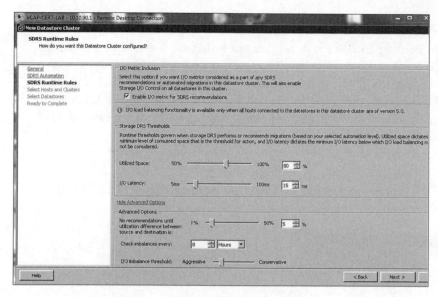

Figure 5-14   The SDRS Advanced Options tab.

SDRS will apply the settings from the Advanced Options page along with its internal algorithms to perform a cost/benefit analysis if a threshold is exceeded and will make a recommendation only if a significant improvement is expected.

Storage DRS Affinity and Anti-affinity Rules

Rules can be used in SDRS to control the affinity of VM files. By default, an intra-VM affinity rule is applied to each VM, forcing SDRS to ensure that all the files for a given VM are stored on the same datastore. If SDRS migrates one of the files of the VM, it must migrate all of that VM's files. An optional rule is **intra-VM anti-affinity**, which forces SDRS to separate the virtual disk files for a VM onto separate datastores. This is only useful for VMs having more than one virtual disk. Another option rule is **VM anti-affinity**, which forces SDRS to separate two ore more VMs onto separate datastores.

To create an SDRS rule, right-click the datastore cluster and select **Edit Settings.** In the datastore cluster settings window, select **Rules**. Provide a name for the rule; select VMs to add to the rule; and select the **Rule Type,** such as VM anti-affinity. For example, consider the following scenario:

Key
Topic

Scenario—Anti-affinity Rule

A Storage DRS cluster contains multiple datastores that are accessed by a cluster of multiple ESXi hosts. A DRS rule is implemented for a pair of Active Directory domain controller VMs, with the setting **separate virtual machines**, which ensures that a single host failure does not cause the failure of the entire AD domain. Likewise, a requirement is defined that the failure of a single datastore should not cause the failure of the AD domain.

To satisfy the requirement in this scenario, you can create an SDRS VM anti-affinity rule on the two domain controllers, as illustrated in Figure 5-15.

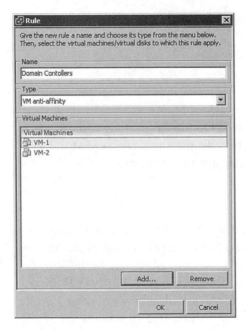

Figure 5-15   Example of SDRS VM anti-affinity rule for domain controllers.

One SDRS best practice is to ensure that all datastores in the cluster are similar and use the same back-end storage, particularly when balancing on I/O latency. Another best practice is to run SDRS in manual mode initially and monitor recommendations before changing to automatic. A final best practice is to follow storage vendor recommendations, especially for automatic tiered arrays. For automatic tiered arrays, the vendor will likely suggest turning off SDRS balancing on I/O latency.

Storage DRS Alarms

SDRS provides two default alarms, **Storage DRS recommendation** and **Storage DRS is not supported on the Host**. If SDRS is set for **Manual** mode, then you should configure the **Storage DRS recommendation** alarm to automatically notify you via email or SNMP. Figure 5-16 shows the default SDRS alarms.

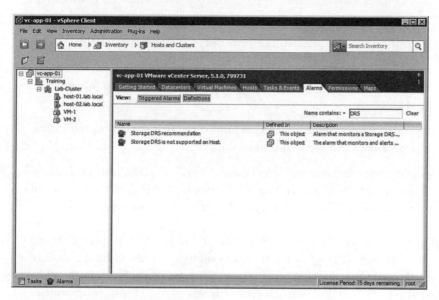

Figure 5-16   The default SDRS alarms.

Scenario—Acknowledge SDRS Alarms

Due to a lack of fully trusting a technology that is new to a particular customer, the administrator elects to configure SDRS Automation to **No Automation (Manual)**. His intent is to be automatically notified when a space usage threshold is exceeded and an imbalance exists, so he can manually investigate the problem and take appropriate actions.

In this case, the administrator configures the action on the **Storage DRS recommendation** alarm to send an SNMP trap to a monitoring system. She defines a procedure to be manually followed whenever the trap is received. The procedure is as follows:

Step 1.   Use the vSphere Client to select a datastore, select its **Alarms** tab, select **Triggered Alarms**, and verify that **Storage DRS Recommendation** alarm is triggered.

Step 2.   Right-click the alarm and select **Acknowledge Alarm**, which indicates to others you are working to address the alarm.

Step 3.   Select the **Summary** tab for the datastore and use it to collect details on the current usage and free space.

Step 4.   Select the datastore cluster in the inventory, and select the **Datastores** tab to examine the usage and free space of all datastores in the cluster.

Step 5.   Identify at least one datastore whose usage is significantly below the threshold.

Step 6.   Manually migrate at least one VM from the first datastore to the second datastore.

Step 7.   Return to the **Triggered Alarms** tab for the first datastore, and locate the **Storage DRS Recommendation** alarm.

Step 8.   Right-click the alarm and select **Clear**. Verify that the alarm is removed from the list and the alert icon is removed from the datastore cluster inventory object. This indicates to others that the issue is resolved.

VAAI-supported arrays that provide storage device thin provisioning can now trigger events in vCenter Server when the thin-provisioning threshold on the storage array is exceeded for the volume(s) backing the datastore. No default alarms are triggered by this condition, but you can create alarms on VAAI thin-provisioned datastores that are triggered by the event. This alarm can be configured only via APIs, but it can be viewed in the vSphere Client as illustrated in Figure 5-17.

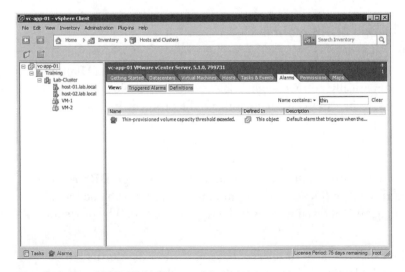

Figure 5-17   SDRS VAAI thin-provisioned alarm.

Use PowerCLI to Configure SDRS

The **New-DatastoreCluster** PowerCLI cmdlet can be used to create new datastore clusters. For example, to create a new datastore cluster named DataCluster-01 in a datacenter named MyDataCenter, the following command can be used:

```
New-DatastoreCluster  -Name 'DataCluster-01' -Location 'MyDataCenter'
```

The **Set-DatastoreCluster** PowerCLI cmdlet can be used to configure the cluster. For example, to set the latency threshold and automation level on a datastore cluster named DataCluster-01, the following command can be used:

```
Set-DatastoreCluster -DatastoreCluster  DataCluster-01
-IOLatencyThresholdMillisecond 10        -SdrsAutomationLevel
FullyAutomated
```

In this example, the latency threshold is set to 10 ms and the automation level is set to Fully Automated.

VMware Distributed Power Management

This section provides details for configuring and managing VMware Distributed Power Management (DPM). It includes details on concepts, implementation, and management, as well as the steps, examples, and scenarios to perform common DPM tasks. These steps involve the use of the vSphere Client and PowerCLI.

DPM Overview

You should already be familiar with the following details in this overview. If any of this information is new to you, be sure to conduct the appropriate research before continuing on to the remainder of the section.

DPM is a DRS cluster feature that can be enabled and used to save electrical power and cooling costs by automatically shutting down some ESXi hosts during periods of low workload. DPM monitors CPU and memory activity across a cluster of hosts and compares it to the current capacity. If it determines that the workload could run effectively on fewer hosts, it recommends shutting down one or more hosts. It first asks such hosts to enter maintenance mode. If DRS is fully automated, it will migrate the VMs from a host that enters maintenance mode to other hosts in the cluster. When the host is in maintenance mode, DPM will instruct the host to enter standby mode, which means the host will gracefully shut down and power down. The host remains available to DPM and can be automatically powered on and added to the cluster if the workload increases.

The main prerequisites for DPM are for DRS to be enabled and for each ESXi host to contain a network adapter capable of powering on the host. DPM appears as a subset feature within the settings of DRS. DRS must be enabled before DPM can be enabled. This implies that all requirements of DRS, such as shared storage and vMotion, are also requirements of DPM. DPM also needs the ability to wake a host from standby mode, which means it needs the ability to send a network command to the host to power on. For this feature, DPM requires iLO, IPMI, or a Wake On LAN adapter to be present in each host of the cluster. DPM must be supplied with the proper credentials to access the interface and power on the host.

DPM Configuration

To enable DPM, edit the cluster settings, navigate to the **vSphere DRS** section, and select the **Power Management** option. Set **Power Management** to either **Manual** or **Automatic**; then set the Aggressiveness, as illustrated in Figure 5-18.

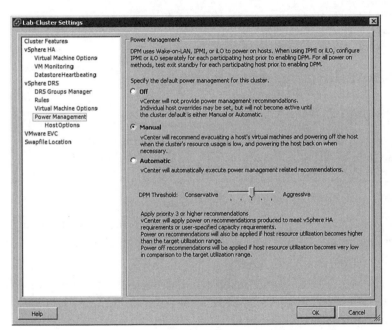

Figure 5-18 DPM Automation and Aggressiveness settings.

For each host in the cluster, navigate to the **Configuration** tab, select **Power Management**, and select **Properties**. Provide the appropriate IP address, MAC address, and user credentials, as shown in Figure 5-19.

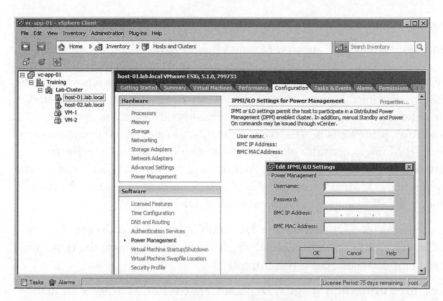

Figure 5-19   Power Management settings for an ESXi host.

DPM offers many configuration options that should be set based on business needs. It provides a threshold control that performs much like the DRS version, but the focus is on how aggressively power operations are performed. These thresholds are separate controls, so, for example, the DRS threshold could be set to aggressive, while the DPM threshold could be set to conservative. The DPM Automation Level can be set to Manual or Full Automation. When set to Manual, DPM only makes recommendations, which require manual approval before action is taken. When set to Full Automation, DPM automatically takes the actions it recommends, which requires no manual intervention.

DPM performs a cost/benefits analysis as part of its decision making. It accounts for costs associated with placing hosts in standby mode, such as compute costs for migrating VMs, cost of compute resources lost while on standby, and cost of potential VM performance degradation. Likewise, it accounts for similar costs incurred when exiting standby mode and the benefits for entering and exiting standby mode. For this computation, DRS must assign CPU and memory costs to each underlying activity. DRS provides Advanced Options that can be configured to granularly impact the analysis. You can use the **Advanced Options** button in the **VMware DRS** section of the Cluster Settings page to set advanced options, such as:

- **PowerPerformanceRatio:** Default value = 40. Range = 0 to 500.

- **HostMinUptimeSecs:** Default value = 600. Range= 0 to maxint.

- **PowerPerformanceHistorySecs:** Default value = 3600. Range = 0 to 3600.

- **MinPoweredOnCpuCapacity:** Default value =1 MHz. Range 0 to maxint.

PowerPerformanceRatio is used as a multiplier for the cost values of power operations before comparing them with the related benefit values. This method ensures that the benefit of a recommendation must significantly outweigh the associated costs. **HostMinUptimeSecs** is used to ensure that hosts run a specific amount of time before DPM might consider placing them in standby mode. **PowerPerformanceHistorySecs** is used to control the period of historical data that is used in the costs/benefits analysis. **MinPoweredOnCpuCapacity** is used to control the minimum amount of CPU capacity to be maintained by DPM.

DPM also provides the advanced options **DemandCapacityRatioTarget** and **DemandCapacityRatioToleranceHost**, which are used to calculate the target utilization range for each host, using this formula:

Target resource utilization range = DemandCapacityRatioTarget ± Demand-CapacityRatioToleranceHost

DPM evaluates the CPU and memory usage of each host and considers taking action when a host's utilization falls outside the target range. The default value for **DemandCapacityRatioTarget** is 63%, and the default value for **DemandCapacityRatioToleranceHost** is 18%. So, by default the target utilization range is from 45% to 81%. You can change the range by adjusting the values of the advanced options. For example, if you are required to adjust the target range from 40% to 80%, set the **DemandCapacityRatioTarget** to 60% and the **DemandCapacityRatioToleranceHost** to 20%.

If business requirements do not permit the automatic shutdown of hosts without manual administrator approval, you might choose to set the automation to Manual and configure alarm actions to notify you when DPM has recommendations to be approved.

Scenario—DPM Settings

In a DRS/HA cluster running on 16 blades evenly split between two enclosures, the administrator wants to implement power management, but business requirements demand a high level of redundancy to be maintained continuously. He needs to ensure that active compute resources are always available in each enclosure in case one enclosure unexpectedly fails.

In this case, the administrator could choose to select two or more blades in each enclosure to disable from DPM. This allows DPM to be fully automated while ensuring that some ESXi hosts are always available in each enclosure. To make these settings, the following steps can be performed:

Step 1.   Right-click the cluster, and select **Edit Settings**.

Step 2.   Select **vSphere DRS > Power Management > Host Options**.

Step 3.   Select one of the ESXi hosts on the right side.

Step 4.   Use the **Power Management** drop-down tool to select **Disabled**.

Step 5.   Repeat steps 3 and 4 for additional hosts.

DPM Alarms

One default alarm exists related to DPM, which is the **Exit Standby Error** alarm. This alarm triggers if DPM fails to bring a host out of standby mode, meaning it does not start and does not make its resources available. You should consider configuring an action to send an SNMP Trap or email on this alarm. Additionally, you can create custom alarms that are triggered when a host attempts and successfully completes entering and exiting standby mode.

Use PowerCLI to Configure DPM

Currently, no PowerCLI commands are available to configure DPM.

VMware Enhanced vMotion Compatibility

This section provides details for configuring and managing Enhanced vMotion Compatibility (EVC). It includes details on concepts, implementation, and management, as well as steps, examples, and scenarios to perform common EVC tasks. These steps involve the use of the vSphere Client and PowerCLI.

EVC Overview

You should already be familiar with the following details in this overview. If any of this information is new to you, be sure to conduct the appropriate research before continuing on to the remainder of the section.

EVC is a cluster feature that is useful in scenarios where not all the hosts in the cluster are compatible with each other for vMotion migration but are from the same CPU vendor. It enables vMotion migration between hosts that have older and newer versions of Intel-based CPUs. It enables vMotion migration between hosts that have older and newer versions of AMD-based CPUs. However, it does not enable vMotion migrations between hosts, where one has an Intel CPU and one has an AMD CPU.

EVC is disabled by default. It can be enabled by selecting either the **Enable EVC for AMD Hosts** or the **Enable EVC for Intel Hosts** option on the cluster settings page.

EVC Configuration

When enabling EVC, you must select the baseline for the appropriate CPU vendor. The choices for the AMD CPU family are shown in Figure 5-20.

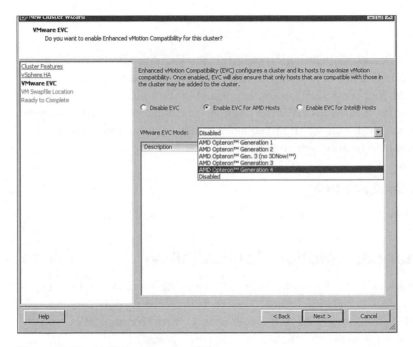

Figure 5-20   AMD baselines for EVC.

The choice for the Intel CPU family are shown in Figure 5-21.

A best practice is to initially set the baseline to the most modern generation of the appropriate chip vendor that is common among all the hosts in the cluster. For example, if in a four-host cluster, three hosts are Nehalem and one is Westmere, select Nehalem. Notice in Figures 5-20 and 5-21 that the **Description** panel provides a list of processor types that are permitted for that selected baseline. EVC will not allow hosts containing a non-listed processor to be added to the cluster.

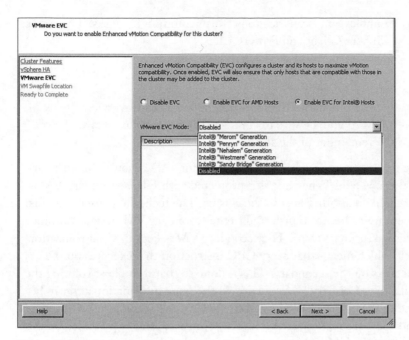

Figure 5-21   Intel baselines for EVC.

A best practice is to initially enable EVC on a new cluster, prior to running any VMs in the cluster. If running VMs need to be migrated into the cluster with vMotion, their actively used CPU feature set must be compatible with the configured EVC generation. Any running VMs with a larger feature set than the selected EVC mode must be shut down and cold migrated into the cluster, which could be planned for during a maintenance window. Another best practice is to enable EVC even when all the hosts in the cluster have identical processors. Simply select the highest generation level that fits the chip type. This makes the potential, future task of adding hosts with newer CPUs much simpler, where the host might simply be added to the cluster without having to modify the cluster settings.

EVC expects software to be written to use CPUID machine instruction to discover its CPU features.

EVC can be set or changed on an active cluster, provided that all the VMs in the cluster are running with a CPU feature set that is lower than the selected EVC mode.

VMware Fault Tolerance

This section provides details for configuring and managing VMware Fault Tolerance (FT). It includes details on concepts, implementation, and management, as well as the steps, examples, and scenarios to perform common FT tasks. These steps involve the use of vSphere Client and PowerCLI.

Overview

You should already be familiar with the following details in this overview. If any of this information is new to you, be sure to conduct the appropriate research before continuing on to the remainder of the section.

FT is a vSphere feature that provides fault tolerance for a VM even if the host currently running the VM fails. When a VM is protected with FT, a secondary VM is automatically created on another host in the cluster. The technology used is similar to vMotion, except users are not transferred to the secondary VM. Users continue to access the original (primary) VM. The secondary VM is kept in synchronization with the primary, which means that every CPU instruction that executes on the primary also executes on the secondary. This is done so that if the host running the primary VM fails, the secondary VM contains all the same information and can be accessed in place of the primary. When a failure occurs, the secondary VM becomes the primary, end users are reconnected to the new primary, and, if possible, fault tolerance re-protects the VM by creating a new secondary on a surviving host.

A secondary VM has the same MAC addresses and IP addresses as the primary, but the secondary is not actually connected to the network. The secondary is fooled into thinking it is on the network and that it is sending and receiving exactly the same packets as the primary. The vmkernel blocks the outgoing packets from the secondary. FT feeds the incoming packets from the primary to the secondary via a dedicated channel, ensuring that every packet that reaches the primary also reaches the secondary. Likewise, the secondary VM is fooled into thinking it is reading and writing to the virtual disk. The vmkernel blocks the outgoing disk I/O from the secondary, and FT delivers the incoming disk I/O that reaches the primary via the dedicated channel. The dedicated channel is a designated vmkernel virtual adapter configured for FT logging.

VMware vLockstep is the name of the record/replay technology that allows all instructions that run in the primary to be captured, sent to the secondary, and executed in the secondary. It provides an acknowledgement to the primary that ensures that each instruction is delivered to the secondary before the primary continues.

Requirements

Key Topic

You should verify that your hosts meet the Fault Tolerance requirements and interoperability as defined in the vSphere Availability Guide and the VMware Compatibility Guide (or online matrix). Fault Tolerant Compatibility Sets are similar, but not identical, to the Enhanced vMotion Capability Modes. The host running the secondary VM must have CPUs in the same family as the host running the primary VM.

FT requires shared storage and compatible CPUs. It requires that a vmkernel port be enabled for FT logging and that it is on a dedicated 1 Gbps or faster network. FT requires that all power management features be turned off in the BIOS of the host. This requirement is to ensure the host running the secondary VM does not enter power savings mode, which could result in insufficient resources to keep the secondary VM running well. The primary VM must be configured with thick eager zeroed virtual disks. FT does not support thin-provisioned or thick lazy zeroed virtual disks. No more than four fault-tolerant VMs (primary VMs or secondary VMs) should exist on any single ESXi host.

Configuration and Best Practices

Ensure that sufficient memory resources are available on the host where the secondary VM will run because FT will automatically reserve the full amount of the secondary VM's configured memory. Ensure that sufficient disk space is available on the datastore because if one or more of the primary VM's virtual disks are thin provisioned, FT will automatically convert them to thick eager zeroed. Ensure that a 1 Gbps network adapter can be dedicated to FT, or ensure that Network I/O Control can be configured on a distributed vSwitch (vDS) with 10 Gbps uplinks. Configure and test VMware HA because FT can be configured only if HA is enabled. Ensure that the VMs to be protected and the hosts they will run on meet the requirement for vMotion as FT uses vMotion-like software to copy the state of the running VM.

Some best practices for FT include

- Use ESXi hosts with approximately the same processor frequencies and same vMotion compatibility group.

- Enable Hardware Virtualization in the BIOS per the manufacturer's instructions.

- Configure all participating ESXi hosts identically including items such as same shared datastores, network configuration, ESXi version, and FT version number.

- Implement 10 Gbps and Jumbo Frames for the FT logging network.

- Use a shared datastore to store actively used ISO files.

- Follow vSphere networking best practices to avoid network partitions.

- Take care during upgrades to ensure the primary and secondary VMs operate on compatible versions of FT.

FT Logging Configuration

Create a vmkernel port on each ESXi host in the cluster, and check the **Use this port group for Fault Tolerance logging** check box on its property page, as shown in Figure 5-22.

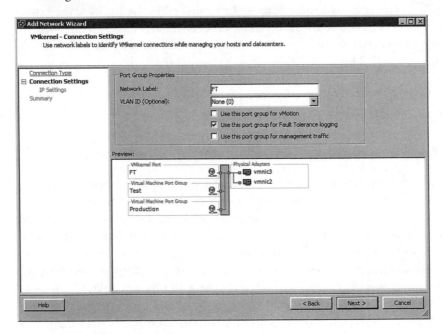

Figure 5-22   FT Logging setting.

Do not select Management or vMotion on these vmkernel ports; instead dedicate it to just **FT Logging**. Insufficient bandwidth or high latency for FT Logging will slow the delivery to and acknowledgement of instructions from the secondary VMs, which in turn will slow down the primary VM. After FT Logging is enabled on the vmkernel port, the Host Configured for FT field on the Summary tab of the host will show Yes.

Operation

Key
Topic

When a VM is protected by FT, the Summary tab of the VM contains status details, such as these:

- **FT Status** indicates whether the VM is Protected or Not Protected.

- **Secondary Location** indicates the host where the secondary executes.

- **Total Secondary PCU** and **Total Secondary Memory** indicate the secondary's total CPU and memory usage.

- **Secondary VM Lag Time** indicates the latency between the execution of commands between primary and secondary.

- **Log Bandwidth** indicates the amount of network being used for sending FT traffic.

To test the failover ability of an FT-protected VM, right-click the VM and select **Fault Tolerance > Test Failover**. This causes the primary VM to be stopped; the secondary VM to be promoted; users to be reconnected to the secondary; and a new secondary to be created on an available, compatible host, if feasible. To migrate the secondary VM to another ESXi host, right-click the VM and select **Migrate Secondary VM** and use the wizard to select the target host and a migration priority.

You can choose between two other actions on a protected VM named **Turn Off FT** and **Disable FT**. Either option will remove FT protection from the VM, but historical data will be lost if the **Turn Off FT** option is selected.

Summary

You should now have the knowledge and skills to successfully perform cluster administration in a vSphere virtualized datacenter. You should also be able to successfully complete cluster configuration, troubleshooting, and management tasks that may be part of the VCAP5-DCA exam. Be sure to take time to practice the steps that are provided in this section until you are confident that you can perform such tasks quickly and without any assistance.

Exam Preparation Tasks

Review All the Key Topics

Table 5-2 provides a list of all Key Topics identified in this chapter along with a few notes intended to refresh your memory of some key details. This can be useful as a quick reference when performing vSphere administration.

Table 5-2 Key Topics for Chapter 5

Key Topic Element	Description	Page
Paragraph	Set Preferred HA Admission Control Policy	214
Paragraph	Control the HA Slot Size: Set **das.vmCpuMinMHz** and Other Advanced Options	216

Key Topic Element	Description	Page
Paragraph	Explanation of how HA determines if a host is isolated	217
Paragraph	Configure HA isolation addresses per best practices	219
Paragraph	Analyze cluster resource usage and availability	220
Step List	Configure DRS affinity rules	226
Paragraph	Configure DRS to keep domain controllers highly available in a blade environment.	228
Step List	Create and configure Storage DRS	230
Paragraph	Configure Storage DRS to balance on I/O latency	231
Paragraph	Configure Storage DRS rules	233
Paragraph	Configure alarms for storage-based thin provisioning	236
Paragraph	Configure DPM	238
Paragraph and Step List	Configure DPM per business requirements	241
Paragraph	Configure EVC per best practices	242
Paragraph	Identify requirements for FT	244
List	Examine FT information for a VM	246

Definitions of Key Terms

Define the following key terms from this chapter, and check your answers in the glossary.

VMware HA, DRS, DPM, Storage DRS, EVC, VMware FT, HA network heartbeat, HA datastore heartbeat, DRS affinity rule, SDRS intra-VM anti-affinity rule, HA Admission Control, vLockStep

Review Tasks

These Review Tasks enable you to assess how well you grasped the materials in this chapter. Because of the advanced and hands-on nature of this particular exam, a set of tasks is provided instead of a set of questions. You should now attempt to perform each of these tasks without looking at previous sections in this chapter or at other materials, unless necessary. The steps for each task are located within the chapter.

1. Configure vSphere HA to use two heartbeat networks and two heartbeat datastores.

2. In a single DRS cluster that consists of 16 ESXi hosts running on 8 blades in one chassis and 8 blades in another chassis, configure a rule that ensures two VM-based domain controllers do not run in the same chassis.

3. Use PowerCLI to configure an existing SDRS cluster's automation level to "fully automated" and its IO latency threshold to 10 milliseconds.

4. Configure an alarm to send an SNMP trap and email whenever DPM fails to start an ESXi host whose resources are needed based on current workload.

5. Configure EVC for a cluster of hosts that contain a mixture of Generation 3 and Generation 4 AMD processors.

6. Configure a cluster of ESXi hosts to support FT.

This chapter covers the following subjects:

- **Install and Configure VMware Update Manager (VUM)**—This section covers installing and configuring VUM.

- **Repositories and Offline Bundles**—This section covers utilizing shared repositories and offline bundles.

- **Create and Modify Baseline Groups**—This section covers creating and configuring baselines and baseline groups.

- **Orchestrated vSphere Upgrades**—This section covers orchestrating vSphere upgrades using VUM.

- **Troubleshooting and Reporting**—This section covers troubleshooting VUM issues and producing VUM reports using Excel and SQL Server Query.

- **Upgrading vApps and Appliances**—This section covers using VUM to update vApps and virtual appliances and controlling the reboot order within vApps.

- **PowerCLI and Update Manager Utility**—This section covers using PowerCLI to export baselines for testing and using Update Manager Utility to reconfigure VUM settings.

This chapter contains material pertaining to the VCAP5-DCA exam objective 5.2.

## CHAPTER 6

Patch Management

This chapter is intended to provide you with the knowledge and skills to successfully perform patch management and the updating of ESXi hosts, virtual machine hardware, VMware Tools, and virtual appliances. It is also intended to ensure that you have the skills to successfully complete the configuration, troubleshooting, and management tasks related to updating that might be part of the VCAP5-DCA exam. As you read this chapter, take time to practice the steps that are provided until you are confident that you can perform the tasks quickly and without any assistance. Some steps involve using the vSphere Client. Others involve using the vCLI and PowerCLI.

"Do I Know This Already?" Quiz

The "Do I Know This Already?" quiz enables you to assess how well you might already know the material in this chapter. Table 6-1 outlines the major headings in this chapter and the corresponding "Do I Know This Already?" quiz questions. You can find the answers in Appendix A, "Answers to the 'Do I Know This Already?' Quizzes." Because of the advanced and hands-on nature of this particular exam, you should read the entire chapter and practice performing all the described tasks at least once, regardless of how well you do on this quiz. This quiz can be helpful to determine which topics will require the most effort during your preparation.

Table 6-1   "Do I Know This Already?" Foundation Topics Section-to-Question Mapping

Foundations Topics Section	Questions Covered in This Section
Install and Configure VMware Update Manager (VUM)	1
Repositories and Offline Bundles	2
Create and Modify Baseline Groups	3
Orchestrated vSphere Upgrades	4
Troubleshooting and Reporting	5
Upgrading vApps and Appliances	6
PowerCLI and Update Manager Utility	7

1. Which of the following options summarizes the steps that can be followed to successfully install VMware Update Manager?

   a. Double-click the **VMware-UMDS.exe** file located on the VUM installation DVD and interact with the installation wizard.

   b. Double-click the **VUM-install.exe** file located on the VUM installation DVD and interact with the installation wizard.

   c. During the installation of vCenter Server, select the **Install VMware Update Manager** option from the wizard.

   d. From the VMware vCenter Installer, select the **VMware vSphere Update Manager** option.

2. Which of the following options summarizes the steps that can be followed to successfully configure VUM to download updates from a shared repository?

   a. Select **Download Settings** > **Use a shared repository**.

   b. Select **Cluster tab** > **Shared Repository**, and then select **Enabled**.

   c. Use the **vmware-umd -E --shared-store** command.

   d. Install the Shared Repository option using the **VMware-UMDS.exe** file.

3. Which of the following options summarizes the steps that can be followed to create a fixed baseline of critical host patches?

   a. In the Create Baseline Wizard, set **Baseline Type** to Critical and set **Patch Option** to Host Patch.

   b. In the Create Baseline Wizard, set **Baseline Type** to Host Patch and set **Patch Option** to Critical.

   c. In the Create Baseline Wizard, set **Baseline Type** to Host Patch and set **Severity** to Critical.

   d. In the Create Baseline Wizard, set **Baseline Type** to Critical and set **Severity** to Critical.

4. Which of the following options summarizes the steps that can be followed to perform an orchestrated host upgrade on a cluster?

   a. Select the cluster, and then select the **Update Manager** tab. Attach at least two baseline groups and select the **Orchestrate** option. Select **Remediate**.

   b. Select the cluster, and then select the **Update Manager** tab. Ensure at least two baseline groups are attached. Select **Remediate**. In the Remediate Wizard, select the **Orchestrate** option.

    c. Ensure at least one baseline group is attached to the cluster. Use a PowerCLI command with the **-enableOrchestration** option to start the remediation.

    d. None of these options is correct.

5. Which of the following options summarizes the steps that can be followed to generate a report from a SQL Server query that shows the results of the latest VUM scan?

    a. Use a **SELECT** statement that contains a **FROM** clause that joins the tables VUMV_UPDATES and VUMV_ENTITY_SCAN_RESULTS.

    b. Use a **SELECT** statement that contains a **FROM** clause that joins the tables VUM_UPDATES and VUM_ENTITY_SCAN_RESULTS.

    c. Use a **SELECT** statement that contains a **FROM** clause that joins the tables VM_UPDATES and VM_ENTITY_SCAN_RESULTS.

    d. Use a **SELECT** statement that contains a **FROM** clause that joins the tables VUM_UPDATES and VM_ENTITY_SCAN_RESULTS.

6. Which of the following options summarizes the steps that can be followed to successfully configure smart rebooting?

    a. In the **Remediation** Wizard, select **Smart Reboot**.

    b. On the **Configuration tab** > **vApp Settings**, check the **Enable smart boot after remediation** box.

    c. In the **Edit Baseline** Wizard, check the **Enable smart boot** box.

    d. Use the **UPD_SmartBoot PowerCLI** cmdlet.

7. Which of the following options summarizes the steps that can be followed to begin using VMware Update Manager PowerCLI after it has been installed?

    a. **Start** > **All Programs** > **VMware** > **VMware Update Manager PowerCLI**.

    b. **Start** > **All Programs** > **VMware** > **VMware vSphere PowerCLI**.

    c. Double-click **VMwareUpdateManagerUtility.exe**.

    d. Double-click **UpdateManagerUtility.exe**.

Foundation Topics

Install and Configure VMware Update Manager

This section provides details for installing and configuring VMware Update Manager.

Overview

You should already be familiar with the following details in this overview. If any of this information is new to you, be sure to conduct the appropriate research before continuing onto the remainder of the chapter.

VMware Update Manager (VUM) is the component of VMware vSphere that can be used to facilitate the patching and upgrading of ESXi hosts managed by vCenter Server. Patching ESXi refers to the process of installing periodically released vSphere patches that are usually intended to repair known bugs and vulnerabilities. Upgrading ESXi refers to the process of installing a newer version of the product, such as when upgrading from ESXi 5.0 to ESXi 5.1. Upgrading ESXi also refers to installing an update for a particular version, such as upgrading from vSphere 5.0 to vSphere 5.0 Update 1. Updates are more significant than patches but are not as significant as new versions. They are typically intended to increase the landscape of supported hardware, operating systems, drivers, and other related items. For example, VMware supports a higher number of processors per ESXi host and more guest operating systems in vSphere version 5.0 Update 1 than VMware supported for vSphere version 5.0. VUM can be used to install patches and updates and install newer versions of ESXi over existing versions while retaining the host configuration.

VUM can also be used to upgrade VMware Tools inside a VM. It can be used to upgrade the VM version, which is commonly referred to as the VM virtual hardware version. Finally, VUM can be used to upgrade virtual appliances.

VUM is a product that can be installed on a Windows-based vCenter Server or on another instance of Windows. It can be configured to check for available patches on a scheduled basis. It provides two default host baselines, Critical and noncritical, and it enables the creation of custom baselines. Baselines contain a fixed set of patches or a dynamically identified set of patches, such as patches that were released prior to a specific date.

VUM enables the administrator to attach a baseline or group of baselines to an ESXi host or container, like a cluster. Attaching does not install the patches; it just associates the hosts with the baseline. Likewise, VUM enables the administrator to attach a baseline or group of baselines to a VM, an appliance, or a container such as a VM folder.

VUM enables the administrator to scan ESXi hosts and VMs to determine whether they are compliant with the associated (attached) baselines. It enables the administrator to remediate hosts and VMs that are not compliant. In other words, it automates the process of installing the missing patches on ESXi hosts and upgrading VMware Tools and the virtual hardware of the VMs.

Some basic VUM terminology includes

- **vSphere Installation Bundle (VIB)**—The smallest unit of software that can be installed in ESXi. It is a software package and a building block for an ESXi image. It consists of the payload files (file archive), a descriptor file (XML file), and a signature file.

- **Bulletin**—A group of one or more VIBs.

- **Patch**—A bulletin that addresses a particular vulnerability, issue, or enhancement.

- **Depot**—A group of VIBs and that is published online.

- **Offline Depot**—A depot that is stored as a Zip file and is available in the LAN.

- **Extension**—A bulletin that is intended to add an optional component to an ESXi host.

You can upgrade ESXi 4x servers to ESXi 5.1, but not if the servers were previously upgraded from ESXi 3.x, due to insufficient free space in the /boot partition. You can use VUM to migrate an ESX 4.x host to ESXi 5.x, which results in a fresh install of ESXi that retains the original ESX configuration. You cannot use VUM to roll back to a previous host version or to uninstall a patch.

VUM Installation

VUM is a 32-bit application that must be installed on a 64-bit version of Windows. It requires a database that, for environments having no more than 5 ESXi hosts and 50 VMs, can be built using SQL Server 2008 R2 Express, which is bundled with VUM. Otherwise, the database can reside on a SQL Server or Oracle server, which must be built prior to VUM installation. For large environments, you should ensure the database server does not run on the same Windows VM as VUM. Because VUM is a 32-bit application, it requires a 32-bit ODBC System DSN. To prepare for VUM installation, first create the SQL or Oracle database, then install the SQL Native Client or Oracle ODBC drivers, and finally create the DSN. Also, ensure that the location on which the VUM is installed has at least 125 GB free disk space because the installer will complain unless it detects a minimum of 120 GB free space.

To install VUM, you can run the same VMware-VIMSetup-all-5.1.0-xxxx (where xxxx is the build number) installer program that you used to install vCenter Server. Select the VMware vSphere Update Manage option, as illustrated in Figure 6-1.

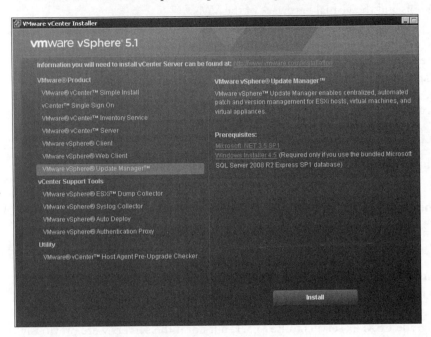

Figure 6-1   Start the VUM Installer.

Use the wizard and follow these steps to complete the installation:

Step 1.   Select the appropriate language, and click **OK**.

Step 2.   On the Welcome page, click **Next**.

Step 3.   On the Patent page, click **Next**.

Step 4.   On the License Agreement page, select **Accept** and click **Next**.

Step 5.   Select the option to download updates immediately, and click **Next**.

Step 6.   Enter the vCenter Server fully qualified name and a user account and password with administrative privileges, as shown in Figure 6-2. Keep the default port setting and click **Next**.

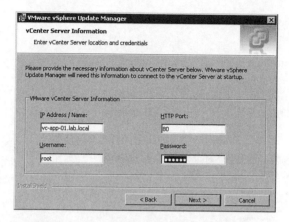

Figure 6-2 Registering VUM with vCenter.

Step 7. Choose to **Use an existing supported database** and select the appropriate DSN; then click **Next**.

Step 8. Select the appropriate IP address or hostname for the VUM instance. Keep the default port configuration. If appropriate, specify a proxy server, as illustrated in Figure 6-3; then click **Next**.

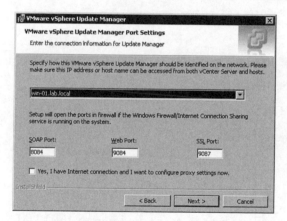

Figure 6-3 VUM ports.

Step 9. Specify a folder to install the software to. Next, specify a folder for the repository where patches will be stored. To make a change, click the **Change** button and then select the folder. Click **Next**.

Step 10. If a message appears warning about the disk free space, click **OK**.

Step 11. Click **Install**.

Step 12. Click **Finish**.

After installing the VUM server, you can add the VUM Client Plug-in to the vSphere Client by following these steps:

Step 1. Open the vSphere Client and log on to vCenter Server.

Step 2. In the menu, select **Plug-ins** > **Manage Plugins**.

Step 3. Click the **Download and install** link for the VUM extension, as illustrated in Figure 6-4.

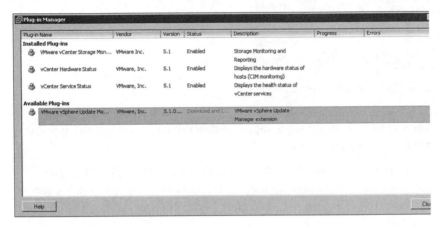

Figure 6-4 VUM Plug-in.

Step 4. In the wizard, select a language and click **OK**.

Step 5. On the Welcome page, click **OK**.

Step 6. On the Patent page, click **OK**.

Step 7. On the License Agreement, click **Next**.

Step 8. Click **Install**.

Step 9. Click **Finish**.

For situations where the VUM server will not have access to the Internet, the VUM Download Service (UMDS) might be needed. UMDS should be installed on a server with Internet access, perhaps a server in the DMZ. UMDS will download updates from the Internet and export the updates to a location that VUM can access. Like VUM, UMDS requires a database and a 32-bit DSN, which must be created prior to installation.

You can use the following steps to install UMDS:

Step 1. On the VUM installation DVD, locate and run **VMware-UMDS.exe**.

Step 2. Select the language, and then click **OK**.

Step 3. If prompted, install any missing items, such as Windows Installer 4.5.

Step 4. On the Welcome page, click **Next**.

Step 5. On the Patent page, click **Next**.

Step 6. On the License Agreement page, click **Next**.

Step 7. Select **Existing database** and select the DSN; then click **Next**.

Step 8. Enter any appropriate proxy settings, and then click **Next**.

Step 9. Select the UMDS installation folder and the UMDS patch download folder. To make a change, click the **Change** button and select the folder. Click **Next**.

Step 10. If warned about disk free space, click **OK**.

Step 11. Click **Install**.

Step 12. If warned about dot-Net 3.5 SP1, click **OK**, which automatically installs the missing component.

Step 13. Click **Finish**.

To verify that VUM Server and vSphere Client plug-in are successfully installed, use the client to navigate to **Home > Solutions > Update Manager**, as shown in Figure 6-5.

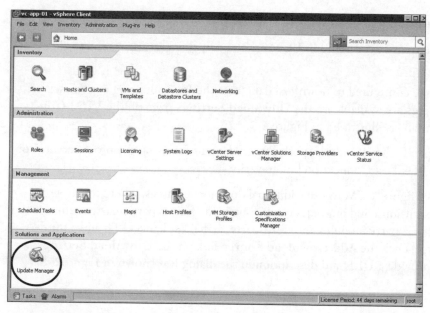

Figure 6-5 VUM icon on the home page.

This selection should open the VUM interface in the vSphere Client, as shown in Figure 6-6.

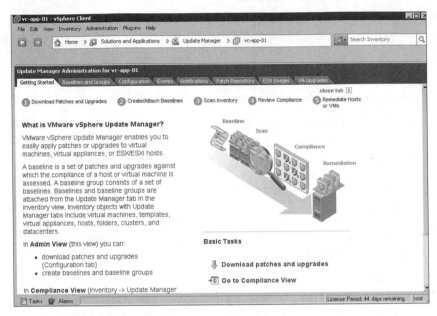

Figure 6-6 VUM interface in the vSphere Client.

VUM Configuration

The initial items to configure in VUM are the download settings and download schedule.

VUM can be configured to download data from the Internet using a proxy server. Proxy settings are available on the **Download Settings** page on the VUM **Configuration** tab, as illustrated in Figure 6-7.

You can specify the IP address, port, and credentials for using the proxy server. You should use the Test Connection link to verify success.

You can configure VUM to use additional download sources, where third-party patches, extensions, and upgrades can be obtained. This is particularly useful for patching third-party modules and third-party virtual appliances. To add a third-party source, click the **Add Download Source** link on the **Download Settings** page and provide a URL and description in the dialog box shown in Figure 6-8.

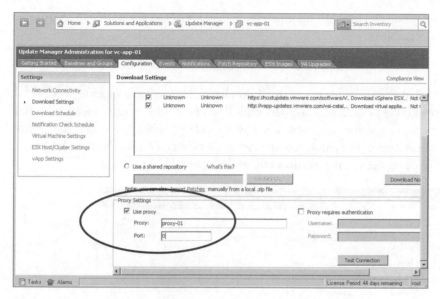

Figure 6-7   VUM proxy settings.

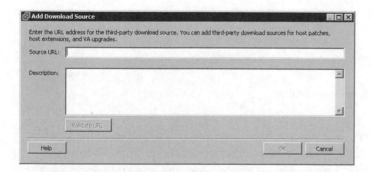

Figure 6-8   Add Download Source.

VUM provides a download schedule that can be configured using these steps:

Step 1.   Navigate to **Home > Solutions > Update Manager**.

Step 2.   Select **Configuration** > **Download Schedule**.

Step 3.   Ensure the **Enable scheduled download** box is checked.

Step 4.   In the upper-right, select **Edit Download Schedule**.

Step 5.   Provide values for **Name** and **Description**, or keep the defaults.

Step 6.   Specify the **Frequency, Start Time**, and **Interval**; then click **Next**.

Step 7.   Optionally, provide administrator email addresses for notifications; then click **Next**.

Step 8.   On the **Ready to Complete** page, click **Finish**.

The VUM Server communicates with VUM client plug-ins via a specific port, which is port 8084 by default. Likewise, each ESXi host must communicate with the VUM server via a specific port, which is 9084 by default. These ports and the IP address (or hostname) of the patch repository can be changed on the **Network Connectivity** page on the **Configuration** tab, as illustrated in Figure 6-9.

Figure 6-9   VUM network connectivity settings.

If the UMDS is installed, then it needs to be configured. To configure the UMDS, log on to Windows on the UMDS server, open a command prompt, and use the **vmware-umds** command. This command provides options to enable or disable the download of host updates and virtual appliance updates, as well as options to enable or disable the download of certain versions of ESX and embedded ESX. This command also provides the ability to change the patch download folder and configure additional download sources.

Scenario—Configure UMDS

You need to configure UMDS to download only ESXi 5.x updates. It must be configured to disallow the download of version 4.x updates and virtual appliance updates.

To meet these requirements, you can issue the following commands from a command prompt on the UMDS server:

```
cd  \program files (x86)\VMware\Infrastructure\Update Manager
vmware-umds -S -enable-host -disable-va
vmware-umds -S -d esx-4.0.0 embeddedEsx-4.0.0
```

Shared Repository and Download to Repository

VUM can be configured to download patches, extensions, and upgrades (data) from the Internet, from an offline bundle, or from a shared repository to the Update Manager repository. By default, VUM downloads data from specific VMware websites and stores the data in its local repository. In some cases, the UMDS is used to download data from the Internet and export it to a shared repository, which VUM can use to download the data into its own repository. In other cases, an offline bundle is downloaded from VMware or a third-party website in the form of a Zip file, which VUM then imports into its repository.

If the UMDS is used to download the data from the Internet, it must be configured (as previously described) and used to perform the initial download. After data is downloaded by the UMDS, it must be exported to a shared repository. To download patches using the UMDS, run this command from a Windows command prompt on the UMDS server:

```
vmware-umds  -D
```

To export the data to a shared repository, use this command:

```
vmware-umd  -E  --export-store  <path>
```

In this command, replace <path> with the fully qualified path of the target folder, such as **e:\UMDS\repository**. The path could also be to a temporary location or to removable media, which could then be presented temporarily to the VUM server.

If VUM is used in the traditional manner, where it downloads data directly from the Internet, the Download Settings page can be used to configure the download sources and to automate the download operation. Alternatively, the Download Settings page provides a **Download Now** button that can be used to download data immediately. Whenever data is downloaded from online sources—either immediately or using the download schedule—the data is stored in the VUM repository, whose path is set during the VUM installation.

You might choose to configure the UMDS to create a shared repository that is hosted on an internal web server or file share. A shared repository is useful in scenarios where the VUM server has no direct access to the Internet. It is also useful in scenarios where more than one VUM server is needed because more than one vCenter Server is implemented.

If a shared repository is used, you can use the vSphere Client to configure VUM to download data from the shared repository using these steps:

Step 1. Navigate to **Home > Solutions > Update Manager**.

Step 2. Select **Configuration > Download Settings**.

Step 3. Select **Use a shared repository**.

Step 4. Enter a folder path or URL to the shared repository.

Step 5. Click **Validate URL**.

Step 6. Click **Apply**.

Step 7. Click **Download Now** to test the configuration.

In step 4, if a folder path is used, it must be local to the VUM server. It cannot be a network path, such as a UNC path, and it cannot be a mapped drive.

In some cases, VMware and third parties package updates in the form of offline bundles (Zip files). You can download these bundles and import the updates from them into VUM using this procedure:

Step 1. Download a Zip file containing the desired patches.

Step 2. Ensure you have the Upload File privilege in vCenter Server.

Step 3. Using the vSphere Client, select **Configuration > Download Settings**.

Step 4. Click **Import Patches** in the **Download Sources** pane.

Step 5. Browse and select the Zip file, click **Next**, and allow time for the download.

Step 6. Click **Finish**.

The location of the VUM repository is set during the installation and is controlled by the **vci-integrity.xml** file. You can use the following procedure to modify its location:

Step 1. Log in to Windows on the VUM Server. Open the **Services** management console.

Step 2. Right-click the **VMware vSphere Update Manager Service** and click **Stop**.

Step 3. Use Windows Explorer to locate and copy the **vci-integrity.xml** file, which is located in the Update Manager folder within the Program Files folder. The copy is intended for backup.

Step 4. Right-click the **vci-integrity.xml** file and select **Edit**. Using a text editor, modify the value between the **<patchStore>** and **</patchStore>** tags. For example, if the repository is moved to a folder named **VUM-Repository** at the root of the **E:** drive, then modify the XML file to contain this string:

<patchStore> E:\VUM-Repository\</patchStore>

Note that the folder path must end with a backslash (\).

Step 5. Start the VUM service.

Create and Modify Baseline Groups

This section describes how to configure and manage baselines in VUM, including how to create fixed and dynamic baselines.

By default, two dynamic baselines are available: critical and noncritical. The Critical baseline contains all patches whose severity is "Critical", regardless of other factors. The noncritical baseline contains all other patches.

You can create a custom, fixed baseline by using these steps:

Key Topic

Step 1. Using the vSphere Client, navigate to **Home** > **Solutions** > **Update Manager**.

Step 2. Click the **Baselines and Groups** tab.

Step 3. In the **Baselines** section, click the **Create** link.

Step 4. In the **New Baseline Wizard**, enter a name to assign to the baseline.

Step 5. Fill in a description for the baseline.

Step 6. Keep the default settings for the Baseline type (Host Patch), and then click **Next**.

Step 7. Select Fixed for the **Patch Options**, and then click **Next**.

Step 8. Select a patch, such as **VMware ESXi 5.0 Complete Update 3**, as shown in Figure 6-10. Click the down arrow.

Step 9. Optionally, select more patches and select the down arrow for each.

Step 10. Click **Next**, and then click **Finish**.

You can create a dynamic, custom baseline in a similar fashion, except instead of choosing fixed, specific patches, identify patches automatically based on property values. For example, dynamic baselines can automatically include patches of a specific severity or time frame.

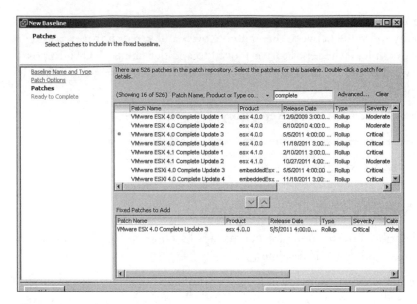

Figure 6-10   Select a patch.

Scenario—Custom Dynamic Baseline

You want to apply only critical ESXi patches that were released prior to October 1, 2013.

To do so, you can create a custom, dynamic baseline using this procedure:

1. Click **Create** in the Baselines section of the **Baselines and Groups** tab.

2. Provide a **Name** and **Description**. Set the **Baseline Type** to **Host Patch**. Click **Next**.

3. Select **Dynamic** for **Patch Options**. Click **Next**.

4. Set **Severity** to **Critical** and **Release Date** to **On or Before released prior to October 1, 2013**.

5. Click **Next** on this page, and again on the next page.

6. Click **Finish**.

To modify a baseline, select the baseline in the **Baselines** section of the **Baselines and Baseline Groups** tab and click **Edit**, which opens the same wizard that was used to create the baseline. Use this wizard to make any necessary changes.

A baseline group is simply a set of related baselines that can be applied and managed as a single entity. To create a baseline group, click **Create** next in the **Baseline Groups** section on the **Baseline and Baseline Groups** tab. For example, to create a host baseline group, the following steps can be used:

Step 1.   Navigate to **Solutions and Applications** > **Update Manager** > **Baselines and Baseline Groups**

Step 2.   To the right of **Baseline Groups**, click **Create**.

Step 3.   In the wizard, set **Baseline Group Type** to **Host Baseline Group** and provide a name in the **Baseline Group Name** box. Click **Next**.

Step 4.   On the **Upgrades** page, select one existing host upgrade baseline. Click **Next**.

Step 5.   On the **Patches** page, select one or more host patch baselines. Click **Next**.

Step 6.   On the **Extensions** page, select one or more host extension baselines. Click **Next**.

Step 7.   On the last page, click **Finish**.

Orchestrated vSphere Upgrades

Orchestrated upgrades, where a set of upgrade and patch operations is automatically performed in the correct order, can be applied to datacenters, folders, and clusters in vSphere. Orchestrated host upgrades involve using baseline groups, where each group contains one upgrade baseline and a set of patch and extension baselines. Orchestrated VM upgrades involve utilizing a baseline group that contains a baseline for updating VMware Tools and a baseline for updating the virtual machine hardware. Updating the ESXi hosts and VMs in a cluster, folder, or datacenter requires two orchestrated updates. The first update is for the ESXi hosts, and the second update is for the VMs.

An orchestrated host upgrade uses a baseline group that contains a single host upgrade baseline and multiple nonconflicting host patch and extension baselines. A host baseline group can be created by using the **Create** link on the **Baseline and Groups** tab. For example, to create a baseline group that can be used to upgrade hosts to version 5.1 and apply all appropriate patches and extensions, the following steps can he used:

Step 1.   Download the ESXi 5.1 ISO file.

Step 2.   Navigate to **Solutions and Applications** > **Update Manager** > **ESXi Images tab** > **Import ESXi Image**, as illustrated in Figure 6-11.

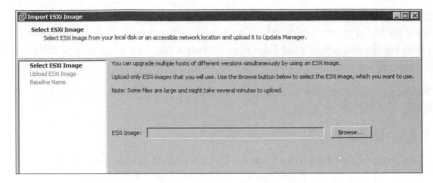

Figure 6-11 Import ESXi image.

Step 3. In the **Import ESXi Image** Wizard, use the **Browse** button to select an ISO file; then click **Next**.

Step 4. Select the **Create a baseline using the ESXi Image** box. Provide a baseline name and description. Click **Finish**.

Step 5. On the **Baseline and Groups** tab, in the **Baseline Groups** section, click **Create**.

Step 6. Provide a unique name for the group and select **Host Baseline Group**, as shown in Figure 6-12. Click **Next**.

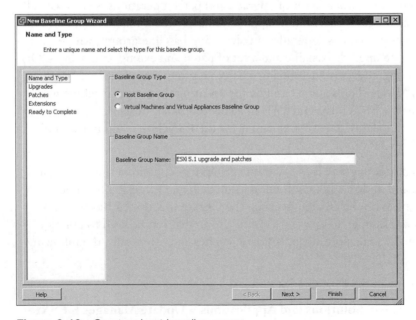

Figure 6-12 Create a host baseline group.

Step 7. Select the ESXi 5.1 upgrade baseline that was created in step 4; then click **Next**.

Step 8. Select or create the patch and extension baselines to add to the baseline group. Click **Next**.

Step 9. On the **Ready to Complete** page, click **Finish**.

After creating the host baseline group, an orchestrated host upgrade can be performed. For example, to perform an orchestrated host upgrade on a fully automated DRS cluster, the following steps can be used:

Step 1. Select the **Inventory > Hosts and Clusters**, and select the cluster.

Step 2. Select the **Update Manager** tab, and click **Attach** in the upper-right corner.

Step 3. Select the baseline group, as shown in Figure 6-13. Click **Attach**.

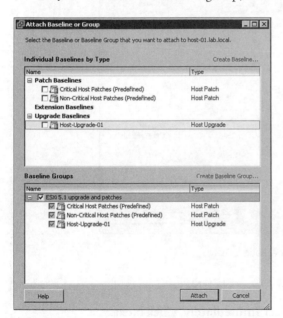

Figure 6-13 Attach a baseline group.

Step 4. On the **Update Manager** tab, select **Scan**.

Step 5. In the wizard, select both **Patches and Extensions** and **Upgrades**, as shown in Figure 6-14.

Step 6. Click **Scan**. Wait for the scan to complete.

Step 7. On the **Update Manager** tab, select **Remediate**.

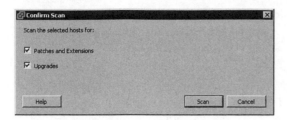

Figure 6-14   Selecting scan options.

> **Step 8.**   On the **Selection** page, select the baseline group as illustrated in Figure
> 6-15. Click **Next**.

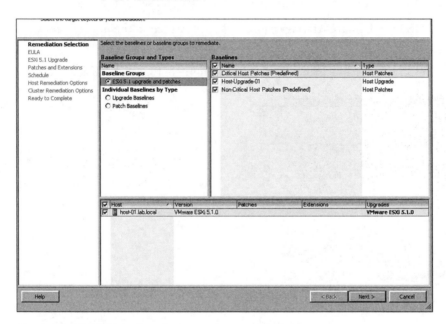

Figure 6-15   Select a baseline group for remediation.

> **Step 9.**   On the **License Agreement** page, click **Next**.
>
> **Step 10.**   On the **Schedule** page, select **Immediately**. Click **Next**.
>
> **Step 11.**   On the next page, ensure the **Do Not Change VM Power State** option
> is selected. Leave the default values for **Retry delay** and **Number of re-
> tries**, as illustrated in Figure 6-16. Click **Next**.
>
> **Step 12.**   For full orchestration and automation, certain vSphere features either
> must not be implemented or must be disabled. To ensure that such fea-
> tures are disabled, on the **Cluster Remediation Options** page, select the
> options to **Disable DPM**, **Disable HA Admission Control**, and **Dis-
> able Fault Tolerance (FT)**, as illustrated in Figure 6-17. Click **Next**.

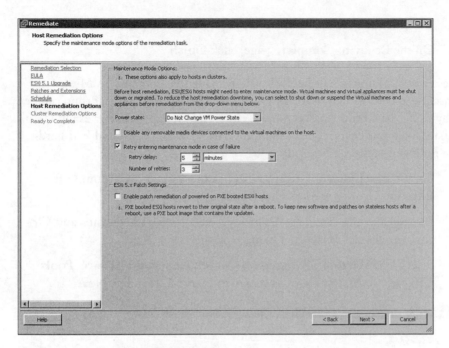

Figure 6-16   Host remediation options.

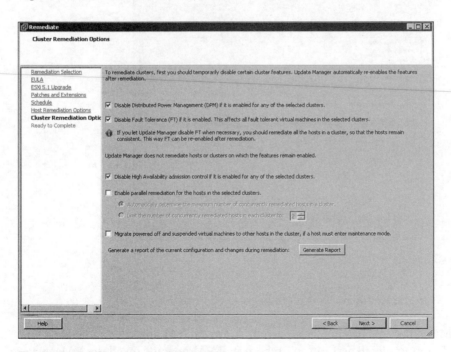

Figure 6-17   Cluster remediation options.

Step 13.   To generate a report, click the **Generate Report** option and click **Next**.

Step 14.   On the **Ready to Complete** page, click **Finish**.

An orchestrated VM upgrade utilizes a baseline group that contains a VMware Tools baseline and a VM Hardware Upgrade baseline. A VM baseline group can be created by using the **Create** link on the **Baseline and Groups** tab. For example, to create a baseline group that can be used to upgrade VMware Tools and VM hardware, the following steps can be used:

Step 1.   On the **Baseline and Groups** tab, click the **VMs/VAs** button. In the **Baseline Groups** section, click **Create**.

Step 2.   Provide a unique name for the group, select **Virtual Machines** and **Virtual Appliances Baseline Group,** and then click **Next.**

Step 3.   Select **VM Hardware Upgrade to Match Host** and **VMware Tools Upgrade to Match Host,** as shown in Figure 6-18. Click **Next**.

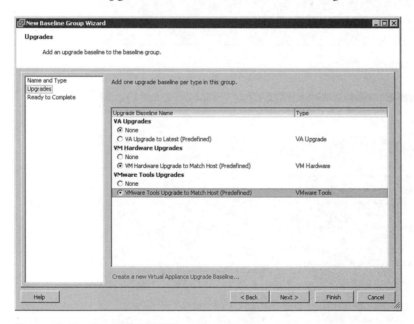

Figure 6-18   Configure a VM baseline group.

Step 4.   On the **Ready to Complete** page, click **Finish**.

After creating the VM baseline group, an orchestrated VM upgrade can be performed. For example, to perform an orchestrated VM upgrade on all the VMs in a specific folder, the following steps can be used:

Step 1.   Using the vSphere Client, navigate to **Inventory** > **VMs and Templates** and select the appropriate folder.

Step 2.   Select the **Update Manager** tab, and click **Attach** in the upper-right corner.

Step 3.   Select the baseline group and click **Attach**.

Step 4.   On the **Update Manager** tab, select **Scan**.

Step 5.   In the wizard, select both **VMware Tools upgrades** and **VM Hardware upgrades**. Uncheck virtual appliance upgrades.

Step 6.   Click **Scan**. Wait for the scan to complete.

Step 7.   On the **Update Manager** tab, click the **Remediate** button.

Step 8.   On the **Selection** page, select the baseline group. On the **Baselines** pane, select **VM Hardware Upgrade to Match Host** and **VMware Tools Upgrade to Match Host**, as shown in Figure 6-19. Click **Next**.

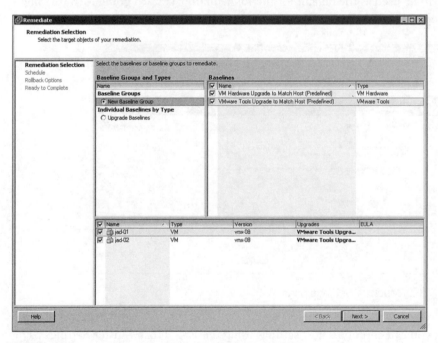

Figure 6-19   Select a VM baseline group for remediation.

Step 9.   On the **Schedule** page, select **Immediately** for each of the three options: **Powered on VM**, **Powered off VMs**, and **Suspended VMs**. Click **Next**.

Step 10.   On the **Rollback** page, select the option to **Take a snapshot of the virtual machine before remediation to enable rollback.** Select the option to **keep the snapshot for 18 hours**, and then provide a name and a description for the snapshot. Ensure that the option **Take a snapshot of the memory for the virtual machine** is not selected. Click **Next**.

Step 11.   On the **Ready to Complete** page, click **Finish**.

Note that on step 9, in addition to upgrading VMware Tools immediately or at a specified time, you can choose the option to Upgrade VMware Tools on power cycle. This selection can be used to perform the VMware Tools update whenever the VM reboots or powers off.

For convenience, you can configure the VM snapshot settings prior to orchestrating host or VM updates. To do this, navigate to **Home > Solutions and Applications > Update Manager > Configuration > Virtual Machine Settings**. Choose whether or not to take snapshots and how long to keep the snapshots. Click **Apply**, and the settings will be used as the default for the Remediation Wizard going forward. The VM settings page is shown in Figure 6-20.

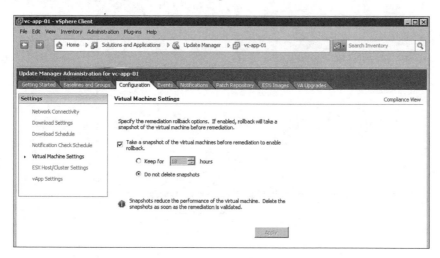

Figure 6-20   Virtual Machine Settings page.

Likewise, you can configure host settings using the ESX Host/Cluster Settings page as illustrated in Figure 6-21.

This page enables you to configure items to apply during remediation, such as the number of retries to enter maintenance mode and which features to disable.

Another automation option that is available concerns VM updates. Under the VMs and Templates view, the Update Manager tab contains a button named VMware

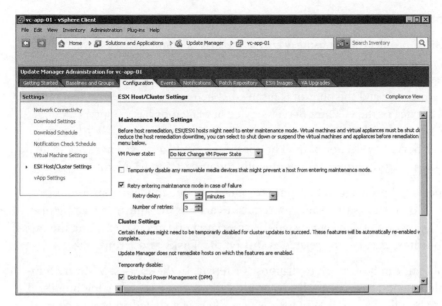

Figure 6-21 ESX host/cluster settings.

Tools upgrade settings, which can be used to configure VUM to automatically check each VM during any power cycle and update VMware Tools, if necessary. This button and the **Edit VMware Tools upgrade settings** window are shown in Figure 6-22.

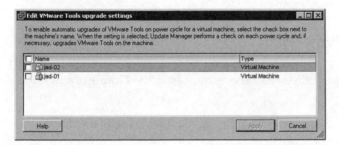

Figure 6-22 VMware Tools Upgrade Settings box.

Troubleshooting and Reporting

This section describes how to troubleshoot VUM issues and how to provide VUM reports using Microsoft Excel and SQL Server Query.

Troubleshooting

One potential problem when using VUM is the loss of connectivity between the VUM server and vCenter Server. A symptom of this issue can be seen when the VUM plug-in displays a reconnection dialog box but attempts to reconnect result in a failure message and the plug-in is disabled. The root cause could be that either the VUM service or the vCenter Server service has failed or has stopped running. In this case, you might be able to correct the issue by restarting the VUM service, the vCenter Server service, or both. The root cause could also be a network issue. In this case, the network administrators must fix the underlying problem.

Another potential problem is the failure to remediate due to missing prerequisites. Whenever VUM detects that some prerequisites are not met during a staging or remediation operation, it does not install the associated updates. To examine the missing prerequisites, examine the related events on the **Tasks and Events** tab.

Some problems can be difficult to diagnose or repair. In these cases, VMware Support should be contacted. Typically, VMware will ask you to create a log bundle. To create a log bundle, log on to Windows where VUM is installed and select **Start** > **All Programs** > **VMware** > **Generate Update Manager log bundle**.

Another potential root cause for issues using VUM could involve the lack of sufficient VUM privileges. The user account that is used to perform VUM tasks must be authorized to perform the necessary tasks. Here are some examples:

- To create or modify a baseline, the user must be granted the **Manage Baseline** privilege.

- To attach a baseline to an inventory object, the user must have the **Attach Baseline** privilege.

- To modify the download schedule, the user must have the **Configure Service** privilege.

- To remediate hosts, the user must have the **Remediate to Apply Patches, Extensions, and Upgrades** privilege.

In each of these examples, permission must be made to grant a role containing the necessary privileges to the user or group on the appropriate inventory object or container. To determine whether an issue is caused by insufficient permissions, examine the applied permissions. For example, if a user cannot remediate a specific ESXi host, select the **Permissions** tab for the host and examine its applied permissions to ensure that at least one permission assigns the necessary privilege to the appropriate user.

VUM provides a mechanism for patch recall. If VMware recalls a patch, VUM learns about the recall during the next scheduled download session as it downloads metadata. Recalled patches cannot be installed by VUM, and VUM removes any re-called patches from its repository. If the recalled patch is already installed and its fix (another patch) is available, VUM notifies you of the fix and prompts you to install the patch.

By default, a task called **VMware vSphere Update Manager Check Notification** is enabled. You can modify the time and frequency at which VUM checks for patch recalls and patch fixes. The task automatically sends notifications via email to the specified email addresses whenever recalls or patches are encountered. The notification checks can be configured using these steps:

Step 1. Verify that the VUM server has Internet access.

Step 2. Navigate to **Home > Solutions and Applications > Update Manager**.

Step 3. Select **Configuration > Notification Check Schedule**.

Step 4. Ensure the **Enable scheduled download** box is checked, as shown in Figure 6-23.

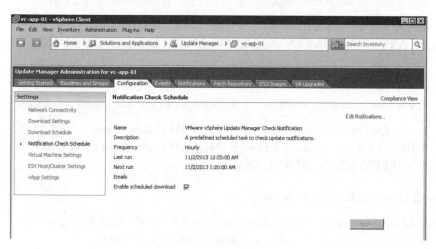

Figure 6-23 Notification Check Schedule page.

Step 5. In the upper-right corner, click **Edit Notifications**.

Step 6. Provide a name and description for the task.

Step 7. Specify the **Frequency**, **Start Time**, and **Interval**; then click **Next**.

Step 8. Provide an administrator email address for notifications; then click **Next**.

Step 9. On the **Ready to Complete** page, click **Finish**.

VUM Reporting Using Excel

Microsoft Excel can be used to generate VUM reports. The main prerequisites are Excel 2003 or higher and an ODBC connection to the VUM database. The main steps are to select the **Import External Data > New Database Query** option and select the columns of data to include in the query.

For example, to display the latest scan results for all inventory objects and for all patches, follow these steps:

Step 1.   On a desktop or server that has Microsoft Excel and network connectivity to the VUM database, configure and test an ODBC connection to the VUM database.

Step 2.   Start the Excel program.

Step 3.   Click **Data > Import External Data > New Database Query**.

Step 4.   In the **Choose Data Source** window, select the ODBC connection. If necessary, provide credentials to connect to the database. Click **OK**.

Step 5.   In the **Query Wizard**, in the **Available tables and columns** pane, select the **VUMV_UPDATES** and **VUMV_ENTITY_SCAN_RESULTS** tables and their associated columns. Examine the columns in your query and the Preview of data in the selected columns. Click **Next**.

Step 6.   If a warning message indicates that the tables cannot be joined, click **OK**.

Step 7.   In the **Query** window, drag the **META_UID** column from the **VUMV_UPDATES** view to the **UPDATE_METAID** column of the **VUMV_ENTITY_SCAN_RESULTS** view.

VUM Reporting Using SQL Server Query

SQL Server Queries can be used to generate reports when a VUM database resides on SQL Server. For example, the following SQL Query can be used to generate a report that displays the latest scan results for all inventory objects and for all patches:

```
SELECT r.entity_uid,r.ENTITY_STATUS,
u.meta_uid, u.title, u.description, u.type, u.severity,
(case when u.SPECIAL_ATTRIBUTE is null then 'false'
else 'true'
end) as IS_SERVICE_PACK,
r.scanh_id, r.scan_start_time, r.scan_end_time
FROM VUMV_UPDATES u JOIN VUMV_ENTITY_SCAN_RESULTS r
ON (u.meta_uid = r.update_metauid)
ORDER BY r.entity_uid, u.meta_uid
```

Upgrade vApps and Appliances

This section covers using VUM to update vApps and virtual appliances.

Upgrade vApps

VUM enables vApps to be updated in the same manner that it enables a VM folder or datacenter to be upgraded. It provides an Update Manager tab for the vApp, where the Attach, Scan, and Remediate options are available to update a vApp, attach a baseline to it, scan it for missing updates, and remediate it. One feature that can be applied to vApps but cannot be applied to other objects is smart rebooting.

Smart Rebooting

Smart rebooting is a feature that can be enabled on vApps. Its purpose is to ensure that after remediation, the VMs in the vApp start in the order specified by the vApp. It is enabled by default, but it can be disabled. If it's disabled, the VMs in the vApp will be restarted in the order specified by the remediation, in the same manner used for VM folders. To view or edit this setting, follow these steps:

Step 1. Navigate to **Home > Solutions and Applications > Update Manager**.

Step 2. On the **Configuration** tab, select **vApp Settings**.

Step 3. Examine the **Enable smart boot after remediation** check box and change it if necessary.

This setting is shown in Figure 6-24.

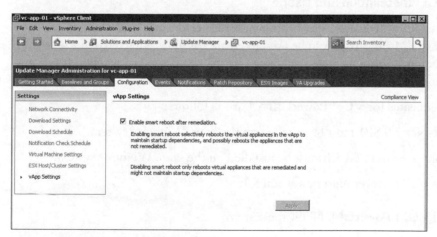

Figure 6-24   Smart Rebooting setting.

Upgrade Virtual Appliances

VMware and other developers of virtual appliances might elect to provide VUM-compatible updates for their appliances. As described previously, additional download sources can be added to the VUM configuration and to the download schedule to accommodate virtual appliances. After a virtual appliance's updates are downloaded and stored in the VUM repository, the following steps can be used to upgrade the virtual appliance:

1. Use the **Baseline and Baseline Groups** tab to create the virtual appliance baseline.

2. In the **Virtual Machines and Templates** view, select a virtual appliance (or a container where it resides). In the **Update Manager** tab, click **Attach** and select the virtual appliance baseline.

3. Click **Scan** to scan the virtual appliance or container for compliance with the baseline.

4. If the appliance is not compliant, click **Remediate** and complete the wizard.

PowerCLI and Update Manager Utility

VMware vSphere Update Manager PowerCLI (VUM PowerCLI) and the VMware Update Manager Utility (VUM Utility) are tools that can be used to modify or automate VUM behavior.

VUM PowerCLI Installation and Usage

VUM PowerCLI provides a set of commands for performing VUM administration tasks. VUM PowerCLI can be used to create baselines, attach baselines, scan virtual machines, stage patches, remediate objects, and download patches. It can be installed and used on a Windows system where vSphere PowerCLI is installed.

The prerequisites for VUM PowerCLI 5.1 are as follows:

- Dot-Net 2.0 SP1 must be installed on the same Windows system.

- vSphere PowerCLI 5.1 must be installed on the same Windows system.

- The VUM Server must be version 5.1.

To install VUM PowerCLI, follow these steps:

Step 1.   Download the installer package from VMware's website. For example, the filename for VUM PowerCLI 5.1 is **VMware-UpdateManager-Pscli-5.1.0.782803.exe.**

Step 2. Start the installer.

Step 3. On the **Welcome** page, click **Next**.

Step 4. Accept the license key.

Step 5. Click **Install**.

Step 6. Click **Finish**.

VUM PowerCLI commands are available in the vSphere PowerCLI console. To get started using the VUM PowerCLI, open the vSphere PowerCLI console. VUM PowerCLI and vSphere PowerCLI commands can be executed within the same console. To open the vSphere PowerCLI console, click **Start > All Programs > VMware > VMware vSphere PowerCLI**. To get a list of all VUM PowerCLI commands, use this command:

Key Topic

```
Get-Command  -PSSnapin  VMware.VumAutomation
```

VUM PowerCLI requires that you begin by using vSphere PowerCLI to set the execution mode and to connect to vCenter Server. After that is done, VUM PowerCLI can be used to perform VUM administration tasks. For example, to create a patch baseline named **Critical 9-30-2013**, the following commands can be used:

```
$patches = Get-Patch  -Before  9.30.2013  -Severity  critical
$staticBaseline = New-PatchBaseline  -Static  "Critical 9-30-2013" -
IncludePatch $patches
```

To attach this baseline to an ESXi host named **host-01.lab.local**, the following command can be used:

```
Attach-Baseline  -Baseline  $staticBaseline  -Entity host-01.lab.
local
```

To scan a VM named **vm-01** against the VMware Tools and VMware hardware baselines that might be attached to the VM, the following command can be used:

```
$task01 = Scan-Inventory  -Entity  vm-01  -UpdateType
VmHardwareUpgrade, VmToolsUpgrade -RunAsync
```

In this example, the object **$task01** will be set to the task that VUM launches to perform the scan. With this approach, you can display the status of the task by entering the following:

```
$task01
```

Or you could use this command to monitor the task and wait until the task completes:

```
Wait-Task  -Task  $task01
```

To remediate a VM name **vm-01** with all its attached baselines, the following commands can be used:

```
$baselines = Get-Baseline  -Entity vm-01

Remediate-Inventory  -Entity  vm-01  -Baseline  $baselines
```

Update Manager Utility

The VUM Utility can be used to make changes to some of the settings that were made during the VUM installation, including

- Proxy settings

- Database user credentials

- vCenter Server IP address or hostname

- SSL Certificate

The VUM Utility is an optional tool that enables you to make changes to any of these settings without having to reinstall VUM. It is included with VUM 4.1 Update 1 and later. It is installed automatically as an additional component on the VUM server.

Key
Topic

To use the VUM Utility to view the options associated with the current VUM installation, use these steps:

Step 1. Use Windows Explorer to navigate to the installation folder for VUM, which by default is

```
c:\Program Files (x86)\VMware\Infrastructure\Update Manager
```

Step 2. Double-click **VMwareUpdateManagerUtility.exe**.

Step 3. When prompted, log in with an appropriate account.

Step 4. Examine the list of options in the **Options** pane, which are **Proxy Settings**, **Database Username and Password**, **vCenter Server IP Address**, and **SSL Certificate**, as illustrated in Figure 6-25.

After viewing the options, you can make any necessary changes. For example, to change the proxy settings, follow these steps:

Step 1. In the **Options** pane, click **Proxy Settings**.

Step 2. Select the **Use Proxy** check box.

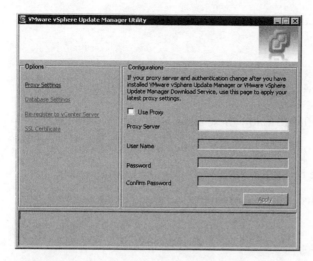

Figure 6-25 Update Manager Utility.

Step 3.   Enter the proxy server name and port number—for example, server01:9119, where server01 is the hostname and 9119 is the port number. Enter a username and password.

Step 4.   Click **Apply**.

Step 5.   Restart the VUM service.

To change the VUM database credentials, follow these steps:

Step 1.   Test the ODBC connection to the database to verify that it works.

Step 2.   Stop the VUM service.

Step 3.   In the **Options** pane of the VUM Utility, click **Database Settings**.

Step 4.   Enter the new username and password for the connection.

Step 5.   Enter the password again in the **Confirm Password** box.

Step 6.   Click **Apply**.

Step 7.   Restart the VUM service.

To re-register VUM with a vCenter Server whose hostname has been changed, follow these steps:

Step 1.   In the **Options** pane of the VUM Utility, click **Re-register to vCenter Server**.

Step 2.   In the **vCenter Server IP Address or Name**, enter the new vCenter hostname.

Step 3.   In the **User Name** and **Password** boxes, enter the appropriate credentials.

Step 4.   Click **Apply**.

Step 5.   Restart the VUM service.

To change the VUM SSL Certificate, follow these steps:

Step 1.   In the **Options** pane of the VUM Utility, click **SSL Certificate**.

Step 2.   Follow the procedure that is provided in the **Configurations** pane.

Step 3.   When completed, select the **Followed and verified the steps** check box.

Step 4.   Click **Apply**.

Step 5.   Restart the VUM service.

Summary

You should now be enabled with the knowledge and skills to successfully patch, update, and upgrade a vSphere environment. You should also be able to successfully complete the VUM configuration, troubleshooting, and management tasks that might be part of the VCAP5-DCA exam. Be sure to take time to practice the steps that are provided in this section until you are confident that you can perform such tasks quickly and without any assistance.

Exam Preparation Tasks

Review All the Key Topics

Table 6-2 provides a list of all Key Topics identified in this chapter along with a few notes intended to refresh your memory of some key details. This can be useful as a quick reference when performing vSphere administration.

Table 6-2   Key Topics in Chapter 6

Key Topic Element	Description	Page
Step List	Install UMDS.	258
Paragraph	Configure VUM Proxy Settings.	260
Step List	Configure a shared repository for VUM.	264
Step List	Import patches from an offline bundle.	264

Key Topic Element	Description	Page
Step List	Create a fixed baseline.	265
Step List	Perform an orchestrated host upgrade.	269
Step List	Perform an orchestrated VM upgrade.	272
Paragraph	Create a VUM log bundle.	276
Step List	Configure VUM Notification Check Schedule.	277
Step List	Generate VUM reports using Excel.	278
Step List	Configure smart rebooting for vApps.	279
Step List	Use Baseline and Groups > Create to create the baseline. Choose an appliance to attach the baseline.	280
Paragraph	Use `Get-Command -PSSnapin VMware.VumAutomation`.	281
Step List	Open **VMwareUpdateManagerUtility.exe** and examine the Options pane.	282

Key Terms

Define the following key terms from this chapter, and check your answers in the glossary:

vSphere Installation Bundle (VIB), patch, extension, host baseline, baseline group, VUM Utility, shared repository, offline bundle

Review Tasks

These Review Tasks enable you to assess how well you grasped the materials in this chapter. Because of the advanced and hands-on nature of this particular exam, a set of tasks is provided instead of a set of questions. You should now attempt to perform each of these tasks without looking at previous sections in this chapter or at other materials, unless necessary. The steps for each task are located within the chapter.

1. Install VMware Update Manager Download Service.

2. Create a shared repository and use it to download updates into Update Manager.

3. Create a host baseline group that contains an ESXi 5.1 upgrade and several patches. Use it to upgrade a cluster of hosts.

4. Use Microsoft Excel to display the latest scan results for all inventory objects and for all patches.

This chapter covers the following subjects:

- **vCenter Server log files and locations**—This section will detail vCenter Server log files that are useful in troubleshooting.

- **ESXi log files and locations**—Log files for ESXi hosts are important when it comes to troubleshooting. A number of log files exist, and some of the more important ones will be detailed in this section.

- **Tools used to view vSphere log files**—Several different tools can be utilized by the system administrator to analyze vSphere log files. This section will discuss tools such as the Syslog Collector and Log Bundles.

The material in this chapter pertains to the VCAP-DCA Exam objectives 6.1.

## CHAPTER 7

Logging

When a computer's operating system begins to have problems, analyzing log files can help to determine the underlying cause. In the early days of Unix, a program called Syslog was created by Eric Allman at the University of California-Berkley. It became a standard for logging errors in many Unix- and Linux-based operating systems. The ESXi hypervisor or vmkernel is proprietary code that uses device drivers written using Linux-like programming due to the engineers' expertise with Linux. The original hypervisor, ESX, included a service console that was derived from Red Hat Linux, although it was not a true Linux host. ESXi eliminates the Service Console and utilizes BusyBox, a small executable that provides several Unix-style tools that allow for the same management tasks the Service Console was capable of. As a result, it stands to reason that ESXi would invoke Syslog as its tool of choice for logging. In previous versions of vSphere, the ESXi host primarily used standard Syslog for logging, and the vCenter Server—which was Windows-based—used its own logging method. So you had this Wild West of logging within vSphere 4.1 and earlier in which there was no standardization. In vSphere 5.0, changes were made by VMware in the way logging was implemented. There was a decision to begin standardizing logging using Syslog, although with some minor changes. In this module we look at some of the changes in logging with vSphere 5.x and how Syslog has been implemented.

One of the important topics that also is discussed in this module is how to create a log bundle. When a support issue exists within vSphere and you contact VMware support, you will most likely be asked to provide a log bundle. In this module, we show several methods you can use to accomplish this task. Of course, any of the choices will work.

Another topic that is discussed is listing the log files and where they are located for the vCenter Server and the ESXi hosts. A section is devoted to listing these log files and giving brief descriptions of their functions. Many system administrators perform their own diagnosis of problems, so we've included a section describing how to view log files and make implementation changes to them.

In addition, this chapter looks at tools built in to vSphere. The Syslog Collector is a tool you can use to gather log files from multiple ESXi hosts and collect them onto a single system. The idea is that by centralizing all the log files in one location, an administrator will have to sift through only one system for troubleshooting information.

"Do I Know This Already?" Quiz

The "Do I Know This Already?" quiz enables you to assess whether you should read this entire chapter or simply jump to the "Exam Preparation Tasks" section for review. If you are in doubt, read the entire chapter. Table 7-1 outlines the major headings in this chapter and the corresponding "Do I Know This Already?" quiz questions. You can find the answers in Appendix A, "Answers to the 'Do I Know This Already?' Quizzes and Troubleshooting Scenarios."

Table 7-1   "Do I Know This Already?" Foundation Topics Section-to-Question Mapping

Foundations Topics Section	Questions Covered in This Section
vCenter Server log files and locations	1, 2
ESXi log files and locations	3
The tools used to view vSphere log files	4, 5

1. Which file represents a default vCenter Server log file?
   a. vpxd.log
   b. shell.log
   c. vCenter.log
   d. syslog.log

2. Which tool will not allow you to create a vCenter Server log bundle?
   a. PowerCLI
   b. vSphere Client
   c. vm-support
   d. vSphere Dump Collector

3. Which log file will contain a history list of all commands run from the command line of an ESXi host?

   a. hostd.log

   b. syslog.log

   c. auth.log

   d. vCenter.log

4. Which two locations do not require installation of the Syslog Collector to provide log centralization? (Select two.)

   a. A Windows-based vCenter Server

   b. The vCenter Server Appliance

   c. A Windows virtual machine

   d. The vSphere Management Appliance

5. The vSphere ESXi Dump Collector can be configured on which two locations? (Select two.)

   a. The vCenter Server Appliance

   b. An Auto-Deployed ESXi host

   c. A manually deployed ESXi host

   d. A Windows virtual machine

Generate vCenter Server and ESXi Log Bundles

Support for software companies has changed over the years. When you call VMware support, they typically request that you send them diagnostic information.

Key Topic

This diagnostic information can be in the form of a log bundle or a diagnostic bundle such as that produced by vCenter Server or a diagnostic bundle containing log files, configuration files, and a capture using esxtop such as that generated by the vm-support utility on an ESXi host. The bundle generated will be either a Zip file or in a tar format gzip depending on the source system. You can unzip or gunzip and extract the log files if you want to inspect the files yourself. **Export System Logs** is a built-in vSphere Client tool that compresses and gzips configuration and log files into one file that can then be sent to VMware support, or it can be used by the system administrator to troubleshoot an issue.

Generate a Log Bundle on the ESXi Host Using vSphere Client

So depending on the method, individual logs can be bundled together or bundled along with configuration files and additional diagnostic information. The primary method many system administrators use to create a log bundle is through the vSphere Client. If you were to call VMware support and they needed to look at log files, this would be the format they would want to receive to diagnose a support issue.

To generate a diagnostic log bundle for an ESXi host using the vSphere Client, first log in to the ESXi host from the vSphere Client. Then from the **Home** view, select **Administration, System Logs**. Figure 7-1 shows an example of using the vSphere Client to view an individual log file, as well as the location of the **Export System Logs** tool.

The current log file being displayed in Figure 7-1 is the **/var/log/hostd.log** file, which is the log file for the ESXi host management agent. The other two log files that can be viewed in the windows by selecting them from the drop-down box are the **/var/log/vmkernel.log** file, which contains messages specific to the ESXi hypervisor, and the **/var/log/vpxa.log** file, which contains messages specific to the vCenter Server agent. To create a log bundle, click the **Export System Logs** button. The window that appears allows you to select the system logs that will be placed into the bundle, as shown in Figure 7-2. Place a check mark next to all the log files you want to incorporate into the log bundle; then decide on whether performance data should be included with the log files as well. Selecting **Next** prompts you to supply the directory location where you want the output file to be created.

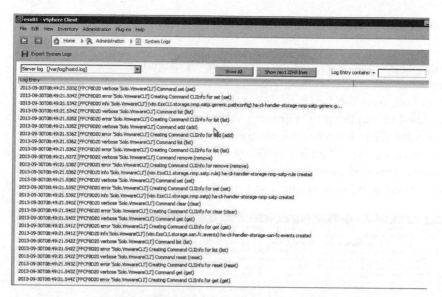

Figure 7-1 The Server log file is being displayed, as well as the Export System Log tool.

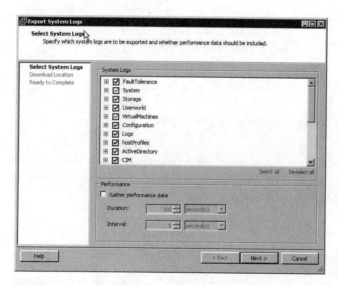

Figure 7-2 Select System Log files to be included in the log bundle.

Generate a Diagnostic Log Bundle on the ESXi Host/vCenter Server Using vm-support

The traditional command-line method of creating the diagnostic bundle can still be accomplished using a Secure Shell (SSH) tool such as PuTTY. After logging in to the ESXi host, from the command line you can run **vm-support** from any directory because **/sbin** is in the path. The script **/sbin/vm-support** is an ASCII file, and you can view the file to learn more about the bundling process. When you run **vm-support** it creates a single Zip file containing log files, configuration files, and a capture of performance data using **esxtop**. In Figure 7-3 you can see the command-line command **vm-support** being executed and creating the diagnostic bundle.

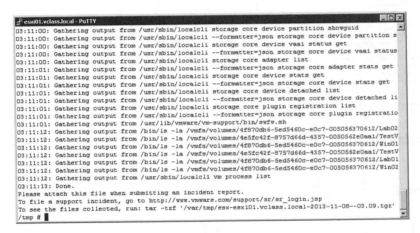

Figure 7-3 Creating a diagnostic bundle using the vm-support utility.

After you create the diagnostic bundle, you can FTP it or upload it to VMware support. A knowledge base document on how to upload diagnostic information is available; the kb.vmware.com document number is 1008525.

NOTE To see additional options to create the support log bundle, use the command **vm-support –h** for a list of additional options.

Generate a Diagnostic Log Bundle on the ESXi Host or vCenter Server Using PowerCLI

After logging in to the vCenter Server or an ESXi host using the **Connect-viserver PowerCLI** cmdlet, you can use the **Get-Log** cmdlet to generate a diagnostic bundle. As shown in Figure 7-4, a progress bar will display the completion status of the diagnostic bundle created using the **Get-Log** cmdlet.

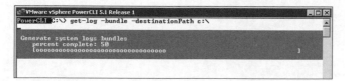

Figure 7-4 The progress bar running during the Get-log PowerCLI cmdlet.

As shown in Figure 7-5, upon completion the PowerCLI console window displays the name of the output file. This Zip file can now be uploaded to VMware support or stored for later use.

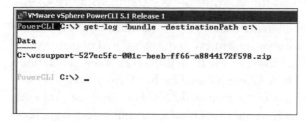

Figure 7-5 A completed log bundle using PowerCLI.

Generate a Diagnostic Log Bundle Directly on the vCenter Server

The Windows vCenter Server machine contains a built-in method to generate diagnostic bundles. Open a menu by clicking the **Start** button located on the vCenter Server desktop. Next, select **All Programs** > and find and select the **VMware** folder. Figure 7-6 displays the available VMware programs. Two of the programs displayed include **Generate vCenter Server log bundle** and **Generate vCenter Server log bundle - Extended**. The extended option adds **msinfo.txt** and **netstat** active connection information.

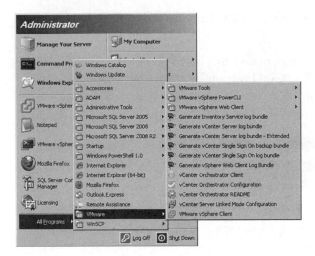

Figure 7-6 VMware programs available, which include the log bundle creator.

Generate a Diagnostic Log Bundle on the vCenter Server Using vSphere Client

The process and the steps performed to generate a diagnostic bundle on the vCenter Server using the vSphere Client are almost identical to the steps used to generate a diagnostic bundle on an ESXi host. However, the main difference when generating diagnostic information using a vSphere Client pointed to the vCenter Server is that information can be collected from any of the managed ESXi hosts and also from the vCenter Server. This can be especially useful when troubleshooting more complex issues not isolated to a single host.

Add a check mark to the vCenter Server and all the ESXi hosts you want included in the log bundle. In Figure 7-7 you can decide which hosts will be included in the log bundle, and you can choose to add the vCenter Server into the log bundle as well. The screenshot shows the objects **vc01.vclass.local**, which is the vCenter Server, and **esxi01.vclass.local**, which is an ESXi host, being included into a log bundle created using **Export System Logs**.

In the **Export System Logs** window in Figure 7-8, you can choose which system log files you want included in the diagnostic bundle. If you decide to add performance data to the Support Bundle, you will need to specify how long to run the script that gathers the data. The maximum gathering period is up to one day, and the interval used to collect data can be up to a maximum of one hour. After determining the appropriate settings, click **Next**.

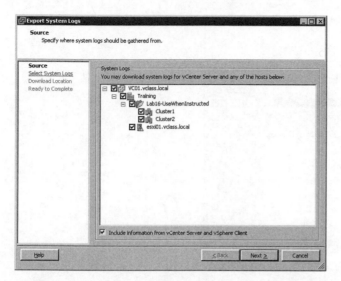

Figure 7-7   Decide which hosts and vCenter Server to include in the diagnostic bundle.

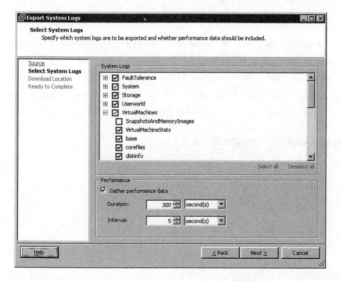

Figure 7-8   Specifying which System Logs and performance information in the log bundle to include.

In the **Download Location** pane in Figure 7-9, you can select **Browse** to choose a location on the client's disk where you want to save the diagnostic bundle. This will be the location where the log bundle file will be saved to on the vCenter Server.

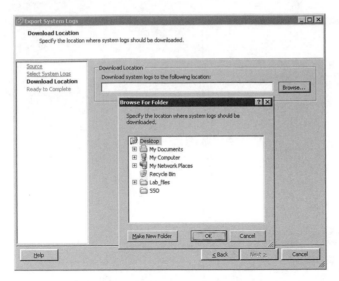

Figure 7-9   Download location for the diagnostic bundle.

After you have selected the download location, click **Next** and the system will begin to bundle all the log files into a single file that is in tar format and is gzipped. Figure 7-10 shows the diagnostic bundle being built. The download location where the diagnostic bundle is going to be placed is listed in the **Download Details**. After the process is completed, you can inspect the compressed tar ball by uncompressing it and extracting the tar ball. Or you can FTP the gzipped tarball to VMware support.

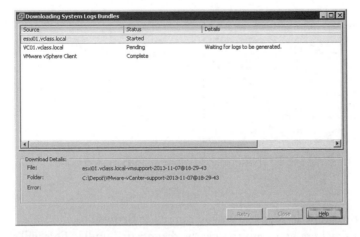

Figure 7-10   Building the log bundle.

Configure Logging Level for the vCenter Server

Adjusting the logging level for the vCenter Server affects the amount of detail the vCenter Server collects in the log files. The logging level options are listed in Table 7-2.

Table 7-2 Logging Levels for vCenter Server

Option	Description
None (Disable logging)	Turns off logging.
Error (Errors only)	Displays only error log entries.
Warning (Errors and warnings)	Displays warning and error log entries.
Information (Default logging)	Displays information, error, and warning log entries. This is the default and recommended setting.
Verbose (Verbose)	Displays information, error, warning, and verbose log entries.
Trivia (Extended verbose)	Displays information, error, warning, verbose, and trivia log entries; this setting gives the most detail.

To modify vCenter Server logging options using the vSphere Client, select the drop-down menu **Administration** and select the **vCenter Server Settings** option. From vCenter Server Settings, select **Logging Options**. The dialog box shown in Figure 7-11 appears, and you can set the vCenter Server logging level to the desired option. The default option is **Information**; if you need a more verbose option, you can select the **Trivia** option. This gives you the most logging information, which can be beneficial in troubleshooting.

Key Topic

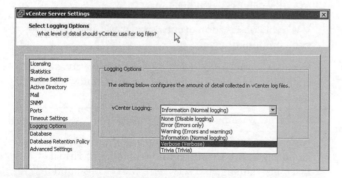

Figure 7-11 Select logging options.

Log Files

The log files for the ESXi host and vCenter Server can be useful in troubleshooting problems with vSphere. Log file entries contain configuration and operational errors as well as performance information. There are many log files on the ESXi host and the vCenter Server. Some of the more important ESXi log files that can be used for troubleshooting are listed in the following section.

ESXi Host Log Files

/var/log/auth.log	ESXi Shell authentication success and failure.
/var/log/dhclient.log	DHCP client logs, including discovery, address lease requests, and renewals.
/var/log/esxupdate.log	ESXi patches and update installation logs.
/var/log/hostd.log	Host management service logs, including virtual machine and host tasks and events, communication with the vSphere Client and vCenter Server vpxa agent, and SDK connections.
/var/log/shell.lo	ESXi Shell usage. This log file contains a history list of all the commands that have been run at the command line on the host, including **enable** and **disable**.
/var/log/sysboot.log	VMkernel startup and module loading.
/var/log/boot.gz	A compressed file that contains boot log information and can be read using **zcat /var/log/boot.gz	more**.
/var/log/syslog.log	Management service initialization, watch dogs, scheduled tasks, and DCUI use.
/var/log/usb.log	USB device arbitration events, such as discovery and pass-through to virtual machines.
/var/log/vob.log	VMkernel observation events, similar to **vob.component.event**.
/var/log/vmkernel.log	Core VMkernel logs, including device discovery, storage and networking device and driver events, and virtual machine startup.
/var/log/vmkwarning.log	VMkernel warning and alert log messages.
/var/log/vmksummary.log	A summary of ESXi host startup and shutdown and an hourly heartbeat with uptime, number of virtual machines running, and service resource consumption.

The vCenter Server log files have different directories depending on the Windows Server version on which the vCenter Server has been installed. The most recent versions of vCenter Server were supported to run on Windows 2003 and Windows 2008. Both versions of Windows have different directories where the vCenter Server log files are located. On the Windows Server 2008, the files are found in the following directory:

```
%ALLUSERSPROFILE%\VMware\VMware VirtualCenter\Logs\
```

Key Topic

vCenter Server Log Files

vpxd.log	The main Server log file that communicates with the vCenter Server Agent (vpxa), which is located on connected ESXi hosts. This log file is useful for troubleshooting configuration and operational errors.
vpxd-profiler	Operational and performance counters used to profile vCenter Server operation. This log file is useful for troubleshooting performance issues.
\drmdump\clusternnn	DRS actions, grouped by the DRS cluster. The log files are gzipped.

Viewing Log Files

ESXi log files can be viewed using the command line by logging in to the ESXi Shell and running commands such as **cat**, **tail**, **more**, **less**, or any command that allows you to view a file. The **tail –f <filename>** is a commonly used command-line command that enables you to see changes being added to the log file as they happen. You run this command in the background, which keeps the log file open. The other option for viewing log files is using the vSphere Client to log directly in to the ESXi host.

The vCenter Server log files can be viewed directly on the Windows host system or by using the vSphere Client, as shown in Figure 7-12.

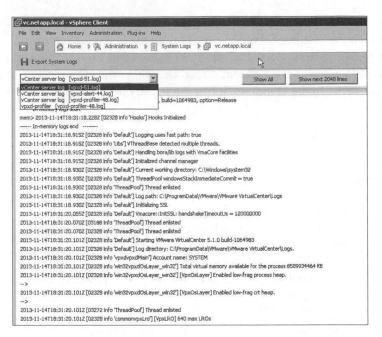

Figure 7-12   Viewing logs using the vSphere Client.

Use ESXCLI System Syslog to Configure Centralized Logging on ESXi Hosts

One of the changes in vSphere 5 is that VMware began to standardize how logging was done by using Syslog for all logging. The Syslog process is designed to handle log messages from the VMkernel, daemons, logger program, and other programs and processes. For remote logging, log messages can be sent to a centralized logging system and system panics can be sent to a remote dump collector. Therefore, troubleshooting log files after a reboot can be performed on the remote Syslog server. Due to the local log files now being stored on a RAM disk in memory, if the ESXi host reboots or crashes, the local log files on the ESXi host are lost. So in vSphere 5, Syslog can now be used to send log entries to a centralized remote log server, instead of storing the log files on the vCenter Server.

System logging using **syslogd** has been a traditional method for performing Unix and Linux logging for a long time. In vSphere 5, VMware modifies Syslog changing the name of the daemon to **vmsyslogd**. Another change is the filename of the socket for incoming logging, which is now **/dev/klog**. So the VMkernel, daemons, and programs will send their initial log messages to the **/dev/klog** socket. The **vmsyslogd** daemon queries **/dev/klog** for incoming logs. When **vmsyslogd** grabs a new log, it then has to figure out what to do with the log information. The configuration of how Syslog is handled is done using the vSphere Client or by using command-line commands. Figure 7-13 shows how Syslog configuration is handled using the vSphere Client. You can see several of the configuration changes that can be made. To configure Syslog in the vSphere Client, highlight the **ESXi host**, click the **Configuration** tab, and then select **Advanced Settings** under the **Software** section.

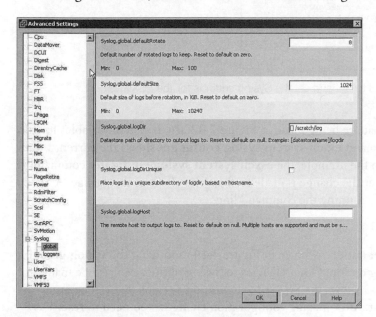

Key
Topic

Figure 7-13   Configuring Syslog using Advanced Settings.

To configure Syslog using the esxcli command line, you first need to authenticate to the ESXi host using an SSH client such as PuTTY. After logging in to the ESXi host, you can execute commands using the vSphere command-line interface. The options that are configurable in the command line in many cases have a similar functionality when using the vSphere client.

An example of using the **esxcli system syslog** namespace is shown in Figure 7-14. The first command shows the **esxcli get** option, which can be used to display several Syslog settings. An example of one of the syslog settings is log file retention for the ESXi host, which defaults to eight log files to retain. These Syslog settings can be modified using the **esxcli set** option. The example in Figure 7-14 shows using the **esxcli set** option to change the current number of log files, which is eight for the ESXi host, and set the new retention value to five.

Key
Topic

```
esxi01.vclass.local - PuTTY
~ # esxcli system syslog config get
   Local Log Output: /scratch/log
   Local Logging Default Rotation Size: 1024
   Local Logging Default Rotations: 8
   Log To Unique Subdirectory: false
   Remote Host: <none>
~ # esxcli system syslog config set --default-rotate=5
~ # esxcli system syslog config get
   Local Log Output: /scratch/log
   Local Logging Default Rotation Size: 1024
   Local Logging Default Rotations: 5
   Log To Unique Subdirectory: false
   Remote Host: <none>
~ # esxcli system syslog reload
~ #
```

Figure 7-14   Using ESXCLI to get and set the Syslog settings for the ESXi host.

The modifications that are being made in Figure 7-14 are to system variables for the ESXi host. The command **esxcli system syslog config get** shows the current values for Syslog options. In the example, the **esxcli system syslog config get** command is shown before and after the change is made to show the effect of the change. A Syslog change is made by running the command line

```
esxcli system syslog config set --<options>
```

An example of the **set** option is shown in Figure 7-14 modifying the **syslog.global. defaultRotate** Syslog option. Other changes to Syslog options can also be made using **esxcli**. Table 7-3 shows the Syslog configuration options that can be modified for the ESXi host. After making configuration changes, you need to restart **vmsyslogd** and load the changes into live memory, which is accomplished using the **reload** option, as shown in Figure 7-14:

```
esxcli system syslog reload
```

The configuration options for Syslog are detailed in Table 7-3. These options can be changed using either the vSphere Client or the command line. An example of making changes to Syslog using the command line is shown in Figure 7-14. Another example of making a change to Syslog, but using the vSphere Client, is shown in Figure 7-13.

Table 7-3   Syslog Configuration Options

Option	Description
Syslog.global.logDir	Location to store local or remote Syslog files
Syslog.global.logHost	Destination host for remote log files

Option	Description
Syslog.global.logDirUnique	A Boolean [True|False] option determines whether a directory using the hostname is created under the configured logDir
Syslog.global.defaultRotate	Number of log files retained on the local ESXi host
Syslog.global.defaultSize	Causes the log file to be rotated when it hits the default size

Install and Configure VMware Syslog Collector

All ESXi hosts run a Syslog service (vmsyslogd), which logs messages from the VMkernel to a log file. In vSphere 5 the log files are stored in the **/var/log** directory, which is a soft link to the **/scratch/log** directory. The **/scratch/log** directory is a scratch partition located in memory. Because the scratch partition is located in memory, updates to the file have a better chance of not being dropped than if the file was located on a hard drive. This benefit, though, is offset by the issue of an ESXi host reboot, which causes all the changes in the in-memory log files to be erased. However, locating logs to a local disk is not always possible because some ESXi hosts do not have hard disks, such as an Auto Deployed ESXi host. Therefore, to set up a location for longer-term storage of log files that can survive a reboot, you need to set up a centralized Syslog Collector. The centralized Syslog server will be advantageous for not only surviving a reboot, but also for providing one place to go to easily access and manage log files that will be collected from all the ESXi hosts in a vSphere implementation.

vCenter Server Appliance and Syslog Collector

The Syslog Collector is bundled into the vCenter Server Appliance. The VCSA server acts as a Syslog server receiving log files from ESXi hosts forwarding their log files, including those provisioned with Auto Deploy. Because the Syslog Collector is installed and built in to the vCenter Server Appliance, no extra setup is required. By default, the log files managed by Syslog will be located in the **/var/log/remote/<hostname>/** directory.

Windows vCenter Server and Syslog Collector

When using vCenter Server on a Windows virtual machine, the vSphere Syslog Collector needs to be installed from the vCenter Server Installer, which is shown in Figure 7-15. You will be given the option during the install process to install the Syslog Collector on the same machine as the associated vCenter Server or on a different machine that has network connectivity to the vCenter Server. You can se-lect a few options during the install process, such as the maximum number of Syslog Collector log rotations to maintain. Following the wizard prompts during the instal-lation enables the Syslog Collector to be functional after the install.

Figure 7-15   Windows vCenter Server Installer choosing Syslog Collector.

Analyze and Test Logging Configuration Information

One of the changes that was made in vSphere 5 logging was separating all the log files to help identify more patterns, which will lead to solving more issues. As an example, say a system-wide outage occurred. In this case, the **vmkwarning.log** and **vmksummary.log** log files would be the best source for log messages to diagnose the problem. The separation of logging to multiple log files helps to categorize log data into specific files to make it easier to locate the information necessary and help solve problems.

In the previous section, we learned how to modify the Syslog configuration options. The system administrator can utilize either the vSphere Client or the esxcli command-line options to make changes to the logging configuration. The esxcli system Syslog has options to display logging information and modify the log file sizes, log rotation, and a few other options as well.

Analyze Log Files to Resolve Issues

In the **/var/log** directory a couple of the important files to view are the **vmkernel.log** file and the **vmksummary.log** file. These log files contain configuration information and tend to be common files to view when troubleshooting problems on the ESXi host. The **vmkernel.log** file contains the main vmkernel log messages as well as events that happen with networking and storage. The other log file is the **vmksummary.log** file. This file contains the logging of the ESXi host when it powers on and powers off, as well as other important events on the ESXi host.

Figure 7-16 shows the **vmkernel.log** file. When you initially observe the file, figuring out how to read it can be confusing. One change that has been implemented in all the major log files is a new date and time stamp at the start of each line. In Figure 7-16, the last two lines in the vmkernel log file were created by running the esxcli command-line command twice:

```
esxcli system syslog mark --message="Test Message!"
```

Figure 7-16 vmkernel.log file.

NOTE Hexadecimal numbers in T10 documentation use the NNNh notation, whereas SCSI status codes logged to the ESXi host use the equivalent 0xNNN notation—for example, 0x2 == 02h.

In Figure 7-16, the log file **vmkernel.log** is displayed. The log file shows VMkernel messages related to storage and contain SCSI Sense codes. The SCSI Sense codes are an industry standard maintained by an independent organization called Technical Committee T10. The ESXi host and all storage arrays conform to this standard.

The Sense codes are sent during the status phase, which occurs prior to the Command Complete Message and indicates success or failure. Any time a SCSI command is sent to a target, the initiator expects a completion status. The various status codes and descriptions are shown in Table 7-4.

Table 7-4 Lockdown Mode Behavior

Status Code	Meaning
00h	Good
02h	Check condition
04h	Condition met
08h	Busy
18h	Reservation conflict
28h	Task set full
30h	ACA active
40h	Task aborted

For more information, see http://www.t10.org/lists/2status.htm.

Here is an example of a **vmkernel.log** file entry:

```
vmkernel:77:17:30:20.109 cpu7:2050)NMP: nmp_CompleteCommandForPath:
Command
0x28 (0x41000b10f000) to NMP device
"naa.600601608c121200f80d33192b62de11"
failed on physical path "vmhba2:C0:T0:L5" H:0x0 D:0x2 P:0x0
Valid sense data:
0x2 0x4 0x3
```

This **vmkernel.log** entry is an example of an error occurring between ESXi and a storage device, which is noted by the Device Status 0x2. When the ESXi host receives the Check Condition status, it sends out a SCSI command 0x3 that equates to REQUEST SENSE to get the SCSI sense data from the device. The sense data is listed after "Valid sense data" and contains (Sense Key, Additional Sense Code, ASC Qualifier).

Isolate the SCSI event in the log file, and focus on the hexadecimal values to evaluate the error message:

Host Status = 0x0 = OK H:0x0

Device Status = 0x2 = Check Condition D:0x2

Plugin Status = 0x0 = No error P:0x0

Sense Key = 0x2 = NOT READY 0x2

Additional Sense Code/ASC Qualifier = 0x4/0x3 = LOGICAL UNIT NOT READY – MANUAL INTERVENTION REQUIRED 0x4 0x3

For more information on the Sense Keys, visit http://www.t10.org/lists/2sensekey.htm.

For more information on Additional Sense Code/ASC Qualifier pairings, see http://www.t10.org/lists/asc-num.txt.

Install and Configure vSphere ESXi Dump Collector

In addition to the Syslog Collector, another new service that was added in vSphere 5.0 is the ESXi Dump Collector. The vSphere Network Dump Collector service is a tool that can be used to collect diagnostic information from an ESXi host that experiences a system panic and generates a purple diagnostic screen. When the VMkernel crashes, the system goes into a fail-safe mode. You could think of it as driving your car at a high rate of speed and hitting a brick wall. Hopefully, your airbag will inflate and your seat belt will lock and save you from bodily injury. Unfortunately, the front of the car will not be saved, but the airbag and seat belt will at least save your life. When the VMkernel panic function begins, it is trying to save the rest of the kernel because something bad just happened on the system. It could be a bad kernel device driver, a bad system call, or an unexpected kernel setting or modification. The system panic is like a seat belt in a car—there is not much you can do about the front of the car or whatever system action started the panic process, but an attempt will be made to save as much of the kernel as possible from the kernel malfunction.

When the system panic starts, it takes the kernel pages of memory and dumps them to disk. When the ESXi host has a local hard drive, the panic routine utilizes it. If the ESXi host does not have an internal hard drive or is an auto-deployed ESXi host, it needs to send the diagnostic information to a Dump Collector. The Network Dump Collector can be configured in addition to or instead of the local hard disk being used to store the dump files. Thus, you need to install the vSphere Network Dump Collector to collect system panics over the network.

During a critical failure on an ESXi host, the panic routine begins and attempts to write a core dump using either or both the DiskDump (local disk) or NetDump (Dump Collector) mechanisms. The panic routine has a magic number at the beginning and end of the core dump and compresses the dump in case there is not enough space on the destination disk. If NetDump has been configured, the host opens a connection from a VMkernel network to the remote IP on UDP port 6500, and transmits a compressed core dump. By default, the NetDump protocol service is registered to the UDP port 6500. The Network Dump Collector service receives the System Dump and checks the magic numbers at the beginning and end to ensure it has all the necessary core dump information. Then the Dump Collector saves the compressed core dump to a file on its own disk in a zdump format. On the Dump Collector host, the zdump files are organized by the sending ESXi host's IP address in a directory format and using the date and time of the Dump Collector Server. If the sending host's IP address was 192.168.33.44, then the directory and file structure would be as follows:

```
C:\ProgramData\VMware\VMware ESXi Dump Collector\Data\192\168\33\44
zdump_192.168.33.44-yyyy-mm-dd-hh_mm-N
```

You can either install the ESXi Dump Collector on a Windows Server using the vCenter Server Installation media or configure the Dump Collector that is included with the vCenter Server Appliance.

vCenter Server Appliance and Dump Collector

The ESXi Dump Collector is bundled with the vCenter Server Appliance. As the VCSA server becomes the preferred choice for vCenter Server, it will be nice to have many of the tools already installed and just requiring configuration. Just like the Syslog Collector, the Dump Collector needs to be configured for it to function using the vCenter Server Appliance.

> **NOTE**   The ESXi Dump Collector is installed and enabled by default on the vCenter Server Appliance. Thus, it just needs configuring on vCenter Server Appliance.

Here are the steps to configure Dump Collector on VCSA:

Step 1.   Log in to the vCenter Server Appliance.

Step 2.   Find the **Services** tab and click **NetDump**.

Step 3.   Type the port number in the **Network Coredump Server Port** text box.

Step 4.   Type the max size in MB in the **Network Coredump Repository**.

Step 5.   Click **Test Settings** to verify that the settings are valid.

Step 6.   Click **Save Settings**.

Step 7.   Restart **ESXi Services**.

Windows-based vCenter Server and the ESXi Dump Collector

If a Windows-based vCenter Server is used, the ESXi Dump Collector needs to be installed from the vCenter Server Installer, which is shown in Figure 7-15, just above the Syslog Collector option. After the central Network Dump Collector is installed, you will need to direct the ESXi hosts to use the Dump Collector for their system core dumps when a ESXi host encounters a critical failure.

Configure ESXi Dump Collector with esxcli

Use the esxcli command to set up an ESXi host to use the Network Dump Collector for their core dumps. You must specify the VMkernel NIC, IP address, and UDP port for the NetDump service on the Network Dump Collector host, like so:

```
esxcli system coredump network set –interface-name vmk0 –server-ipv4
192.1.2.3 –serverport 6500
```

Then, you enable ESXi Dump Collector:

```
esxcli system coredump network set –enable true
```

Summary

This module describes logging in vSphere. Although how logging works and is used in vSphere 5 has changed from previous vSphere versions, behind the scenes Syslog is still used and in general works in a similar fashion. There are a variety of methods to bundle the log files that can be sent to VMware support or used by the local system administrator for analysis. Of course, knowing where and what the log files are is helpful to the system administrator. After learning where to find the log files, the module discussed how to view the log files as well as how to change the settings for how Syslog is implemented in vSphere 5.x. Finally, the module finished with how to install and configure Syslog Collector and ESXi Dump Collector. Both tools can be used to help when issues arise in the vSphere environment.

Exam Preparation Tasks

Review All the Key Topics

Table 7-5 provides a list of all Key Topics identified in this chapter along with a few notes intended to refresh your memory of some key details. This can be useful as a quick reference when performing vSphere administration.

Table 7-5 Key Topics for Chapter 7

Key Topic	Description	Page Number
Diagnostic Log Bundles	Diagnostic and log files can be sent to VMware support by using a number of methods, such as the command-line tool **vm-support PowerCLI Get-Log** cmdlet, Generate System Log Bundle option directly on vCenter Server, or Generate System Log Bundle on vCenter Server using vSphere Client.	290
Selecting ESXi Hosts to Include in the System Log Bundle	When you are stepping through the windows while building the vSphere system log bundle, one of the windows is the Source window, which allows you to select ESXi hosts and whether you want the vCenter Server log files in the System Log Bundle.	294
Configure Logging Level for vCenter Server	Figure 7-11.	297
ESXi Log Files Location	**/var/log**.	298
vCenter Server Log Files on Windows Server 2008	**%ALLUSERSPROFILE%\VMware\ VMware VirtualCenter\Logs**	299
Advanced Settings	Figure 7-13 displays where to configure Advanced Settings on an ESXi host for syslog.	301
esxcli system syslog	To configure Syslog for an ESXi host using the command line.	301
Syslog Configuration Options	Table 7-3 displays Syslog configuration options that can be modified.	302

Key Terms

Define the following key terms from this chapter, and check your answers in the glossary.

tar, gzip, PuTTY, System Log Bundle, vm-support, Syslog, Syslog Collector, Dump Collector.

Review Tasks

These review tasks allow you to assess how well you grasped the materials in this chapter. Because of the advanced and hands-on nature of this particular exam, a set of tasks is provided instead of a set of questions. You should now attempt to perform each of these tasks without looking at previous sections in this chapter or at other materials, unless necessary. The steps for each task are located within the chapter:

1. Generate a system log bundle using any method from the module.

2. Generate a system log bundle, but do not include the vCenter Server.

3. Modify the vCenter Server logging level to none.

4. Change the number of log files that an ESXi host retains to five.

5. Install Syslog Collector.

6. Install Dump Collector.

This chapter covers the following subjects:

- **Users and Groups**—This section covers how to secure the ESXi host with users, groups, and roles. It also looks at SSH, SSL, certificates, and lockdown mode.

- **Strong Passwords**—The strength of a user's password and the password policies are covered in this section.

- **Hardening Virtual Machines**—An often-overlooked part of security is the security of the virtual machine itself. This section covers how to secure the virtual machine.

- **Firewall**—This section covers which ports and services are open on the ESXi built-in firewall. It also discusses how to enable and disable services, as well as open and close firewall ports using the vSphere Client, CLI, and PowerCLI.

- **Custom Service and Firewall Security Level**—This section covers how to create a custom service and explains the firewall security levels.

The material in this chapter pertains to the VCAP-DCA Exam objectives 7.1 and 7.2.

## CHAPTER 8

Security and Firewall

The way in which security in vSphere works and the various methods used to secure the environment are discussed in this chapter. Many security settings in vSphere are controlled by variables located on the hypervisor's file system. These security-related files can be modified to control the behavior of the various security tools within vSphere, and these changes are part of the focus of this chapter. The process of configuring Active Directory integration with vSphere is also explained. A demonstration on how to configure Secure Sockets Layer (SSL) timeouts and customize Secure Shell (SSH) settings is provided. In addition, this chapter examines users and groups on the ESXi host and how to add, edit, and remove them. Another feature discussed is how users and groups log in using passwords, as well as how passwords can be strengthened. Other security functions covered in this chapter include how to enable and disable certificates (CA-signed) and how to enable lockdown mode in a vSphere environment.

This chapter also includes a section about the ESXi firewall. We identify the esxcli configuration commands that affect the ESXi firewall, as well as explain how to modify the firewall by performing actions such as opening and closing ports. This section also looks at how to enable and disable services, including how to create custom services.

The latest version of vSphere offers many ways to secure the environment and is the most secure version of vSphere to date. Unfortunately, as more source code and new features get added to the hypervisor, new risks will emerge that need to be addressed. Securing a vSphere environment really boils down to two areas: authentication and authorization. Authentication focuses on proving you are who you say you are, and we look at the ways this is done in vSphere. Authorization focuses on allowing or not allowing a user or group access to an object. In this chapter, we examine a lot of features that control both authentication and authorization.

"Do I Know This Already?" Quiz

The "Do I Know This Already?" quiz enables you to assess whether you should read this entire chapter or simply jump to the "Exam Preparation Tasks" section for review. If you are in doubt, read the entire chapter. Table 8-1 outlines the major headings in this chapter and the corresponding "Do I Know This Already?" quiz questions. You can find the answers in Appendix A, "Answers to the 'Do I Know This Already?' Quizzes and Troubleshooting Scenarios."

Table 8-1   "Do I Know This Already?" Foundation Topics Section-to-Question Mapping

Foundations Topics Section	Questions Covered in This Section
Users and Groups	1, 2
Strong Passwords	3
Hardening Virtual Machines	4
Firewall	5, 6
Custom Service and Firewall Security Level	7

1. Which is not a predefined system role?

   a. No access

   b. Read-only

   c. Virtual machine user

   d. Administrator

2. Which predefined role can assign permissions to users?

   a. Administrator

   b. Resource Pool Administrator

   c. Virtual Machine Administrator

   d. Role Administrator

3. Which two statements regarding the pam_passwdqc plugin are accurate? (Select two.)

   a. An uppercase letter used as the first character counts toward the number of character classes.

   b. An uppercase letter used as the first character does not count toward the number of character classes.

    c. A number used as the last character counts toward the number of character classes.

    d. A number used as the last character does not count toward the number of character classes.

4. Which option is not a method for hardening virtual machines?

    a. Installing antivirus software

    b. Preventing copy and paste to a remote console from the clipboard

    c. Restricting the VMCI Interface

    d. Closing the SSH Server firewall port

5. Which two versions of vSphere contain a built-in firewall? (Select two.)

    a. ESXi 4.0

    b. ESX 4.1

    c. ESXi 4.1

    d. ESXi 5.0

6. Which statement is accurate regarding the default status of system services on an ESXi host?

    a. Telnet is stopped and SSH is running.

    b. Telnet is running and SSH is stopped.

    c. Telnet is running and SSH is running.

    d. Telnet is stopped and SSH is stopped.

7. Which of the following is the default firewall security level?

    a. Maximum Security—Firewall is configured to block all incoming and outgoing traffic except for port 902.

    b. High Security—Firewall is configured to block all incoming and outgoing traffic, except for ports 22, 123, 427, 443, 902, 5989, and 5988.

    c. Medium Security—All incoming traffic is blocked, except on the default ports and any ports you specifically open. Outgoing traffic is not blocked.

    d. Low Security—There are no ports blocked on either incoming or outgoing traffic. This setting is equivalent to removing the firewall.

Foundation Topics

Users and Groups on an ESXi Host

The VMkernel identifies a user by a unique integer called a user ID (UID). A user can also be a member of a group of users identified by an integer called a group ID (GID). For security reasons, the VMkernel imposes strict rules governing user access. The login process is generally responsible for setting the UID and GID for the user's session. These variables are inherited by other processes run by the user using interfaces such as the vSphere Client, the vCLI, or PowerCLI.

Users can be broken down into several types but basically fall into two classifications. Regardless of whether a user is created as a local user or integrated from a directory service, users on ESXi and vCenter Server can be classified as root or non-root users.

The root user on an ESXi host is given the capability to administer the host. The root user is exempt from limitations on the ESXi host and has the ability to maintain the security of the system and to make configuration changes, just to name a few of the things the root user can do. In general, the root user, or super user, can do everything and is the only user defined by default on the ESXi host. If you authenticate as the root user, then you really do not need to spend time worrying about roles or how to get the necessary permissions to perform tasks or functions.

Non-root users, however, must have proper permissions to perform tasks on an ESXi host. These users are also defined on the host or using Active Directory (AD) authentication. Although in both cases users can be defined in either fashion, in a large environment with multiple ESXi hosts, it is advantageous to use a centralized management system such as AD. This can be accomplished by configuring the hosts to join an AD domain. In fact, a group called ESX Admins is preconfigured on ESXi hosts by default. Creating this group and assigning users to the group in AD automatically provides those users with Administrator-equivalent permissions on the ESXi hosts in the environment.

By default, the root equivalent user on vCenter Server is the Administrator account, when vCenter Server is deployed on a Windows virtual machine. If the vCenter Server is a member of the AD domain, any Active Directory user with Domain Administrator privileges has Administrator-equivalent permissions. This behavior can be insecure, and you might need to adjust AD and vCenter Server settings appropriately to ensure that the desired AD users are given Administrator-equivalent permissions.

A non-root local user defined on a vCenter Server virtual machine is considered a separate user and is defined independently from users defined on an ESXi host.

Figure 8-1 shows a vSphere Client logged directly in to an ESXi host. Selecting the **Local Users & Groups** tab displays the local users on the host.

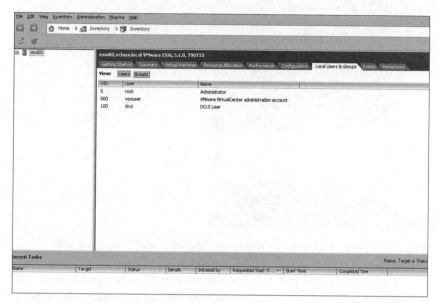

Figure 8-1   A list of users for the selected ESXi host.

Using the mouse, you can right-click the open space on the page and select **Add**. This opens the **Add New User** window (see Figure 8-2), which you can use to populate users directly on an ESXi host. Each user will have a unique UID, login, and username. You will also need to add a password and assign the user to a group, if applicable.

A user starts with no privileges. To perform actions on inventory objects, a user must be assigned a role containing the necessary privileges. Roles are used in vSphere to give privileges to non-root users. A role created on a vCenter Server applies privileges to users on objects in the vCenter Server inventory only and does not apply to ESXi users or inventory objects not managed by vCenter Server. The various types of roles available include default system roles, sample roles, and custom roles.

The three default system roles can be assigned to ESXi users and/or vCenter Server users; these are as follows:

- No access—No abilities are given.

- Read-only—The user can view but not modify objects.

- Administrator—Can do everything. By default, root, dcui, and vpxuser have this role on an ESXi host.

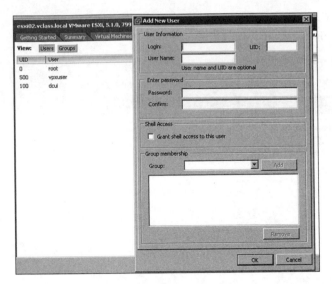

Figure 8-2   The Add New User window enables you to add a local user to an ESXi host.

vCenter Server has six additional premade sample roles that can be used as is, or you can take a sample role and modify it. Ideally you would take the sample role, make a copy of it, and then modify it. To modify the sample role, you will need a user with Administrator privileges, such as one of these:

- Virtual machine power user

- Virtual machine user

- Resource pool administrator

- VMware Consolidated Backup user

- Datastore consumer

- Network consumer

The only user that is defined by default on an ESXi host is the root user. The initial root password is typically set using the Direct Console User Interface (DCUI). It can be changed afterward using the vSphere client. Whether adding more users to vCenter Server or ESXi, these non-root users begin with no permissions and then roles are assigned to these users to give them appropriate privileges on selected objects. The roles assigned can be the default or sample roles, but in some cases a custom role might be needed, which can be generated only by a user with the Administrator role. Figure 8-3 displays an example of the current roles for a vCenter Server. As you highlight each role, the users who have been assigned the particular role are shown on the right side of the window.

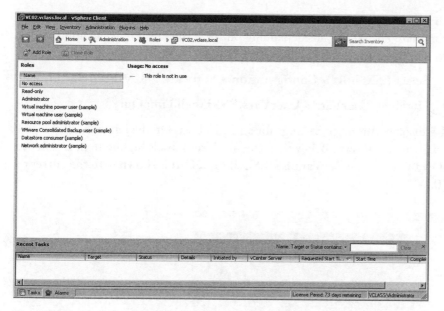

Figure 8-3   To display a current list of roles, select Home > Administration > Roles.

Customize SSH Settings for Increased Security

To access ESXi hosts remotely using a command line, you need an SSH client. A software program like PuTTY is a nice SSH client that will enable you to connect to a remote host. PuTTY is an open-sourced SSH client that has been in use for a number of years and is well trusted. It is fairly simple to quickly set up a PuTTY connection to an ESXi host. The PuTTY client is already installed in the VCAP-DCA lab environment, but to use it with a freshly installed ESXi host, you first need to know how to enable SSH connections to the host. By default, SSH is not enabled on an ESXi host. Using the vSphere client, you can connect either directly to the ESXi host or to a vCenter Server for managed hosts. From there, the following steps can be used to enable access to an ESXi host using SSH.

Figure 8-4 shows enabling SSH to an ESXi host while connected to a vCenter Server using the vSphere Client. The steps are identical if connected directly to the host:

Step 1.   Highlight the **ESXi host > Configuration > Software > Security Profile**.

Step 2.   Select the **Services Section > Properties > Highlight SSH**.

Step 3.   Select the **Options** tab **> Service Commands > press Start > OK**.

Note that selecting the **Start and stop manually** option will not keep the SSH service running if the host is restarted. This is a more secure option, but security can be further increased on the SSH connection by setting a timeout value. The value can range from 0 seconds, which is equivalent to no timeout value and is the default, to a maximum of 86,400 seconds depending on what you deem to be an appropriate value. Do the following:

Step 1. Select **ESXi host > Configuration > Software > Advanced Settings**.

Step 2. Highlight **UserVars > UserVars.ESXiShellTimeOut**.

Figure 8-5 displays Advanced Settings for an ESXi host. On the left side, all the different categories are shown. Below the category **UserVars** is highlighted, and in the left window the variable **UserVars.ESXiShellTimeOut** is shown with the current value of 0.

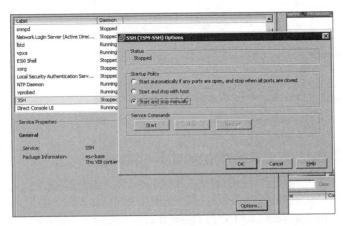

Figure 8-4 Enabling SSH for an ESXi host.

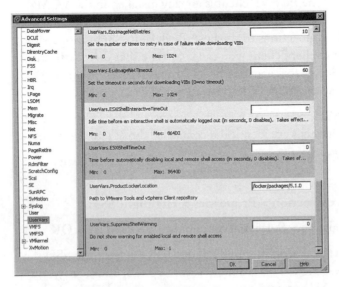

Figure 8-5 Modifying the ESXi Shell Timeout value.

Enable/Disable Certificate Checking

Cryptography is used to secure the data on a network and to authenticate the users of that data. The data that travels between clients and ESXi hosts is encrypted to ensure that the transactions are private and authenticated. The SSL is used to create a secure connection between the clients, ESXi hosts, and/or the vCenter Server. The SSL protocol runs above TCP/IP and below higher-level protocols such as HTTP. SSL uses TCP/IP on behalf of the higher-level protocols, allowing SSL-enabled ESXi hosts and/or vCenter Server to authenticate with SSL-enabled clients. This enables the client to establish encrypted connections with hosts and/or the vCenter Server. When an ESXi host or vCenter Server is installed, the installation includes SSL certificates. These preinstalled, autogenerated certificates are not from an official certificate authority (CA), but they can be used to establish an initial connection. The vCenter Server uses an SSL certificate when adding ESXi hosts and to connect to managed ESXi hosts whose passwords are stored in the vCenter Server database. After an authenticated encrypted connection is established, a smaller session key is encrypted and exchanged using public and private key pairs. This shared session key is then used to encrypt and decrypt the data between client and server. Shared secret key encryption generally requires very little processing time, which makes it a viable solution for encrypting large amounts of data between a client and a server.

In vSphere 5.1, vCenter Servers always connect through SSL when connecting to an ESXi host.

In vSphere 5.0, the following procedure is used to configure SSL settings:

Step 1. In the vSphere client, navigate to the vCenter Server instance.

Step 2. Click the drop-down box labeled **Administration**, and select **vCenter Server Settings**. In the **vCenter Server Settings** window's right pane, select **SSL Settings**.

Generate ESXi Host Certificates

VMware products use standard X.509 version 3 (X.509v3) certificates to encrypt session information sent over Secure Socket Layer protocol connections between the client and the server.

When you replace the default vCenter Server and ESXi certificates, the certificates you obtain for your servers must be signed and must conform to the Privacy Enhanced Mail (PEM) key format. The key used to sign certificates must be a standard RSA key with an encryption length that ranges from 512 to 4,096 bits. The recommended length is 2,048 bits.

Certificates signed by a commercial certificate authority, such as Entrust or Veri-Sign, are pre-trusted on the Windows operating system. However, if you replace a certificate with one signed by your own local root CA, or if you plan to continue using a default certificate, you must pre-trust the certificate by importing it into the local certificate store for each vSphere Client instance.

You must pre-trust all certificates that are signed by your own local root CA, unless you pre-trust the parent certificate, the root CA's own certificate. You must also pre-trust any valid default certificates you will continue to use on vCenter Server.

Replace default certificates with those signed by an internal certificate authority or public key infrastructure (PKI) service. Alternatively, purchase a certificate from a trusted commercial security authority.

The two certification files located on an ESXi host are

- Private key file: **/etc/vmware/ssl/rui.key**
- Certification file: **/etc/vmware/ssl/rui.crt**

NOTE   Use commercially signed certificates for systems that are exposed to the Internet.

When you replace default server certificates in a production environment, deploy the new certificates in stages, rather than all at the same time. Make sure that you understand the process as it applies to your environment before performing these actions.

You will need to generate a new certificate if the ESXi host or vCenter Server certificate gets deleted, or if you change the hostname of the system. These would be the most common reasons to generate a new SSL certificate.

The steps to generate a new ESXi host certificate are detailed here:

Step 1.   Log in to the ESXi shell as the root user.

Step 2.   Back up any existing certificates, just in case.

```
# mv /etc/vmware/ssl/rui.crt /etc/vmware/ssl/rui.crt.old
# mv /etc/vmware/ssl/rui.key /etc/vmware/ssl/rui.key.old
```

NOTE   If the **rui.crt** and **rui.key** files do not exist then you do not need to back them up; you can just go to the next step.

Step 3. Generate the new certificates:

```
# /sbin/generate-certificates
```

Step 4. Reboot the ESXi host or restart the hostd process:

```
# /etc/init.d/hostd/restart
```

Replace Default Certificate with CA-Signed Certificate

A default certificate is generated automatically for the ESXi host during installation. Because the certificate for the ESXi host was self-generated, it has not been signed and will not be given a trusted status when attempting to communicate with other servers and clients. Other network devices might not allow communication with the ESXi host until it is certified by a well-known CA. X.509 certificates are supported over SSL connections for the encrypted session.

NOTE When replacing the default certificate of the ESXi host, if the vCenter Server stops managing the host, check whether the ESXi host has Verify Certificates enabled. If this is the case, reconnect the ESXi host to the vCenter Server using the vSphere Client.

The steps to add a CA-signed certificate are as follows:

Step 1. Log in to the ESXi shell. As an example, use PuTTY to SSH into the ESXi host.

Step 2. Change the directories to **/etc/vmware/ssl**, and give the original certificate files a backup by using the **move** command:

```
# mv rui.crt rui.cert.orig
# mv rui.key rui.key.orig
```

Step 3. Go to the location where the new authenticated certificate **rui.crt** and key file **rui.key** are located; copy the CA-signed certificate files to the directory **/etc/vmware/ssl**.

Step 4. Either restart the services using

```
# services.sh restart
```

or reboot the ESXi host.

Enable ESXi Lockdown Mode

To increase the security of ESXi hosts that have been added to a vCenter Server, you can enable the **Lockdown Mode** option. Enabling lockdown mode restricts users from performing actions directly on an ESXi host using SSH or the ESXi Shell. Many businesses and government organizations use this mode to limit access to the server. It also restricts users from accessing the DCUI unless they have the **DCUI Access** privilege.

Subsequent actions performed on managed ESXi hosts in this mode must be made by connecting to a vCenter Server using an account that has been given the necessary permissions to perform those actions. Access to the ESXi Shell locally or remotely using SSH is completely restricted. Access to the DCUI is restricted to users that have the DCUI Access privilege. By default, no local user accounts exist on the ESXi system. Such accounts would have to be created and assigned this privilege before enabling lockdown mode.

Table 8-2 shows which type of access is allowed in normal and lockdown modes.

Table 8-2   Mode Behavior

Access Mode	Normal Mode	Lockdown Mode
vSphere API (for example, vSphere client, PowerCLI, or vCLI)	Any user, based on local roles/privileges	None (except vCenter "vpxuser")
CIM	Any user, based on local role/privilege	None (except via vCenter ticket)
DCUI	Root and users with admin privileges	Root only
Tech support mode (local)	Root	None
Tech support mode (remote)	Root	None

Lockdown mode is available only when an ESXi host is being managed by a vCenter Server. The following four tools can be used to enable or disable lockdown mode:

- The vSphere client
- The ESXi shell (using the **vim-cmd** command)
- The Direct Console User Interface
- PowerCLI

Modify Lockdown Mode Using the vSphere Client

To modify lockdown mode using the vSphere Client, do the following:

Step 1.   Highlight **ESXi host > Configuration > Security Profile**.

Step 2.   When the **Security Profile** panel appears, click **edit** in the **Lockdown Mode** section of the panel.

Step 3.   The Lockdown Mode Window appears with a box labeled **Enable Lockdown Mode** (see Figure 8-6). With the mouse, check the box to enable lockdown mode.

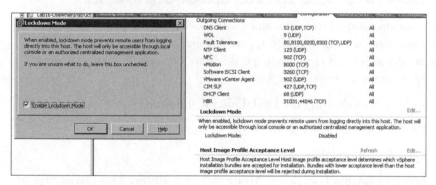

Figure 8-6   Enabling lockdown mode.

Modify Lockdown Mode Using ESXi Shell Command Line

In vSphere 5.x one method to enable lockdown mode is to use the ESXi Shell command line. The ESXi Shell in vSphere 5.x used to be referred to as Tech Support Mode (TSM) in ESXi 4.0 and 4.1. The ESXi Shell is a service that is not enabled by default. To enable the ESXi Shell, refer to the Security Profile Services and Firewall Section at the end of this module. An example of using the CLI to modify the status of lockdown mode is shown in Figure 8-7.

To get the current status of lockdown mode:

```
# vim-cmd -U dcui vimsvc/auth/lockdown_is_enabled
```

To enable lockdown mode:

```
# vim-cmd -U dcui vimsvc/auth/lockdown_mode_enter
```

To disable lockdown mode:

```
# vim-cmd -U dcui vimsvc/auth/lockdown_mode_exit
```

```
esxi02.vclass.local - PuTTY
~ # vim-cmd -U dcui vimsvc/auth/lockdown_is_enabled
false
~ # vim-cmd -U dcui vimsvc/auth/lockdown_mode_enter
~ # vim-cmd -U dcui vimsvc/auth/lockdown_is_enabled
true
~ # vim-cmd -U dcui vimsvc/auth/lockdown_mode_exit
~ # vim-cmd -U dcui vimsvc/auth/lockdown_is_enabled
false
~ # █
```

Figure 8-7 Enabling and disabling lockdown mode using the CLI.

Configure Lockdown Mode Using the Direct Console User Interface

The DCUI can also be used to enable and disable lockdown mode. If you enable or disable lockdown mode using the DCUI, permissions for users and groups on the ESXi host are discarded. To retain these permissions, perform the action using a vSphere Client connected to vCenter Server.

To enable lockdown mode using the DCUI, do the following:

Step 1.   Connect to the DCUI on the ESXi 5.x host.

Step 2.   Press **F2** for Initial Setup.

Step 3.   Scroll to **Enable Lockdown Mode** and press **Enter**. This places an X in the check box for **Enable Lockdown Mode**. If there is no check in the box, lockdown mode is disabled.

Enable or Disable Lockdown Mode with PowerCLI

Lockdown mode can also be performed using PowerCLI cmdlets. Before changing the status of lockdown mode, you can run a PowerCLI cmdlet to determine the current value. The following PowerCLI cmdlet, as shown in Figure 8-8, will check the status of lockdown mode for the ESXi host:

```
Powercli > Get-VMHost | Select Name,@{N="Lockdown";
E={$_.Extensiondata.Config.adminDisabled}}
```

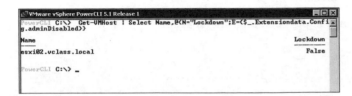

Figure 8-8 Using PowerCLI to check lockdown mode.

Enabling lockdown mode can help secure access to an ESXi host. The following PowerCLI cmdlet enables lockdown mode. In Figure 8-9 the first and last cmdlets list the status of lockdown mode. The middle cmdlet modifies the lockdown status as shown here:

```
Powercli>  (Get-VMHost <hostname> | get-view).EnterLockdownMode() |
Get-VMHost | select Name,@{N="LockDown";E={$_.Extensiondata.Config.
adminDisabled}} | ft -auto Name LockDown
```

This cmdlet is used to enable lockdown mode. Notice in Figure 8-9 that the status of lockdown mode changes to True after running the cmdlet:

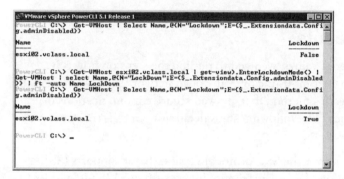

Figure 8-9   Enabling lockdown mode using PowerCLI.

Enabling and disabling lockdown mode can be accomplished using PowerCLI as well. Again, the first and last cmdlets in the figure show the status of lockdown mode. The following PowerCLI cmdlet changes lockdown mode back to the default, which is disabled or false:

```
Powercli> (Get-VMHost <hostname> | Get-View).ExitLockdownMode()
```

In Figure 8-10 notice that when the initial PowerCLI cmdlet is run that displays the status of lockdown mode, it shows that the status is set to true. Then the PowerCLI cmdlet is run that modifies the status to false and is executed on the command line. So, after the PowerCLI cmdlet that modifies the status of lockdown mode is run, the PowerCLI cmdlet that displays the status of lockdown mode is again run and shows the new status of false or disabled.

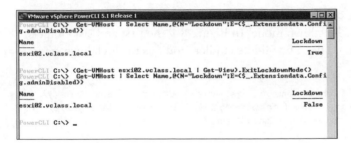

Figure 8-10 Disabling lockdown mode using PowerCLI.

Configure SSL Timeouts

Before we look at the timeout values, we need to outline the steps on how SSL works. SSL can be used to encrypt traffic over any open network. SSL was originally created by Netscape to create a method that allowed secure communications over the Internet using a browser. The following steps detail how an SSL transaction occurs:

1. The client sends the server the SSL protocol version that it supports (SSLv2 or SSLv3), some random data, its maximum bit size (40 bit, 128 bit, and so on), plus some other information needed for performing an SSL transaction.

2. The server replies with a similar set of data to the client, except that it also sends the client a copy of the server's certificate and its public key. The certificate contains information that vouches for the server's identity.

3. The client decides whether the server can be trusted from the information received from the server.

4. If the client does not trust the server, it disconnects from it. If, however, the client does trust the server, then it sends back an initial secret key that is signed with the server's public key.

5. The server decrypts the message and can also ask for client SSL authentication (this latter part is optional). The server then sends back some information that the client and server will use to encode their messages, which will now be encrypted with SSL.

Now that we have looked at the process of how an SSL connection works, we need to define two of the timeout values that can affect SSL connections. After an SSL connection becomes idle, two SSL timeouts can be configured for ESXi. By default, the SSL connection between the server and client does not timeout; however, if a timeout value is set, it will be in milliseconds. The two timeout settings that affect SSL are

- Read Timeout

- Handshake Timeout

The Read Timeout setting applies to connections that have completed the SSL handshake process using port 443 of the ESXi host.

The Handshake Timeout setting applies to connections that have not completed the SSL handshake process with port 443 of ESXi.

Configure Timeout Values via the SSH Command Line

The timeout values can be modified using an SSH command-line connection. Log in to the ESXi host via an SSH client and modify the **/etc/vmware/hostd/config. xml** file.

To change the Read Timeout to 20 seconds, add the following line:

```
<readTimeoutMs>20000</readTimeoutMs>
```

To change the Handshake Timeout to 20 seconds, add the following line:

```
<handshakeTimeoutMs>20000</handshakeTimeoutMs>
```

After adding the two lines to the **config.xml file**, save the file. Now that the file has been modified to include the two timeout values, the **vmware-hostd** process needs to be restarted:

```
# service mgmt-vmware restart
```

Configure vSphere Authentication Proxy

The vSphere Authentication Proxy service is also known as the CAM service. This service enables an ESXi host to join an Active Directory domain without requiring AD credentials. The CAM service is required when using autodeployed stateless ESXi hosts because the credentials of the users cannot be stored on a host that is created in memory. The service stores the user credentials for autodeployed hosts and is utilized when the autodeployed host that resides in memory is being created.

NOTE By default, ESXi must authenticate the vSphere Authentication Proxy server when using it to join a domain. Make sure that this authentication functionality is enabled at all times. If you must disable authentication, you can use the Advanced Settings dialog box to set the **UserVars.ActiveDirectoryVerifyCAMCertificate** attribute to 0.

To configure the vSphere Authentication Proxy service in the vSphere client follow these steps:

Step 1.   Highlight the **ESXi host**.

Step 2.   Click on the **Configuration** tab.

Step 3.   Under **Software** select **Authentication Services** and then select **Properties**.

The **Directory Services Configuration** window is displayed, showing the domain settings (see Figure 8-11). Change the **Select Directory Service Type** from **Local Authentication** to **Active Directory**. The **Use vSphere Authentication Proxy** option is now no longer grayed out. Check the **Use vSphere Authentication Proxy** check box, and enter the **Domain Name** and the IP address of the proxy server.

Figure 8-11   Configuring the vSphere Authentication Proxy Service.

Enable Strong Passwords and Configure Password Policies

Ensuring that user accounts are not compromised is an important function of any computer system. In vSphere, different types of users have different requirements for their respective passwords. Also, there are local users and AD users that have to be taken into account. There are no restrictions set on the local root user account of an ESXi host. However, local non-root users must observe rules when creating passwords, and the strength of their password is defined using a plug-in called a

Pluggable Authentication Module (PAM). By default, the ESXi host checks for password compliance using the **pam_passwdqc.so** PAM. If the password is not compliant, the following error appears:

```
A general system error occurred: passwd: Authentication token
manipulation error.
```

The **pam_passwdqc** plug-in is inserted into the PAM stack so that when a user creates a password, **pam_passwdqc** enforces rules on the password chosen for his account on the ESXi host. The plug-in enables you to determine the password requirements that all local non-root user passwords must meet.

To modify the non-root user password complexity, edit the **/etc/pam.d/passwd** file by finding the line that looks like this:

Key Topic

```
password requisite /lib/security/$ISA/pam_passwdqc.so retry=4
min=8,7,6,5,9
```

where the syntax is:

```
password requisite /lib/security/$ISA/pam_passwdqc.so retry=N
min=N0,N1,N2,N3,N4
```

The last five numbers control the complexity of the password and refer to the four character classes (numbers, lowercase letters, uppercase letters, and special characters). Thus, the password requirements would be as follows:

- **retry=4**—A user is allowed four attempts to enter a strong password.

- **N0=8**—Passwords containing characters from at least one character class must be at least eight characters long.

- **N1=7**—Passwords containing characters from at least two character classes must be at least seven characters long.

- **N2=6**—Passphrases. ESXi requires three words for the SSL certificate passphrase. Each word in the passphrase must be between 8 and 40 characters long.

- **N3=5**—Passwords containing characters from at least three character classes must be at least five characters long.

- **N4=9**—Passwords containing characters from all four character classes must be at least nine characters long.

NOTE   The **pam_passwdqc** plug-in does not count uppercase letters used as the first character in the password and numbers used as the last character of a password when the number of character classes is being counted.

Setting any of these options to -1 directs the **pam_passwdqc.so** plug-in to ignore the requirement. The change will take effect immediately, and non-root users can change their passwords with the **passwd** command.

Identify Methods for Hardening Virtual Machines

By design, virtual machines (VMs) are isolated from other virtual machines. Part of the hardening process for each VM is to look at the security guidelines of the guest operating system for the VM.

Each VM has a .vmx file, otherwise known as the Virtual Machine Configuration File. This file governs the behavior of the virtual hardware and contains many settings for the VM. There are two ways to view the parameters and values for the VM.

One way to view the config file, which is an .ascii file, is from a command line. In a PuTTY session, go to the directory containing the VM files:

```
# cd /vmfs/volumes/[storage]/[vm_name]/
```

- **[storage]** = the current datastore for the VM
- **[vm_name]** = the name of the VM

Next, run a command such as **ls** to see the files in the VM's encapsulated directory (see Figure 8-12).

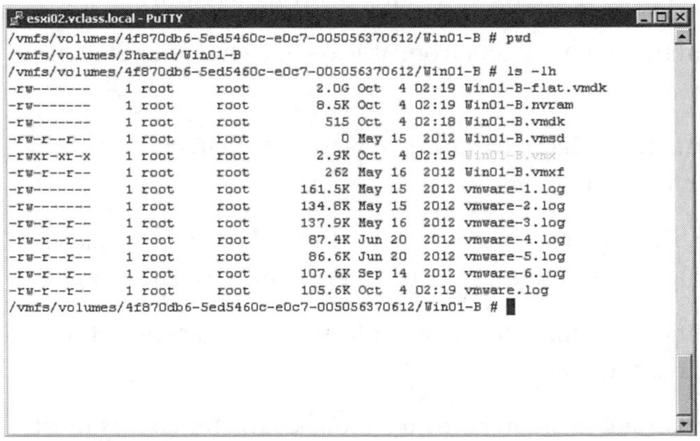

Figure 8-12   Listing of files for a VM.

Now using command-line tools such as the vi editor, you can modify the VM's .vmx config file. You can also use the vSphere Client to make additions or modifications to the VM's configuration. You must restart the VM for most changes to take effect when you modify VM settings using this method.

In the vSphere Client, highlight the VM, right-click, and select **Edit Settings > Options > General > Configuration Parameters** (see Figure 8-13).

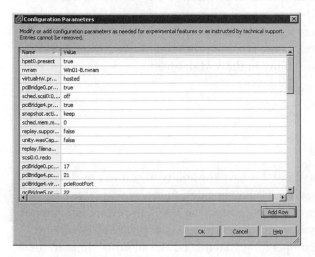

Figure 8-13   Configuring parameters for a VM using vSphere Client.

Protect the Number of Consoles for the Virtual Machine

By default, remote console sessions to a VM can be connected to by more than one user at a time. If an administrator in the VM logs in to the remote console, a non-administrator in the VM could connect to the console during the session and observe the administrator's actions. Thus, to limit the number of entry points to a VM to a single point, you need to apply a security setting by adding the following line to the VM's config file:

```
RemoteDisplay.maxConnections="1"
```

Prevent Virtual Disk Shrinking

The shrinking of a virtual disk reclaims space in the virtual disk. If this process is done repeatedly, the virtual disk can become unavailable and cause a denial of service. You probably should check with your storage administrator to find out whether this is necessary. If these values are set to true in the VM's config file, the administrator cannot shrink the disk:

```
isolation.tools.diskWiper.disable="TRUE"
isolation.tools.diskShrink.disable="TRUE"
```

Prevent Copy and Paste to a Remote Console from the Clipboard

Although this has been disabled by default since vSphere 4.1, you might want to check the status of the copy-and-paste capability. After you install VMware tools into a VM, you have the ability to copy and paste between the guest operating system and the computer where the remote console is running. VMware recommends that you keep the copy-and-paste ability to the VM disabled:

```
isolation.tools.copy.disable="TRUE"
isolation.tools.paste.disable="TRUE"
```

Control Virtual Hardware Usage

Non-root users and processes within VMs have the ability to connect or disconnect devices, such as CD-ROM drives or a USB controller. One way to disable the virtual hardware is to simply remove the device from the VM. However, if you do not want to remove the device but still want to prevent a user or process from connecting to the device within the guest operating system, you can add these lines to the VM .vmx config file:

```
isolation.device.connectable.disable="TRUE"
isolation.device.edit.disable="TRUE"
```

Restrict the VMCI Interface

The Virtual Machine Communication Interface (VMCI) is designed to allow communication from VM to VM. The main objective of VMCI was to provide a socket-based framework for a new generation of applications that will exist only on VMs. If VMCI is compromised, one VM could be used to attack another VM, so this value should be disabled, which is the default.

To display the status of VMCI, highlight the ESXi host, right-click the mouse, and select **Edit Properties**. The **Virtual Machine Properties** window displays, as shown in Figure 8-14. The **Hardware** tab lists all the hardware devices including the VMCI device, which is currently in the state of **Unrestricted** or disabled.

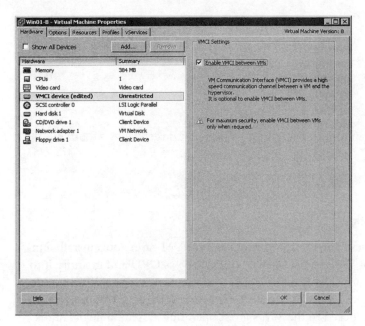

Figure 8-14 Enable VMCI between VMs.

Limit Messages Sent to VMX Files (setinfo)

A setinfo message is where the guest operating system of a VM can send informational messages to the ESXi host through VMware tools. Usually the message contains information about the VM, such as the IP address. Unfortunately, the setinfo message can be any length, and back in the ESX 3.0 days there was a denial-of-service attack that filled up the setinfo message buffer of 1MB. An example of how setinfo messages work is when you look at the summary page of a VM you can see an IP address, that address is populated from a setinfo message.

Control VM Logging Functions

There are four options you can modify to change logging behavior for VMs. Each VM has a log file called **vmware.log**, which is stored in the same directory with all the other files for the VM. By default, a new **vmware.log** file will be created when the host is rebooted; therefore, the size of the log file can become quite large. These changes are made in the VM's .vmx config file:

```
logging="false"  will turn logging off

log.rotateSize="1000000"  log file will rotate when it reaches 1MB.
log.keepOld="10"  will keep 10 log files  the default value is 3
log.fileName="VMlog"  will change the name from vmware.log to VMlog
```

> **NOTE** You can direct log files to be written to a different directory by modifying the **log.fileName** value:
>
> ```
> log.filename="/vmfs/volumes/SAN1/newVMDir/VM.log"
> ```

Secure Perfmon Integration

Microsoft Windows guest operating systems that have VMware Tools installed include the integration of VM performance counters such as CPU and memory into Perfmon. This feature provides accurate performance analysis. The problem with the Perfmon DLL integrated into VMware tools is that some sensitive information about the host can be exposed to the VM's guest operating system. The default is not to expose sensitive information about the host, which is in the VM's .vmx config file:

```
tools.guestlib.enableHostInfo-"FALSE"
```

Install Antivirus Software

In addition to the configuration files that can be changed to restrict certain activities, there are software programs you can install that will harden the security of your VMs. You can also install antivirus, antispyware, intrusion detection, and other applications to protection your VMs. If you were working with a physical host, you would install many of these same programs to protect the operating system. Just like a physical host, for better performance, turn off any screen savers and disable any unused services in the guest operating system of your VMs.

Manage Active Directory Integration

After the initial install, an ESXi host is authenticated by the local files on the host. This lack of centralized management creates an environment in which each individual host requires management, which is not ideal in most companies.

An alternative is to configure each host to join an Active Directory domain, so that a user attempting to access the host will be authenticated against the centralized authentication authority. Any time you are asked to provide credentials—for example, while logging in directly to an ESXi host using the vSphere Client—you can enter the username and password of a user in the domain to which the host is joined. The advantage of this model is that you can now manage user accounts using Active Directory, thus creating the ability to manage all the users from one centralized server.

Even after AD integration, the only user defined on the ESXi host locally is the root user for the host, and the root user will not be mapped to Active Directory.

Configure Active Directory using the vSphere Client by doing the following:

Key Topic

Step 1. Select an ESXi host in the vSphere Client, and click the **Configuration** tab.

Step 2. Under the **Software** section, select **Authentication Services**.

Step 3. In the **Authentication Services Settings**, select **Properties**. The **Directory Services Configuration** dialog box appears.

Step 4. In the **Directory Services Configuration** dialog box, select the **Active Directory** service from the drop-down menu.

Step 5. In the **Domain Settings**, enter a domain or enter Active Directory OU information.

Step 6. Click **Join Domain**.

Step 7. Enter the username and password of an Active Directory user that has permissions to join the host to the domain, and click **OK** (see Figure 8-15).

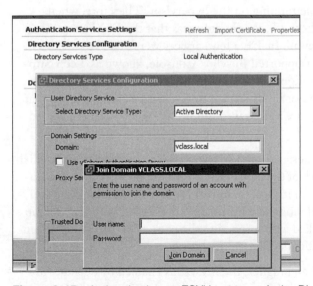

Figure 8-15   Authenticating an ESXi host to an Active Directory Service.

Configure Active Directory Using the Command Line

The configuration of Active Directory settings can also be accomplished by using the **vicfg-authconfig** command. When adding the host to the AD domain, the appropriate AD permissions are needed and you must have administrative privileges on the ESXi host:

```
# vicfg-authconfig -server esxi01 -authscheme AD -joindomain addomain
-addusername root -adpassword passone
```

Configure Active Directory Using PowerCLI

One method to view the status of AD integration for all the ESXi hosts connected to a vCenter Server is using PowerCLI. Check each ESXi host and their domain membership status using the following PowerCLI cmdlet:

```
Powercli> Get-VMHost | Get-VMHostAuthentication | Select VMHost,
Domain, DomainMembershipStatus
```

Security Profile—Services and Firewall Section

One of the features system administrators used to find on an ESX 4.1 and earlier host was a firewall built in to the Service Console. This firewall was based on Linux iptables. When VMware was making the switch from ESX to ESXi in vSphere 4.0, no firewall was included in the ESXi 4.0 server. This was mostly due to the fact that the ESXi 3.5 server was small and did not have a firewall and the code was designed to have as few services as possible running on the hypervisor. Therefore, when VMware was upgrading to vSphere 4.0, the thought was that the ESXi host was so secure that it did not need a firewall. In 4.1, a few services were added to make it easier to enable the "hidden" unsupported Busybox Console, known as **Tech Support Mode**. Although these additional services were added, ESXi 4.1 still did not contain a firewall. As the hypervisor in 4.x started to grow, it became apparent that the next ESXi release would require a firewall—and the ESXi 5.0 release included this.

The new ESXi 5.0 firewall was designed by VMware to be a stateless firewall, which means that it does not keep track of the conversations on the network and it evaluates each packet that goes through it. Access control is provided by a vmknic (VM-kernel network adapter) firewall module. This module resides between the vmknic and the virtual switch and is tasked with inspecting the packets on the management network utilizing the firewall rules defined on the host.

When you first install ESXi 5.0 and higher, the firewall is enabled by default. All incoming and outgoing ports are blocked, except the default TCP and UDP ports used for management purposes. The ESXi firewall protects the management interface of the ESXi host, but no protection is given to the individual VM.

The Preconfigured Services Open by Default

When an ESXi host is first installed, several Management services are open by default. The following lists them:

- **lbtd (/sbin/net-lbtd)**—Load-based teaming for distributed switches is an option that evaluates the uplink load, which was added in ESXi 4.1.

- **vpxa (/usr/lib/vmware/vpxa/bin/vpxa)**—The Virtual Center Agent can be referred to as vpxa or vmware-vpxa. This service enables communication from the Virtual Center Server to hostd located on the ESXi host.

- **NTP Daemon (/sbin/ntpd)**—The Network Time Protocol Daemon is used to synchronize time between the ESXi host and either a stratum or an atomic clock over the network.

- **Direct Console UI**—The Direct Console User Interface **(/sbin/dcui)** enables you to start and stop the system and perform a limited amount of setup, maintenance, and troubleshooting tasks.

- **CIM Server (/bin/cimslp)**—The Common Information Model (CIM) is an interface used to monitor and manage the health of the managed server hardware. The implementation is based on the System Management Architecture for Server Hardware (SMASH) initiative Service Location Protocol version 2.

The Firewall Ports Open by Default

In addition, after an ESXi host is installed, these firewall ports are open by default for management access:

- **22**—SSH server for incoming TCP
- **53**—DNS client for incoming and outgoing UDP
- **68**—DHCP client for incoming and outgoing UDP
- **161**—SNMP server for incoming UDP
- **80**—Fault tolerance for incoming TCP and outgoing TCP and UDP
- **427**—CIM client SLPv2 to find server for incoming and outgoing UDP
- **443**—HTTPS access for incoming TCP

- **902**—Host access and heartbeat for incoming and outgoing TCP and outgoing UDP

- **1234 and 1235**—vSphere replication for outgoing TCP

- **5988**—CIM transactions over HTTP for incoming TCP

- **5989**—CIM XML transactions over HTTPS for incoming and outgoing TCP

- **8000**—vMotion requests for incoming and outgoing TCP

- **8100 and 8200**—Fault-tolerance traffic for incoming and outgoing TCP and UDP

> **NOTE** ICMP ping requests will be replied to by default.

What Is a Firewall Ruleset?

The ESXi firewall ports and services are configured together in the vSphere client. To protect the management interface, the ESXi host uses firewall rulesets to allow and disallow access to the ESXi host. The firewall is strictly designed to protect the management interface and not individual VMs. The firewall default rulesets are initially defined in the read-only **/etc/vmware/firewall/service.xml** file.

To get a list of the known firewall rulesets, use the following command:

```
#esxcli network firewall ruleset list
```

Example 8-1 shows partial output of the firewall rulesets.

Example 8.1 Partial Output of the Firewall Rulesets

```
# esxcli network firewall ruleset list
NAME
-------------------
sshServer            true
sshClient            false
nfsClient            true
dhcp                   true
dns                     true
snmp                   true
ntpClient            false
```

```
CIMHttpServer           true
CIMHttpsServer          true
CIMSLP                  true
iSCSI                   false
vpxHeartbeats           true
```

In addition, more information about the firewall rulesets, such as the port type and protocol, can be displayed by adding the option **rule** to the **esxcli** command. The following **esxcli** command provides a lot of detailed output about the various rulesets (see Example 8-2). The inclusion of the firewall port number and whether the rule is for incoming sessions or outgoing sessions can be useful information. Each ruleset can be either an incoming connection or an outgoing connection of the firewall:

```
# esxcli network firewall ruleset rule list
```

Example 8-2   Using the esxcli Command to Display Firewall Information

```
# esxcli network firewall ruleset rule list
Ruleset         Direction   Protocol   Port Type   Port Begin   Port End
-----------     ---------   --------   ---------   ----------   --------
sshServer       Inbound     TCP        Dst                 22         22
sshClient       Outbound    TCP        Dst                 22         22
nfsClient       Outbound    TCP        Dst                  0      65535
dhcp            Inbound     UDP        Dst                 68         68
dhcp            Outbound    UDP        Src                 68         68
```

Configure the ESXi Firewall

The ESXi firewall ports and services are configured together in the vSphere Client using the **Configuration** tab **> Software > Security Profile**. The **Security Profile** page is broken down into **Services Properties** and **Firewall Properties**. The services are processes that access the management network and pass through the firewall if they are enabled. Configuration changes can be made either using the vSphere Client or using the esxcli command-line tool. Figure 8-16 shows the security profile and both the preconfigured services and the firewall properties.

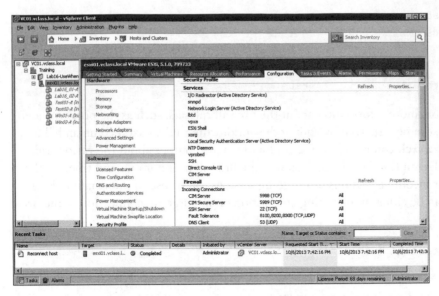

Figure 8-16   Security profile showing services and firewall information.

Configure the Firewall Service Properties Using vSphere Client

To configure services in the vSphere Client, highlight an ESXi host and select **Configuration** tab > **Software** > **Security Profile** > **Properties**, which is located to the right of **Services**. This opens a new window called **Services Properties**; it lists the daemons that are stopped and running, as shown in Figure 8-17.

The ESXi services are daemons that will start automatically, unless the service is programmed otherwise. An example of a service is SSH, which is configured not to start automatically. When you start the SSH service, it allows authorized users to access the ESXi host via command line. To change the status of a service from the Services Properties window, highlight the service you want to change and select **Options** to start, stop, or restart a process. Figure 8-18 shows the vSphere Client window that enables you to start, stop, or restart a process. After a service is started, the daemon's status changes from **Stopped** to **Running**.

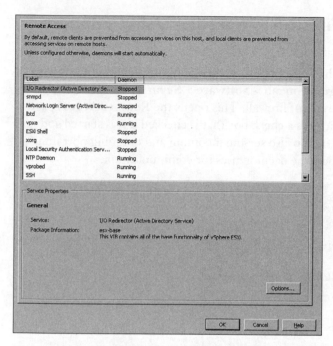

Figure 8-17   The Services Properties window showing whether each service is running or stopped.

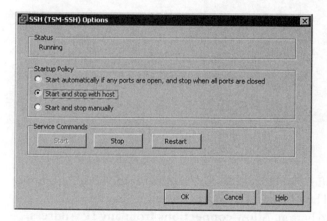

Figure 8-18   Start, stop, or restart a process.

Configure the ESXi Firewall Properties Using vSphere Client

To configure properties of the ESXi firewall in the vSphere Client, highlight the ESXi host and select **Configuration** tab > **Software** > **Security Profile** > **Properties**, which is located to the right of firewall. This opens the **Remote Access** page (see Figure 8-19). Each service has a check box that is checked if it is started and unchecked if it is not started. You can also see the incoming and outgoing port numbers and which type of protocol the daemon uses for communication.

Figure 8-19 Firewall properties.

Firewall settings can be modified by clicking the **Firewall** tab at the bottom right on the **Remote Services** page. The **Allowed IP Addresses** setting has a couple of options available. If the top radio button, **Allow connections from any IP Address,** is enabled, the firewall performs exactly as the name indicates (see Figure 8-20). The bottom radio button limits which hosts or networks have access to a particular service.

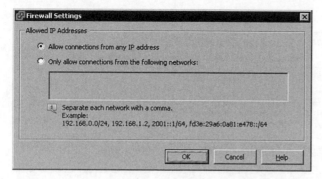

Figure 8-20 This shows which IP addresses are allowed for a particular firewall service.

Configure the ESXi Firewall Using esxcli

The vSphere Client is the most common method for modifying ESXi firewall ports and services. However, in certain circumstances or environments, there needs to be a way to make changes using command-line commands. To modify the firewall from the command line in vSphere 5.x, use the **esxcli** command with the appropriate options. Examples of using **esxcli** commands to perform firewall-related actions are shown in Table 8-3.

Table 8-3 Examples of esxcli Commands and the Actions They Perform

Command	Description
`esxcli network firewall get`	Displays the status of the firewall, enabled or disabled.
`esxcli network firewall set --defaultaction`	Updates default actions of the firewall.
`esxcli network firewall set --enabled`	Enables or disables the ESXi firewall. If **--enabled false**, then the ESXi firewall is disabled.
`esxcli network firewall load`	Loads the firewall module and ruleset configuration files.
`esxcli network firewall refresh`	If you edit a custom service, you will need to refresh the firewall. This command reloads the firewall configuration by reading the ruleset files.
`esxcli network firewall unload`	Destroys filters and unloads the firewall module.
`esxcli network firewall ruleset list`	Lists the rulesets in the firewall and state of enabled or disabled.
`esxcli network firewall ruleset rule list`	Lists the rules of each ruleset in the firewall.

Command	Description
`esxcli network firewall ruleset set --allowedall`	Sets the **allowedall** flag.
`esxcli network firewall ruleset set --enabled`	Enables the ruleset.
`esxcli network firewall ruleset allowedip list`	Lists the allowed IP addresses for the rulesets.
`esxcli network firewall ruleset allowedip add`	Adds the allowed IP address or range to the ruleset.
`esxcli network firewall ruleset allowedip remove`	Removes the allowed IP address or range from the ruleset.

Configure the ESXi Firewall Using PowerCLI

A third option is using PowerCLI to supply information about the ESXi firewall. The **Get-VmHostService** cmdlet can supply useful information about services running on an ESXi host. Maybe you want to log in via SSH or check whether the NTP service is running on the host. The **Get-VmHostService** cmdlet can return the status of those and other services. Run the **Get-VmHostService** cmdlet as shown in Figure 8-21 to display details about the various services on the ESXi host:

```
Powercli > Get-VmHost esxi01.vclass.local | Get-VmHostService
```

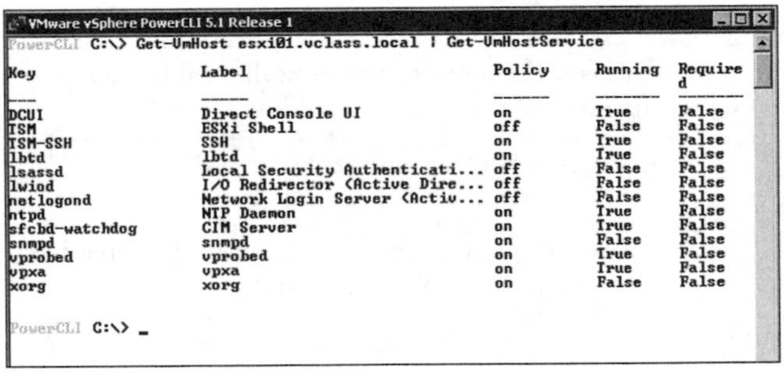

Figure 8-21   Using PowerCLI to display services running on an ESXi host.

Information on firewall services running on an ESXi host can also be attained using the **Get-VmHostFirewallException**, a PowerCLI cmdlet. In Figure 8-22 a cmdlet is used to return all the enabled firewall services and to show which incoming and outgoing port each service is using:

```
Powercli> Get-VmHost esxi01.vclass.local |
Get-vmhostfirewallException | Where{$_.Enabled}
```

The output of this is shown in Figure 8-22.

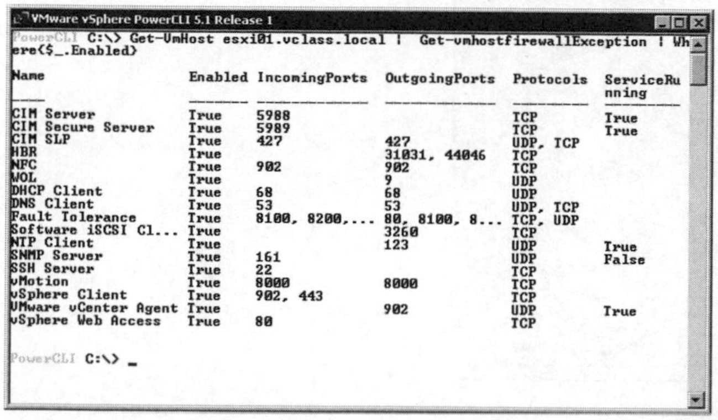

Figure 8-22   Using PowerCLI to show more details on the enabled firewall services.

Enable/Disable Preconfigured Services

By default, management services are enabled on the ESXi host. These management processes enable local and remote clients to access services on a host. The services are allowed through the firewall if they are enabled. As an example, the SSH daemon is stopped by default on a new ESXi host. To utilize PuTTY or other SSH clients to connect to the ESXi host, the SSH daemon has to be enabled.

Figure 8-23 shows that the SSH service has been started using the vSphere Client, which is noted by the **Running** status of the daemon. This was done by highlighting the SSH daemon and selecting the **Options** button, which displays the SSH options window. The **Options** window for a service can be used to enable and disable that service. To enable the SSH service, click the **Service Command** button **Start**. To disable the SSH service, click the **Service Command** button **Stop**. In addition, you can restart the SSH service by clicking the **Service Command** button **Restart**.

To enable or disable preconfigured services using the command line, start an SSH session using an SSH client such as PuTTY. An **esxcli** command is used to change the firewall settings for the ESXi 5.x firewall. Example 8-3 shows the **esxcli network firewall** command working with the syslog service, which is an example of one of the many firewall services. There is an example of listing, enabling, and disabling the syslog service.

Key
Topic

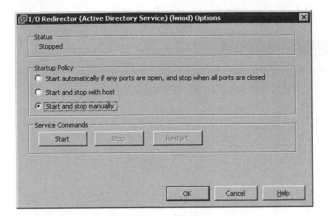

Figure 8-23   Start or stop a process.

Example 8.3   Enable/Disable a Firewall Ruleset Using the Command Line

```
# #### Listing the firewall rulesets, showing only the syslog rulset
status
# esxcli network firewall ruleset list
# syslog        false
#
# #### Enable the syslog firewall service
# esxcli network firewall ruleset set -e true -r syslog
# esxcli network firewall ruleset list
# syslog        true
#
# #### Disable the syslog firewall service
# esxcli network firewall ruleset set -e false -r syslog
# esxcli network firewall ruleset list
# syslog         false
```

Open/Close Firewall Ports

By default, only necessary management ports are open on the ESXi host. In the vSphere Client, firewall ports that have a check next to their check boxes are open; if the check box is empty, the port is closed (see Figure 8-24).

Click the **Firewall** button to define which networks are allowed to connect to each service that is running on the host. All connections may be allowed, or the connection can be restricted to a single IPv4/IPv6 address or a range of allowed IP addresses in a network. You can enter IP addresses in the following formats: 192.168.0.0/24, 192.168.1.2, 2001::1/64, or fd3e:29a6:0a81:e478::/64. The vSphere Client or the command line can be used to modify the allowed IP list for a service.

Figure 8-24   Distinguishing between open and closed ports.

By default, all IP addresses are allowed.

NOTE   All ICMP ping requests will be replied to by default.

Figure 8-25 displays an example of a firewall service's **Allowed IP Addresses**. By default, a connection from any IP address is allowed. Selecting the second radio button restricts connections to specific IP addresses.

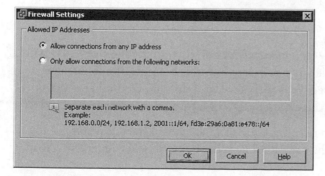

Figure 8-25   Using the vSphere Client to establish network access.

Create a Custom Service

The ESXi firewall ports and services are configured together. The services are processes that access the network. The services pass through the firewall if they are enabled. Although ESXi includes a set of predefined services, you can add more services. These services must be initially defined from a command line, but they are then accessible through the vSphere Client or Web Client.

Step 1. From the ESXi Shell, the first step is to change directories to the **/etc/vmware/firewall** directory:

```
# cd /etc/vmware/firewall
```

Step 2. Next, create an XML file containing the custom service using a text editor such as the vi editor. The service file will contain rules and needs to be located in the **/etc/vmware/firewall** directory. Each rule will open a port, with a direction of either inbound or outbound, and the port number for the service. Following is a sample of what the XML file needs to resemble:

```
# more testserv.xml
<!-- Firewall configuration information for testservice -->
<ConfigRoot>
  <service>
    <id>testyserv</id>
    <rule id='0000'>
      <direction>inbound</direction>
      <protocol>tcp</protocol>
      <porttype>dst</porttype>
      <port>2345</port>
    </rule>
    <enabled>false</enabled>
    <required>false</required>
  </service>
</ConfigRoot>
```

Save the file in the **/etc/vmware/firewall** directory. The ruleset ID will be located in the file you just created. In this example, the filename is **testserv.xml**, the service is **testyserv**, and the ruleset number is **0000**. You will need to change these pieces of information to match the service.

Step 3. The third step is to reload the firewall, which will start or restart all the services listed for the firewall. The refresh option will trigger the reload of the processes:

```
# esxcli network firewall refresh
```

Step 4.   Finally, now that the firewall service is loaded into memory, verify that the new service is running using either the **esxcli** command or the vSphere Client. Following is an example of the **esxcli** command:

```
# esxcli network firewall ruleset list
# esxcli network firewall ruleset rule list | grep testyserv
```

Or you can use the vSphere Client to check whether the firewall service has been loaded into memory. Highlight the **ESXi host > Configuration** tab **> Software > Security Profile**. Then use the mouse to click **Refresh** for either the **Services** or the **Firewall**, as shown in Figure 8-26.

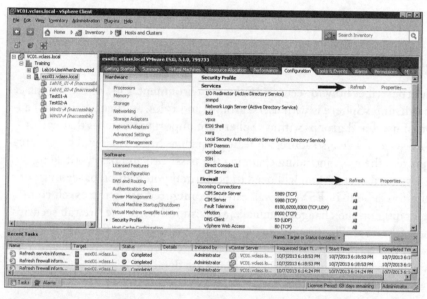

Figure 8-26   Use the mouse to click the Refresh option to restart the firewall and services.

Set Firewall Security Level

There are three firewall security levels on an ESXi host. The difference between the levels is how open and accessible the ports are. The most secure level is called **High Security**, and it blocks every incoming and outgoing connection except for specified ports. This narrows down the possible entry and exit points for communications to and from the ESXi host. The other two firewall security levels allow for more open ports. The least-secure level is **Low Security,** which allows all traffic to enter and exit as if there was no firewall on the ESXi host.

If you change the firewall configuration to open the firewall ports, you essentially move in between the **High Security** and **Medium Security** levels on the ESXi host. The security levels differ in the following ways:

1. **High Security**—This is the default. The firewall is configured to block all incoming and outgoing traffic, except for ports 22, 123, 427, 443, 902, 5989, and 5988. These ports are used for basic ESXi communication.

2. **Medium Security**—All incoming traffic is blocked, except on the default ports and any ports you specifically open. Outgoing traffic is not blocked.

3. **Low Security**—No ports are blocked on either incoming or outgoing traffic. This setting is equivalent to removing the firewall.

Summary

This module describes how to secure a vSphere environment. One of the first places to begin hardening vSphere is with users, groups, and roles. Authentication and authorization of users and groups within vSphere are important features that will enable a secure system. We also addressed features such as SSL; SSH; and certificates that help protect the user, including changing the password and password aging. There are also certain steps you will need to perform if you plan on hardening your VM. In addition, a built-in ESXi firewall can be configured using the **esxcli** command. Depending on the changes you make, you can influence the firewall security level of the ESXi host. The firewall services can be enabled or disabled using several methods within this chapter. Ports can be opened or closed in the firewall, and a few methods for performing the appropriate action were detailed.

Exam Preparation Tasks

Review All the Key Topics

Table 8-4 provides a list of all Key Topics identified in this chapter along with a few notes intended to refresh your memory of some key details. This can be useful as a quick reference when performing vSphere administration.

Table 8-4   Key Topic for Chapter 8

Key Topic	Description	Page
List	Three default system roles	317
Step list	Generate ESXi host certificate	322

Key Topic	Description	Page
Command list	Enable/Disable lockdown mode using CLI	325
Step list	Configure vSphere Authentication Proxy	330
Paragraph	Modify password requirements for non-root users	331
Paragraph	Protect the number of consoles for VM	333
Paragraph	Prevent users of a VM from connecting or disconnecting hardware	334
Command list	Control VM logging functions	336
Step list	Configure Active Directory using CLI	337
Command line	List and learn more about known firewall rulesets	340
Paragraph	To start the SSH daemon on an ESXi host	347
Step list	Create a custom service that passes through the firewall	350

Key Terms

Define the following key terms from this chapter, and check your answers in the glossary.

Default System Roles, ESXi Lockdown Mode, vSphere Authentication Proxy, VMCI, Firewall Ruleset, Firewall Services.

Review Tasks

These Review Tasks enable you to assess how well you grasped the materials in this chapter. Because of the advanced and hands-on nature of this particular exam, a set of tasks is provided instead of a set of questions. You should now attempt to perform each of these tasks without looking at previous sections in this chapter or at other materials, unless necessary. The steps for each task are located within the chapter.

1. Enable SSH for an ESXi host.

2. Generate an ESXi host certificate.

3. Enable or disable lockdown mode for an ESXi host.

4. Configure vSphere Authentication Proxy service for an ESXi host.

5. Modify the non-root user's password requirements.

6. Limit the number of remote console sessions for a virtual machine to 1.

7. Change the number of default log files for a virtual machine to 10.

8. Configure Active Directory for an ESXi host.

9. Create a custom firewall service.

This chapter covers the following subjects:

- **Auto Deploy Architecture**—There are many parts that can be set up in the Auto Deploy environment. This section looks at the primary pieces of Auto Deploy.

- **Identify Auto Deploy Requirements**—To successfully use Auto Deploy, you need to understand the architecture and the Rules Engine and be aware of the parts and requirements needed to deploy an ESXi host into production.

- **Edit a Host Profile with Profile Editor**—The Profile Editor can be used to modify a host profile. Host profiles can be used to establish a baseline ESXi host configuration and to ensure that multiple hosts in a vSphere implementation conform to that configuration. Host profiles can be used individually or with Auto Deploy.

The material in this chapter pertains to the VCAP-DCA Exam objectives 9.1, 9.2, and 5.2.

## CHAPTER 9

Auto Deploy

Auto Deploy is a feature that was introduced in VMware vSphere 5. It enables system administrators to significantly cut down the time they usually spend when provisioning vSphere servers. The true benefit Auto Deploy provides is when you need to provision tens or hundreds of physical hosts with ESXi. This ability to add large numbers of ESXi hosts or reimage a single ESXi host quickly is what makes Auto Deploy a useful feature in large and small implementations of vSphere.

Auto Deploy works by using PXE to boot a physical ESXi host and then load into memory an image profile, host profile, and state information managed by the vCenter Server. The ESXi server stores this information into memory on the physical box and continues to function in a stateless mode. Because the ESXi host is stateless, you can deploy a new ESXi host in a few minutes or reimage an existing ESXi host by rebooting and grabbing a new image from the PXE boot server.

To begin understanding how Auto Deploy works, let's look at the components the Auto Deploy infrastructure needs to provision a physical ESXi host. Because the ESXi host runs in memory, several components need to be gathered from different locations to build the physical ESXi server image—and that is what the Rules Engine will do.

"Do I Know This Already?" Quiz

The "Do I Know This Already?" quiz enables you to assess whether you should read this entire chapter or simply jump to the "Exam Preparation Tasks" section for review. If you are in doubt, read the entire chapter. Table 9-1 outlines the major headings in this chapter and the corresponding "Do I Know This Already?" quiz questions. You can find the answers in Appendix A, "Answers to the 'Do I Know This Already?' Quizzes and Troubleshooting Scenarios."

Table 1-1   "Do I Know This Already?" Foundation Topics Section-to-Question Mapping

Foundations Topics Section	Questions Covered in This Section
Auto Deploy Architecture	1, 2, 3, 6
Identify Auto Deploy Requirements	4, 5
Edit a Host Profile with Profile Editor	7

1. Which tool defines (creates) the image profiles used with Auto Deploy?

    a. The vSphere Client via the **Image Profiles Management** plug-in

    b. The vSphere Image Builder CLI cmdlet

    c. The vSphere CLI **esxcli image add** command

    d. The vSphere Client via **Host Profiles**

2. Which installation method installs the ESXi image directly into host memory?

    a. Scripted ESXi installation

    b. Interactive ESXi installation

    c. VMware Update Manager

    d. vSphere Auto Deploy ESXi installation option

3. Which feature of vSphere 5 is used to create ESXi installation images with a customized set of updates, patches, and drivers?

    a. Auto Deploy

    b. Host profiles

    c. esxcli

    d. Image Builder

4. What are two attributes that can be used by the rules engine to match a target? (Select two.)

    a. MAC address

    b. Inventory tag

    c. FQDN

    d. BIOS UUID

5. Auto Deploy uses which method to boot an ESXi host to deploy an image from a software depot?

  a. ISO

  b. PXE

  c. Altiris

  d. TFTP

6. Which PowerCLI cmdlet adds a rule into the ruleset?

  a. New-RuleSet

  b. Add-EsxImageRule

  c. Add-DeployRule

  d. New-DeployRule

7. Which condition might prevent the application of a host profile to an ESXi host?

  a. Multiple profiles are attached to the host.

  b. The host was declared noncompliant when a compliance check was issued.

  c. The ESXi host's cluster has VMware HA enabled.

  d. The ESXi host has not been placed into maintenance mode.

Auto Deploy Architecture

The layout of Auto Deploy can be as simple as a few components, or it can be a rather intricate layout with many parts; some of the less frequently used parts are not listed here. All these parts are dependent on how much configuration is needed for the ESXi host to boot up in memory. There is a process that the ESXi host must follow to successfully be deployed or redeployed. To form the ESXi host image, you need a host profile; an image profile; and a few other pieces of information that you will gather during the boot process, such as an IP address. Figure 9-1 shows the components of an Auto Deploy configuration and a high-level view of the host deployment workflow.

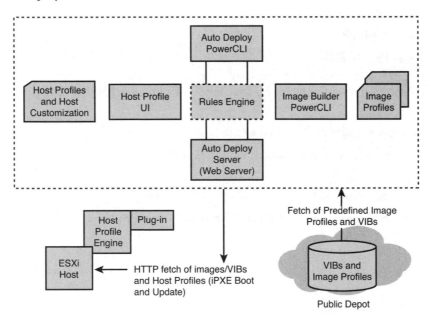

Figure 9-1   The Auto Deploy server helps to build the ESXi image.

The components include (from the bottom right):

- The public depot, where vSphere Installation Bundles (VIBs) and image profiles can be obtained

- The image profiles, which are created and maintained using the Image Builder PowerCLI cmdlet

- The Auto Deploy server, which is accessed using the Auto Deploy PowerCLI cmdlet

- The Rules Engine, which contains the active and working rulesets

- The host profiles and answer files, which are created and maintained using the Host Profile UI

- The ESXi host, which is deployed using a combination of host profiles and image profiles in accordance with the active ruleset

The components work to create the parts that make up the ESXi image. The main components are discussed in more detail in the upcoming sections. After all the components are set up, the Auto Deploy uses a defined workflow to deploy or redeploy ESXi hosts. We are going to concentrate on how the physical host deploys for the first time. An example of the workflow is detailed in Figure 9-2.

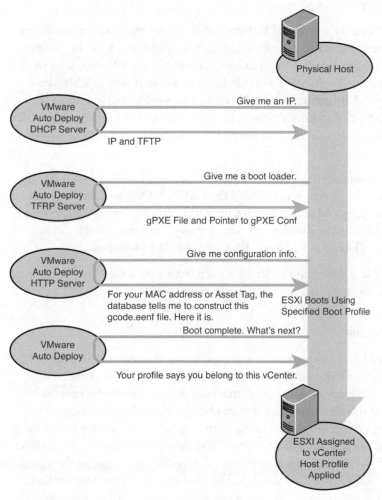

Figure 9-2 A typical Auto Deploy workflow.

An Auto Deploy workflow begins with an ESXi host performing a Preboot eXecution Environment (PXE) boot. When the boot process starts, the ESXi host attempts to find a DHCP server to get an IP address, and from the DHCP scope options the ESXi host is pointed to the correct TFTP server. The TFTP server contains the actual PXE boot loader image and also the PXE configuration files, which then point to the Auto Deploy Server.

Using this information, the ESXi host performs an HTTP connection to the Auto Deploy server and makes a request for the proper ESXi image. The only way the Auto Deploy server is going to push out an image is if the ESXi host matches a rule. The rules engine matches the rule based on the attributes of the host, examples of which were given in the previous section.

An ESXi image is based on a standard VMware ESXi deployment image combined with optional vSphere installation bundles (VIBs). Standard images can be downloaded from VMware's website, or you can obtain them from a VMware sales or technical representative. An example of a standard download image is **VMware-VMvisor-Installer-5.1.0.update01-1065491.x86.iso**, which can be used to boot and install an ESXi host. You can take the standard image and combine it with VIBs to form a single image using Image Builder, which is discussed in an upcoming section.

Also from the download page on VMware's website you can find the download image for auto deploy. This image is now called the ESXi5.X Offline Bundle. It will contain the VIB packages and image profiles for ESXi. You can use image profiles and VIB packages with Image Builder and Auto Deploy. An example of an image you can use for Auto Deploy is **VMware-ESXi-5.0.0-441354-depot.zip**.

After an image profile (a collection of VIBs) is associated with a rule, the rule is then matched with the ESXi host to deploy the image to the host.

Auto Deploy Rules Engine

After designing a VMware infrastructure and purchasing the necessary equipment, it would be nice to make the process of installing new ESXi hosts or reinstalling existing hosts easy. One way to accomplish that goal is to automate the process by creating an image of the ESXi software that can be quickly and easily installed (or reinstalled). This can be accomplished using Auto Deploy. Auto Deploy uses a rules engine to build and manage ESXi host images. The rules engine uses rules to associate hosts with an ESXi image and a host profile. The set of rules used by the rules engine are written using PowerCLI cmdlets. For example, the **New-DeployRule** cmdlet can be used to create a rule that associates a host with an IP address, a MAC address, a vendor name, a BIOS UUID, or SMBIOS information to identify the ESXi host that will be built. The same cmdlet can be used to specify the location to place the host in a folder or cluster on a vCenter Server. For example, to create a simple rule named **newrule1** that associates the host **192.168.10.10** to the host profile **hostprofile1**, the following PowerCLI cmdlet can be used to accomplish this task:

```
Powercli> New-DeployRule -Name "newrule1" -Item hostprofile1 -Pattern
"ipv4=192.168.10.5"
```

For a rule to be utilized, it must be added to a ruleset. Rulesets are used to evaluate requests from ESXi hosts attempting to boot using Auto Deploy. Two rules sets are used with Auto Deploy: the active ruleset and the working ruleset. The active ruleset contains the current set of rules used to deploy new ESXi hosts. The working ruleset can be used to test changes to rules before they are made active. By default, when a rule is created, it is added to the working ruleset and becomes part of the active ruleset. A rule can be added only to the working ruleset by using the **NoActivate** parameter in the PowerCLI cmdlet. The following example shows a new rule being added to both the working and active rulesets:

```
Powercli>  Add-DeployRule newrule1
```

In addition to writing rules that match particular hosts, you also can write a rule to match any host that communicates and queries the Auto Deploy server for a match. The PowerCLI cmdlet and option that are used are the **NewDeployRule** cmdlet and the **–Allhosts** option:

```
Powercli>  New-DeployRule -Name "newrule2" -Item hostprofile2
-AllHosts
```

The rules engine combines an ESXi image and a host profile. The Image Builder is not needed if you plan to use a standard ESXi image. However, if you need to customize the ESXi image, then you will need to create an image profile.

Image Profiles Using Image Builder

The concept of building an operating system image is nothing new, and it is an important part of delivering an OS image that can be installed on a physical server. If you install the ESXi image directly from VMware, it works just fine and it installs a standard copy of ESXi. However, there may be VIBs for the physical server. If so, these would not be included on the DVD you downloaded from VMware. These VIBs would provide additional pieces of code that bind a vendor's hardware with ESXi, including specific CIM providers and device drivers.

The hardware vendor could deliver the hardware, the ESXi image on a DVD, and a separate DVD with the CIM providers and device drivers for the physical server you purchased, but it would be a simpler installation process if the ESXi image and the vendor's drivers were provided on a single image. To remedy this issue, VMware created a utility for third-party hardware vendors called the Image Builder. An example of the Image Builder architecture is shown in Figure 9-3.

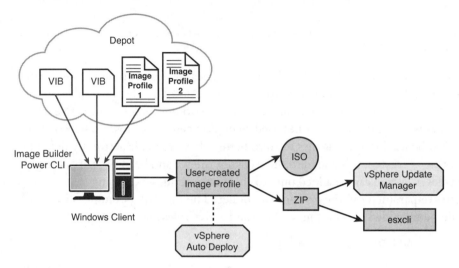

Figure 9-3 The Image Builder architecture.

The Image Builder cmdlet is an extension of PowerCLI that can be used for creating custom images. So, you can download the original ESXi image from VMware, which will be a Zip file. After downloading the Zip file, you should create a new image by adding the hardware vendor's drivers using a VIB to create one big image that can be burned onto a DVD. This process allows third-party hardware vendors to generate a single DVD with the ESXi image, the vendor's CIM providers, and their device drivers, which could then be presented to the customer.

The idea is to deliver an image that the customer can easily install and that the software vendor can easily deliver. This is instead of delivering one CD-ROM or DVD with the ESXi software and one CD-ROM or DVD with the third-party vendor's drivers. If the third-party vendor could add its drivers to the CD-ROM or DVD, it would appear more professional to the customer. The Image Builder is one process that makes this possible. This same process can be used to create an online PXE image that Auto Deploy can use to push out to Auto Deploy clients.

NOTE Using Image Builder for customization is required only if you have to add or remove VIBs.

Software or Public Depot

Image Builder must be able to access one or more software depots before you can create or customize an ESXi image. The software depot can be either online or offline. An online software depot is one that is connected to via a web service over the Internet. An offline software deport is local and contains Zip files you downloaded from www.vmware.com. The Zip files are a collection of VIBs that are commonly referred to as an image profile. You can use Auto Deploy to deploy an ESXi image from a software depot to a physical host doing a PXE boot. Use the **Add-EsxSoftwareDepot** PowerCLI cmdlet to add a software depot to Image Builder. An example of the command is shown here, and the results are displayed in Figure 9-4:

```
Powercli>  add-esxsoftwaredepot C:\Depot\LabDepot.zip
```

Figure 9-4   Offline software depot connecting to Image Builder.

Next, you use the PowerCLI cmdlet **Get-EsxImageProfile** to verify that the image depot has been imported. This cmdlet retrieves a list of all published image profiles in the software depot. Figure 9-5 demonstrates running the **Get-EsxImageProfile** cmdlet, which shows two image profiles, ESXi 5.0 (no vmware tools) and ESXi (standard):

```
Powercli>  Get-EsxImageProfile
```

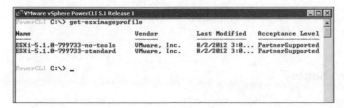

Figure 9-5   Using **Get-EsxImageProfile** to show the images in the depot.

Install and Uninstall Custom Drivers

The previous section added a standard ESXi image into the software depot. If all you want to do is install the standard image to the physical hosts making requests for an image, then you are finished. However, if you need to customize the ESXi image, you must create a new image. The first step in generating a new image is to clone an existing image profile and then modify the new profile.

Cloning an existing published profile is a fast and easy method to create a custom image profile that can include additional drivers for ESXi. The **New-EsxImage-Profile** cmdlet enables you to either create a new image profile or clone an existing image profile. An example of the command is shown here, and the results are displayed in Figure 9-6:

```
Powercli> New-EsxImageProfile -cloneprofile ESXi-5.1.0-799733-
standard -name myprofile -vendor myvendor
```

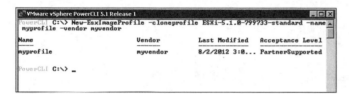

Figure 9-6   Cloning an image profile in the depot.

So now you have a new image profile called **myprofile**. You can add any more VIBs by using the **Add-EsxSoftwareDepot** cmdlet. After you have all the VIBs added to the software depot that are going to be used to build the ESXi Image, you should generate an ESXi image. The **Export-EsxImageProfile** cmdlet can be used to create an installable image from the image profile in one of two possible formats. You can either generate a Zip file that vSphere Update Manager can utilize to remediate ESXi hosts or generate an ISO image that Auto Deploy can use to PXE boot physical hosts and deploy the new image. An example of using the cmdlet to create an ISO image follows:

```
Powercli> export-esximageprofile -imageprofile myprofile -exporttoiso
-filepath c:\depot\myprofile.iso
```

Identify Auto Deploy Requirements

The Auto Deploy system is made up of four components. These parts interact to form the system that can take a physical host and deploy ESXi to it. The components that make up the Auto Deploy environment are PowerCLI, the PXE boot environment, the Auto Deploy Server, and vCenter Server with host profiles. These four components interact to create the ability to install ESXi hosts.

PowerCLI

When you install PowerCLI, you are installing a snap-in to Microsoft Windows PowerShell that hooks in through an SDK. Originally Microsoft wrote PowerShell for system administrators (sysadmins) in a way in which the sysadmin would not have to spend a lot of time learning to write code. The snap-in provides a series of cmdlets created to ease the management and automation of vSphere. PowerCLI is completely object oriented and is built on Microsoft's PowerShell, which is built on Microsoft's .NET. The cmdlets that enable you to manage the complete lifecycle of an object, including **new**, **get**, **set**, **move**, and **remove**, are the most common types of cmdlets in vSphere PowerCLI. You can locate the PowerCLI installation either on the same system as vCenter Server or on a separate Windows machine.

The first step in installing PowerCLI is to verify that a supported version of the Microsoft .NET Framework is installed, and if it is not, install it from Microsoft's website. The next prerequisite is to have a supported version of Microsoft Power-Shell installed or install it from Microsoft's website. The final piece to install is the vSphere PowerCLI package, which adds the vSphere snap-ins to Windows Power-Shell. One of the snap-ins is named **VMware.ImageBuilder**, which provides the cmdlets for managing software depots, image profiles, and VIBs. After PowerCLI is installed, double-click the VMware vSphere PowerCLI icon to begin the process of logging in to PowerCLI, as shown in Figure 9-7.

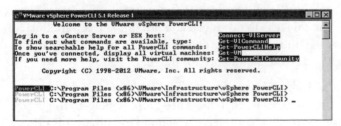

Figure 9-7   PowerCLI prompt.

The PXE Boot Environment

The second component that makes up the Auto Deploy system is the PXE Boot Environment. What makes this component different from the other components is that you need to get both parts from a vendor other than VMware. Both the DHCP and

TFTP servers will come from third parties, so their setups will vary from vendor to vendor. The DHCP server has two options that need to be set up in the DHCP scope. The first option is the IP address of the TFTP server, which directs the ESXi host to the TFTP server. In the scope options, option 066 specifies the IP address of the TFTP server. The other option that is set in the DHCP scope options is option 067, which is the name of the Preboot eXecution Environment (PXE) file that is downloaded from the TFTP server during the PXE boot process. Depending on the third-party software you are using, open the scope on your DHCP server and add the following options:

Scope Options

```
066  Boot Server Host Name    172.3.2.1  → Add the IP address of the
DHCP/TFTP Server.
067 Bootfile Name    undionly.kpxe.vmw-hardwired
```

How the scope options are set up depends on which TFTP server you are using. Regardless of which implementation you use, the information still needs to be added using the appropriate method. The previous information, including the IP address of the TFTP server and the name of the bootfile, are the important pieces of information that help the ESXi host image to acquire the proper IP address and help load the proper image.

Trivial File Transfer Protocol (TFTP) is a simple protocol that uses UPD port 69 to transfer files. The protocol is implemented using the client-server model, and Auto Deploy requires the server component. The TFTP server does not come with the vSphere software, so you will need to download and install a third-party TFTP server. Fortunately, a number of viable options exist. WinAgents' TFTP server has a 30-day trial. Another popular choice is to download and install the freeware Solarwinds TFTP server; the installation is easy. After download, all you should need to do is start the TFTP Service and create a directory for the files.

To set up the TFTP server, add a boot image to your TFTP server root directory. In the vSphere client, from the home view, click the **Auto Deploy** plug-in to get to the Auto Deploy configuration screen. Then select the action **Download TFTP Boot Zip**, which is used to download the TFTP boot Zip file and unzip it to your TFTP server's root directory. The Auto Deploy configuration screen is shown in Figure 9-8.

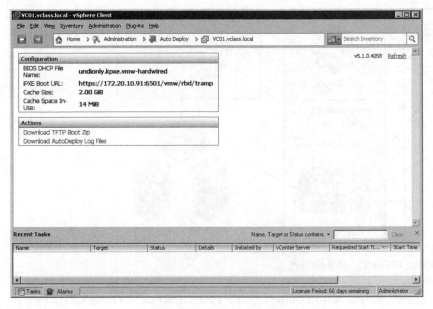

Figure 9-8 Auto Deploy and TFTP boot association.

The Auto Deploy Server

The third component is the Auto Deploy server, which is a web service that is associated with a vCenter Server and needs to be installed. You can install the Auto Deploy server directly on a Windows or Linux vCenter server or directly on a Windows system not running vCenter server, but in either case it will still need to be associated with a vCenter server. When you install the Auto Deploy server, it downloads the image profile and configuration files that are required for the boot process.

The image profile is stored on the Auto Deploy server before it is pushed out to the actual ESXi host. A high-level view of the components used by Auto Deploy is shown in Figure 9-9. Refer to this figure when reviewing the following steps.

The steps to install, configure, and prepare Auto Deploy are as follows:

Step 1.   Install the TFTP server, which sends the gPXE image to the host.

Step 2.   Install PowerCLI, which adds the Auto Deploy and Image Builder cmdlets.

Step 3.   Prepare the target hosts, and check the MAC address and BIOS requirements.

Step 4.   Prepare the DHCP server, which serves IP addresses to each host.

Step 5.   Install the Auto Deploy server software.

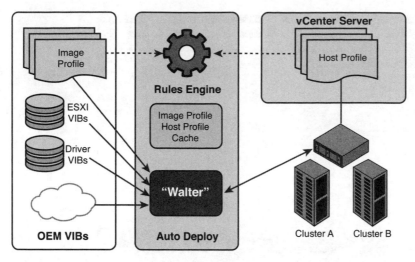

Figure 9-9 The Auto Deploy environment.

Step 6. Configure the Auto Deploy and TFTP environment. Download a TFTP boot Zip file from the Auto Deploy server.

Step 7. Prepare the ESXi software depot. Add an image profile that includes all the VIBs that will be deployed to the host. If you want to customize the download image, use the Image Builder cmdlet.

Step 8. Use the **New-DeployRule** cmdlet to write a rule that assigns an image profile to a host, multiple hosts, or all the hosts:

```
NewDeployRule -Name "newrule5" -Item "newimageprofile5"
-AllHosts
```

Step 9. Boot the host to have Auto Deploy provision the host with the specified image profile.

Step 10. Set up the new host as a reference host to provision other hosts.

Step 11. Create a host profile from the referenced host.

Step 12. Power on the hosts you want to provision using Auto Deploy.

vCenter Server with Host Profiles

The fourth component of the Auto Deploy environment is the vCenter server, which has the option to provide a host profile and vCenter server location information. The host profile is used to maintain consistent ESXi configuration across hosts, particularly for repetitive configuration steps like setting up network and storage connections. The system administrator can create a host profile image for a specific host or for any host. Creating a host profile for a specific host enables that host's configuration to be saved and provides an excellent way to redeploy that host by reimaging the host with the same network, storage, and configuration settings. Creating a host profile for any host is done by creating a reference host or golden image that can be used to provide the same ESXi configuration to any physical ESXi host during deployment. In environments with a large number of hosts, this can save a lot of time and help manage the host configuration.

Auto Deploy stores the information for the ESXi hosts to be provisioned in different locations. Information about the locations of image profiles and host profiles is initially specified in the rules that map machines. When a host boots for the first time using Auto Deploy, the vCenter server system creates a corresponding host object and stores the information in the database.

Host profiles can be used to set up an ESXi host by populating the host with many potential configuration settings. The configuration parameters and values include

- CPU

- DNS and routing

- Licensing

- Memory

- Networking

- Storage

The host profiles feature can be used in conjunction with Auto Deploy to supply the configuration data after Auto Deploy has imaged the ESXi host. By using a profile of configuration settings, the new host will be quickly set up to match the properties of the other hosts in a vSphere implementation.

Host profiles can also be used to ensure that all ESXi hosts in a cluster have the same configuration. This is done by running a compliance check on the hosts in the cluster. The compliance check detects whether any hosts in the cluster are not compliant with the reference or golden host. A periodic check of the configuration settings can be useful in large environments where changes can occur from many different sources.

The four parts mentioned here are important, but there are other parts that can optionally exist as well. To serve up the information the ESXi host needs to be incorporated into a vSphere environment, the Auto Deploy environment has several pieces that make up the infrastructure that provisions the hosts. The various parts of the infrastructure have to be set up, but not all the pieces are needed with every implementation. For example, a basic ESXi server installation can be performed by Auto Deploy without ever using Image Builder.

Install and Build Auto Deploy

Use the vCenter Server Installer to install the Auto Deploy server. The installer is the utility that is also used to install vCenter server, vSphere client, and other tools. Select the option **VMware vSphere Auto Deploy**, as shown in Figure 9-10, and follow the steps to install the Auto Deploy server. The steps are fairly straightforward.

Figure 9-10   Install the Auto Deploy server from the vCenter Server Installer.

The vCenter Server Installer steps you through the installation process. When the installation process is finished, the **Auto Deploy Waiter** service starts. The **Auto Deploy Waiter** service runs as a process on the host. If you installed the Auto Deploy server on a Windows server, you can search through Windows Services to find the **Auto Deploy Waiter** process.

NOTE   Check that the Windows Service Auto Deploy Waiter is started; this is an excellent method to reaffirm that the Auto Deploy process is installed and running on this machine.

If the service has not started, you will need to start or restart this service. Figure 9-11 shows the **Auto Deploy Waiter** process on a Windows server.

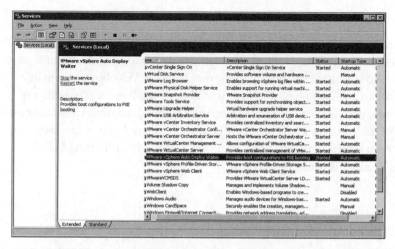

Figure 9-11 Auto Deploy Waiter process running on a Windows server.

The next step after installing the Auto Deploy server is to install the Auto Deploy client plug-in in your vSphere client. The plug-in is used for configuration of the Auto Deploy server. You can perform tasks such as associating the Auto Deploy server with a TFTP boot server. If you go to the main **Home** tab on the vSphere Client, you will see the **Auto Deploy** icon, as shown in Figure 9-12. If you do not see the **Auto Deploy** icon, click **Plug-ins** and then select **Manage Plug-ins**. Find the Auto Deploy Plug-in and enable it, or disable and then enable it.

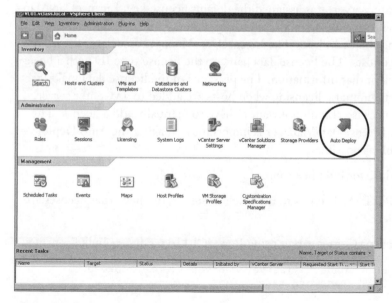

Figure 9-12 Auto Deploy icon on the vSphere client.

Bulk Licensing

There is no option built in to Auto Deploy or host profiles to attach a license to an ESXi host that is built using Auto Deploy. Because one of the main ideas behind using Auto Deploy is to automate the installation process of an ESXi host, manually adding a license key to an Auto Deployed host would be considered a problem. To get around this issue, you can configure bulk licensing to use predefined license keys to automatically be added to an ESXi host that is Auto Deployed. There are two ways to assign license keys to an ESXi host. The first method is using the vSphere client; the second method is using PowerCLI.

Method #1

You can use the vSphere client to attach an individual license key to an ESXi host. This is the standard method for licensing: you assign a license key to a specific host when you add the host to the vCenter server. The issue is that this is not an automated process.

Method #2

Bulk licensing uses PowerCLI to add predefined license keys to ESXi Auto Deployed hosts, so that a license key is automatically assigned to the host—or if the host reconnects to the vCenter server, it is assigned a license. A license key assigned using PowerCLI is treated as a default license. If an unlicensed host is added or reconnected to vCenter server, it is assigned the default license key. LicenseDataManager makes it possible to retrieve, add, remove, and modify the association between the license data and the ESXi host. The LicenseDataManager associates the license data with the ESXi hosts. The license data pairs up the license type ID with a license key and keeps track of that information. The presence of the license data makes it possible to support automatic licensing when hosts are added to a vCenter server. This is important because you do not want to have to manually add a license. The automation of the LicenseDataManager is important to making the Auto Deploy process as hands-off as possible.

Here is the procedure for bulk licensing:

Step 1.   Add CPU ESXi licenses to the vCenter server, or check that licenses are available.

Step 2.   Connect to vCenter server using PowerCLI to configure bulk licensing:

```
Powercli>  Connect-Viserver -Server vcenterAddress
-User root -Password passw
```

Step 3.   Bind the **licenseDataManager** objects to the variable **$licenseData-Manager**:

```
Powercli>  $licenseDataManager = Get-LicenseDataManager
```

Step 4.   Bind the variable **$dataCenter** to the datacenter where the ESXi hosts that will be licensed are located:

```
Powercli>  $dataCenter = Get-DataCenter -Name
dataCenterNameX
```

Step 5.   Create a new **licenseData** object and then a new **licenseKeyEntry**, with associated type ID and license key:

```
Powercli>  $licenseData = New-Object VMware.VimAutomation.
License.Types.LicenseData
Powercli>  $licenseKeyEntry = New-Object Vmware.
VimAutomation.License.Types.LicenseKeyEntry
Powercli>  $licenseKeyEntry.TypeId = "vmware-vsphere"
Powercli>  $licenseKeyEntry.LicenseKey = "XXXXX-XXXXX-XXXXX-
XXXXX-XXXXX"
```

Step 6.   Associate the **LicenseKeys** attribute of the **LicenseData** object you created in step 5 with the **LicenseKeyEntry** object:

```
Powercli>  $licenseData.LicenseKeys += $licenseKeyEntry
```

Step 7.   Update the license data for the datacenter with the **LicenseData** object:

```
Powercli>  $licenseDataManager.UpdateAssociatedLicenseData
($hostContainer.Uid, $licenseData)
```

Step 8.   Verify that the license is associated with the host container:

```
Powercli>  $licenseDataManager.QueryAssociatedLicenseData
($hostContainer.Uid)
```

Provision and Re-provision ESXi Hosts Using Auto Deploy

You can use Auto Deploy to provision and re-provision one or many ESXi hosts. To provision or re-provision an ESXi host with Auto Deploy, the first step is to create the Auto Deploy infrastructure. After the environment is set up, which can include adding a host profile or an image profile, you set up rules to match the ESXi host with an image. When you provision a host using Auto Deploy, the rules engine determines which ESXi image gets loaded directly into memory.

When you provision an ESXi host for the first time using Auto Deploy, the host is going to follow the Auto Deploy process. During the boot process, the BIOS attempts to boot off of the network looking for the Auto Deploy environment. The host PXE boots and establishes contact with the Auto Deploy server. The Auto

Deploy process loads the ESXi image into the physical server's memory. This is done when the physical host that is going to become an ESXi host begins to power on. During the boot process, the image profile, the host profile, and any software configuration add-on pieces are loaded into RAM. The host then proceeds to finish booting and starts regular processing.

Because the entire ESXi host is loaded into memory, a power-off of the ESXi host causes the image to be lost, and the ESXi host has to PXE boot again to re-provision an ESXi image. If the ESXi host reboots, it PXE boots—or it can boot from cache using its same image and host profile. If you want to use a different image profile, then you need to change the rule that the rules engine supports. Point the rule to the new image profile and/or host profile.

The true test of the Auto Deploy process is to PXE boot the physical host. As the physical host establishes communication with the Auto Deploy server, during the boot process you should see an IP address being assigned. Then the PXE boot finds a TFTP boot image and starts to load the image profile and any host profile into memory. Then Auto Deploy assigns the host to the appropriate vCenter server.

Using a Host Profile from a Reference Host with Auto Deploy

A reference host is an ESXi host that contains a known good set of configuration parameters that will be standardized across a vSphere implementation. A host profile can be created from this host, which can then be used by Auto Deploy to configure newly deployed hosts and can also be used by the vCenter server to verify the configuration of existing hosts. The host profile can be created using either the vSphere client or the vCLI. The reference host should already have all the required host configuration information, including the storage, networking, and security settings that are required for other hosts deployed to the same vSphere environment.

One method to create the host profile to be used with Auto Deploy is to use the vSphere client. Select the ESXi host to be used as a reference host. Right-click and select **Host Profile > Create Profile from Host**, as shown in Figure 9-13.

Key Topic

On the next screen, give the profile a name, such as **NewProfile1**. Press Enter and vSphere begins to create a host profile based on the ESXi host.

Now that the reference host has been used to create a host profile, you need to verify that the profile was created successfully. In the vSphere client, click **Home** to go to the **Home** view. In the **Home** view under **Management**, find the icon **Host Profiles** and select it. Figure 9-14 shows the **Host Profiles** window. In the left pane under Host Profiles, you can see the new profile that was created named **NewProfile1**.

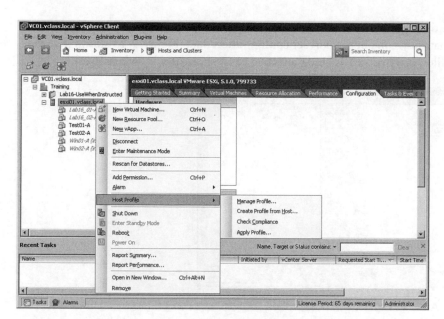

Figure 9-13   Creating a reference host using the vSphere client.

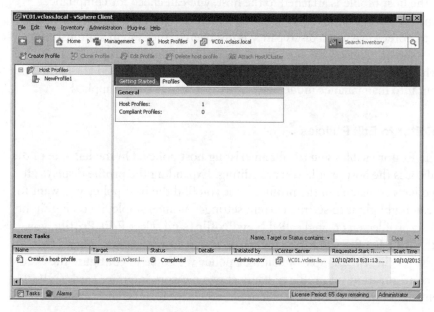

Figure 9-14   The Host Profiles screen.

There is also an option on this screen to create a host profile as well. **NewProfile1** is an example of a host profile that contains the standard collection of configuration settings that will be applied to new ESXi hosts deployed with Auto Deploy. After you have this "golden image," you can attach the host profile to hosts/clusters to ensure that they contain the correct configuration data. Figure 9-15 shows that the host profile **NewProfile1** is being attached to the host **esxi01.vclass.local**.

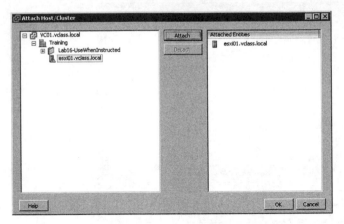

Figure 9-15 Attaching a host to a host profile.

Now that the host profile is attached to the host, you can check for compliance. This compliance check can be used to maintain configuration consistency throughout the datacenter. So when a discrepancy is discovered, the system administrator can fix the issue by applying the host profile to the noncompliant host. Because network changes for the host might be necessary as part of the remediation, the host must be put into maintenance mode before the host profile can be applied.

Use Profile Editor to Edit Policies

The Profile Editor enables you to edit an existing host policy. On the left side of the Profile Editor is the host profile you are editing. Expanding the profile displays all the host policies contained in the profile. After you find the host policy you want to edit, you can highlight it to see the current settings. As an example, if you highlight the new host profile you created called **NewProfile1** and select **Edit Profile**, you then see the **Edit Profile** window that enables you to customize the policies that make up the profile. An example of editing a policy would be to configure the **Networking configuration** subprofile to connect two network interface cards (NICs) to vSwitch0. Then when vCenter server applies the profile, it assigns two free NICs to the vSwitch.

A number of policies can be edited within a profile. Each host profile contains a number of subprofiles, as shown in Figure 9-16.

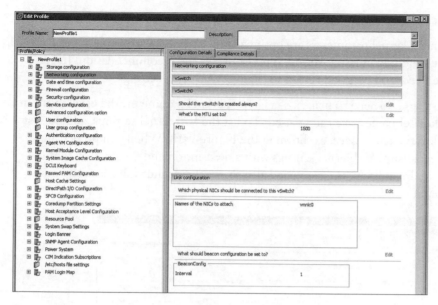

Figure 9-16   Editing a host profile using the Policy Editor.

Configure Advanced Boot Loader Options

When an ESXi host begins to boot up, you can enter **<shift>+o** in the boot loader. The system then displays the **boot:** prompt, which enables you to enter advanced boot loader options. An example of what the prompt looks like after you enter "**<shift>+o**" is shown in Figure 9-17.

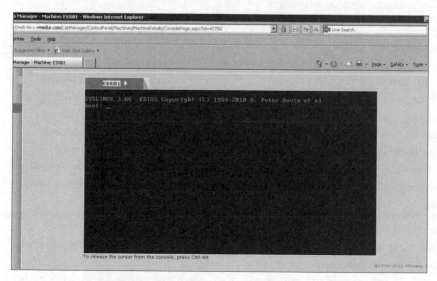

Figure 9-17   Boot Loader prompt.

Configure Kernel Options

The advanced kernel parameters are optimized by VMware and do not typically need to be modified unless VMware Support makes the recommendation. In general, there needs to be a good reason to change VMkernel settings.

However, if you do need to make a change to a kernel parameter, the **esxcli system settings kernel** namespace can be used. To list the VMkernel settings, add the **list** command to the namespace, as shown in the Figure 9-18. When you press Enter, you will see a list of VMkernel settings with a description and the current configured setting. In addition, the command also shows the default value as well as the runtime value.

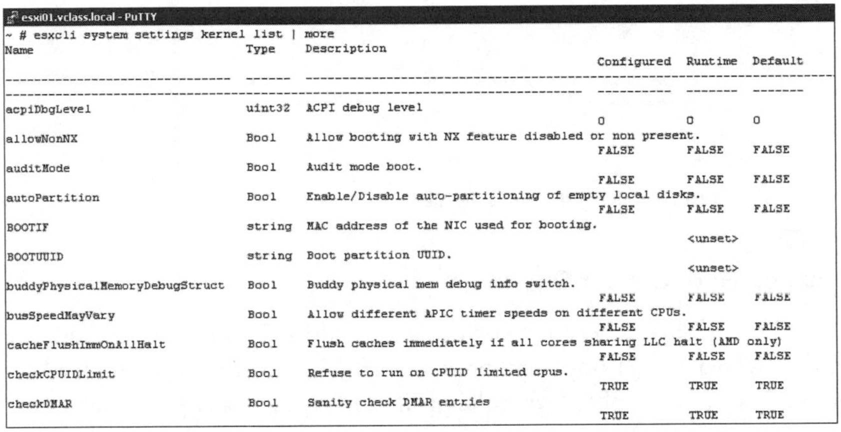

Figure 9-18   Using esxcli to list kernel options.

The same namespace can be used to modify VMkernel options. Keep in mind you can cause serious problems if you make mistakes when you change VMkernel settings because you are modifying the kernel. To make a change, you need to add the **set** command to the namespace, along with the proper name for the VMkernel setting and the value to which you want to change the setting. Several VMkernel settings can be changed, such as the setting **maxPCPUS**, which is the maximum number of physical CPUs the VMkernel should use. Another example is **fsCheck**, which is a Boolean value that determines whether to run the filesystem check on the system partitions. An example of using the **set** command to set the maximum number of physical CPUs to 2 is shown in Figure 9-19.

Another method to modify VMkernel options is to use the vSphere client. First, select an ESXi host in the hierarchical view. Next, select the **Configuration** tab, and then in the **Software** box select the **Advanced Settings** option. The left column lists a number of parameters that can be modified, such as settings for the processor, memory, and SCSI. Although several changes can affect the vSphere environment, any changes made to the VMkernel.Boot parameter will not take effect until after a reboot of the ESXi host. An example of using the vSphere client to view the VMkernel boot advanced settings is shown in Figure 9-20.

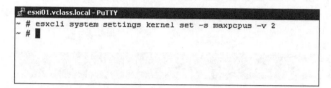

Figure 9-19   Using esxcli to configure kernel settings.

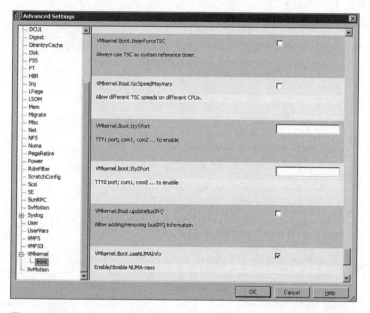

Figure 9-20   Using Advanced Settings option to view and modify VMkernel settings.

Summary

This module describes how to set up and utilize an Auto Deploy environment. There are standard steps that need to be done to use Auto Deploy, and there are optional methods and steps that can be performed as well. The reasons to use Auto Deploy include the ability to rapidly automate the provisioning of new ESXi hosts and reimaging an existing host. In this chapter, you learned about Image Builder, which can be used to modify a standard ESXi image. Auto Deploy can then use the image built by Image Builder to deploy ESXi hosts. You also learned about adding and removing custom drivers as well as how to use advanced boot options. We reviewed how host profiles can be added to the deployment process. Host profiles enable settings from a reference host to be used in conjunction with Auto Deploy to deploy ESXi hosts with the same configuration information and base ESXi image. The host profile and the ESXi image can be combined within the Auto Deploy server using the rules engine. The rules engine is used to determine which image and host profile an ESXi host will receive when it attempts to PXE boot.

Exam Preparation Tasks

Review All the Key Topics

Table 9-2 provides a list of all the Key Topics identified in this chapter along with a few notes intended to refresh your memory of some key details. This can be useful as a quick reference when performing vSphere administration.

Table 9-2 Key Topics for Chapter 9

Exam Topic	Notes	Page
Auto Deploy Rules Engine	The rules engine uses rules to associate a host with an ESXi image and a host profile.	362
Four Parts to Auto Deploy	PowerCLI, PXE boot environment, Auto Deploy server, vCenter server with host profiles.	367
PXE Boot Environment	The parts that make up the PXE boot environment are the DHCP and TFTP servers.	367
Auto Deploy Server	The Auto Deploy Server is a web service that associates the image profile and configuration files, and the client downloads the PXE image from the Auto Deploy server.	369
vCenter Server with Host Profiles	The ESXi host that is being deployed will be located on the vCenter server. If using a host profile, the ESXi host can receive network and storage information from the host profile.	376

Key Terms

Define the following key terms from this chapter, and check your answers in the glossary.

Auto Deploy, Auto Deploy Rules Engine, VIB, CIM, Image Builder, Image Profile, Host Profile, Software Depot, PowerCLI, TFTP Server, PXE

Review Tasks

These Review Tasks allow you to assess how well you grasped the materials in this chapter. Because of the advanced and hands-on nature of this particular exam, a set of tasks is provided instead of a set of questions. You should now attempt to perform each of these tasks without looking at previous sections in this chapter or at other materials, unless necessary. The steps for each task are located within the chapter.

1. Install an Auto Deploy environment.

2. Create a rule and add the rule to the ruleset.

3. Create a host profile from a reference host.

4. Create and use an Auto Deploy cmdlet to deploy an ESXi host.

This chapter provides testing scenarios on the following subjects:

- **Implement and Manage Storage**—This section provides scenarios that focus on vSphere administration tasks involving storage management.

- **Implement and Manage Network**—This section provides scenarios that focus on vSphere administration tasks involving network management.

- **Deploy DRS Clusters and Manage Performance**—This section provides scenarios that focus on vSphere administration tasks involving DRS cluster and performance management.

- **Manage Business Continuity and Protected Data**—This section provides scenarios that focus on vSphere administration tasks involving vSphere HA and fault tolerance (FT) configuration.

- **Perform Operational Maintenance**—This section provides scenarios that focus on vSphere administration tasks involving host profiles and Update Manager utilization.

- **Perform Advance Troubleshooting**—This section provides scenarios that focus on vSphere administration tasks involving vSphere troubleshooting.

- **Secure a vSphere Environment**—This section provides scenarios that focus on vSphere administration tasks involving vSphere security.

- **Perform Scripting and Automation**—This section provides scenarios that focus on vSphere administration tasks involving vSphere Management Assistant (vMA) and PowerCLI utilization.

- **Perform Advanced vSphere Installations and Configurations**—This section provides scenarios that focus on vSphere administration tasks involving Image Builder and Auto Deploy usage.

This chapter contains material pertaining to all objectives in the VCAP5-DCA Exam Blueprint.

## CHAPTER 10

Scenarios

This chapter is intended to challenge you to apply your skills to address multiple scenarios that call for advanced vSphere administration. It provides one scenario for each major objective identified in the VCAP5-DCA Exam Blueprint. In each scenario, assume you are the assigned vSphere Administrator, review the brief overview and objectives, and address the specific requirements.

This chapter is intended to help you assess your ability to address scenarios that might be similar to scenarios in the VCAP5-DCA exam involving configuration, troubleshooting, and management tasks. As you read each scenario, attempt to address each requirement and perform the necessary tasks without looking at the provided possible solution. Take time to practice the steps that are provided until you are confident that you can perform such tasks rather quickly and without any assistance. Some steps involve using the vSphere Client. Others involve using the vCLI and PowerCLI.

Foundation Topics

Implement and Manage Storage—Scenarios

This section provides real-world scenarios related to implementing and managing storage in a vSphere environment. These scenarios will help you assess your knowledge and skills that are covered in Objectives 1.1–1.3 in the VCAP5-DCA Blueprint. These skills include implementing complex storage solutions, managing storage capacity, and configuring multipathing and PSA plug-ins.

Scenario 10-1—Mask LUNs

Overview: A new fiber-based logical storage device (LUN) has been presented to your host cluster and is managed by the VMware Native Multipathing Plug-in. The logs on one ESXi host indicate intermittent issues with the new LUN. No datastores or virtual machines (VMs) are currently using the LUN.

Objectives: Temporarily change the masking on the host such that it cannot access the LUN.

Specific Requirements: You need to use the ESXi shell or vCLI to execute commands to mask a LUN whose ID is naa.600601604550250018ea2d38073 cdf11 from an ESXi host.

Scenario 10-2—Configure Datastore Alarms

Overview: After analyzing virtual disk usage for a given set of VMs, you feel comfortable deploying a group of VMs using thin-provisioned disks, such that the total size of the provisioned space is as much as 1.5 times the size of the usable datastore capacity. For example, a 1TB datastore could be used to deploy VMs that have a total of 1.5TB provisioned space. A set of datastores of various sizes is used to store the VMs. You do not plan to use SDRS.

Objectives: Configure an alarm to notify you whenever the provisioned space on a datastore is greater than planned or when the space utilization is greater than best practices.

Specific Requirements: Create an alarm that alerts you if you provision more than 1.5 times the size of usable space on a datastore. Configure the alarm to alert you if used datastore space is more than 80 percent, regardless of the provisioned space. Apply the alarm to only the datastores used by this specific set of VMs.

Scenario 10-3—Configure iSCSI Software Adapter Networking

Overview: You are provided a single standard vSwitch with two vmkernel ports and two physical NICs attached.

Objectives: You want to add iSCSI storage to the host using the software iSCSI adapter, but you first need to configure the vmkernel ports. You want the solution to allow for storage multipathing.

Specific Requirements: Configure the two vmkernel ports, and configure an iSCSI software adapter to bind to the vmkernel ports per VMware best practices.

Implement and Manage Network—Scenarios

This section provides real-world scenarios related to implementing and managing networks in a vSphere environment. These scenarios will help you assess your knowledge and skills that are covered in Objectives 2.1–2.4 in the VCAP5-DCA Blueprint. These skills include implementing complex virtual networks, managing VLANs / PVLANs, deploying scalable virtual networking, and administering vNetwork distributed vSwitches.

Scenario 10-4—Virtual Network Commands

Overview: Your environment is built on vSphere Enterprise, so you cannot use distributed vSwitches. Because it is rather large, you frequently use scripts to perform common administration tasks.

Objectives: Create and configure a standard vSwitch using vCLI commands.

Specific Requirements: Use vCLI commands to

- Create a standard vSwitch named vSwitch3
- Set the switch's MTU = 9000
- Attach vmnic1 and vmnic2
- Attach a VM port group named Test50
  - Assign VLAN = 50
- Attach a VM port group named Test51
  - Assign VLAN = 51
- Attach a vmkernel port named vmk2 to the Test50 port group
  - IP = 192.168.1.199
- Set the mask = 255.255.255.0

Scenario 10-5—Private VLANs

Overview: You recently implemented distributed vSwitches in your environment and are ready to implement private VLANs (PVLANs) for a specific use case involving IT training.

Objectives: Configure the distributed vSwitch to provide a secondary PVLAN for each classroom, a secondary PVLAN for shared servers, and a secondary PVLAN for student desktops.

Specific Requirements: Configure the distributed vSwitch and its port groups meeting these specifications:

- Port group name = Shared:
- Secondary PVLAN Type = Promiscuous
  - PVLAN ID = 10
- Port group name = Classroom-A
- PVLAN ID = 10-101
  - Set type to
    - Allow all VMs in this port group to communicate with each other
    - Allow all VMs in this port group to communicate with the Public port group
    - Do not allow the VMs in the port group to communicate with VMs in any other port group
- Port group name = Classroom-B
- PVLAN ID = 10-102
  - Set type to
    - Allow all VMs in this port group to communicate with each other
    - Allow all VMs in this port group to communicate with the Public port group
    - Do not allow the VMs in the port group to communicate with VMs in any other port group
- Port group name = Student-Desktops
- PVLAN ID = 10-201
  - Set type to
    - Not allow the VMs in this port group to communicate with each other
    - Allow all VMs in this port group to communicate with the Public port group
- Do not allow the VMs in the port group to communicate with VMs in any other port group

Scenario 10-6—Explicit Failover

Overview: Your ESXi host has a standard vSwitch where the Management Network vmkernel port, a VMotion vmkernel port, and two NICs (vmnic0 and vmnic3) are connected.

Objectives: You need to configure virtual networking per VMware best practices.

Specific Requirements: Configure explicit failover to conform to VMware best practices, without removing or adding vmkernel ports, vmnics, or vSwitches.

Scenario 10-7—Network I/O Control

Overview: Your distributed vSwitch has two high-speed (10 Gbps) uplinks per ESXi host and provides networking for VMs, vMotion, and management.

Objectives: You intend to allow vMotion to maximize its utilization of available (unused) network bandwidth whenever hosts attempt to enter maintenance mode. However, you are concerned that uncontrolled network utilization by vMotion could cause competition with production VM network traffic and management traffic.

Specific Requirements: You need to configure network I/O control to ensure that vMotion traffic is set with the lowest priority of all network traffic types during times of network contention.

Deploy DRS Clusters and Manage Performance—Scenarios

This section provides real-world scenarios related to implementing and managing DRS clusters and performance in a vSphere environment. These scenarios will help you assess your knowledge and skills that are covered in Objectives 3.1–3.4 in the VCAP5-DCA Blueprint. These skills include tuning vSphere performance, optimizing VM resources, implementing complex DRS solutions, and using advanced performance monitoring tools.

Scenario 10-8—Configure SplitRxMode

Overview: You are concerned about the performance of some VMs that receive multicast network traffic. You want to ensure the ESXi host is properly configured to process the multicast traffic in the most efficient manner and is configured to allow multiple CPU cores to process the network packets from a single network queue.

Objectives: You need to configure the ESXi host to allow multiple CPU cores to process network packets from a single network queue.

Specific Requirements: You need to ensure the **Net.NetSplitRxMode** advanced setting is enabled.

Scenario 10-9—Modify Swap File Location

Overview: You manage a DRS/HA cluster containing VMs that are stored in a storage area network (SAN) with array-based replication to a remote site for DR purposes. You want to reduce the amount of replicated data.

Objectives: You need to configure the VMs such that their swap files are not replicated.

Specific Requirements: Configure the swap files to a specific nonreplicated datastore named *Swap-file-01*.

Scenario 10-10—Configure EVC

Overview: Your DRS cluster contains identical server hardware. You need to add a new host to the cluster that is not identical.

Objectives: You need to add a new host with CPUs from the same manufacturer and family as other hosts in the cluster, but with a slightly improved feature set.

Specific Requirements: You need to enable EVC on the cluster without disrupting the running VMs. The current hardware uses Intel "Sandy Bridge" generation CPUs. The new host uses Intel "Ivy Bridge" generation CPUs.

Scenario 10-11—Use resxtop in Batch Mode

Overview: A specific set of VMs running on an ESXi host named **host-01.lab. local** is not performing well. You intend to determine the root cause.

Objectives: You need to collect resource usage data at a level that is more granular than the vSphere Client performance graphs can provide.

Specific Requirements: Use resxtop to collect all statistical data for 12 hours, at 5-minute intervals, and export the data to a CSV file named **results.csv**. Import the **results.csv** file into Windows Performance Monitor, and show the CPU ready time for all VMs over the 12-hour period.

Manage Business Continuity and Protected Data— Scenarios

This section provides real-world scenarios related to implementing and managing business continuity and data protection in a vSphere environment. These scenarios will help you assess your knowledge and skills that are covered in Objectives 4.1–4.2

in the VCAP5-DCA Blueprint. These skills include implementing complex VMware HA solutions and deploying VMware FT.

Scenario 10-12—Configure HA Admission Control

Overview: Your HA cluster currently has four hosts but is expected to grow over time. Regardless of the number of hosts in the cluster, you need to configure HA to tolerate just one host failure. The memory reservation on one VM is set to 4GB. The memory reservation on all other VMs is 0MB. You are concerned that if that HA slot size is 4GB, then the total number of slots will be too low to support your VMs.

Objectives: You need to configure HA admission control to tolerate just one host failure, but you want to limit the maximum size of the slot size to 2GB.

Specific Requirements: You need to configure HA for one host failure and use advanced settings to ensure the slot size used by admission control is no more than 2GB.

Scenario 10-13—Configure FT

Overview: Your HA cluster contains hosts with identical hardware. It provides automatic high availability for all VMs but is not configured to support continuous availability for any VM.

Objectives: Due to recent changes in service level agreements, you need to provide fault tolerance protection for some of your VMs.

Specific Requirements: Configure the hosts in the cluster to support FT. Protect a specific VM named Test-01 with FT and test failover.

Perform Operational Maintenance—Scenarios

This section provides real-world scenarios related to performing maintenance in a vSphere environment. These scenarios will help you assess your knowledge and skills that are covered in Objectives 5.1–5.2 in the VCAP5-DCA Blueprint. These skills include implementing host profiles and managing complex VMware Update Manager environments.

Scenario 10-14—Configure Host Profiles

Overview: You use host profiles to manage the configuration of a specific host cluster. You noticed that when checking for compliance, it complains a lot about differences in locally attached drives and private iSCSI LUNs.

Objectives: Implement a plan to work around the issue by editing the host profile and disabling checks for specific items.

Specific Requirements: Disable checking for the **PSP and SATP configuration for NMP devices, PSA device configuration**, and **Software iSCSI Initiator Configuration** items.

Scenario 10-15—Configure UMDS and a Shared Repository

Overview: Your vSphere environment resides in a network where you must comply with strict, company-imposed network security policies. One policy requires the network to prevent any servers in the local area network (LAN) from connecting to any external servers, including via firewalls.

Objectives: Implement Update Manager Download Service (UMDS) in a VM residing in the demilitarized zone (DMZ), and use it to download updates to a shared folder in the network. Configure the VMware Update Manager (VUM) server in the network to use the shared folder to obtain updates.

Specific Requirements: Install UMDS server in a VM that runs in the DMZ. Export downloaded updates to a specific server location (e:\UMDS\repository), and configure VUM to use a shared repository (z:\UMDS\repository).

Perform Advance Troubleshooting—Scenarios

This section provides real-world scenarios related to performing advanced troubleshooting in a vSphere environment. These scenarios will help you assess your knowledge and skills that are covered in Objectives 6.1–6.5 in the VCAP5-DCA Blueprint. These skills include troubleshooting the performance of CPU, memory, network, and storage, as well as troubleshooting vCenter Server and ESXi host management.

Scenario 10-16—Central Logging

Overview: Your vSphere environment currently does not provide any centralized logging. You use a Windows-based vCenter Server, whose FQDN is *vcenter01.lab.local*.

Objectives: Provide a central location to automatically collect all ESXi logs.

Specific Requirements: Install vSphere Syslog Collector, set its log file repository to *E:\ProgramData\VMware\VMware Syslog Collector\Data*, and configure each ESXi host.

Scenario 10-17—Troubleshoot CPU and Memory Performance

Overview: One of the VMs in your vSphere cluster is performing poorly. You suspect the VM either is not configured with sufficient resources or is contending with other VMs for available resources.

Objectives: Determine whether the issue is CPU or RAM related. Determine whether it is due to a lack of provisioned resources or due to contention.

Specific Requirements: Use real-time performance charts or resxtop to determine whether the issue is one of the following:

- The VM is contending too much with other VMs for CPU usage.
- The VM is contending too much with other VMs for RAM usage.
- The VM needs additional configured virtual CPUs.
- The VM needs additional configured virtual RAM.

Scenario 10-18—Network Troubleshooting

Overview: Your network administrators have the ability to use Wireshark on a Windows laptop to inspect network traffic as it travels across physical network switches. They are interested in extended this ability to examine traffic in vSwitches using a Windows-based VM running Wireshark.

Objectives: Perform a proof of concept test by simply using a VM-based Wireshark instance to inspect network packets traveling to and from a specific web server VM.

Specific Requirements: Configure port mirroring on a dvSwitch to replicate all incoming and outgoing network packets from port 10, where the web server VM is attached to port 110, where the Wireshark VM is attached.

Scenario 10-19—Analyze Disk Latency

Overview: Several of the VMs you manage are performing poorly, and you suspect the root cause might be storage related.

Objectives: Use resxtop to closely examine storage statistics during a time of peak disk I/O activity.

Specific Requirements: Use resxtop to determine the disk I/O latency from the guest perspective for each LUN. For any LUN whose guest perspective latency is frequently higher than 15ms, determine whether most of the latency occurs during vmkernel processing or during the HBA and SAN activities. For any LUN whose kernel latency is more than 2ms, determine whether it is mostly due to queue latency.

Examine the I/O latency for each VM's virtual disk and determine whether any VM is frequently experiencing read latency or write latency higher than 15ms.

Scenario 10-20—Gain Familiarity with vCenter Server Connection Issues

Overview: In your vSphere environment, the vCenter Server frequently indicates that some ESXi hosts are not responding. Sometimes the connections automatically fix themselves, and sometimes you have to manually fix the connections.

Objectives: You need to gain familiarity with symptoms of and possible causes for lost connections between ESXi hosts and vCenter Server. To do so, you plan to use a test environment to deliberately break connections in various ways and examine the symptoms, alarms, and logs.

Specific Requirements: Perform each of the following "breaks." After performing each break, attempt to use the vSphere client and the web client to log in to vCenter Server and examine the **Hardware Status** of the host. Pay attention to any errors, warnings, alarms, or other signs of connectivity issues. Examine the log files on the ESXi host and vCenter Server, and pay attention to any related entries. Undo each break before moving on to the next break:

- Stop the vCenter Server agent on the ESXi host.

- Disallow vCenter Server agent traffic through the host firewall.

- Allow vCenter Server agent traffic through the host firewall, but only from a range of IP addresses that do not include the vCenter Server.

- Change the permissions of the local **vpxuser** account to **Read Only**.

Secure a vSphere Environment—Scenarios

This section provides real-world scenarios related to securing a vSphere environment. These scenarios will help you assess your knowledge and skills that are covered in Objectives 7.1 and 7.2 in the VCAP5-DCA Blueprint. These skills include securing ESXi hosts and configuring the ESXi firewall.

Scenario 10-21—Generate New Host Certificates

Overview: You recently changed the name of an ESXi host and are concerned about its certificates.

Objectives: Generate new certificates on the host.

Specific Requirements: Use the ESXi Shell to generate new certificates for the ESXi host.

Scenario 10-22—Configure a Custom Firewall Rule

Overview: Your network requires customized ports for many applications and services.

Objectives: Configure each ESXi host to use a customized port for DNS.

Specific Requirements: Although the ESXi firewall allows you to control DNS over UDP port 53, you are required to enable DNS on TCP port 53. You need to create a custom DNS service on port 53 over TCP in the ESXi firewall on each host.

Perform Scripting and Automation—Scenarios

This section provides real-world scenarios related to implementing and managing a vSphere environment using scripts and commands. These scenarios will help you assess your knowledge and skills that are covered in Objectives 8.1 and 8.2 in the VCAP5-DCA Blueprint. These skills include using cmdlets in PowerCLI and commands in the vSphere Management Assistant to perform administration tasks.

Scenario 10-23—Use PowerCLI to Manage VMs

Overview: Your vSphere environment is managed by a vCenter Server named **vcenter-01**. You have determined that no VM needs to currently utilize a virtual CD drive. You notice that the vSphere client provides no direct means to easily disconnect the CD drive for a set of VMs.

Objectives: Develop a means to quickly disconnect the CD drive for each running VM.

Specific Requirements: Build and execute a PowerCLI script to disconnect the virtual CD drive of each powered-on VM.

Scenario 10-24—Configure the vSphere Management Assistant

Overview: Your vSphere environment consists of one vCenter Server named **vcenter-01** and three ESXi hosts named **host-01**, **host-02**, and **host-03**. The domain name is **lab.local**. You deployed a vMA and are now ready to configure it.

Objectives: You need to configure the vMA to connect to the vCenter Server and each ESXi host in such a manner that you will not have to provide credentials each time you connect.

Specific Requirements: Use **fastpass** commands to make a connection to vCenter Server and to each of the three hosts. To check your work, list all the **fastpass** connections. Finally, set **host-02** as the target and verify that you can issue the **vicfg-nics –l** command without having to provide any additional connection information, such as username and password.

Perform Advanced vSphere Installations and Configurations—Scenarios

This section provides real-world scenarios related to performing advanced installations and configurations in a vSphere environment. These scenarios will help you assess your knowledge and skills that are covered in Objectives 9.1 and 9.2 in the VCAP5-DCA Blueprint. These skills include installing ESXi hosts with custom settings and using Auto Deploy.

Scenario 10-25—Use Image Builder to Add a Custom Driver

Overview: The host hardware on which you need to install includes an OCZ Technology Z-Drive R4 Solid State Drive (SSD). The standard ESXi installer contains all the drivers you need, except the best driver for the SSD.

Objectives: Use Image Builder to build a custom ESXi installer where the standard ESXi Installer is merged with the custom OCZ Z-Drive R4 C Series and R Series SSD driver.

Specific Requirements: Use Image Builder to use a depot file named **VMware-ESXi-5.1.0-799733-depot.zip** that contains the standard ESXi profile and a depot file named **ocz10xx-1.0.0-751505.zip** that contains the custom SSD driver. Create a new image profile that merges the driver with the standard profile. Export the ISO file to a file named **Custom-ESXi.iso**.

Scenario 10-26—Auto Deploy

Overview: Your vSphere environment is quickly growing. Deploying new ESXi hosts and updating ESXi hosts is taking a lot of your time.

Objectives: Simplify the process for deploying and updating ESXi servers by implementing Auto Deploy, importing the standard image profile, and creating appropriate rules.

Specific Requirements: Enable Auto Deploy on a vCenter Server Appliance. Use PowerCLI to

- Add a software repository file named **update-from-esxi5.1-5.1_ update01.zip** as an offline software depot.

- List the image profiles in the repository, and verify one is named **ESXi-5.1.0-20130402001-standard**.

- Create a rule that assigns the **ESXi-5.1.0-20130402001-standard** profile to all ESXi hosts.

- Create a rule that assigns all hosts to a cluster named **Cluster-01**.

- Add both rules to the current working rule set.

- List the rules in the current working rule set.

Summary

You should now have had an opportunity to practice the skills needed to successfully tackle various scenarios directly related to objectives covered by the VCAP5-DCA exam, including scenarios around vSphere configuration and troubleshooting. Be sure to take time to practice the steps that are provided in this section until you are confident that you can perform such tasks rather quickly and without any assistance.

Answers to the "Do I Know This Already?" Quizzes

Chapter 1

1. c
2. d
3. a
4. c
5. c
6. a

Chapter 2

1. c
2. b
3. c
4. b
5. d
6. a
7. c
8. b

Chapter 3

1. d
2. b, c
3. a, c
4. a
5. b, d

Chapter 4

1. c
2. c
3. a
4. d
5. d
6. b
7. b

Chapter 5

1. a
2. a
3. a
4. d
5. c
6. c

Chapter 6

1. d
2. a
3. c
4. d
5. a
6. b
7. b

Chapter 7

1. a
2. d
3. b
4. b, d
5. a, d

Chapter 8

1. c
2. a
3. a, c
4. d
5. b, d
6. d
7. b

Chapter 9

1. b
2. d
3. d
4. a, d
5. b
6. c
7. d

Hands-On Solutions to Chapter 10 Scenarios

The hands-on solutions in this appendix apply to the scenarios presented in Chapter 10, "Scenarios."

Implement and Manage Storage—Hands-On Solutions

This section provides hands-on solutions to the real-world scenarios related to implementing and managing storage in a vSphere environment provided in Chapter 10.

Hands-On Solution 10-1—Masking LUNs

1. Execute these commands to list all the paths for the LUN:

   ```
   esxcfg-mpath -b -d naa.600601604550250018ea2d38073cdf11
   ```

2. Examine the results. For this example, assume the paths are vmhba33:0:0:0, vmhba33:0:1:0, vmhba33:0:2:0, and vmhba33:0:3:0.

3. Execute this command to display the current claim rules:

   ```
   esxcli storage core claimrule list
   ```

4. Examine the results. For this example, assume the rule numbers 192–195 are unused and the rule that currently claims the LUN has a number greater than 195.

5. Execute these commands to add claim rules (to assign each of the LUN's paths to the MASK_PATH plug-in):

   ```
   esxcli storage core claimrule add --rule 192 -t location -A
   vmhba33 -C 0 -T 0 -L 0 -P MASK_PATH
   esxcli storage core claimrule add --rule 193 -t location -A
   vmhba33 -C 0 -T 1 -L 0 -P MASK_PATH
   esxcli storage core claimrule add --rule 194 -t location -A
   vmhba33 -C 0 -T 2 -L 0 -P MASK_PATH
   esxcli storage core claimrule add --rule 195 -t location -A
   vmhba33 -C 0 -T 3 -L 0 -P MASK_PATH
   ```

6. Execute this command to load the new rule set:

```
esxcli storage core claimrule load
```

7. Execute these commands to unclaim all the LUN's paths from the currently assigned plug-in and reclaim the paths on the newly assigned plug-in.

```
esxcli storage core claiming reclaim -d naa.600601604550250018ea
2d38073cdf11

esxcli storage core claiming unclaim -d naa.600601604550250018ea
2d38073cdf11 -t location

esxcli storage core claimrule run
```

8. Rescan the HBAs and verify the LUN is no longer present.

Hands-On Solution 10-2—Configure Datastore Alarms

1. Under **Datastores and Datastore Clusters**, create a folder and populate it with the datastores used by this set of VMs.

2. Select the folder and select the **Alarms** tab. Create a conditional alarm that monitors datastores.

3. Add two triggers:

   - **Datastore Usage on Disk** is greater than 80%.

   - **Datastore Disk Provisioned** is greater than 150%.

4. Select Trigger if any of the conditions are satisfied.

Hands-On Solution 10-3—Configure iSCSI Software Adapter Networking

1. Configure one vmkernel port such that the first NIC is active and the second is unused.

2. Configure the other vmkernel port such that the second NIC is active and first is unused.

3. Add the iSCSI software adapter.

4. Verify that it is enabled.

5. Select **Properties**. On the **Network Binding** tab, use the **Add** button to add each of the two vmkernel ports.

Implement and Manage Network—Hands-On Solutions

This section provides hands-on solutions to the real-world scenarios related to implementing and managing networks in a vSphere environment provided in Chapter 10.

Hands-On Solution 10-4—Virtual Network Commands

```
esxcli network vswitch standard add v vSwitch3
esxcli network vswitch standard set m 9000 v vSwitch3
esxcli network vswitch standard uplink add --uplink-name=vmnic1 v
vSwitch3
esxcli network vswitch standard uplink add --uplink-name=vmnic2 -v
vSwitch3
esxcli network vswitch standard portgroup add -p Test50 -v vSwitch3
esxcli network vswitch standard portgroup add -p Test51 -v vSwitch3
esxcli network vswitch standard portgroup set -p Test50 --vlan-id 50
esxcli network vswitch standard portgroup set -p Test51 --vlan-id 51
esxcli network ip interface add --interface-name=vmk2 -p Test50
esxcli network ip interface ipv4 set --interface-name=vmk2
ipv4=192.168.1.199      netmask=255.255.255.0 type=static
```

Hands-On Solution 10-5—Private VLANs

- Edit the settings of the distributed vSwitch and use the **Private VLAN** tab to define these PVLANs:
  - PVLAN = 10. Type = Promiscuous
  - PVLAN = 10-101. Type = Community
  - PVLAN = 10-102. Type = Community
  - PVLAN = 10-201. Type = Isolated
- Right-click the distributed vSwitch and use **New Port Group** to add each of the following:
  - Port group name = Classroom-A. PVLAN = 10-101
  - Port group name = Classroom-B. PVLAN = 10-102
  - Port group name = Student-Desktops. PVLAN = 10-201
  - Port group name = Shared. PVLAN = 10

Hands-On Solution 10-6—Explicit Failover

- On the NIC Teaming tab of each vmkernel port, check the **Override switch failover order** box.

- On the NIC Teaming tab for the Management Network vmkernel port, set **vminic0** as an **Active** uplink and **vmnic3** as **Standby**.

- On the NIC Teaming tab for the VMotion vmkernel port, set **vminic3** as an **Active** uplink and **vmnic0** as **Standby**.

Hands-On Solution 10-7—Network I/O Control

- Select **Inventory** > **Networking**. Select the distributed vSwitch.

- On the **Resource Allocation** tab, enable **Network I/O Control**.

- In the **System Network Resource Pools** section, select the vMotion pool.

- Set the vMotion network pool's shares to *Low*.

- Ensure that all other network pools' shares are *Normal* or *High*.

Deploy DRS Clusters and Manage Performance— Hands-On Solutions

This section provides hands-on solutions to the real-world scenarios related to implementing and managing DRS clusters and performance in a vSphere environment provided in Chapter 10.

Hands-On Solution 10-8—Configure SplitRxMode

- Use the vSphere Client to select the ESXi host and navigate to **Configuration** tab > **Advanced Settings**. In the left pane, navigate to **Net**. In the right pane, navigate to **NetSplitRxMode**.

- Ensure the value 1.

Hands-On Solution 10-9—Modify Swap File Location

- Edit the cluster settings, and set its **Swap file Location** to *Store the swapfile in the datastore specified by the host*.

- Edit each ESXi host in the cluster, and set its **Virtual Machine Swapfile Location** to *Swap-file-01*.

- Edit the VM and ensure its **Swapfile Location** is set to *Store in the host's swapfile datastore* or *Default*.

Hands-On Solution 10-10—Configure EVC

- Right-click the cluster. Select **Edit Settings**.

- Select **VMware EVC** and click **Change EVC Mode**.

- Select **Enable EVC for Intel Hosts**.

- Set **VMware EVC mode** to **Intel Sandy Bridge Generation**.

- Click **OK**.

Hands-On Solution 10-11—Use resxtop in Batch Mode

- Use this command from the vMA to collect data at 5-minute intervals for 144 samples:

```
resxtop--server host-01.lab.lcoa-b -d 300 -n 144>> results.csv
```

- Use a tool such as WinSCP to copy the results.csv file from the vMA to the Windows desktop.

- On the Windows desktop, launch Perfmon. Use the **Source** tab of its **Properties** page to change the source to the results.csv file.

- Use the **Data** tab to change the counters to include just the CPU Ready Time.

Manage Business Continuity and Protected Data— Hands-On Solutions

This section provides hands-on solutions to the real-world scenarios related to implementing and managing business continuity and data protection in a vSphere environment provided in Chapter 10.

Hands-On Solution 10-12—Configure HA Admission Control

- Right-click the cluster and select **Edit Settings**.

- In the vSphere HA section, set **Admission Control** to **Enable**.

- Select the **Host failures the cluster tolerates** option and set its value to 1.

- Click the **Advanced Options** button.

- On the Advanced Options page, add a row for the option *das.slotMemInMB* and value the *2048 MB*.

Hands-On Solution 10-13—Configure FT

- Verify that the host meets the FT requirements:

  - Examine the current compatibility matrices to ensure the CPU hardware in the cluster is supported for FT.

  - Modify the BIOS settings on each host to disable the power management features.

- Modify the BIOS to ensure that hyperthreading is configured identically (preferably enabled) on each host.

- Modify the BIOS to apply the same instruction set extension on each host. (Refer to the documentation for your hosts' BIOS.)

- Modify the BIOS to enable hardware virtualization (HV) in the BIOS.

■ Add a vmkernel port to each host and enable FT logging.

■ Verify the VM meets the FT requirements, such as the following:

- Verify it meets all vMotion requirements.

- Ensure its virtual disks are eager zero thick provisioned (or that room exists for FT to automatically inflate the disks).

- Right-click the VM, and select **Fault Tolerance > Turn on Fault Tolerance**.

- Monitor the progress of the associated task.

- On the VM's summary tab, verify that it is protected and determine the location of the secondary VM.

- To test failover, right-click the VM and select **Fault Tolerance > Test Failover**.

- Verify that no user interruption occurs during the test, and confirm that the primary VM is running on a different host.

Perform Operational Maintenance—Hands-On Solutions

This section provides hands-on solutions to the real-world scenarios related to performing maintenance in a vSphere environment provided in Chapter 10.

Hands-On Solution 10-14—Configure Host Profiles

■ Right-click the profile and select **Enable/Disable Profile Configuration**.

■ In the Profile Structure, deselect the **Storage configuration > Native Multi-Pathing (NMP) > PSP and SATP configuration for NMP devices** check box.

■ In the Profile Structure, deselect the **Storage configuration > Pluggable Storage Architecture (PSA) configuration > PSA device configuration** check box.

■ In the Profile Structure, deselect the **Storage configuration > iSCSI Initiator Configuration > Software iSCSI Initiator > vmhba*XX* > PSP and**

SATP configuration for NMP devices check box (where *XX* refers to the appropriate vmhba device number assigned to the software iSCSI initiator).

Hands-On Solution 10-15—Configure UMDS and a Shared Repository

- Prepare a compatible database, prepare an ODBC System DSN connection to the database, and test the connection.

- Use the **VMware-UMDS.exe** file located on the VUM installation DVD to install UMDS in the DMZ-based VM. Be sure to choose the ODBC connection in the installation wizard.

- Use these commands to download the updates and export the updates to the specified location:

```
vmware-umd -D
vmware-umd -E --export-store e:\UMDS\repository
```

- In the vSphere Client, select **Home > Solutions > Update Manager**.

- Select **Configuration** tab > **Download Settings**.

- Select **Use a shared repository**, and set the folder path to **z:\UMDS\ repository**.

- Click **Validate URL** and click **Apply**.

- Click **Download Now** to test the configuration.

Perform Advance Troubleshooting—Hands-On Solutions

This section provides hands-on solutions to the real-world scenarios related to performing advanced troubleshooting in a vSphere environment provided in Chapter 10.

Hands-On Solution 10-16—Central Logging

- Verify that the Windows-based vCenter Server meets all the prerequisites for installing vSphere Syslog Collector.

- Log on to Windows on the vCenter server. Launch the same installer that was used to install vCenter, but in the installation menu select **VMware Syslog Collector** and click **Install**.

- Use the installation wizard to complete the installation:
    - Accept the patent and license agreements.

- Set the installation and repository directories appropriately.

- Select **VMware vCenter Server installation**.

- Provide the appropriate vCenter name and credentials.

- Keep the default value for the **Syslog Collector Server Port** (514), and verify that **TCP protocol** and **UDP protocol** are enabled.

- Ensure the collector is identified by the fully qualified name *vcenter01. lab.local*.

- Use the vSphere Client to configure central logging for each ESXi host. Perform these steps on each ESXi host:

  - Select the host, and select **Configuration** tab > **Advanced Settings**.

  - Select **Syslog > global**.

  - Set **Syslog.global.logHost** to *vcenter01.lab.local*.

  - Select **Configuration** tab > **Security Profile** > **Firewall** > **Properties**.

  - Ensure that **syslog** is enabled (checked) and the outgoing ports are UDP/TCP 514.

- Use the vSphere Client to select **Home** > **Administration** > **Network Syslog Collector**.

- Review the **VMware Syslog Collector Overview** details and ensure its Configuration details indicate that it is listening on each host. Verify the logs are stored at *E:\ProgramData\VMware\VMware Syslog Collector\Data*.

- Log in to Windows on the vCenter Sever, and examine the files located at *E:\ProgramData\VMware\VMware Syslog Collector\Data*.

Hands-On Solution 10-17—Troubleshoot CPU and Memory Performance

- Use resxtop or performance graphs (real-time) to display CPU statistics for the VM.

- Examine the current CPU ready time for the troubled VM. If the value is less than 5% (in resxtop) and 1000 ms in the performance graphs, the problem is not CPU contention.

- Examine the current memory ballooning, compression, and swapping values for the VM. If the values are zero for each item, the problem is not RAM contention.

- Examine the CPU usage. If it is consistently near 80% or more or if it frequently spikes to 90% or more, it might benefit from additional vCPU.

- Examine the memory usage of the VM. If it is consistently near 80% or more or if it frequently spikes to 90% or more, it might benefit from additional vRAM.

Hands-On Solution 10-18—Network Troubleshooting

- In the vSphere Client, select **Inventory > Networking**.

- Right-click the distributed vSwitch and select **Edit Settings**.

- Select the **Port Mirroring** tab, and click **Add**.

- Provide a name for the port mirroring session—for example, use *Wireshark*.

- Select **Allow normal I/O on destination ports**.

- Click **Next**.

- Select **Ingress / Egress**.

- Enter the port ID of the source port, *10*. Click **Next**.

- Enter the port ID of the source port, *10*. Click **Next**.

- Click the **>>** link and enter the port ID of the Wireshark VM, *110*.

- Click **Next**, and then click **Finish**.

Hands-On Solution 10-19—Analyze Disk Latency

- Start **resxtop**. Press the **u** key to examine storage devices.

- For each row, examine the **GAVG** (guest latency) column.

- For any device whose **GAVG** is higher than 15ms, examine these columns:

  - **KAVG** (kernel latency)

  - **DAVG** (physical latency)

- For any device whose **KAVG** is more than 2ms, examine the **QAVG** (queue latency) column.

- Press the (lowercase) **v** key to display virtual disk statistics.

- For each virtual disk, examine the **LAT/r** and determine whether it is higher than 15ms.

- For each virtual disk, examine the **LAT/w** and determine whether it is higher than 15ms.

Hands-On Solution 10-20—Gain Familiarity with vCenter Server Connection Issues

- Select the ESXi host; then select **Configuration** tab > **Security Profile**.

- Select **Services** > **Properties**.

- Select the *vpxa* service. Click the **Options** button.

- Click **Stop**.

- Test the vCenter Server to ESXi host connectivity.

- Restart the *vpxa* service and return to **Security Profile**.

- Select **Firewall** > **Properties**.

- Uncheck the **VMware vCenter Agent** box.

- Test the vCenter to ESXi host connectivity.

- Recheck the **VMware vCenter Agent** box, and stay on the **Firewall Properties** page.

- Select (highlight) the **VMware vCenter Agent** row, and click the **Firewall** button.

- Provide a range of IP addresses that does not include the vCenter Server's IP address.

- Test the vCenter Server to ESXi host connectivity.

- Undo the Firewall settings and verify that all settings are back to normal state.

- Use the vSphere Client to log on directly to the ESXi host.

- On the **Permissions** tab, locate the permission for the *vpxuser* account.

- Select the assigned vpxuser role, which should be **Administrator**, and change it to **Read Only**.

- Test the vCenter Server to ESXi host connectivity.

Secure a vSphere Environment—Hands-On Solutions

This section provides hands-on solutions to the real-world scenarios related to securing a vSphere environment provided in Chapter 10.

Hands-On Solution 10-21—Generate New Host Certificates

- Log in to ESXi Shell as root account and issue these commands:

```
cd   /etc/vmware/ssl
```

```
mv   rui.crt   orig.rui.crt
mv   rui.key   orig.rui.key
/sbin/generate-certificates
```

- Restart the host.

Hands-On Solution 10-22—Configure a Custom Firewall Rule

- Enable the ESXi Shell on an ESXi host.

- Modify the permissions of the **/etc/vmware/firewall/service.xml** file to allow write access, using this command:

```
chmod 644 /etc/vmware/firewall/service.xml
```

- Use the **vi** editor to modify the **/etc/vmware/firewall/service.xml** file.

- Add these lines to create the appropriate rule:

```
<service id="0032">
  <id>DNSTCPOut</id>
  <rule id='0000'>
    <direction>outbound</direction>
    <protocol>tcp</protocol>
    <porttype>dst</porttype>
    <port>53</port>
  </rule>
<enabled>true</enabled>
<required>false</required>
</service>
```

- Modify the permissions of the **/etc/vmware/firewall/service.xml** file to reset it to the original state, using this command:

```
chmod 644 /etc/vmware/firewall/service.xml
```

- Refresh the firewall by running **esxcli network firewall refresh**.

- Repeat these steps for each ESXi host.

Perform Scripting and Automation—Hands-On Solutions

This section provides hands-on solutions to the real-world scenarios related to implementing and managing a vSphere environment using scripts and commands provided in Chapter 10.

Hands-On Solution 10-23—Use PowerCLI to Manage VMs

- Use PowerCLI to connect to the vCenter Server and disconnect the CD drive for all running VMs using these commands:

```
Connect-VIServer  vcenter-01
Get-VM | Where-Object {$_.PowerState -eq "PoweredOn"} | Get-
CDDrive | Set-CDDrive -NoMedia -Confirm:$False
```

Hands-On Solution 10-24—Configure the vSphere Management Assistant

- Log on to the vMA and execute these commands:

```
vifp addserver vcenter-01.lab.local
vifp addserver host-01.lab.local
vifp addserver host-02.lab.local
vifp addserver host-03.lab.local
vifp listservers
vifptarget -s host-02.lab.local
vicfg-nics -l
```

Perform Advanced vSphere Installations and Configurations—Hands-On Solutions

This section provides hands-on solutions to the real-world scenarios related to performing advanced installations and configurations in a vSphere environment provided in Chapter 10.

Hands-On Solution 10-25—Use Image Builder to Add a Custom Driver

- Download the depot files to a folder named *d:\depot* on a Windows desktop or server where PowerCLI is installed.

- Issue the following commands:

```
Add-ESXSoftwareDepot d:\depot\ocz10xx-1.0.0-offline_
bundle-751505.zip


Add-ESXSoftwareDepot d:\depot\VMware-ESXi-5.1.0-799733-depot.zip


Get-ESXImageProfile


New-ESXImageProfile -CloneProfile ESXi-5.1.0-799733-standard
-Name "ESXi-5.1.0-799733-custom"


Get-ESXSoftwarePackage
```

```
Add-EsxSoftwarePackage -ImageProfile ESXi-5.1.0-799733-custom
-SoftwarePackage scsi-ocz10xx

Export-ESXImageProfile -ImageProfile ESXi-5.1.0-799733-custom
-ExportToISO -FilePath d:\ESXi-5.1.0-799733-custom
```

Hands-On Solution 10-26—Auto Deploy

- Use PowerCLI to execute these commands

```
Add-EsxSoftwareDepot d:\ update-from-esxi5.1-5.1_update01.zip
Get-EsxImageProfile  | Select Name
New-DeployRule -name Rule01 -item ESXi-5.1.0-20130402001-
standard      -allhosts
New-DeployRule -name Rule02 -item "Cluster-01"
Add-DeployRule -deployrule Rule01
Add-DeployRule -deployrule Rule02
Get-DeployRuleSet
```

Glossary

Auto Deploy   A feature that enables system administrators to automate the process of provisioning ESXi hosts. It runs in memory as a web service.

Auto Deploy rules engine   Uses rules to associate a physical host that is going to be an ESXi host with an ESXi image and a host profile.

baseline group   A set of baselines.

CIM   Also known as the Common Information Model, it monitors plug-ins that are developed and released by the server, storage, or I/O device vendors for monitoring the respective vendor's hardware.

DCUI   The direct console user interface that is available on the ESXi host console. It provides a menu of options for performing the initial ESXi host configuration and for troubleshooting issues that are difficult to resolve by other means.

default system roles   The three default system roles that are on every ESXi host are No access, Read-only, and Administrator.

device latency   Storage latency from the point of view of the storage adapter driver in the VMkernel. This is the amount of time a storage operation requires to complete as it travels from the HBA, through the storage network, to the storage array, and back.

direct path I/O   A technology that allows a virtual machine (VM) to have direct access to a hardware device. A supported network device can be configured for Pass Through, which means the device is not accessed by the vmkernel but instead is accessed directly by a VM.

Distributed vSwitch (vDS)   A vSwitch that is controlled by vCenter Server, with a data plane that is distributed across all connected ESXi hosts. The data plane is provided using hidden virtual switches that run on each connected ESXi host.

DPM   Distributed Power Management (DPM) is a DRS cluster feature that can be enabled and used to save electrical power and cooling costs by automatically shutting down some ESXi hosts during periods of low workload.

DRS   Distributed Resource Scheduler (DRS) is a vSphere feature that provides automatic balancing of CPU and memory workloads across a cluster of ESXi hosts. It achieves the balancing by placing new VMs on hosts and by migrating running VMs with vMotion as needed.

DRS affinity rule   A rule that forces DRS to keep two or more VMs running on the same host in the cluster.

Dump Collector   A vCenter Server support tool used to dump the vmkernel memory to a network server, rather than to disk.

esxcli   A modern namespace utility for managing ESXi hosts via the command line from within ESXi Shell and the vSphere Management Assistant (vMA).

ESXi Lockdown Mode   Affects how users access an ESXi host using DCUI, SSH, and ESXi Shell.

ESXi Shell   A command-line interface available directly on the ESXi host.

EtherChannel   A link aggregation protocol developed by Cisco that treats multiple physical links as a single logical link to provide fault tolerance and increased bandwidth.

EVC   Enhanced vMotion Compatibility (EVC) is a cluster feature that is useful in scenarios where not all the hosts in the cluster are compatible with each other for vMotion, but they are from the same vendor.

extension   A set of related vSphere Installation Bundles (VIBs) that add an optional feature or component to an ESXi host.

firewall ruleset   Defines whether a service is allowed or disallowed on the ESXi host.

firewall services   These are processes that access the management network and pass through the firewall if enabled.

guest latency   Storage I/O latency from the VM's point of view. The VMkernel latency plus the device latency.

gzip   This command originated as a replacement for the compress program in Unix and was created for the GNU Project to compress and uncompress files.

HA Admission Control   A mechanism aimed at ensuring sufficient resources are available in case of VM failover. It is applied as VMs attempt to power on to prevent the action if it would violate the Admission Control Policy, which can be based on reservations, dedicated failover hosts, or slot size calculation.

HA datastore heartbeat   A datastore-based heartbeat that is transmitted between ESXi hosts in an HA cluster to signal the nodes are available.

HA network heartbeat   A network-based heartbeat that is transmitted between ESXi hosts in an HA cluster to signal the nodes are available.

host baseline   A set of patches or extensions.

host profile   Configuration information about the host, the VMs that are registered to it, the HA cluster it is in, licenses, and so on.

Image Builder   A part of PowerCLI, it's basically a set of cmdlets you can use for creating more images by adding VIBs.

image profile   Defines an ESXi image and is made up of a collection of VIBs.

Jumbo Frames   Frames that are transmitted at a size larger than the default MTU size of 1500. The maximum size is 9000.

MPP   Multipathing Plug-in can be either the internal MPP which is the NMP, or it can be a third-party MPP supplied by a storage vendor. MPP=NMP+SATP+PSP

MTU   Maximum Transmission Unit, which is the maximum size of a data unit that can be sent on the virtual switch. The default size is 1500, but it can be increased to support Jumbo Frames.

net-dvs   A vCLI command that displays configuration and statistics details on dvSwitches.

Network I/O Control   A technology that allows a vDS to allocate network bandwidth according to traffic type by automatically generating network resource pools that correspond to each type of network traffic recognized by vSphere. This includes VM, management, vMotion, Fault Tolerance, vSphere Replication, iSCSI, and NAS traffic types. It also allows the use of user-defined network resource pools.

network resource pool   Containers that include multiple vSwitch port groups and ports that enable administrators to assign shares and limits. Automatically created system network pools correspond to various types of traffic, such as vMotion Administrators that can easily set shares and limits that are applied to all ESXi hosts that are connected to a vDS.

NFS   Network File System (NFS) provides a file-based access to remote storage without the VMFS overhead of a logical unit number (LUN).

NIC teaming   Two or more physical uplinks that are connected to a vSwitch or port group that are intended to provide redundancy and increased bandwidth.

NMP   Native Multipathing Plug-in is the default MPP in vSphere, and provides a default claim rule which associates an SATP and a PSP.

NPIV   N-Port ID Virtualization, which is used when you want a virtual machine to be assigned a World Wide Port Name (WWPN) with the SAN fabric.

offline bundle   A Zip file containing patches, extensions, and upgrades. It can be imported into VMware Update Manager (VUM).

patch   A set of related VIBs that addresses a particular vulnerability, issue, or enhancement.

performance graphs   Customizable graphs provided in the vSphere Client for reporting resource usage and performance metrics for VMs and ESXi hosts.

PowerCLI   A command-line interface used to manage all of vSphere, including vCenter and applications requiring vCenter, like VMware DRS.

promiscuous mode   A feature of a vSwitch port group that permits the port group to receive all network packets that are sent to and from all other ports in a port group or on the vSwitch.

PSA   Pluggable Storage Architecture is an architecture that defines how multipathing works within vSphere.

PSP   Path Selection Plug-in performs the task of selecting which physical path to send I/O requests.

PuTTY   A free and open-source terminal emulator. It is commonly used to support SCP and SSH protocols.

PXE   Also known as the Preboot eXecution Environment, a file is downloaded from the TFTP server during the PXE boot process.

RDM   Raw Device Map, which allows storage to directly be accessed to and from the ESXi host.

SATP   Storage Array Type Plug-in is a driver for a storage array that monitors the health of each physical path on the array, and can handle path failover.

SDRS intra-VM anti-affinity rule   A rule that forces SDRS to keep two or more virtual disks belonging to the same VM running on separate hosts in the cluster.

shared repository   A shared folder or website from which VUM can download updates with the WAN.

SNMP   Simple Network Management Protocol, which is a protocol used by monitoring systems to query managed objects for status information. It is also used by managed systems to automatically notify monitoring systems of status changes and events. It is commonly used to detect faults, unauthorized access, and usage of network devices and servers.

software depot   Stores ESXi images and additional VIBs. The Image Builder groups the necessary VIBs to form an ESXi image to be deployed. It can be either online or offline.

Standard vSwitch (vSS)   A vSwitch that is controlled by a specific ESXi host.

Storage DRS   Storage DRS (SDRS) is a vSphere feature that provides automatic balancing of disk space usage and disk I/O latency across a cluster of data stores.

storage replica   A copy of a LUN to another LUN that is created by the storage system.

storage snapshot   A point-in-time capture of the data in a LUN that is created by the storage system.

syslog   Developed by Eric Allman as a standard for Unix logging.

Syslog Collector   A vCenter Server support tool that allows for the combining of system log files to a single server for syslog processing.

system log bundle   VMware Technical Support might request log files and configuration files during a support call. When you create a system log bundle, you are forming one file to upload to VMware Support.

tar   This command originated in Unix and is short for tape archive. The command itself is being used to combine multiple files in a single file. There is also an option to untar or uncombine them into multiple files.

TFTP server   A third-party server that serves the boot images that Auto Deploy provides.

traffic shaping   A method for limiting some network traffic to effectively improve the performance of other network traffic. In vSwitches, traffic shaping can be used to configure limits on the average and peak traffic per virtual switch port group.

UUID   Universal Unique Identifier, which is used to match a LUN to a specific Virtual Machine File System (VMFS) datastore.

VAAI   vStorage API for Array Integration is a set of APIs and SCSI commands used to offload certain functions that are performed more efficiently on the storage array.

VASA   VMware vSphere vStorage APIs for Storage Awareness, which is a set of APIs that a storage vendor can provide to advertise information about the storage array.

vCLI   A command-line interface for managing ESXi hosts from a remote Linux or Windows machine. It provides the esxcli and vicfg commands.

VIB   Also known as a vSphere Installation Bundle, it's a collection of files packaged into a single Zip or tar archive. VMware and its partners package the ESXi base image, drivers, CIM providers, and vendor plug-ins.

VLAN   Virtual LAN, which is a logical network partition of a physical network. VLANs are used to segment traffic and isolate broadcast domains.

VLAN Trunking   VLAN Trunking Protocol (VTP) is a protocol that allows a network port to transfer packets for multiple VLANs. VTP is commonly configured on ports used to connect two switches.

vLockStep   The play/replay technology in Fault Tolerance (FT) that is used to keep the secondary VM in sync with the primary VM, such that each instruction that executes in the primary immediately executes in the secondary.

vMA   The vSphere Management Assistant is a virtual appliance used to remotely manage vSphere. It provides vCLI and fastpass.

VMCI   The Virtual Machine Communication Interface allows direct communication between one virtual machine to another virtual machine.

VMFS   The Virtual Machine File System is a block-based file system that is only used with local disk or LUNs.

VMkernel latency   The amount of time a storage operation is processed by the VMkernel, including queuing and driver processing time.

VMkernel log   The VMkernel.log file on the ESXi host.

vmkfstools   A command utility to manage VMFS datastores and virtual disks from within ESXi Shell and the vMA.

vm-support   A command-line utility that produces a gzipped tarball system log bundle.

VMware FT   VMware FT is a vSphere feature that provides fault tolerance for a VM even if the host it is running on fails.

VMware HA   VMware HA is a vSphere cluster feature that provides automatic high availability for VMs and applications.

vscsiStats   A utility in the ESXi Shell that collects storage metrics and produces histograms. Metrics include latency, seek distance, I/O size, and inter arrival time.

vSphere Authentication Proxy   This service is also referred to as the CAM service and enables an ESXi host to join an Active Directory domain without using Active Directory credentials.

vSphere Client   A C#-based graphical user interface to manage vSphere.

vSphere Installation Bundle (VIB)   The smallest software package that can be installed on an ESXi host.

VUM Utility   A tool that can be used to view and change settings that were made during the VUM installation.

Index

A

Active Directory, configuring
with command line, 338
with PowerCLI, 338

Active Directory integration, 336-337

AD domain, vMA, 31

Add Host wizard, 63

Add Network wizard, 49

adding
custom drivers with Image Builder, 396
download sources in VUM, 260
software iSCSI adapter, 124

Admission Control, HA (High Availability), 214-215

advanced Boot Loader options, configuring, 379

advanced cluster attributes, 154

advanced ESXi host attributes, configuring, 150

advanced virtual machine attributes, 150-152

advanced vSphere installations and configurations, scenarios, 395-396

affinity rules
DRS (Distributed Resource Scheduler), 226-228
Storage DRS, 233-234

Alarm Settings window, 118

alarms
DPM (Distributed Power Management), 241
DRS (Distributed Resource Scheduler), 229
HA (High Availability), 221
Storage DRS, 235-236

Alert triggers, 118

-AllHosts option, 363

Allman, Eric, 286

alternative virtual machine swap locations, configuring, 162-163

analyzing
disk latency, scenarios, 393
log files, 305-307
to identifying storage and multipathing problems, 201-202
virtual switches using ESXCLI, 67

anti-affinity rules, 222
DRS (Distributed Resource Scheduler), 226-228
Storage DRS, 233-234

antivirus software, installing, 336

application workload, sizing VMs, 158-159

architecture, Auto Deploy, 360-362

attaching baseline groups, 269

O

P-Q

S

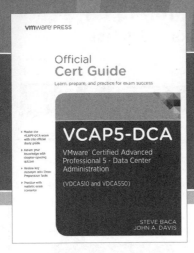

FREE
Online Edition

Your purchase of **VCAP5-DCA Official Cert Guide** includes access to a free online edition for 45 days through the **Safari Books Online** subscription service. Nearly every VMware Press book is available online through **Safari Books Online**, along with thousands of books and videos from publishers such as Addison-Wesley Professional, Cisco Press, Exam Cram, IBM Press, O'Reilly Media, Prentice Hall, Que, Sams.

Safari Books Online is a digital library providing searchable, on-demand access to thousands of technology, digital media, and professional development books and videos from leading publishers. With one monthly or yearly subscription price, you get unlimited access to learning tools and information on topics including mobile app and software development, tips and tricks on using your favorite gadgets, networking, project management, graphic design, and much more.